Luca Marenzio and the
Italian Madrigal
1577–1593

Studies in British Musicology

Nigel Fortune, Series Editor

Reader in Music
The University of Birmingham

Other Titles in This Series

Luca Marenzio and the Italian Madrigal

1577–1593

Volume 1

by
James Chater

UMI RESEARCH PRESS
Ann Arbor, Michigan

Produced and distributed by
UMI Research Press
an imprint of
University Microfilms International
Ann Arbor, Michigan 48106

Library of Congress Cataloging in Publication Data

Chater, James (James Michael)
   Luca Marenzio and the Italian madrigal, 1577-
93.

   (British studies in musicology)
   "A revision of the author's thesis, Oxford University,
1980."–T.p., verso.
   Bibliography: p.
   Includes index.
   1. Marenzio, Luca, 1553-1599. Madrigals. 2. Madrigal.
I. Title. II. Series.

ML410.M326C5 1981   784.1'2'00924   81-13095
ISBN 0-8357-1242-7 (set)   AACR2
ISBN 0-8357-1255-9 (v.1)

Contents

Volume I

Volume II

List of Abbreviations

1. Primary musical sources in the main comprise the madrigal books of Marenzio and his contemporaries. These are referred to with a Roman numeral, the preposition "a," and an Arabic numeral: the Roman numeral stands for the number of the book, the Arabic for the number of voices used. Thus *II a 5* indicates *Il secondo libro . . . a cinque* or *Madrigali a cinque voci . . . libro secondo.*

2. Secondary sources are sometimes referred to by their initials. The following abbreviations are used:

AMW: Archiv für Musikwissenschaft

Brown: Brown, H.M., *Instrumental music printed before 1600*

CEMF: Corpus of Early Music (in facsimile)

CMM: Corpus Mensurabilis Musicae

CW: Das Chorwerk

DBI: Dizionario Biografico degli Italiani

DDT: Denkmäler deutscher Tonkunst

Domenichi, i etc.: L. Domenichi (ed.), *Rime diverse di molti eccellentiss. auttori,* 9 vols., Venice etc., 1546-1560. (Separate volumes listed in Appendix IV, poetic anthologies.)

DTB: Denkmäler der Tonkunst in Bayern

EISLA: Enciclopedia Italiana di Scienze, Lettere ed Arti

EMS: English Madrigal School (later, *English Madrigalists*)

Festschrift: denotes any collection of essays in honour of a scholar regardless of whether the word "Festschrift" appears in the title or not. Used in short references (see preface).

Flanders: Flanders, P., *A thematic index to the works of Benedetto Pallavicino*

Grove: Grove's Dictionary of Music and Musicians, 6th edn., London (forthcoming)

HAM: Historical Anthology of Music

IMAMI: Istituti e Monumenti dell'Arte Musicale Italiana

JAMS: Journal of the American Musicological Society

JRBM: Journal of Renaissance and Baroque Music (= *Musica Disciplina*, i)
MGG: Die Musik in Geschichte und Gegenwart
ML: Music and Letters
MT: Musical Times
MQ: Musical Quarterly
NA: Note d'Archivio
NRMI: Nuova Rivista Musicale Italiana
NV: "New Vogel": Vogel, Einstein, Lesure, Sartori, *Bibliografia della musica italiana* . . . (1977)
RIDM: Rivista Italiana di Musicologica
RISM: Répertoire International des Sources Musicales
RMI: Rivista Musicale Italiana
SCA: Smith College Archives: P. de Monte, madrigals, transcr. by A. Einstein
SM: Studi Musicali
UM: University Microfilms
VE: Vogel, E. and Einstein, A., *Bibliothek der gedruckten weltlichen Vokalmusik*
VJM: Vierteljahrsschrift für Musikwissenschaft
ZMW: Zeitschrift für Musikwissenschaft
3. The following library sigla are used:
D-Mbs: Munich, Bayerische Staatsbibliothek
D-Rp: Regensburg, Proskesche Musikbibliothek
F-Pn: Paris, Bibliothèque Nationale
GB-Lbm: London, British Museum, now British Library
GB-Ob: Oxford, Bodleian Library
I-Bag: Bologna, Biblioteca dell'Archiginnasio
I-Bc: Bologna, Biblioteca del Conservatoria (Civico Museo Bibliografico Musicale)
I-Bu: Bologna, Biblioteca Universitaria
I-Fl: Florence, Biblioteca Mediceo-Laurenziana
I-Fn: Florence, Biblioteca Nazionale Centrale
I-Fr: Florence, Biblioteca Riccardiana
I-Rsm: Rome, Archive of the Basilica of Santa Maria Maggiore
I-Rvat: Rome, Biblioteca Apostolica Vaticana
I-Rvic: Rome, Viccariato
I-Sc: Siena, Biblioteca Comunale
I-Vnm: Venice, Biblioteca Nazionale Marciana
I-VEaf: Verona, Biblioteca dell'Accademia Filarmonica

List of Tables

Preface

This study is concerned mainly with the madrigals Marenzio published between 1577 and 1593. My original plan was to devote almost equal space to the madrigals of the first decade (the 1580's) as to those of the second. Limitations of time and space dictated otherwise: eight chapters were needed for the first decade, while the last chapter examines briefly the nature of and reasons for the abrupt change of style in the second decade. Thus the last chapter may in part be considered a resumé of an unwritten "second part" dealing with the madrigals published between 1594 and 1599. The concluding bibliography embraces both periods.

At all times (but especially in chapters 1, 2, 3, and 9) it should be remembered that this study is concerned both with Marenzio as an individual composer and with the total development of the late sixteenth-century madrigal. This fact has necessitated the acceptance of certain limitations other than the already mentioned chronological one: thus non-madrigalian forms (*villanella, intermedio,* motet) have not been considered except where they were found to have a direct connection with the madrigal. Likewise with the composers discussed in chapter 2: the chanson and all other non-madrigalian genres were excluded from consideration, as were the works of all composers preceding Rore, including such important figures as Willaert and Arcadelt.

An excellent biography of Marenzio was recently completed by Steven Ledbetter. The life and works of Marenzio were previously the subject of a monograph by Hans Engel. This uneven work contains a number of insights mingled with unnumerable inaccuracies, while the section dealing with the works is curiously fragmented. The best critical works remain Einstein's chapter in *The Italian Madrigal* and Denis Arnold's monograph, though much remains to be added to these. It should be added that Dürr's thesis on rhythm and metre, and two more recent theses (by Bennett and Kishimoto) approach the task of analysis from standpoints sufficiently distant from this study to ensure widely different results.

It is salutary that more works of Marenzio have recently become available; less salutary that there are no less than four "complete editions" in various stages of non-completion. The first is Einstein's edition of the first six books *a 5* (*PÄM*, iv/1 and vi); after a long gap, Les Editions Renaissantes published *Il settimo libro . . . a 5* (1595), but, since 1975, nothing more of this projected *Opera Omnia* has been issued. In 1977 and 1980 the first two volumes of Broude's edition of *The Secular Works* appeared, edited by Steven Ledbetter and Patricia Myers. In 1978 the American Institute of Musicology published the first four volumes of the *Opera Omnia*—three volumes of motets and one of madrigals (*CMM*, lxii/4). It is assumed the reader will have easy access to all these works.

References to works of Marenzio have been made in the awareness that more works will presumably become available within a short space of time. While it is inconceivable that Broude and *AIM* will both publish the complete madrigals, it is still doubtful which edition will prevail over the other. I have therefore referred to madrigals by the original book, date, and number so as to make it easy to locate references in whichever modern edition might be available. During detailed discussion, madrigals published by Broude, *AIM*, or any other edition *except* Einstein's (*PÄM*), are referred to first in their primary, then their secondary source, e.g.,

I a 6 (1581), no. 3: *Opera,* iv (ed. Meier), p.18, b.1 ff.

However, to save space, I have omitted specific references to Einstein's edition of the first six books *a 5* (*PÄM*). All that the reader need remember is that the *first* three books *a 5* are available in *PÄM*, iv/1, the *next* three in *PÄM*, vi, after which the edition was discontinued. Also to save space, brief references to madrigals are to primary sources only: the reader should remember that all the modern reprints consulted are cross-referenced with the list of books and madrigals in appendix II. The first section of appendix II is a list of all madrigal publications by Marenzio together with all the pieces they contain: the second section lists all anthologies in which madrigals by Marenzio are published for the first time. The reader is encouraged to use these lists while reading the text. Modern editions are listed in appendix II, and general reference works containing reprints of works by Marenzio are listed in appendix VI and marked with an asterisk.

This study is illustrated by six transcriptions and numerous examples drawn from Marenzio and other composers. These are contained in volume II of this work, and are referenced in volume I, e.g., [ex. 5].

For the rest, this study follows the system used in F.W. Sternfeld's *History of Western Music,* i, in which works are referred to by self-explanatory short titles, e.g. Einstein, *Madrigal,* listed in Appendix VI by its full title, A. Einstein, *The Italian Madrigal,* 3 vols., Princeton, 1949.

Acknowledgments

During the writing of this study I have received financial support from Exeter College, Oxford (Amelia Jackson Award), the Department of Education and Science (Major State Studentship), the Italian Government (through the British Council), and the British School at Rome. I would like to thank Dr. F. W. Sternfeld, Professor Denis Arnold, and Professor Joseph Kerman for their advice and supervision, Lorenzo Bianconi and Hiroko Kishimoto for much useful information, Professor Arnold, Keith Bennett, David Butchart, and Rosalind Halton for lending or presenting copies of their transcriptions of madrigals by Marenzio, and Katherine Bosi for providing me with copies of transcriptions of madrigals by Pallavicino. (It must be stressed, however, that all transcriptions and examples were checked against original sources and that therefore any inaccuracies are the author's sole responsibility.) I would like also to thank the librarians of all the libraries I have worked in—especially of the Civico Museo Bibliografico Musicale, Bologna—for their prompt service and kind assistance. Above all, I must thank my parents for their moral support during the hectic days preceding submission, and Patricia Garrett, who typed my manuscript and whose eagle eye spotted a number of inconsistencies and inaccuracies that have been corrected.

In addition, I would like to acknowledge the following publishers and individual editors whose editions of madrigals were consulted during the preparation of this study: Smith College Werner Josten Library; Breitkopf and Härtel; Penguin Books Ltd.; Oxford University Press; Bärenreiter-Verlag; Broude Brothers Ltd.; A-R Editions, Inc.; the American Institute of Musicology and Armen Carapetyan, Director of the AIM; Rosalind Halton; and W. Richard Shindle. Specific citations appear with the examples in volume 2, and the editions are referenced in the text as explained in the preface, p. xii.

1

Marenzio and His World

Life of Marenzio

Marenzio was born most probably in 1553[1] in the north of Italy. His birthplace, Coccaglia, near Brescia, occupied a distant corner of the still powerful and then very extensive Republic of Venice. Brescia boasted an academy and a flourishing musical establishment.[2] The *maestro di cappella,* Giovanni Contino, may well have been Marenzio's first teacher.[3] Marenzio's compatriots include madrigal composers such as Bertani (b. c. 1554) and Virchi (b. 1552),[4] both of whom, with Marenzio, collaborated in the composition of eighteen settings of a poem by the Brescian nobleman, Marcantonio Martinengo.[5] After Contino's death in 1574, Marenzio passed into the service of Contino's former protector, Cristoforo Madruzzo, Cardinal of Trent. The latter, who lived mainly in Rome from 1567 till his death in 1578, was a friend of Cardinal Luigi d'Este, and it was therefore natural that Marenzio should have joined Luigi's employment less than a month after Madruzzo's death.[6]

Luigi d'Este (1538-1586), the brother of Alfonso, Duke of Ferrara, became a cardinal in 1561, much against his own wishes. His extravagant and secular lifestyle was much at odds with the spirit of the Counter-Reformation, though not, it seems, such as to discourage secular music making. In fact Luigi kept a large *capella* (contrary to what Engel states)[7] and Marenzio was not boasting when he refers to himself as *maestro di capella* on the titlepage of his *I a 6* (1581). Despite one complaint of Marenzio about the nonpayment of his salary,[8] it seems that Marenzio occupied a privileged position at Luigi's court: he is not mentioned in the account books as a teacher and was therefore free to devote all his time to composition and freelance singing.[9] An additional advantage in being employed by Luigi was the connection with Ferrara, whose reigning duke was much more devoted to music than Luigi. However, owing to ill health and the strained relationships with his brother, Luigi visited that court only once during Marenzio's employment with him: in 1580-1581, taking Marenzio with him.[10]

On Luigi's death (30 December 1586) Marenzio seems to have been unemployed, though a trip to Verona is indicated in the dedication of the *I a 4, 5, 6* to Count Mario Bevilacqua (signed on 10 December 1587).[11] From February 1588 to November 1589 Marenzio was in Florence, collaborating with Cristoforo Malvezzi, Jacopo Peri, Caccini, Cavalieri, and Antonio Archilei on the famous *intermedi* on the occasion of the marriage of Grand Duke Ferdinand with Christine of Lorraine.[12] During his stay in Florence Marenzio probably met Virginio Orsini, the Duke of Bracciano since the death in 1585 of his father, Paolo Giordano Orsini. Virginio married Flavia Peretti, grandniece of Sixtus V, by proxy in 1589, traveling to Rome soon afterwards to join his new wife. With them went Marenzio as a member of the household: the *V a 6,* as the dedicatory letter states,[13] was composed in the young couple's home (Via Parione, 8).[14]

In June 1588, while in Florence, Marenzio may also have met Cinzio, nephew of Ippolito Aldobrandini, the future Pope Clement VIII, shortly before Cinzio was made cardinal on 17 September 1593.[15] In his rooms in the Vatican, Cinzio gathered round him some of the most distinguished poets and philosophers of his time, including Guarini, Torquato Tasso, and Angelo Grillo. Marenzio's *VI a 5* (1594) was merely one of a number of musical or poetical works dedicated to him.[16]

Cinzio Aldobrandini's diplomatic connections with Poland were instrumental in the appointment of Marenzio as *maestro di capella* at the court of Sigismund III[17] who was married to a member of the Sforza family. Marenzio had arrived in Cracow by March 1596, during which year the entire court (including no doubt Marenzio) was transferred to Warsaw. In September 1598 he was dismissed (or dismissed himself)[18] and in October was back in Venice in time to sign the dedication of the *VIII a 5.* There appears to have been no resumption of connections with the Aldobrandini circle; rather, the last few books indicate a renewal of contact with the Ferrarese and Mantuan courts. On 22 August 1599 Marenzio died in the gardens of the Villa de' Medici at Monte S. Trinità and was buried in the nearby church of San Lorenzo in Lucina.[19]

Musical Patronage

By 1580, fifty-three years after the devastating sack of Rome, the city had begun to display very clear signs of spiritual and moral resurgence. Architecturally, the city was transformed by the construction of new churches, fountains, obelisks, and avenues; the aim was to surpass the grandeur of ancient Rome by dedicating public works to the glory of God. An element of spontaneity was provided by the growth of popular religious movements like that of the Jesuits (St. Ignatius Loyola) and the Congregazione dell'Oratorio whose founder, St. Philip Neri, encouraged the adaptation of the light, secular canzonet style to religious or didactic texts.[20]

That the energy generated by the reform movement spilled over into the arts in general is manifested through the formation of guilds with the purpose of holding lay religious meetings and performing charitable works. One such guild was the Vertuosa Compagnia dei Musici di Roma, whose original name points to its religious origins: "Congregazione dei musici di Roma sotto l'invocazione della Beata Vergine di Gregorio Magno e di S. Cecilia."[21] The papal bull confirming the society's official existence was signed by Sixtus V on 1 May 1585. In 1589 an anthology appeared with madrigals by members of the society;[22] however, there are much earlier signs of a cohesive group of composers working in Rome: important in this respect are the anthologies *RISM* 1574[4] and *RISM* 1582[4], besides Moscaglia's compilation of 1582.[23] To all of these, except RISM 1574[4], Marenzio contributed.

The official churches, many of which had only recently been built, needed musicians; nevertheless, Marenzio was employed exclusively in the secular sphere. Contemporary sources give us a tantalizing glimpse at what must have been a rich variety of secular music making in the palaces of Roman cardinals and priests. Thus, in the dedication of Rota's *I a 5* (1579) we read of a circle of musicians and learned men around Lodovico Bianchetti, Chamberlain to Gregory XIII.[24] Rota's collection is a mixture of sacred and secular texts; Marenzio, in 1584, dedicated a collection of *Spirituali* to the same patron. Nor was purely secular music making spurned: Raval's *I a 5* (1593) is one such collection, the dedication of which speaks of a musical gathering in the palace of Cardinal Montalto, the Cancelleria: among the participants, we read, was "Sig. Luca Marenzio divino compositore."[25]

Patronage Outside Rome

Owing to the pre-eminent position of Rome in Christendom, the city had numerous links with cities throughout Europe, especially in the Italian peninsula. Thus many of the reigning families were represented by cardinals: Florence, by Cardinal (later Grand Duke) Ferdinando de' Medici; Ferrara, by Cardinal Luigi d'Este; and Mantua, by Cardinal Scipione Gonzaga.[26] Marenzio came into contact with all three of them and was thus enabled to forge valuable links with all three courts.

In the case of Florence the links are particularly intimate. Of interest is the appearance in Roman part-books of a number of poems by the Florentine nobleman Giovambattista Strozzi the Elder.[27] His poems remained popular with musicians long after his death in 1571;[28] Marenzio set at least six of his poems, most obtainable only in manuscript. The two earliest known settings were published in the *III a 6* (1585), dedicated to Bianca Cappello, the

Venetian wife of Grand Duke Francesco. Marenzio's desire for a post at the Medici court is shown by his early publication (in the *IV a 5,* 1584) of his contribution to the collection of sonnet settings honoring the marriage of Francesco with Bianca in 1579.[29] This interest in Bianca Cappello, of whom the new Grand Duke Ferdinand had thoroughly disapproved, proved no obstacle to Marenzio's employment at his court in 1589: together with Malvezzi he received the lion's share of the commission for the music for the 1589 *intermedi.*

If the Florentine madrigal style is still difficult to assess,[30] it is nevertheless possible to make a few general observations about the madrigal at Ferrara, the court ruled by the brother of Marenzio's patron. Many leading Renaissance literary and musical figures are associated with Ferrara; among the former are Ariosto, Torquato Tasso, and Guarini, all of whom are represented in Marenzio's madrigal books along with the lesser known Pigna, Pocaterra and Arlotti.

Among the characteristics of Ferrarese music making in the 1580's, two are important for Marenzio. The first is the development of the ornamental or "luxuriant"[31] singing style as manifested in the *musica secreta,* the virtuoso group formed for the Duke's personal delectation.[32] Marenzio is perhaps the first important composer to form his style with the sound of these Ferrarese voices still fresh in his ears.[33]

The second characteristic is the predominance of certain stereotyped literary motives. Thus in the anthologies *Il lauro secco* and *Il lauro verde*[34] the prime movers are not musicians but literary figures, Torquato Tasso and Ippolito Gianluca, both of the Accademia dei Rinnovati.[35] The central image is the laurel tree, symbol of love and poetic inspiration, withered and parched in the first collection, restored to life and health in the second. The latter commemorates the marriage of the singer, Laura Peperara,[36] to Count Annibale Turco in 1583, and the two collections together allude perhaps to the vicissitudes of the love affair preceding the match.[37] Marenzio's prominence in both collections reflects the impact his music had already made in Ferrara by 1582-83[38] and was to sustain in the subsequent years. Of interest in this regard is Gianluca's next anthology, *I lieti amanti (RISM* 1586[10]),[39] where poetic ideas determine not only the content of the poems but their sequence and the choice of composer to set them. The odd-numbered poems are *partenze* (songs of parting), while the even-numbered are scornful outbursts in the manner of the *Lauro secco* poems. The first group is contributed by composers working in Ferrara, the second by composers from elsewhere. Marenzio falls into the second category,[40] but seems to have exerted considerable influence on the first, Ferrarese category, in that many of the dialogue *partenze* closely resemble a *partenza* published by Marenzio himself two years previously.[41]

Both *I lieti amanti* and *La gloria musicale* (*RISM* 1592[14]) indicate a connection between the academies of Ferrara and Verona in their common dedication to Count Mario Bevilacqua,[42] the most distinguished music patron of his time. Historians speak of several musical establishments in Verona, the two most prominent being the Accademia dei Filarmonici and Bevilacqua's personal *ridotto*.[43] The membership of the two institutions probably overlapped, for Bevilacqua himself was the Academy's *padre* (president) from 17 April 1582 to 22 April 1583.[44] Therefore Marenzio must have already known Bevilacqua when he dedicated his *III a 5* to the Filarmonici on 1 December 1582. To Bevilacqua Marenzio was later to dedicate the *I a 4, 5, 6* (1588), a collection which differs enormously from the *III a 5* in both the higher literary standard and the more elevated, less popular tone. Though the 1588 collection was a commercial failure, a passage from the dedication reveals Marenzio's confidence of its success at least in Bevilacqua's private circle:

> . . . havendo, & per l'imitatione delle parole, & per la proprietà dello stile atteso ad una (dirò così) mesta gravità, che da gl'intendenti pari suoi & dal virtuosissimo suo ridutto sarà forse via più gradita.[45]

In friendly competition with Ferrara was Mantua, the seat of the Gonzaga family which had close family ties with the Este family of Ferrara.[46] Vincenzo, Prince and later Duke of Mantua (from 1586), was a frequent visitor to Ferrara; one of his visits (1580-1581) coincided with Marenzio's.[47] Later, Marenzio was to dedicate to him his last book, the *IX a 5* (1599). In fact the dedications of the later books suggest an awakening of interest in Marenzio's music at the Mantuan court. This is not surprising, given the stylistic *rapprochement* with Wert, Pallavicino, and the young Monteverdi, all active at Mantua between 1593 and Marenzio's death.

Venice, still an important trading center in the late sixteenth century, also held a virtual monopoly of music printing in Italy. All but two of Marenzio's madrigal books were first printed there,[48] while a number of anthologies printed in Venice and featuring composers from the Veneto also contain madrigals by Marenzio: G. B. Mosto's *Primo fiore della ghirlanda musicale* (*RISM* 1577[7]), which contains Marenzio's first madrigal,[49] Angelo Gardano's *Musica spirituale* (*RISM* 1586[1])[50] and *Il trionfo di Dori* (*RISM* 1592[11]) which celebrates the marriage of a Venetian couple.[51]

The Relationship Between Patronage and Literary Choice

Though little is known about the literary preferences of Marenzio's patrons, we may be sure that the poetic content of each book was often influenced by patrons whose favors Marenzio sought to gain or retain. It is probable, for instance, that Marenzio frequented the *ridotto* of Lelio Pasqualino, canon of Santa Maria Maggiore, patron of Stabile and G. M. Nanino, and author of the text of Marenzio's popular *Liquide perle.*[52] Other suppliers of texts may have been the patrons Girolamo Ruis, Virginio Orsini, and Ferrante Gonzaga.[53]

Another way in which patrons exercised direct influence on choice of poetry was through occasional texts. The celebration of marriages was the most important social function of the madrigal composer. This involved the setting of very stereotyped, ornamental verse in which the wedded couple is depicted in transparent pastoral surroundings. The poetry is so standardized that names may be substitued without impairing the meaning of the text.[54] A number of poems celebrate the virtue or beauty of a patron,[55] or allude by means of puns to the patron's name.[56] However, before further discussion of the literary texts is possible, we must consider the musical background against which Marenzio emerged.

2

The Musical Background:
The Madrigal Before Marenzio

Introduction

The development of the late sixteenth-century madrigal may be seen as an ever increasing urge towards extreme expression and extreme artifice.[1] "Expression" is a vague concept, but a useful one only if we do not attempt to narrow down its meaning too much; it embraces all the known techniques of representing the meaning of words, from "expressivity"—such devices as chromaticism and dissonance that are designed to achieve pathos—to the more "artificial" forms of word-painting such as eye-music. Artifice, viewed nowadays with suspicion but upheld as a virtue in the sixteenth century, may be partially redefined as style consciousness and self-consciousness:[2] Marenzio actually goes as far as describing his change of style in the dedication of his *I a 4, 5, 6* (1588).[3]

Another kind of artifice, one designed to appeal to a learned minority, was parody, including self-parody. The latter may be illustrated by two compositions from the *III a 5* (1582): *Ohimè, il bel viso* (text by Petrarch) and *Ohimè, se tanto amate* (text by Guarini).[4] Petrarch's elegiac sighs are humorously parodied by Guarini's repeated "ohimè," while the patter-rhythms introduced by Marenzio in the final lines of both pieces underline their interrelationship.[5] As an example of a Petrarchan parody providing the stimulus for a musical parody, we may further mention a quotation from Striggio's *Là ver l'aurora* (text by Petrarch) at the opening of Marenzio's *Là 've l'aurora* [ex. 1].

Rore and His Successors

If we proceed on the basis of comparing Marenzio's works with those of composers whose works he quotes from time to time, we are inevitably led back to Rore, in whose works the madrigal may be said to have come of age.

Despite the interval of time between the two men, Rore's example seems to have been as vivid to Marenzio as it had been to the intervening generations; nor should we forget that Giulio Cesare Monteverdi heads his list of composers of the Seconda Prattica with Rore's name.[6]

Rore's elegiac descending phrases and phrygian cadences find a distinct echo in Marenzio's music; however, Marenzio clearly prefers intensification to mere copying. This is seen not only in the terrifying distortions of *Crudele acerba*[7] but also in an earlier piece the opening of which contains a discreet but direct parody of the opening of one of Rore's madrigals [ex. 2]. Marenzio's tenor transposes the first eight notes of Rore's canto down a fourth, while Rore's canon between canto and alto is transferred to alto and tenor. Marenzio is more compact and more disturbing in his daring use of the six-four on the fourth semibreve and chromaticism in the canonic alto and tenor themes.

Not only could one point to similar instances of quotation,[8] but one can see in Rore's stylistic development a finger pointing directly to the future. The gradual paring down of the dense polyphonic texture of the earlier works for the sake of greater clarity and lightness, together with the increase in chordal writing, has been described elsewhere.[9] Consistent with this desire for clarity is the pairing together of vocal entries; that Marenzio quotes two examples of this favorite device betrays the extent to which he and his generation were still indebted to Rore in the matter of contrapuntal technique [ex. 3].[10]

At this point we need mention only two of Rore's successors: Contino and Ingegneri. From Giovanni Contino Marenzio is unlikely to have learned much; despite the former's indebtedness to Rore in the matter of counterpoint, he shrinks from chromatic experiments of any kind. However influential Contino was as a teacher (if indeed he was ever Marenzio's teacher) his compositions do not seem to have had any influence.[11] The two men's settings of *Se voi sete cor mio* are vastly dissimilar.[12]

A far more imaginative composer—and one more fully aware of the expressive power of chromaticism—was Ingegneri, whose sphere of activity, Cremona, lay only a few miles south of Brescia.[13] In 1580 both composers published their settings of a popular stanza by the Neapolitan poet, Tansillo.[14] Marenzio follows Ingegneri closely, and the very short time separating the publication of the two settings leads one to suspect that Marenzio may have known Ingegneri's setting in manuscript.[15]

The first known setting of Tansillo's text is Monte's of 1558,[16] but it is less influential than Isnardi's of 1577, which served as a model not only for Ingegneri and Marenzio, but also for the Romans, G.M. Nanino (1581 and 1586) and Soriano (1592). Common to these five composers is the choice of phrygian mode, the *misura di breve,* and a five-voice texture with two tenors.

A comparison of the openings by Isnardi, Ingegneri, and Marenzio reveals instructive similarities and differences [ex. 4]. Isnardi and Ingegneri employ two overlapping groups of three voices; Isnardi's second statement includes a disturbing leap in the alto and a conspicuous melisma in the tenor. Ingegneri, too, aims at an unsettling effect, with three different themes deployed in the quinto, tenor, and bass followed by inversion of two of these in the canto and alto. The listener is thus confronted with five apparently different themes. Marenzio's approach is entirely different. Superficially, he resembles Isnardi by allowing two themes to diverge from the same note at the beginning; however, he abstains from wide leaps and *melismata* likely to distract attention away from the contrapuntal argument. The theme for "fieri tormenti" ("bitter torments") grows naturally from the opening descending motive, the final, *e*, which acts as a pivotal note both times. As with Ingegneri this phrase is a descending theme in the canto which is isolated by a wide vertical gap from the next highest voice. Marenzio even imitates Ingegneri's countersubject in the alto (Ingegneri, b.5; Marenzio, b.6); for greater clarity, however, he suppresses the alto's ascending fifth and the subsequent melisma (Ingegneri, bb.5-6). Marenzio further borrows Ingegneri's theme for "empi lacci" ("pitiless chains"), transferring it to the preceding phrase, "duri ceppi" ("harsh fetters").[17] Throughout his setting Marenzio employs the clear vertical structures typified by the opening paired motives. Horizontally, however, Marenzio is capable of finer gradations of texture: especially remarkable is the three-voice texture for "aspre catene" ("harsh chains"),[18] while in the next section, scored for four voices by both composers, Marenzio emphasizes the words "misero piango" ("sadly I weep") through the momentary reintroduction of the bass (b.22 ff).[19] Similarly phrases characterized by different types of rhythm merge in such a way that no precise dividing line can be drawn between them (see b.11 ff and b.28 ff). Marenzio's polish and clarity are far removed from the slightly clumsy but expressive severity of Ingegneri.

The Three Oltremontani: Lassus, Monte, and Wert[20]

The influence of Lassus would be highly apparent even if we did not know that Marenzio had possessed a copy of the 1573 reprint of Lassus *I a 5* (1555).[21] The two texts in Lassus' First Book later reset by Marenzio are both by Petrarch: *Crudele acerba* and *Solo e pensoso,* but it was only at the very end of his life that Marenzio felt able to compete with the great cosmopolitan who had died five years previously.[22]

The awe which Marenzio must have felt for arguably the greatest composer of the second half of the century did not however prevent him from acquiring some of the techniques deployed in Lassus' *I a 5*. Thus Marenzio's *O voi che sospirate*[23] includes a direct borrowing from a Petrarch setting by

Lassus[24] [ex. 5]. Noteworthy is the rhythmic contrast between the first and second parts of Lassus' opening line, copied by Marenzio at the opening of a setting of a sonnet by Della Casa, where the same chromatic theme appears in inversion [ex. 6] On the whole, however, such rhythmic contrasts are rarely used in the sombre, turbulent manner of the earlier madrigals of Lassus; on the contrary, the emphasis in Marenzio's works of the early 1580's is on lightness, grace, and pungent, easily memorable rhythmic motives.[25]

The madrigals of Lassus' friend and contemporary, Filippo de Monte, are more difficult to assess owing to the scarcity of reprints. By far the most remarkable feature of his madrigal writing is his discriminating literary choice; indeed his wide knowledge of the latest Italian poetry is remarkable for a foreigner. In this he resembles Marenzio; indeed, the two share an estimated forty-two texts in common.[26] According to Einstein, Monte moves from a style that is "animated and at the same time subdued"[27] to "a more facile way of writing, characterized by greater transparency and the use of smaller motives."[28] It was about this time when, after 1581, Monte's style drew closer to Marenzio's, that the younger composer appears to have modeled one of his own pieces on one by the Flemish composer.[29]

There could be no greater contrast between Monte's gallic refinement and the sombre emotionalism of another Northerner, Giaches de Wert. His settings of *Solo e pensoso* and *Crudele acerba* are an important link between Lassus in 1555 and Marenzio in 1599. The former was published by Wert in his *VII a 5* (1581),[30] a milestone in both the career of Wert and the development of the Italian madrigal. The impact this book made on Marenzio is visible as early as 1584, when he resets a passage from Tasso's recently published epic, *La Gerusalemme liberata,* adding two further stanzas to the two already set by Wert.[31] The passage beginning "Giunto a la tomba . . ." is Tancredi's lament at having slain his beloved Clorinda in battle, a lament made more lugubrious through Tancredi's presence at Clorinda's tomb. As a "set piece" of pathos it surpasses even the most lyrical moments of Guarini's *Pastor fido,* on which Wert, Marenzio, and Monteverdi drew in the 1590's. Not only does Marenzio choose the same mode, clefs, and mensuration as Wert,[32] but he quotes Wert's music for the opening of Tancredi's speech.[33] Similar, too, is the exploitation of the low E in the first line to represent the descent to the tomb, and the suitably lifeless recitative on line 3.[34] There are however some fundamental differences. Whereas Wert repeats whole lines and phrases for the sake of emphasis and word audibility,[35] Marenzio is more prone to repeating individual words.[36] In addition, Wert restricts his harmonies in the *prima parte* to *c* and *g* major, *a* minor, and *e* major or minor. This limited harmonic range chillingly evokes the narrow confines of a tomb,[37] whereas Marenzio's harmonic spectrum is much wider and his expressive means lacking Wert's emotional directness. Marenzio depicts the tomb through white, boulder-like semibreves and relies more on contrapuntal artifices such as contrary motion and double counterpoint.

Wert's unaffected emotionalism and seriousness gained him the admiration of Tasso himself, who could well have known Wert's setting when, in his dialogue *La Cavaletta* (1587)[38], he urged Striggio, Wert, and Luzzaschi to restore music to the dignity of ancient times.[39] With Striggio, if not with Luzzaschi, Marenzio seems to have had some connection. The phenomenal success of the *I a 6* (1560) may have been partly due to the popularity of *Nasce la pena mia*,[40] which in one madrigal by Marenzio becomes the subject of an amusing *jeu d'esprit*. Striggio's first line is parodied in the final line of a six-line poem by Pigna, *La dipartita è amara:* "Nasce la *gioia* mia."[41] On repetition, Marenzio discards Striggio's music and introduces faster music to symbolize the transition from "pena" ("pain") to "gioia" ("joy") [ex. 7].

Later, it is possible the two composers became personally acquainted:[42] this is suggested by the appearance of one setting each of a stanza from the same *sestina,* both published in the 1592 edition of *Spoglia amorosa* (*RISM* 1592[15]). Marenzio's stanza, *Rivi, fontane e fiumi,* had already appeared in an exclusively Roman collection (*RISM* 1589[7]) and appears now as the *seconda parte* of Striggio's *All'hor che lieta l'alba,* the first stanza of the same *sestina.* The poem, set entire by Monte in his *I a 7* (1599), celebrates a wedding or wedding anniversary. Both *parti* use the untransposed aeolian mode and the bright sonority of two sopranos. Striggio seems to have absorbed the younger composer's more florid writing in his later years and may in this respect be grouped with Monte, A. Gabrieli, Lassus, and Ingegneri, whose styles changed along similar lines around 1580 or a little after.

Marenzio and the "New Manner"

Before continuing, it would be well to pause and consider what Marenzio's contemporaries regarded as important in his music.[43] The tone is set in 1597 by Thomas Morley, who speaks of "good ayre and fine invention": the implication is that Marenzio's music is more pleasing to the ear than Alfonso Ferrabosco's "deepe skill."[44] The word "ayre" is echoed by Peacham in 1622,[45] while its Italian equivalent, "aria," appears in the writings of Vincenzo Giustiniani and G.B. Doni. Giustiniani implies that the novelty of the early madrigals made an immediate impact:

> In poco progresso di tempo s'alterò il gusto della musica e comparver le composizioni di Luca Marenzio e di Ruggero Giovannelli, con invenzione di nuovo diletto [...] l'eccellenza delle quali consisteva in una nuova aria et grata all'orecchie, con alcune fughe facili e senza straordinario artificio.[46]

G.B. Doni also uses the words "bell'aria" and the nearly synonymous "grazia" in connection with Marenzio.[47]

From the above examples it is clear that the fashionable view of Marenzio's music was based more on the earlier than on the controversial, but lesser known, later style. Morley and Peacham based their judgments on those madrigals available in English anthologies and Giustiniani clearly refers to the madrigals published in the 1580's. Significant too is the viewpoint of Alessandro Guarini who in his *Farnetico savio* (1610) compares Luzzaschi with Dante, and Marenzio with the more euphonious and fashionable Petrarch.[48] Had he been more familiar with the later works (and with the Dante setting, *IX a 5*, 1599, no. 1) he might have had occasion to modify this comparison!

Thus it was not intensity of expression, bold chromaticism, or dissonance that contemporaries preferred to see in Marenzio's music. Rather they imply that his music is more pleasant to listen to than that of earlier composers, owing to the new melodic style and the avoidance of over-complicated contrapuntal textures. One madrigal which helped to form this verdict must have been *Liquide perle* (*I a 5*, 1580, no. 1), commended by Pietro della Valle in an essay of 1640 together with a *sdrucciole* setting of Giovanelli.[49] As this piece is the most popular item of Marenzio's most popular book, it is well to consider what may have been the "grazie" found by della Valle. He would no doubt have found the opening passage of double counterpoint "new and delightful";[50] while such combinations are by no means entirely new, nevertheless the lightness of touch, clear harmonies, and the opening dactylic rhythm distinguish it from previous examples by composers such as Lassus. This combination of erudition and sheer musical delight caught the imagination of composers who emerged during the 1580's, as can be seen by the number of resettings and quotations. Among the latter is the one in Pallavicino's *Donna, se quel "ohimè"*; however, the rearrangement for five voices lacks the delicacy of Marenzio's four-voice opening [ex. 8].

Premonitions of the "New Manner"

How was Marenzio's "new manner" arrived at, and how new was it? A glance at the Venetian and Roman madrigal c.1565-1580 will provide several clues.

Andrea Gabrieli's madrigals foreshadow Marenzio's in a number of ways. Chordal writing, and the repetition and transposition of homophonically declaimed phrases are more common than with Rore. The paired entries at the opening of *Due rose fresche* are each composed of two voices sounding the words simultaneously rather than in overlapping succession, as in the previously mentioned examples by Rore. Marenzio's *Due rose fresche* quotes Gabrieli's earlier setting, smoothing out the opening paired entries [ex. 9]. The greater concern for harmonic colour affects the way Gabrieli uses chromaticism. Direct chromaticism is rare; more common are indirect chromaticism[52] and indirect false relations such as the diminished fifth or octave, or the false unison.[53]

A younger composer working in Venice, Claudio Merulo, provides a stylistic link between Gabrieli and Marenzio. Lively declamation and warm chromaticism characterize his most popular composition, *Da le perle e rubini*.[54] Marenzio enlivens Merulo's reiterated chords with touches of direct chromaticism [ex. 10].

Merulo belonged to that generation of madrigalists who turned away from Petrarch to embrace the new, lighter kind of *poesia per musica*. This trend is already discernible in 1561, the year of Merulo's first setting of an epigrammatic *canzone* stanza, *Madonna poi ch'uccider mi volete*.[55] This text became very popular in the Veneto and was eventually set by Marenzio in 1582 (*III a 5*, no. 1). Marenzio's setting contains only one possible reference to Merulo's [ex. 11]. The real model, however, is provided by another composer of the Veneto, Ippolito Baccusi. Baccusi was active at Verona, and his *III a 6* (1572) is dedicated to the famed *Accademici* of that city. It can hardly be a coincidence that two of the texts set by Baccusi recur as the texts of the opening two numbers of Marenzio's *III a 5* (1582), dedicated to the very same *Accademici*. Marenzio's first composition, *Madonna, poich'uccider mi* copies Baccusi's slow, invocatory rhythms for the initial "Madonna," following this with the same snatches of rapid declamation playfully bounced from one half-choir to another [ex. 12].

Playfulness is an important element of the newer *poesia per musica*, with its short phrases and concentrated, witty argument. This quality is epitomized by the technique which Artusi calls *gioco*,[56] meaning a short snatch of melody reiterated by the same voice or another voice of equal pitch. This results in a sound reminiscent of medieval *stimmtausch* and in static harmonies animated by strongly rhythmical motives. G.M. Nanino, one of the more original Roman composers before Marenzio, achieves precisely this effect at the opening of one of his most popular madrigals [ex. 13]. Nanino's text, with its play on the theme of death, was set as often as the similar *Madonna, poich'uccider mi*.[57] Its repeated tonic and dominant harmonies foreshadow Macque and Marenzio.

If the madrigal was beginning to assimilate lighter, canzonet-like elements, the converse process was also happening. Girolamo Conversi's *Canzoni alla napolitana* (1572) are all in one stanza and approach the madrigal in the polyphonic and often lengthy manipulation of small motives. This blend of playfulness and erudition left a decisive imprint on Marenzio and his generation. Particularly important is the sense of functional harmony, as may be seen, for example, in the IV-V-I progression and sequential passage at the end of *Ma se tempo giamai*.[58] But the converging of the lighter madrigal and the "new *canzone*"[59] was a two-way process, for Conversi's setting of Petrarch's *Zefiro torna* is reminiscent of his *canzoni*, less sophisticated than Marenzio's richly suggestive setting of 1585. Nevertheless, Marenzio occasionally recaptures Conversi's brisk rhythms [ex. 15].

If the lightness of such pieces as Nanino's *Morir può'l vostro* owe something to the new canzonet style of Conversi, the quality of the madrigals produced in Rome in the decade before Marenzio is by no means even. As far as generalizations from limited sources allow, we can be reasonably certain that the chromatic experiments of the North are avoided, with a compensating emphasis on texture and vocal color. Restraint and understatement are the hallmarks of Dragoni's *Lieti, verdi, fiorite* (*III a 5*, 1579; text by Sannazaro), which contains some striking anticipations of Marenzio's setting (*V a 5*, 1585). The final line uses a similar scalar theme and relies on passing dissonances (rather than chromaticism) to achieve the required emotional effect [ex. 16].

At other times however, the Romans showed a disregard for expression and appropriate word-setting which is at the best of times naïve, at the worst, barbaric. Thus Palestrina, the leading church composer, sets the phrase "Morì quasi il mio core" to a rising phrase which negates the meaning of the words, even though at other times he was capable of great expressivity.[60] Equally uneven is Zoilo, whose *Chi per voi non sospira*[61] was justly popular; however, the same composer's *Io piango* (*II a 4, 5*, 1562; text by Petrarch)[62] is marred by an unnecessary melisma on the word "questo" ("this") in the final line. Both Zoilo and Nanino habitually place melismas on the penultimate syllable of the line; Marenzio however uses them only when the word requires emphasis.

Whether or not the inhibitions of the Roman madrigalists are due to their indifference to the madrigal and their preference for church music at a time of religious revival, it was a foreigner, Jean de Macque, who gave the madrigal in Rome a decisive creative impetus. Macque had been in Rome as early as 1574, in time to contribute to the *Quarto libro delle muse* (*RISM* 1574[4]), a collection dominated by Roman composers. Stylistically the turning point is five years later, for the *I a 4, 5, 6* of 1579 sets him widely apart from his Roman colleagues. Greater rhythmic variety and fluidity and clearer harmonies are the main characteristics. Quavers, used rarely in the earlier madrigals, now from an integral part of his melodic thought, often appearing in a melismatic group of four in ascending or descending motion, as with Marenzio.[63] The two composers' remarkable affinity is apparent in the way they use *gioco*, which usually appears as a series of overlapping paired entries in canon at the unison [ex. 17]. Not merely affinity, but mutual acquaintance and collaboration is suggested by Marenzio's and Macque's settings of the third and fourth stanzas of Horace's ode *Donec gratus eram tibi* in Alamanni's translation (*RISM* 1582[4]).[64] The final couplets have similar syntactical and semantic structures, reflected by musical motives common to Marenzio and Macque. Macque even takes the trouble of altering Alamanni's text in lines 4-5 so as to incorporate a textual-musical reminiscence of the stanza set by Marenzio.[65] The two movements typify the two composers' contrasting use of *gioco:* Marenzio achieves breadth and serenity in his depiction of Amaranta's playing and singing (b.22 ff); Macque's swirling quavers (b.1 ff) suggest sudden infatuation, while the dotted rhythms and ternary rhythms (b.25ff) sound suitably lascivious. It is clear that the techniques of the lighter forms have been manipulated with a virtuosity and expressive power unprecedented in the Roman madrigal.

The Virtuoso Madrigal

Of the "three great virtuosi" of the late Italian madrigal—Marenzio, Gesualdo, and Monteverdi[66]—Marenzio is chronologically the first. In fact he is surrounded by a host of lesser *virtuosi* an awareness of whom is essential if we are to appreciate Marenzio's early style to the full. Of these lesser figures, Macque is the most crucial. Nor must we neglect the hypersensitive Luzzaschi, the two Brescians, Bertani and Virchi, contemporaries as well as compatriots of Marenzio, and the extrovert Giovanelli, Marenzio's most formidable rival in Rome.

Of Luzzaschi's madrigals we know less than we know of his musical philosophy, thanks to a letter of dedication addressed to Lucrezia d'Este in 1596. In it, the author[67] expounds the familiar Renaissance idea that artistic and cultural standards improve with each generation.[68] Thus the madrigal as a poetic form has been improved out of all recognition, while musicians of the day have striven to attain

> . . . nuovi modi, e nuove invenzione (*sic*) più dell'usate dolci, e leggiadre (. . .) delle quali hanno formata una nuova maniera, che non solo per la novità sua, ma per l'isquisitezza dell'artificio potesse piacere, e conseguir l'applauso del mondo.[69]

Novelty[70] and artifice are inseparable from a third quality, namely, expressive variety:

> [Il musico] piagne, se il verso piagne, ride, se ride, se corra, se resta, se priega, se niega, se grida, se tace, se vive, se muore, tutti questi affetti, ed effetti così vivamente da lui vengon espressi . . .[71]

Affect and effect, novelty and artifice, go hand in hand in the *virtuosi* who achieved prominence in the 1580's. The newly found emotional energy and technical assurance typified by the Horace settings are essential to what Luzzaschi calls the "nuova maniera" with its seemingly inexhaustible possibilities. An undoubted stimulus was provided by the new singing style cultivated at Ferrara in the early 1580's: in Marenzio's *I a 6* (1581), dedicated to the Duke of Ferrara, the new "luxuriant" style makes deeper inroads than before, reaching its peak in the *IV a 6* (1587), just before Marenzio's artistic attitude underwent an irreversible change.[72]

The *IV a 6* may be described as a compendium of fashionable texts set in a fashionable style, compiled possibly with the aim of procuring a new patron following the imminent death of Luigi d'Este. The two sonnets by Tasso represent the most ambitious choice, and may be regarded as showpieces of the luxuriant style. The expressive use of *melismata,* intricate rhythms, wide ranges and rapid shifts in texture, sets them in a higher artistic bracket than many of the earlier experiments of the 1580's.[73] Lighter, but at times equally intricate, is the setting of G.B. Strozzi's *Questa ordì'l laccio* (no. 12). This text exists in several versions; Marenzio's is exactly the same as one set three years earlier by a fellow Brescian, Lelio Bertani. The two compositions are similar in a general sense, in that they both make use of motives in canon at the crotchet and exploit the equal range of two interweaving sopranos [ex. 18]. *Questa ordì'l laccio* is close in mood to the sprightly *Vaneggio od è pur vero* (no. 13), the opening paired entries of which seem related to Stabile's setting of 1581 [ex. 19]. It is however the concluding piece that tells us the most about Marenzio's activities in Rome. The nine-voice *Donne, il celeste lume* was almost certainly written for a performance of Cristoforo Castelletti's *Stravaganze d'Amore,* a five-act comedy staged in the palace of Giacomo Boncompagni, the natural son of Pope Gregory XIII, on 3 March 1585.[74] The other surviving piece which was probably destined for this performance, *Donne, la pura luce,* is by Ruggiero Giovanelli.[75]

Giovanelli's career parallels Marenzio's in many respects. His madrigal books were all reprinted several times, and he is mentioned alongside Marenzio in the writings of both Pietro della Valle and Vincenzo Giustiniani.[76] His broad harmonies and predilection for quaver declamation bring him close to Marenzio, even if he could not match his emotional range. He too was drawn to the Ferrarese poets, Guarini and Tasso, and to the *versi sdruccioli* of Sannazaro's *Arcadia.* One of his distinguishing characteristics is his acute sense of rhythm: in the way he can use a rhythm thematically, he is at least the equal of Marenzio. There is in fact an extraordinary family resemblance between the three settings of Tasso's *Amatemi ben mio* by Bertani (1585), Giovanelli (1586), and Marenzio (1591),[77] a resemblance derived from the introduction of similar rhythmic motives to underline the two verbs "V'amerò [. . .] Morirò" in lines 4 and 8 [ex. 20].

We have further opportunity to compare these three composers through their appearance in the Brescian anthology, *L'amorosa Ero* (*RISM* 1588[17]), for their settings in many ways form a group distinct from the sixteen remaining settings.[78] Not only are they more melismatic, but they employ rhythmic motives of a type sometimes met in Conversi's *canzoni,* but here expressive of heroic dignity.[79] Remarkable also is the extent to which successive fragments of text are combined contrapuntally, especially at the opening and close.[80] There is a strongly competitive element in such anthologies as *L'amorosa Ero* and *I lieti amanti* (*RISM* 1586[10]) where originality of content is less important than the novelty and artifice which each individual composer is able to inject into a familiar or stereotyped text.

Summary

The earliest composer whose influence is clearly discernible is Rore. Of the composers of the immediately succeeding generations, Lassus may have had a decisive influence in the spheres of rhythm and counterpoint, Ingegneri in that of chromaticism, and Gabrieli and Merulo in their colorful, declamatory style. In the last two composers a lighter style of madrigal is gradually forming, characterized by less ambitious poetic texts, more incisive rhythms, and clearer harmonies. At the same time, the invention of the "new canzone" (Conversi) reinforces the combination of hedonism and erudite wit which characterizes the "new manner" of Marenzio, Giovanelli, and Bertani. However, the *virtuosi* who rose to prominence in the 1580's would have made less impact without the sharp stimulus provided by a Northerner, Macque.

Conclusion

With Marenzio, the lighter madrigal, single-stanza *canzone,* and the new singing style all converge to form the virtuoso madrigal. However, if this were all, Marenzio would be no finer a composer than Macque, Bertani, or Giovanelli. What distinguishes Marenzio is the thoroughness with which these virtuoso elements have become infused with an expressive capacity at least equal to that found in the madrigals of Rore. The new-fangled motives, contrapuntal techniques, rhythms, harmonies, and textures are not used for their own sakes, but are subordinated to the requirements of expression. In order to find out what it is that is being expressed, let us now turn to the literature chosen by Marenzio.

3

The Literary Sources

Introduction

The object of this chapter is partly to correct and amplify Einstein's[1] extensive researches in the field of Marenzio's poetic choice, and partly to interpret the significance of this choice, especially with regard to the four favorites, Petrarch, Sannazaro, Tasso, and Guarini. Where possible the identified texts have been traced back to the earliest surviving source, whether a miscellaneous anthology, a publication of a single poet's works, a manuscript, or a musical source which Marenzio would have known.

Marenzio's Preferences

Marenzio's choice reveals a striking preference for Petrarch, Sannazaro, Guarini, and Tasso, in almost equal proportions (see table 1). All other poets are represented by a maximum of eight texts (Celiano), most by only one. The astonishing variety of souces (forty-six poets) betrays a wide knowledge of literature culled no doubt from his association with literary patrons such as Cleria Cesarini, Girolamo Ruis, and Cinzio Aldobrandini. The table also shows the abrupt change in the pattern of literary choice after 1593: no Sannazaro, more Guarini (*Il Pastor fido*), and the emergence of Celiano—altogether a less heterogeneous, more narrow selection.

Petrarch

Of the two greatest *trecento* poets, it was Petrarch rather than Dante who inspired the poets and musicians of the sixteenth century. Typical signs are Bembo's analysis of the potentially musical qualities of Petrarch's poetry (1525),[2] innumerable reprints and commentaries of the *Canzoniere,* and the whole literary movement named after him.[3] As late as 1597, when Petrarch's popularity with musicians was already on the wane, Morley defines the madrigal as "a kinde of musicke made upon songs and sonnets, such as

Table 1.   Marenzio's Poetic Choice Before and After 1593

Poet	Number of texts to 1593	Number of texts after 1593	Overall total
Guarini	11	24	35
Petrarch	21	8	29
T. Tasso	18	9	27
Sannazaro	26	0	26
Celiano	0	8	8
Strozzi	3	3	6
Della Casa	5	0	5
Ariosto	3	0	3
Ongaro	0	3	3
Quirino	3	0	3
Tansillo	2	1	3
Troiano	3	0	3
Alamanni*	2	0	2
Castelletti	2	0	2
Gottifredi	2	0	2
Molza	2	0	2
Pigna	2	0	2
Arlotti	0	1	1
Barbati	1	0	1
Barignano	1	0	1
Bembo	0	1	1
Caro	0	1	1
Casone	1	0	1
Cini	1	0	1
Coppetta	1	0	1
Dante	0	1	1
Gambara	1	0	1
Grillo	0	1	1
Groto	1	0	1
Guiccardi	1	0	1
Guidi	1	0	1
Manfredi	1	0	1
Marcellini	1	0	1
Martinengo	1	0	1
Moscaglia	1	0	1
Nannini	1	0	1
Orsi	1	0	1
Pace	1	0	1
Parabosco	1	0	1
Pasqualino	1	0	1
Pavesi	1	0	1
Pocaterra	1	0	1
Sacchetti	1	0	1
B. Tasso	1	0	1
M. Veniero	1	0	1
Zuccarini	1	0	1

* Includes one translation from Horace.

Petrarcha and many Poets of our time have excelled in."[4] In fact, Petrarch was much more frequently set in the first two thirds of the century than during the last third, the generation of Tasso and Guarini. It is therefore something of an anachronism to find Marenzio in the 1580's and 1590's returning so frequently to the *Canzoniere*.

The poems set by Marenzio date from about 1326-1351. The first extant version of the *Canzoniere* was completed in 1362 and constantly revised until the year of Petrarch's death (1374).[5] The dominant motive is the poet's unrequited love for Laura, whom he met in Avignon in 1327 and who died there of the plague in 1348. This event accounts for the distinction between the poems written before her death (*in vita di madonna Laura*) and those written after (*in morte di madonna Laura*).[6] The idealization of Laura owes much to Dante and the *stilnovisti;* in addition Petrarch was much influenced by the rhetorical tradition of antiquity,[7] a fact which accounts for the elegance and erudition which sixteenth-century poets found so worthy of imitation.

Marenzio's Petrarch settings may be divided very loosely into three consecutive groups (see table 2). In the first and third there is a preference for the relatively sombre poetry *in morte,* while in the very brief second period (1585), Marenzio shows a preference for the more cheerful poems from the first part of the *Canzoniere*.

Owing to the preponderance of poems *in vita* in the *Canzoniere* (266 *in vita* to 95 *in morte*) we can conclude that Marenzio displays a *relative* preference for the poems *in morte* (thirteen settings) to those *in vita* (fifteen settings). The overall preference for the poems *in morte* is explained by the selection of eight stanzas from the double sestina, *Mia benigna fortuna* (*Canzoniere,* no. 332). In this monotonously gloomy poem, to which Marenzio turned repeatedly from 1581 till 1599 (the year of his own death), Petrarch laments the death of Laura, and contrasts his present gloom with his former happiness. In almost every stanza, Death is called upon to put an end to the poet's misery with his own death. There is no variation in mood, only in the way it is expressed;[8] for this reason, Marenzio, like Lassus, sets each stanza as a separate composition rather than risking the monotony of a unified cycle. His decision is vindicated by the intensity of expression achieved in every one of the settings, all of which are cast in "minor" modes[9] and use the archaic, even rhythmic tread characteristic of *tempus imperfectum diminutum* (barred C).

The other remarkable characteristic about Marenzio's selection concerns the poems *in vita*. Many of these appear in the *I a 4* (1585) where the pastoral setting and classical allusions form an ideal complement to the settings from Sannazaro's *Arcadia*. Marenzio sets three out of the four madrigals Petrarch ever wrote (*Canzoniere,* nos. 52, 121, and 106), all of them describing an encounter between the poet and his beloved in pastoral, idyllic surroundings.

Table 2.   Marenzio's Settings of Petrarch

Incipit	Number of Canzoniere	Vita or Morte	Work
L'aura serena	196	Vita	*I a 6* (1581)
O voi che sospirate	332	Morte	*II a 5* (1581)
I piango ed ella	359	Morte	*II a 5* (1581)
Se'l pensier che	125	Vita	*II a 5* (1581)
Oimè il bel viso	267	Morte	*III a 5* (1582)
Nessun visse giamai	332	Morte	*II a 6* (1584)
Del cibo onde	342	Morte	*II a 6* (1584)
Consumandomi vo	237	Vita	*V a 5*(1585)
Due rose fresche	245	Vita	*V a 5* (1585)
Non vidi mai	127	Vita	*I a 4* (1585)
O bella man	198	Vita	*I a 4* (1585)
Non al suo amante	52	Vita	*I a 4* (1585)
Hor vedi Amor	121	Vita	*I a 4* (1585)
Apollo s'ancor vive	34	Vita	*I a 4* (1585)
Nova Angeletta	106	Vita	*I a 4* (1585)
Ahi dispietata morte	324	Morte	*I a 4* (1585)
Tutto'l dì piango	216	Vita	*I a 4* (1585)
Zefiro torna	310	Morte	*I a 4* (1585)
Ov'è condotto	332	Morte	*I a 4, 5, 6* (1588)
Se la mia vita	12	Vita	*I a 4, 5, 6* (1588)
Fuggito è'l sonno	332	Morte	*I a 4, 5, 6* (1588)
Giovane Donna	30	Vita	*VI a 5* (1595)
Amor i ho	332	Morte	*IX a 5* (1599)
Dura legge d'Amor	—	—	*IX a 5* (1599)
Chiaro segno Amor	332	Morte	*IX a 5* (1599)
Se sì alto pon	332	Morte	*IX a 5* (1599)
L'aura che'l verde	246	Vita	*IX a 5* (1599)
Solo e pensoso	35	Vita	*IX a 5* (1599)
Crudele acerba	332	Morte	*IX a 5* (1599)

All of the madrigals use classical motives or allegory; the same may be said for the sonnet, *Apollo, s'ancor vive,* an invocation to Apollo, God of medicine, comparing Laura to Daphne who was transformed into a laurel bush while fleeing from Apollo. For these more idyllic poems *in vita,* Marenzio uses the same continuous polyphonic texture as found in the settings from *Mia benigna fortuna;* the rhythm however is more varied and Marenzio uses the usual *tempus imperfectum* (unbarred C).

Petrarchism

The most important literary movement of the sixteenth century is Petrarchism, without which it is impossible to envisage the development of secular music.[10] In Petrarch's poems, as in the musical form of the madrigal, Love is raised to the level of a transcendent force, at once a cruel tyrant and an embodiment of ideals. This contradictory quality is reflected in the poet's varied moods, for Love is the cause of life and death, hope and fear; its power is expressed through conventional symbols such as darts, chains, and flames. The omnipotence and omnipresence of Love is fundamental to the sixteenth-century madrigalists to such a degree that Morley speaks of the madrigal as "lovers musicke"[11] and draws an implied parallel between Petrarchan sentiment and musical style.[12] Contrast is a quality as important to the madrigal composers of the sixteenth century as to Petrarch. The sonnet *Zefiro torna* (*I a 4*, 1585, no. 18) exhibits a form of contrast (between the exuberant quatrains and the despair of the two tercets) which was seminal in its influence. Thus in both *Già torna* (*II a 5*, 1581, no. 15) and *Ecco L'aurora* (*IV a 5*, 1584, no. 9) the first six lines describe springtime and dawn respectively, the last two lines, the poet's inconsolable grief.[13] Another, more obvious form of Petrarchism is the parody or quotation of first lines of Petrarch's poetry. There is a clear parallel between the intellectual pleasure derived from poetic quotation and musical quotation, especially when the two are found together.[14]

Petrarchan Metrical Forms

In his poetry, Petrarch uses the forms of *ballata, canzone, sestina,* sonnet, *terza rima,* and madrigal.

The one *ballata* which Marenzio selected is made unrecognizable through the omission of the first three lines. The poem *Amor quando fioria,* of which Marenzio sets lines 4-12,[15] has the metrical structure ABB/DeF/EdF/fBB.[16] With the initial *ripresa* omitted, the rhyme scheme is the same as for a *canzone* stanza: two balancing *piedi* (or *mutazioni*) of three lines each, and a concluding *volta.*

The *canzone* is a ballata without ripresa, the former presumably derived from the latter.[17] The canzone consists of two piedi with corresponding line lengths and rhyme content,[18] followed by a concluding *sirma* (or *sirima*). The latter is relatively free in form; normally however it takes for its first rhyme the last rhyme of the second piede. This linking rhyme is called the *concatenazione.* After the last stanza of a canzone there is often an *envoy* or *commiato* of about three to seven lines, in which the poet takes his leave from the poem, or sends it on its way.

Marenzio sets two canzone stanzas from Petrarch (*Canzoniere*, nos. 125 and 127), and one fragment (no. 359). In addition, some of the canzone stanzas from Sannazaro and Della Casa are modeled on examples of Petrarch. For example, *Ben mi credeva*[19] is taken from a canzone which shares the same form as Petrarch's *Se'l pensier che mi strugge* (abC/abC/cdeeDff).[20] Stanzas based on the Petrarchan model usually amount to thirteen lines (two piedi of three lines each and a volta of seven lines);[21] in addition there exists a shorter type of canzone stanza quite distinct from the Petrarchan tradition (see below).

The form of the *sestina* (invented by Arnaut Daniel in the twelfth century) is far stricter than that of the canzone: six stanzas (or twelve if a double sestina) in which the six rhyme words rotate in the pattern ABCDEF FAEBDC CFDABE [. . .]. The final stanza concludes with a commiato combining all six rhyme words in three lines. Marenzio sets not only numerous single stanzas, but also three sestinas in their entirety: two by Sannazaro published in 1584 and 1585, and one by Petrarch dating from ten years later.[22]

The sonnet shows all the signs of being a consciously invented art form,[23] and was therefore the most appropriate vehicle for the spread of Petrarchism throughout Europe in the sixteenth century. As used by Petrarch and his successors, the sonnet consists of two quatrains in the fixed form ABBA/ ABBA[24] and two tercets using two or three different rhymes with relatively greater freedom.[25] The final tercet provides the poem with a climax, usually effected through the introduction of some previously withheld rhetorical device.[26] Sustained thought is assured through long and involved sentences, as in Petrarch's *Se la mia vita*[27] which consists of a subordinate clause in the two quatrains and a main clause in the tercets. In *L'aura che'l verde lauro*[28] the syntactical order is the reverse. In *Laura serena* and *Solo e pensoso*[29] the syntactical division occurs after the first tercet; however, Marenzio adheres to the conventional division into two quatrains. A similar division affects *Affliger chi per voi*[30] on a text by Della Casa, a poet whose handling of rhythm and sonority had a liberating influence on later poets, especially Tasso.[31] The sombre menace and metaphorical boldness of the final tercet of the above-named is typical:

> Aspro costume in bella donna e rio
> Di sdegno armarsi, e romper l'altrui vita
> A mezzo il corso, come duro scoglio.[32]

Terza rima is the rhyme-scheme of Petrarch's *Trionfi*[33] and consists of a series of tercets in the form ABA/BCB/[. . .]/YXY/Z. A poem in this form is called a *capitolo* after the division of Petrarch's *Trionfi* into chapters.[34] The one *capitolo* Marenzio set in its entirety is Tansillo's *Se quel dolor.*[35] In addition, the same rhyme scheme frequently occurs in Sannazaro's *Arcadia.*

The *trecento* madrigal is represented by three examples from Petrarch all set in the *I a 4* (1585). These all display the characteristic division into tercets, with an optional final rhyming couplet.[36]

Other Metrical Forms

Metrical forms not used by Petrarch comprise the *caccia, ottava rima,* the shorter canzone and related strophic forms, the *villanella,* and the *cinquecento* madrigal.

The only *caccia* is Sacchetti's *Passando con pensier,* which uses dialogue to depict young girls picking flowers before a rain-shower. Marenzio's setting[37] is the only setting since Nicola da Perugia's in the fourteenth century.

The *ottava rima* (ABAB/ABCC) is, like *terza rima,* traditionally associated with drama and the epic.[38] It is used for long poems like Ariosto's *Orlando Furioso* (1516) and Tasso's *Gerusalemme* (1580), both popular with composers. The latter is the source of the four-part cycle which opens Marenzio's *IV a 5* (1584). Most in fact of the *ottava* stanzas set by Marenzio are from long poems; many are taken from Lodovico Dolce's two-volume *Stanze di diversi* (1556 and 1572). Marenzio was particularly attracted to two elegiac poems, *O bionde Iddio* (Anon)[39] and *Hor che nell'Oceano* (Quirino).[40] Marenzio exercises great discrimination in his choice of stanzas. Thus *Con dolce sguardo*[41] is taken from a spiritual poem which describes the conflict between divine and profane love; from it Marenzio selects the most profane and sensuous passage of all, in which the poet's mistress attempts, through gentle glances, laughter and tears, to dissuade him from abandoning her. Similarly, in the *I a 4* (1585), Marenzio draws on a passage from Tasso's *Rinaldo* in which the heroic mask is allowed to slip: *Lasso, dicea* is the love-lament of a shepherd after he has been repulsed for stealing a kiss.[42] Despite the popularity of the *ottava rima* form with Marenzio before 1593, there are no further settings beyond that date.

In the sixteenth century there emerged a new type of canzone with much shorter stanzas than those previously discussed, and frequently lacking the *concatenazione.* Such a one is Maffeo Veniero's *canzon pastorale, Florinda e Armillo,* with the form of Ab/Ab/cC.[43] A similar form (six lines, three rhymes) is found in *Madonna, poich'uccider mi volete* and *Togli dolce ben mio* (*III a 5,* 1582, nos. 1 and 16), both with single stanzas in the forms Ab/Ab/cC and aB/aB/cC.[44]

Irregular and free strophic forms often take the canzone as their formal basis. Thus *Deggio dunque partire* (*II a 5,* 1581, no. 1) would be a regular canzone but for the irregularity in the second piede of the first stanza.[45]

Equally close to the canzone is the two-stanza dialogue *Caro Aminta pur vuoi* (ab/b*A*/cC).[46] Cesare Pavesi's *Cinthia tu sei più bella* (set by Marenzio as *Filli tu sei più bella*)[47] borrows from the canzone the device of syntactically paired openings ("Cinthia, tu sei più bella . . . Cinthia, tu sei più cruda . . . Io son il più costante . . . Io, che morir . . .").[48] The same pairing together of the first stanza with the second, and the third with the fourth, affects the composite setting of Alamanni's translation of an ode by Horace ("Mentre ti fui sì grato . . . Mentre ti fui sì cara . . . Hor pien d'altro desio . . . Hor un laccio, un'ardore).[49] The poem is a dialogue between two lovers, each of the six stanzas being in the form aBbaA.[50] Alamanni's is one of many translations of this and other odes of Horace made in the sixteenth century.[51] It resembles the original Italian odes of Bernardo Tasso in the use of five lines and two rhymes in every stanza. Like Tasso, Alamanni is content to capture the Horatian spirit without reviving the classical metre.[52]

A number of texts recall the tercet structure of the villanella-without-refrain.[53] The clearest example is the anonymous *Basciami mille volte* whose nine lines may be divided into three ministrophes with the form of aBB.[54] The resemblance to the villanella is less clear when the tercets do not contain mutually distinct rhymes, in which case they may be nearer to the *cinquecento* madrigal.[55]

The Cinquecento Madrigal

The madrigal is Marenzio's favorite poetic type. We may surmise that a number of madrigals were written with no other purpose than to be set to music.[56] This would apply equally to the numerous anonymous texts as to those by such celebrities as Strozzi, Tasso, and Guarini whose poems were set to music (often in many versions) long before being published by those poets themselves.

The *cinquecento* madrigal is freer than its *trecento* namesake, but occasionally relies on pre-existing stricter forms, such as the *trecento* madrigal itself, the canzone stanza, or the ballata.[57] The influence of Petrarch's *Nova angeletta* (ABc/ABc/DD)[58] is seen in the exact adherence to the same form in Sannazaro's *Quando i vostri begl'occhi*,[59] which reproduces the Petrarchan form exactly. Other poems modify Petrarch's forms by replacing some of the *endecasillabici* with *settenari,* yet retaining the same rhyme scheme.[60]

More common than madrigals with *trecento* rhyme schemes are madrigals based on the canzone stanza whose second piede is irregular. One such text, *Liquide perle* (*I a 5;* text by Pasqualino), became a "hit number" in Marenzio's setting; it served as the model for the text of Bicci's *Candide perle* (published in Marenzio's *V a 6,* 1591, no. 3). Both poems have the six-line, three-rhyme form typical of the sixteenth-century canzone stanza: Ab/ba/cC and Ab/*ba*/Cc.[61] Another type exists with seven or more lines and a linking rhyme between the second piede and the sirma. As it happens, these texts occur only in the first three books *a 6*.[62]

The few ballata madrigals, like the many canzone madrigals, are found mainly in the earlier books. *Amor io non potrei*[63] differs from the ballata only inasmuch as it is the first, not the last rhyme of the ripresa that is recalled in the final volta: aBB/cDcD/dAA. This piece is followed by *Amor, poiche non vuole* (text by Parabosco) which likewise ends in an "A" rhyme: aBcbA/ BCCBA. Lines 5 and 10 of this poem are identical both poetically and musically.

Whatever its resemblance to other forms, the essential hallmark of the *cinquecento* madrigal is its formal freedom. The majority of the madrigals set by Marenzio are characterized by a loose succession of rhymed couplets relieved perhaps through the occasional *rime incrociate* (ABBA) or *alternate* (ABAB). The last two lines nearly always form a rhymed couplet, while the first line is often unrhymed (*verso sciolto*).

Such formal looseness is often compensated for by a corresponding tightness in the internal structure, especially in the concentrated use of rhetorical devices such as repetition, antithesis, and exclamation. There is a tradition of wit and ingenuity stretching back to the Latin epigrams of Pontano,[64] through the *strambotti* of Serafino dall'Aquila and the madrigals of Parabosco,[65] Groto and Guarini. Many of the madrigals set by Marenzio share these qualities: *Liquide perle* (*I a 5*, 1580, no. 1) may be described as a reduction to the barest essentials of a paradoxical conceit invented by Petrarch.[66] The poem divides into three parts: the first two lines describe the poet's tears; the second pair, the burning heart, still unquenched by the tears; while the third pair rounds off the poem with an elegiac exclamation. In *Donne il celeste lume* (*IV a 6*, 1587, no. 15) we may discern a similar tripartite form, in which the final couplet encapsulates the paradox developed during the first five lines.[67] The image of the flame which burns forever is used in many poems of this type: for example *Qual vive Salamandra*, the epigrammatic madrigal *par excellence*, which concludes with the couplet "O che felice sorte/ Viver in fiamma e non haver la morte."[68]

Other devices used to achieve structural cohesion in the *cinquecento* madrigal include the use of repeated sounds (alliteration and assonance). The musical or melic madrigal has aims very far removed from those of the epigrammatic madrigal, even if the two genres are not completely watertight.[69] The emphasis on sonority characteristic of the melic madrigal is clearly discernible in the lyrical masterpieces of G. B. Strozzi the Elder and Torquato Tasso. The sensuous, hypnotic quality of the following madrigal is due to the way in which the rhyme sounds are integrated with the total sonority. The result could hardly have been surpassed by the nineteenth-century French symbolists:

Dai bei labri di rose *aura* tranquilla,
 *Aura soav'*hor m*ovi*,
 E con Amor t'inst*illa*
M*ille* e *mille* piacer diversi e nuovi;
 Dolce spirando piovi,
 Dolce spirando fiocca
Dall'angelica b*occ'ond'io* sospiro,
 Ond'io respiro solo
E se n*on* gli mi do*n'io* gli m'inv*olo*[70]

Insistent word repetition is a favorite device of Strozzi's. The words in question are often printed in capitals in the original poetic source and some of them refer to specific personages.[71] Thus we encounter groups of poems featuring different words: "Filli,"[72] "Posa," "Zefiro," "Luce,"[73] "Pietra,"[74] "Maggio,"[75] etc.

Sannazaro

The sources by Iacopo Sannazaro used by Marenzio are the *Arcadia*[76] and the *Rime.*[77] The former was printed sixty-six times between 1504 and 1600.[78] It was regularly recited at meetings of the Accademia dei Rozzi in Siena,[79] and it is possible to see musical performance of certain passages—many of them containing the songs of shepherds—as growing out of that academic tradition. The informal *ridotti* of Roman patrons interested in both literature and music would have provided the right atmosphere for the numerous settings by Marenzio and his contemporaries active in Rome.[80] This interest is due to the nostalgia for antiquity prevalent in most Renaissance arts and branches of learning. Poets and musicians looked back to a Golden Age when poetry and music, art and life were one. As in Virgil's eclogues, Sannazaro's shepherds are innately musical[81] and cultivate their art in tranquil and natural surroundings. From the ancient Mantuan poet, Sannazaro drew many elements: the singing competition, the funeral oration, and many specific turns of phrase. The autobiographical element is also Virgilian: Sannazaro represents himself as Sincero, the name he went under in the Accademia Pontaniano in Naples. Alongside the humanistic influences must be noted the influence of that great humanist, Petrarch. For example, the passage beginning "Menando un giorno . . ." describes an encounter similar to the one described in Petrarch's madrigal, *Non al suo amante.*[82]

The *Arcadia* is divided into twelve books of richly descriptive prose each concluding with an eclogue in one or more of a variety of metrical forms. Marenzio draws on the first nine books only—a fact possibly explained by the omission of the last two books from the very first edition. The settings are concentrated in four books published between 1581 and 1588.[83] More than half are from the *I a 4* (1585), Marenzio's pastoral book *par excellence.* The mood varies from lyrical calm (*Fillida mia, II a 5*, 1581, no. 6) to the boisterous rhythms used in the settings of *versi sdruccioli*. *Fillida mia* is the first strophe of a song sung in alternation by Montano and Uranio. A setting of the second strophe by Rinaldo del Mel dating from 1584[84] reveals something of Marenzio's influence on composers resident in Rome, for several musical motives are common to both compositions. Particularly marked is the resemblance in the final lines [ex. 21].

A more boisterous, popular style invest the four settings of passages with *versi sdruccioli,* a type of *terza rima* with a weak syllable added to the end of the iambic hendecasyllable. The tripping, almost clumsy effect of the dactylic ending is designed to portray the accents of rustic speech. The last three syllables normally appear as a dotted rhythm ♩·♪♩ or ♩·♪♩ . The obtrusive effect of this cadential rhythm is lessened by the all-pervasiveness of lively rhythmic motives. This is especially the case in the two settings of passages describing idyllic scenes: *Vedi le valli* and *I lieti amanti* (*I a 4*, 1585, nos. 9 and 16). Rustic simplicity is suggested by other means: for example, parallel thirds recalling the sound of pipes are persistently used in the third part of *Vienne Montan*, the tripartite scene which concludes the *I a 4*.[85] Elenco and Ofelia indulge in a slanging match before deciding to settle their differences by holding a singing competition with Montano as adjudicator. The opening of the *gara di canto* coincides with the opening of Marenzio's *terza parte*. Elenco and Ofelia sing alternate tercets, the former represented by the two lower, the latter, by the two higher voices.[86] After a prayer addressed respectively to Pallas and Pan, the singers continue to sing of their repective loves. The parallelism of subject matter and syntax is matched by the recurrence of simple musical motives; in particular, the cadence patterns remain the same from one tercet to another [ex. 22]. From line 67 the treatment is more elaborate in that Elenco's song (lines 67-69) and Ofelia's (lines 70-72) are sung simultaneously, the word order thus being obscured [ex. 23]. It is clear that Marenzio was addressing a sophisticated audience already familiar enough with the text not to be perturbed by this simultaneous combination of successive tercets.

Even though Marenzio and Giovanelli set only three texts in common, the two composers' publications alternate in a manner that suggests a *gara di canto* rather like the one just described (see table 3). Marenzio's resetting of the singing competition overlaps with Giovanelli's by fifteen lines. This resetting may have provoked Giovanelli to reset two passages already selected by Marenzio. In his *II a 4*, Giovanelli copies Marenzio's dotted rhythms and the opposition of the two higher and two lower voices. However, he is unable to attain the pathos of Marenzio where the text requires it [ex. 24].

Sannazaro's *Rime* are subdivided into two unequal parts (thirty-three poems in the first part, ninety-eight in the second). All but one of Marenzio's

Table 3.   Texts from Sannazaro's *Arcadia*
Set by Giovanelli and Marenzio

Marenzio	Giovanelli
III a 5 (1582):	*I a 4* (1585):*
La pastorella mia (i.91-106)	Dimmi, caprar (ix.1-36, 43-57)
I a 4 (1585):*	*II a 4* (1589):
I lieti amanti (v.103-111)	I lieti amanti (v.103-111)
Vienne, Montan (ix.37-75)	La pastorella mia (i.91-106)

* Giovanelli's dedication is dated 1.1.1585, Marenzio's, 15.7.1585. Both books were published in Rome by Alessandro Gardano.

sixteen settings are from the larger second part. That Marenzio was relying more on one of the many reprints of the *Rime* than on anthologies is suggested by the inclusion in the *Spirituali* (1584) of three poems printed consecutively in all the editions.[87] However, the variants between Marenzio's versions of the text and those in the printed sources are more considerable than in the case of Petrarch, who is treated with more reverence.[88] The influence of Petrarch is evident both from the choice of subject matter and metre. Thus *Venuta era Madonna,* one of three madrigals set very early on,[89] depicts the appearance of the *Madonna* in a dream, uttering words of comfort.[90] In the sestina, *Non fu mai cervo,* rhyme words are used that had previously been used by Petrarch. Marenzio's musical settings are as varied and often as profound as his settings of Petrarchan poetry. There are in fact some interesting resemblances between settings of similar passages by both poets. One has only to compare the classically imitative openings of *Nova angeletta*[91] and *Sola angioletta* (*V a 5,* 1585, no. 1), or the distant modulations in the two sestina settings, *O voi che sospirate* and *O fere stelle.*[92]

Tasso

Tasso is Marenzio's fourth favorite poet; in the earlier period, Marenzio draws on his poetry more than on his Ferrarese contemporary, Guarini. Even without the recent identification of six settings of passages from two of Tasso's four eclogues,[93] it would be necessary to modify Pirrotta's statement that Marenzio showed an "apparente scarso interesse" in Tasso's poetry.[94] Among the reasons for Marenzio's interest we must count the fame brought by the *Gerusalemme liberata* (the first complete edition of which dates from 1581) and the two men's common involvement with the Ferrarese court. Despite Einstein's conjecture that the two men met and exchanged ideas (an opinion based on a highly selective reading of Tasso's dialogue *La Cavaletta*)[95] it is now generally accepted that the two men could not have met until 1592-1593 when Tasso was residing with Cardinal Cinzio Aldobrandini in Rome.[96]

It is not surprising that the first known Tasso settings tend to derive from Ferrarese and Mantuan circles: Fiesco in 1569, and Wert and Isnardi in 1577.[97] In 1582 Tasso became actively involved with the composition and compilation of the two anthologies honouring Laura Peperara (*RISM* 1582[5] and 1583[10]). It is in this decade that Tasso's poetry (along with Guarini's) became highly fashionable among musicians.

The five sonnets and thirteen madrigals set by Marenzio are nearly all love poems addressed to Lucrezia Bendidio and Laura Peperara, later singers at the Ferrarese court.[98] The poetry addressed to the former was published in the *Rime de gli Academici Eterei* (1567) which contains three sonnets later selected by Marenzio.[99] The first publication devoted exclusively to Tasso is Manuzio's *Rime . . . parte prima* (1581); neither this nor subsequent editions satisfied Tasso, owing to numerous misprints and misattributions.[100] From Manuzio's edition of the *Seconda parte* (1582) Marenzio may have taken only one sonnet,[101] while from the *Aggiunta alle rime et prose* (1585) he selects two madrigals for the *V a 6* (1591).[102] Of interest is the appearance of three madrigals in the *Parte quarta* (Venice: G. Vasalini, 1586) all set to music and published by Marenzio in 1583 and 1584; these must have been accessible only in manuscript form.[103]

Nearly all the many writers on Tasso's lyric poetry emphasize his sensuous qualities. As Fubini puts it so concisely: "come alla musica, alla luce tende la sensualità tassesca."[104] In *La Cavaletta* (a large portion of which is devoted to the discussion of music) Tasso himself emphasizes the importance of rhythmic and phonetic elements in establishing the mood of a poem.[105] With Tasso even more than with Strozzi, or Della Casa, the words pulsate with a life and vigor that is intensified even further when they are set to music.

This sensuous element accounts for Marenzio's rather special approach to the problem of setting Tasso's poetry to music. The vocal forces used are consistently larger than those used for Sannazaro's or Guarini's poetry: each of the six-voice books contains an average of two poems definitely ascribable to Tasso, whereas in the five-voice books the interest in Tasso appears to be more sporadic. The reason for this becomes clear if we compare two poems both set by Marenzio: Guarini's *Tirsi morir volea* (*I a 5*, 1580, no. 5) and Tasso's *Nel dolce seno* (*V a 6*, 1591, no. 8). The latter is modeled on the former: it describes love making in the guise of a metaphor of agonised dying.[106] Tasso's poem is more openly erotic than Guarini's epigram; as if aware of this difference, Marenzio sets the Tasso poem for the more colorful combination of six voices.

Marenzio's preference for poems of a richly descriptive or metaphorical character is evident if we study other six-voice settings. That these settings from a stylistic group is evident form certain shared musical characteristics such as recurring word-painting devices, a superabundance of *melismata* and other "luxuriant" features, and unusually large voice ranges.[107] There are more specific resemblances too, as may be seen if we compare the openings of *In un bel bosco* (*II a 6*, 1584, no. 9)—an encounter similar to that described by Petrarch in his madrigal *Nova angeletta*—and *In un lucido rio* (*III a 6*, 1585, no. 4), an ingenious deployment of the Narcissus myth to depict a shepherd's unrequited love [ex. 25]. In both compositions the introductory description is scored *a 3*, the Canto soaring above the two lower voices as if emphasizing the protagonists' loneliness. Meanwhile the interweaving of the two lower voices is suggestive of rich vegetation. A similar opening is used for the anonymous stanza set in the *V a 6* (1591), no. 6 in which the theme of Narcissus recurs [ex. 26]. Noteworthy is the use of the "narrative rhythm" ($\downarrow\,\downarrow\,\downarrow$) in all the three openings just discussed.[108]

Sustained allegory or metaphor characterizes both *In un bel bosco* and *Di nettare amoroso* (*IV a 6*, 1587, no. 2). In the first Love appears as a huntsman and the poet compares himself to a trapped animal. In the second the metaphor is military: the embrace of two women is likened to the jousting of two knights. The two settings abound in themes suggestive of hunting or searching and military, fanfare-like motives, and are among Marenzio's most colorful pieces.

The pieces for four or five voices form a less distinctive and more uneven group. In *Su'l carro della mente* (*I a 4*, 1585, no. 19) the celebrated beauty, Leonora Sanvitale, is compared to the sun being driven in a chariot across the sky. Marenzio's clumsy, halting rhythms fail to capture the majestic mood of the poem.[109] More expressive is *Se tu mi lasci* (*RISM* 1583[11]), the bitter denunciation of unfaithfulness, in which the emotional intensity of the declamatory madrigals of the *VI*, *VIII*, and *VIII a 5* is foreshadowed. The use of repeated notes for the cries of "misera" or "misero" betray the possible influence of Wert.[110] *Giunto a la tomba* (*I a 4*, 1584, no. 1) also owes much to Wert not only musically but in the choice of one textual reading. Unfortunately space does not permit a full discussion of the conflicting versions of the stanzas set by Marenzio.[111] It must suffice to observe that the version used by Marenzio finds no exact duplicate in any known source. The same applies to the madrigal *In un lucido rio* (*III a 6*, 1585, no. 4), an early version of *Sovra un lucido rio*, though not, it seems, as early as the version which now survives in a Sienese manuscript. Other poems may be early versions of works revised so radically that they are recognizable only after careful scrutiny (e.g. *Bianchi cigni e canori*[112]); some betray stylistic resemblances to other poems known to be by Tasso.[113]

Guarini

As a supplier of musical texts, Battista Guarini perhaps exceeded Tasso in popularity. Born in Ferrara, he was, from 1564, a member of the *Accademia degl'Eterei* at Padua.[114] In 1567 he was back in Ferrara by personal invitation of Alfonso II.[115] Two years later a number of his sonnets appear set to music by Giulio Fiesco.[116] However, it was only in the 1570's and 1580's (after the decline of Tasso's prominence at the Este court) that his madrigals were systematically commissioned and disseminated for musical setting.[117] Marenzio's emergence as a madrigalist around 1580 coincides exactly with the sudden growth in the poet's popularity.

Of the seventeen texts not taken from the *Pastor fido* the first five and last five are all scored *a 5,* the intervening seven being scored *a 6.* The overall preference for the five-voice combination[118] is in contrast to the six-voice scoring of most of Tasso's sonnets and madrigals, a fact arising no doubt from the two poet's stylistic differences. Whereas Tasso, the more sensuous of the two, wishes to overwhelm or excite the reader, Guarini seeks to entertain by appealing to the reader's sense of humor or intellect. It was Guarini who perfected the epigrammatic madrigal, a genre for which Tasso, master of the melic madrigal, had a profound suspicion.[119] Guarini's choice of subject matter is deliberately narrow and stereotyped: the first edition of the *Rime* (1598) is in fact arranged according to subject matter. The themes themselves—usually concerned with love and often descriptive of love making, leave taking, jealousy, scorn, etc.—seem less important than their ingenious manipulation through antithetical word-pairs and the double meaning of such words as "core" ("heart"), "morte" ("death"), or "vita" ("life") which may be taken literally as well as figuratively.

Antithesis is a rhetorical device derived ultimately from Petrarch; however, the resemblance to Petrarch remains a superficial one related to technique. Whereas the sincerity of Petrarch's idealistic love is never in doubt, Guarini openly admits the fictitious nature of the emotions expressed in his poems.[120] Moreover, whereas Tasso's poetry is a sensitive reaction to female beauty, Guarini's standpoint is more cynical, more comic, and more hedonistic: love implies gratification when it is reciprocated, jealousy and scorn ("sdegno") when refused. Eroticism plays a large role in the Guarini texts chosen by Marenzio. The kiss (a motive derived ultimately from Catullus and used also by Tasso) is the central theme of the notorious *Canzon de'baci* (*V a 6,* 1591, no. 12) and the long-winded madrigal, *O che soave e non inteso bacio.*[121]

Marenzio's settings differ in character from those of the three poets so far discussed. There is less brilliance and color contrasts than in the case of the Tasso settings, because Guarini's more abstract language lends itself far less to the depiction of natural objects, sounds, or movement. They are less contrapuntal than those of Petrarch and Sannazaro owing to Guarini's simpler syntax and more frequent use of the *settenario.* Livelier rhythms and playful repetitions (*gioco*) are often combined with melancholy undertones

(*Tirsi morir volea, I a 5*, 1580, no. 5).[122] Irony is evident in *Donò Cinthia a Damone* (*III a 6*, 1585, no. 10) at the words "All'hor disse il pastor/Con un sospir d'amore"[123] musically conveyed by indirect parallel fifths, the pause before "sospir" ("sigh") and the fussy dotted rhythm before "d'amore" [ex. 27].

As with Tasso's poetry, there are considerable variants between the versions found in music books and those published in Guarini's own edition (1598)—not to mention those published in poetic anthologies. For example, *Tirsi morir volea* exists in almost as many versions as there are musical settings.[124] Marenzio's reading follows Meldert's[125] closely if not exactly, and at one point quotes his setting [ex. 28]. Pallavicino in his turn was to quote Marenzio's setting [ex. 29] as well as to adhere rigidly to Marenzio's textual reading.[126] Later on in Marenzio's career the problem of finding a reliable version of the text is removed by the publication of the *Rime* in 1598. The five settings of 1598-99[127] mark a revival of interest in the *Rime*, spurred no doubt by their publication: they all follow the 1598 edition closely. *Parto o non parto* and *Credete voi* (*IX a 5*, 1599, nos. 11 and 12) are related in subject matter and stand in close proximity in the 1598 edition. Marenzio uses the same mode for both.

As with Tasso, one suspects that some early versions of Guarini's poems survive set to music and are only recognizable as such after close scrutiny. One of the most remarkable instances is the madrigal set by Marenzio in the Ferrarese anthology, *I lieti amanti* (*RISM* 1586[10]); it is almost certainly an early version of the madrigal which begins "Donna voi vi credete/D'avermi tolto il core":[128]

> Falsa credenza havete,
> Donna, se voi credete
> Ch'io non sia vivo poi
> Che più non amo voi.
> Anzi morrò s'io v'amo,
> Che tanto io vivo quanto vi disamo;
> E se'l portarvi amore
> Fù sempr'ed è cagion ch'altri si more,
> Mort'e chi v'ama e vive in dura sorte,
> Che ben vivo non è l'huom ch'ama morte.[129]

Similarly scornful tirades flowed freely from the pens of both Guarini and Tasso. The former's *Ardo sì ma non t'amo* served as the single text of the collection *I sdegnosi ardori* (*RISM* 1585[17]).[130]

Summary

Marenzio's four favorite poets are Petrarch, Sannazaro, Tasso, and Guarini. Marenzio shows a preference for Petrarch's poems *in morte,* especially the sestina, *Mia benigna fortuna.* Many settings are in the *misura di breve* and are markedly polyphonic. Among the metres used by Petrarch Marenzio selects at least one example of a ballata, canzone, sestina, sonnet, *terza rima,* and madrigal. Of the metres not used by Petrarch, Marenzio prefers the free sixteenth-century type of madrigal, many examples of which were written for musical setting. Sannazaro's *Arcadia* exhibits a strong dependence on the classical tradition as well as on Petrarch. The influence of the latter is discernible also in the *Rime,* and Marenzio's settings of the latter are close in style to his Petrarch settings. Tasso's poetry reveals an altogether different facet of Marenzio's musical personality; its richly descriptive and metaphorical qualities call for larger voice combinations and a more brilliant singing style. Guarini's drier, more epigrammatic style, however, requires smaller voice combinations, conscious lightness sometimes ironically mingled with melancholy. Both Tasso and Guarini are contemporaries of Marenzio and had intimate links with the Ferrarese court. In the case of both poets the versions set by Marenzio often differ from the definitive edition; both poets are almost certainly represented in Marenzio's works by more poems than can definitely be attributed to them.

4

Texture, Mensuration, and Mode

After choosing his text, the composer must choose the voice combination, mensuration, and mode for each composition. In our reconstruction of the order of decisions taken while composing, we start by examining the first of these three elements.

Voice Combinations

We have here to consider the broad implications of the choice of the voice combination for a whole composition. Marenzio wrote a total of 171 madrigals for five voices, 86 for six voices, only 26 for four voices, and 7 for eight or more voices. The emphasis on five-voice writing is usual for the late Renaissance, the four-voice combination having been in favor up to the time of Rore. Despite this preference, the four-voice combination was still apparently regarded as an ideal standard against which larger combinations were to be measured. This may be deduced from the terminology which distinguishes the canto, alto, tenor, and bass from any additional voices such as quinto, sesto, etc. The symmetrical, even-numbered scoring for four voices was considered to be a reflection of natural order, and was compared by Glareanus and Zarlino to the four elements.[1] The moment this system is augmented, that is, whenever composers insert extra voices according to individual expressive aims, it is as though an attempt were being made to surpass Nature.[2] Thus the self-conscious and subjective will of composers increases in importance, at the expense of the Renaissance idea of obeying the proportions of Nature.[3].

This tendency towards the individualistic and the arbitrary reaches its peak with Marenzio. To clarify what exactly is meant by "arbitrary," let us compare two passages scored for five voices, one by Marenzio, and one by an older composer, G.M. Nanino, [ex. 30]. The latter's *Là, dove par* (*RISM* 1589[7]) starts with a rigorous contrapuntal argument. The two fragments of the opening line are each assigned a different motive, heard at least once, the second following the first without a pause. In Marenzio's *Perchè adoprar*

(*RISM* 1583[12])the first line is scored for two voices, the second line entering in overlap in the tenor and bass. The two motives used by Marenzio for the second line are similar to those used by Nanino, but they are deployed differently. Marenzio does not shrink from allowing the two motives to appear in the wrong order in the quinto (bb. 8-14), repeating the first segment before proceeding to the next (bass, bb. 6 ff), or separating the two segments by a rest (canto, bb. 11-12; tenor, bb. 9-10). All these characteristics are symptomatic of a more modern approach to the manipulation of five-voice texture. Where Nanino treats the voices as independent units, weaving them together to create a larger, more perfect unity, Marenzio takes as his starting point the total sonority achieved by the play of motives in all five voices, the contribution of each voice being merely incidental.

Such an effect of "vocal orchestration" can be aimed only at the listener rather than the performer, who is left to make of an incomplete or garbled text whatever sense he can. This textual incompleteness is especially characteristic of the *III a 6* and *IV a 6* (1585 and 1587); often in these books the complete six-voice texture provides little more than a frame of reference. Perhaps the most extreme case is *Piangea Filli,* the vast majority of the phrases of which are scored for four or five voices.[4] The form of this piece depends on the repeated cries of "O Tirsi!" (lines 3-6). Though Marenzio reintroduces the same music at these points, the five-voice scoring is nearly always varied through the omission of a different voice. Moreover, each textual fragment coincides with a change of scoring. This applies equally to *Tirsi morir volea* (*I a 5,* 1580, no. 5) which is best described not as a five-voice composition, but as an interweaving of two-, three-, and four-voice homophonic blocks, either in combination or antiphonically. Einstein has drawn attention to the frequent two-voice writing,[5] but several other combinations occur: canto versus alto, tenor, quinto, and bass;[6] canto and alto versus tenor, quinto, and bass;[7] and various four-voice combinations. In general, the contrasts are less stark than in *Piangea Filli;* this is in keeping with the six-voice madrigals' greater reliance on sonority and textural contrasts.

In both the five-voice madrigals the position of the quinto and sesto plays a large part in determing the composition's mood and character. Marenzio usually follows contemporary practice by assigning the extra voice or voices to the tenor or canto ranges. In the six-voice pieces, a second alto is also common. The more brilliant or ornamental madrigals tend to have a greater number of higher voices, the more sombre ones, of lower voices. In the six-voice madrigals, the combination of double canto and double tenor[8] is the most frequent. The brightest possible sonority is the rarely used combination of double canto with double alto.[9] For mournful pieces Marenzio prefers double alto and double tenor—or perhaps triple tenor. Two extremes are reached in the successive books of 1588 and 1591. The *I a 4,5,6,* Marenzio's most gloomy work, contains four six-voice madrigals, none of them using double canto, and two of them using triple tenor.[10] The *V a 6* (1591), however, contains nine pieces (out of thirteen) with double canto; these include all the wedding madrigals.[11]

Remarkable, in the five-voice madrigals, is the gradual decrease in the use of the double canto and the increased preference (especially after 1588) for the darker sonority of two tenors. The result, more freedom and independence for the canto, greatly enhances the so-called "pre-monodic" character of the last four books *a 5* (see table 4). In the increased preference for double tenor over double canto Marenzio was swimming against the current. The books by Wert, Monte, Monteverdi, A. Gabrieli, and Dragoni,[12] published c. 1580-1600, all display an ever increasing preference for high voices, due perhaps to the rise of professional sopranos in Northern Italian courts. Marenzio's later preference for the double tenor puts him alongside the earlier Rore and Palestrina, and the slightly younger Luzzaschi.

Mensuration

Another factor affecting the mood of a composition is the choice of using the *tempus imperfectum diminutum* (*misura di breve*, with mensuration ₵) or the *tempus imperfectum* (*misura comune*, with mensuration C).[13] The former had gradually superseded the latter in madrigalian music, though the *misura di breve* was still preferred in sacred music. Marenzio uses it only for those compositions characterized by a steady, uniform rhythmic tread in a highly serious or even tragic mood. In these Marenzio seems to be turning his back on the modern madrigal, with its contrasts, its dance-like rhythms and melismatic style, and returning to the older rhythmic style prevalent before the advent of the *note nere* madrigal. This retrospective quality is confirmed by the frequent recourse to the texts of earlier poets: Petrarch, Sannazaro, Della

Table 4.   Position of the Quinto in the Five-Voice Madrigals

	With Canto	With Tenor	Other	Total
I a 5	6	6	1	13
II a 5	6	6	3	15
III a 5	11	6	0	17
Spirituali	3	7	2	12
IV a 5	3	7	5	15
V a 5	6	9	2	17
I a 4, 5, 6	0	6	0	6
VI a 5	0	14	2	16
VII a 5	0	17	0	17
VIII a 5	0	16	0	16
IX a 5	0	14	0	14

Casa, and Tansillo, but never Tasso or Guarini. This is particularly the case in the *I a 4,5,6* (1588), where Marenzio uses the *misura di breve* throughout, and whose "mesta gravità" ("sombre gravity") he specifically emphasizes in the dedication.

The Modes

If theorists were unanimous in stressing the importance of selecting a mode appropriate to the text, they did not always agree as to the number of modes that existed. Glareanus'[14] addition of four new modes to the original eight was not universally accepted, even though Zarlino[15] inherited the twelve-mode system and altered only the numbering. Among those who still thought in terms of the eight-mode system were Leonhard Lechner[16] and Aiguino, a compatriot of Marenzio who in 1581 dedicated a treatise defending the older system to Marenzio's patron, Luigi d'Este.[17]

There are a number of reasons for preferring to discuss Marenzio's madrigals with reference to the twelve-mode reformed system. First, the ideas of Glareanus' *Dodecachordon* (1547) had had ample opportunity to gain ground, and Glareanus' main argument, that the chief criterion for determining the mode lies in its octave species, is hard to refute. Moreover, two contemporary manuscript sources, Andrea Raselius' *Dodecachordi vivi* (1589),[18] and Orazio Vecchi's *Mostra delli tuoni* (1630),[19] contain expositions of the twelve-mode system with citations from Marenzio's madrigals. Vecchi's description of the mood generally associated with each mode corresponds closely with the way Marenzio uses the modes. With Marenzio, each mode is distinguished not only through its mood, but also through its melodic material and cadence structure. This applies equally to the modes with finals on *a* and *c* (in untransposed form) as to the other ones. We may therefore safely assign the names aeolian and hypoaeolian to modes with finals on *a*, and ionian and hypoionian to modes with finals on *c*.

We may now turn to each mode and describe the mood or moods associated with each. We will follow Glareanus' numbering, modifying it as follows: 1, 2, 3, 4, 9, 10, 5, 6, 7, 8, 11, and 12. This ordering has been adopted in order to show the affinities between modes 3 and 10, and modes 4 and 9.

The dorian and hypodorian modes, the first and second in Glareanus' system, are also the most commonly used by Marenzio. They are best described as all-purpose modes, capable of a great variety of mood and expression. Vecchi's description of the first mode, "misto con l'allegrezza e con la gravità,"[20] is wholly appropriate to Marenzio's use of it. In dorian compositions, happy and sad states are blended or juxtaposed. Thus in *Mentre l'aura spirò (RISM 1582[5])* and *Cantai già lieto (II a 6,* 1584, no. 10) the poet contrasts his former happiness with his present grief, while the octave and sestet of *Zefiro torna* (*I a 4*, 1585, no. 18) present a contrast between the joy of nature and the poet's affliction at the death of Laura. Mode 1 is the mode of antithesis and oxymoron: for example, the bittersweet epigram, *Non porta ghiaccio* (*IV a 6*, 1587, no. 9), and *Amatemi, ben mio*, also probably written in 1587.[21] Their mutual affinity is evident from their similar openings [ex. 31]. The hypodorian, much more commonly found in its transposed than its natural form, is quieter and more relaxed than its authentic counterpart. This is clear from the melodic patterns associated with the two modes, introduced early on to establish the mode (and the mood) clearly in the listener's mind. Thus the pattern *a'* - *d'* - *d"* (*d"* - *g'* - *g"* if transposed), typical of mode 1,[22] has no place in mode 2. Pieces in the latter mode often begin with an undulating theme which suggests anacreontic grace, or a state of relaxed happiness[23] [ex. 32]. In this type of progression the canto starts on *b'*-flat (the modal *repercussio*), departs, then returns to this note. The same progression is occasionally found in mode 1 [ex. 33]. The upper third, as *repercussio*, often serves as the highest note of a prominent phrase near the opening and achieves further emphasis through the use of long notes [ex. 34].

The phrygian and hypophrygian modes are described by Vecchi respectively as "molto in uso perchè s'accomoda [a] le parole dolorose, e piene di pianto"[24] and "atto ad ogni sorte di parole che sentin il grave."[25] Not surprisingly, the third and fourth modes often coincide with the *misura di breve* and, in the case of the five-voice madrigals, the use of the dark sonority of two tenors. The extreme emotional quality of these modes is reflected in their interval structure: they are the only modes in which the first and second degrees are separated by semitone, not a tone. This has a number of important consequences. First, it means that perfect[26] cadences on the final are not possible without chromatic sharping of the second degree. Instead, the final is reached through a descending fourth (or rising fifth) in the bass—in modern terms, a half cadence in *a* (*d* when transposed). The effect is often less conclusive than that obtained by the perfect cadence, and therefore appropriate for the expression of frustration or unfulfilled wishes and hopes. Secondly, the semitone between the final and the second degree plays an important part in the melodic structure—especially near the opening. The gloomy quality of the semitone is apparent in such pieces as *Tutte sue squadre* with its semitonal clashes.[27] Other melodic *topoi* appear in the third and fourth modes which are not directly related to the semitone. These include the outline of an *e*-minor or *e*-major triad [ex. 35] and the more modern-sounding exclamatory formula of a falling fourth, *e"* - *b'* [ex. 36].

In the late sixteenth century the phrygian and hypophrygian and the aeolian and hypoaeolian become closely associated with each other.[28] This is apparent not only from the voice ranges but also from the cadence patterns: in all four modes the principal cadences are on *a* (perfect or half cadence) and *c*.

In mood, too, there is considerable overlap. The piercing intensity of a piece like *Caro dolce mio ben*[29] brings it very close to the phrygian in mood. If the aeolian can also be joyful, as for example in *Rivi, fontane* (*RISM* 1589[7]), the hypoaeolian is more subdued, "atto alle parole flebili, et minacciose di vendetta."[30] It is the mode of unrequited love (*Lasso, ch'io ardo,*[31] *Piango che Amor*[32]) and spurned love (*Falsa credenza*[33]). Thus the aeolian resembles the dorian and hypodorian in its broad expressive range, but is also capable of the intensity of the phrygian and hypophrygian.

Before considering the three modes with major thirds, a further comment on the proximity of modes 3 and 10, 4 and 9, is necessary. There exist three compositions which share characteristics of more than one mode:

1. *La rete fu* (*V a 5*, 1585, no. 6): mode 3 (with characteristics of mode 10).
2. *Stringeami Galatea* (*III a 6*, 1585, no. 3): mode 3 (with characteristics of mode 10).
3. (a) *Signor, che già te stesso* (*RISM* 1586[1]): mode 4 (with characteristics of mode 9).
   (b) *Vergine gloriosa* (*seconda parte* of no. 3a)[34]: mode 4 (with characteristics of mode 9).

In all these cases the melancholy of modes 3 and 4 is avoided through the more varied rhythms and lightness often found in modes 9 and 10. The case for assigning them to modes 3 and 4 lies solely in the fact that they all end on imperfect rather than perfect cadences. The third composition is a bipartite *spirituale* exhibiting a cadence pattern characteristic of mode 4: *a* (perfect) at the end of the *prima parte, a* (imperfect) at the end of the *seconda parte.*

If we adhere to the classification of Glareanus and Vecchi, whereby all compositions with final on *f* and a flat signature are ionian and not lydian, we find that the lydian and hypolydian appear rarely in early Marenzio and not at all after the *V a 5* (1585). Generalizations about its mood are therefore dangerous: Vecchi describes mode 5 as "atto alla modestia, et alla solevatione de gl'animi noiosi"[35] and cites *Venuta era Madonna* (*I a 5*, 1580, no. 9) as an example.

The seventh mode is described by Vecchi as "molto atto a i componimenti lascivi, come si può vedere nel Madrigale del Marentio, *Spuntavan già . . .*"[36] By "lascivious" Vecchi presumably means light, cheerful, and profane. To mode 8 Vecchi assigns "le cose soavi, e dolci, et anco gravi";[37] it is less demonstrative and more subdued than mode 7. This is shown by a comparison of two settings from Sannazaro's *Arcadia, La pastorella mia,*[38] and *I lieti amanti.*[39] In the former, the protagonist depicts his unrequited love, the roaming of the flocks, and the acoustical phenomenon of echo with an almost naive indifference. In the latter, Opico wistfully recalls the Golden Age (depicted in the music through triple time and dotted rhythms), but reaches the depressing conclusion that the world grows more evil as it grows older.[40] Lyricism characterizes a number of other mode-8 pieces all published in 1582-83: *Se tu mi lasci* (*RISM* 1583[11]), *Perchè adoprar catene* (*RISM* 1583[12]), and *In quel ben nato* (*RISM* 1582[4]). The difference in mood between authentic and plagal is matched by their different melodic *topoi*. In mode 7 the *repercussio*, *d″*, often opens the piece and acts as the point of departure for ascending motion [ex. 38] or turning motion [ex. 39]. As opposed to the confident nature of these mode-7 themes, those for mode 8 are more subdued, often rising to the fourth degree (the *repercussio*) to emphasize one important word [ex. 40]. In example 40 (e) the dream-like atmosphere is enhanced by groping chromatics and the avoidance of characteristic cadences. Only at the hyperbolic final line "Con parole ch'i sassi romper ponno" is the repercussion interval *g′ - c″* "broken" in the canto by the intrusion of *d″* for the first time in the piece.[41]

The eleventh and twelfth modes may be considered as successors to the fifth and sixth, which had practically become obsolete by Marenzio's time. However, they also resemble modes 7 and 8 with respect to mood and melodic behavior. Vecchi regards mode 11 as "atto a soggetti danzevoli, e giocosi"[42] and mode 12 as "atto al triomfo."[43] The latter is used for two wedding pieces from the *IV a 5* (1584).[44] It is noteworthy that the festive *Bianchi cigni*,[45] written for Laura Peperara's wedding, uses many of the same motives found in other mixolydian and ionian pieces. In particular, at the end of the *seconda parte*, triple time is used to represent dancing in much the same way as in *I lieti amanti*.[46]

Not only weddings, but any happy scene or event, such as the return of spring or any country scene, tends to suggest mode 11 or 12. Triadic motives of a type also found in mode 7 often occur [ex. 41]. In all of the above examples the major triad, as a natural acoustical phenomenon, symbolizes nature in its primitive, unspoilt state. Not only triads, but sustained notes and chords built on the final, have the same meaning: *Strider faceva*[47] begins with a drone in the lowest voice in the manner of shepherds' pipes; in *Scaldava il sol*[48] the words "giaceva il villanel"[49] are set to an *f* chord (*f* being the final of mode 11 transp.) in order to represent the humble, primitive, and natural.[50]

The melodic characteristics of the ionian modes are derived partly from the mixolydian, partly from the lydian modes. Michael Praetorius gives exactly the same repercussion notes for the ionian modes as for the lydian: the fifth degree for mode 11, the third for mode 12.[51] Particularly striking is the way that, in modes 6 and 12, the *repercussio* serves as progenitor for the melodic material of whole composition. Thus in *Dolor, tant'è la gioia*[52] the note *a′* appears in the canto more frequently than any other, and often as the first note of a phrase.[53] The same technique may be found in *Fillida mia*[54] which begins with a series of descents from the *repercussio, e''*. It is only at the word "più" ("more") that the canto exceeds the *e''* and attains *g''*. The fourth line once again takes *e''* as its point of departure, the key adjective "proterva"[55] and "tremula"[56] both being set to this note. In mode 12 untransposed, another method of emphasizing the *repercussio* is to rise from the final in slow notes [ex. 42].

Other melodic characteristics are derived from mode 7: for example, the cadence formula with the flattened seventh [ex. 43]. Also characteristic of both modes is direct descending motion in even note values (usually minims or semibreves) to create a feeling of breadth and regular metric pulse. Thus a passage near the opening of *Sapete amanti*[57] combines long values in the top voice with shorter note values in the lower voices, with crisp effect.[58] Similar formulae appear in two wedding pieces published in 1591 [ex. 44]. Such broad, confident themes are indeed "apt for triumph."

Clefs

The question of clefs, and consequently of voice ranges, is inextricably tied up with modality. We may distinguish two types of clef combination: the high clefs (*chiavette*) and medium clefs (*chiavi naturali*); in general the former are more brilliant and festive, the latter more pensive, sombre, and introverted. The piercing cries of "O Tirsi" in *Piangea Filli*[59] may be contrasted with the sepulchral sounds at the opening of *Giunto a la tomba*.[60] We may assume that, because of their expressive and symbolic function, the higher clefs actually did indicate higher pitches and not, as it sometimes thought, downward transposition.[61]

The *chiavette* combination is G_2, C_2, C_3, and F_3 (or C_4), corresponding to canto, alto, tenor, and bass. Extra voices may duplicate or (more rarely) use a new clef, e.g. G_2, C_1, C_2, C_3, and F_3 (or C_4).[62] The *chiavette* are used in modes 1 transposed, 2 untransposed, 3 transposed, 4 untransposed, 5 untransposed, 7 untransposed, 8 transposed, 9 untransposed, 10 transposed, 11 transposed, and 12 untransposed. The *chiavi naturali* normally consist of C_1, C_3, C_4, and F_4 with the option C_1, C_2, C_3, C_4, and F_4 in 5-voice combinations, and C_1, C_1, C_2, C_3, C_4, and F_4 in six-voice combinations; they are used in modes 1 untransposed, 2 transposed, 3 transposed down a major second,[63] 4 transposed, 6 untransposed, 6 transposed, 7 transposed, 8 untransposed, 11 untransposed, and 12 transposed. The clef combinations of each mode generally coincide with those prescribed by the theorists of the time, in particular Vecchi[64] and Praetorius.[65] In addition, one lower combination, C_2, C_4, F_3, and F_4, is once used for one piece in mode 7 transposed.[66]

The clefs are determined by the voice ranges, which in turn depend on the mode. Normally the canto and tenor move between the final and the upper octave if the mode is authentic, and between the lower fifth and upper fifth if it is plagal. The ranges are commonly extended by one scale degree on either side of the octave in such a way as to span a tenth. Notes above and below the basic octave become less common as they become more remote; they are used only at special moments.

There are two exceptions to this rule: the tenor in mode 12 transposed and the canto and tenor in mode 4 transposed. In mode 12 the tenor normally encompasses both the plagal and authentic ionian ranges (*c - c'*, overlapping with *f - f'*). This total range of an eleventh (*c - f'*) is used for the first time as a *normal* range in *Disdegno e gelosia* (*IV a 5*, 1584, no. 3), and the use of the extended range becomes more frequent in later works. The preference for notes above the regular octave instead of those below it presumably serves the practical purpose of avoiding an uncomfortably low tenor part, a fact which tends to confirm that there is a real pitch difference between the high and medium clefs.

The second exception is the rarely used hypophrygian mode, in which the ranges of the canto and tenor tend to outline the octaves *e' - e''* and *e - e' (a' - a''* and *a - a'* if transposed) rather than the range usually prescribed by the theorists, namely *c' - c''* and *c - c' (f' - f''* and *f - f'* when transposed).[67] Thus the ranges for mode 4 are similar to those for mode 9—yet another point of similarity between hypophrygian and aeolian.[68]

Expressive Use of Mode

Any mode may express any concept in a positive or a negative way: positively, by introducing melodies characteristic of the mode, and negatively, by contravening the limitations of the mode, or introducing material characteristic of another mode. Positive concepts such as "justice," "love," "piety," or "triumph" call forth modally assertive melodies or progressions. Thus in *Arsi gran tempo* (mode 2 transposed) a modally characteristic motive[69] underlines the idea of "just scorn" [ex. 45].

More common is deliberate contravention of the modal rules in order to isolate a word or phrase from its context. Thus one or more voices may exceed the range normal for that mode, or cadences or melodic material characteristic of another mode may be introduced.

Unusually high or low notes appear for brief moments in the course of the composition. These moments are not hard to identify: the individual voice ranges correspond with the clefs in such a way as to avoid ledger lines as much as possible; when these cannot be avoided, upper ledger lines are deemed more convenient than lower. Thus, to a singer using the original clefs, any pitch irregularity is immediately recognizable.

A pitch irregularity may be expressive or nonexpressive. The latter occur in tenor voices when they are the lowest voice, the bass being silent.[70] In these cases an unusually low note is approached by a descending leap, usually of a fifth. In *Fuggito è 'l sonno*[71] the normal tenor range is f-f', but this is exceeded by the harmonically motivated leaps of a - D, g - C and f - D.[72]

More widespread is the expressive use of very high or low notes. High notes may be introduced 1) for emotional or dramatic emphasis, 2) to depict certain natural phenomena, 3) to depict the concepts of nobility, pride, triumph, etc., and 4) to emphasize a name or important personage.

1. In *O voi che sospirate* the canto completes its expected voice range by attaining e'' for the first time on "attrista" ("saddens");[73] at the same time the tenor reaches the lowest note, C, on "pianto" ("tears") and "attrista." In *Piangea Tirsi*, the upper octave, a'', is reserved for the piercing cries of "O Tirsi!"[74] In *Giunto a la tomba*, the tenor exceeds the normal octave by a fourth, rising to a' for "prendi" ("take").[75]

2. Unusually high notes may depict the "sky," "stars," "Paradise," "mountains," etc. Mention of the "wind" may call forth high pitches: in *Ohimè, il bel viso*, the canto ascends to a'' on the last line, "Ma 'l vento ne portava le parole" ("But the wind took her words away");[76] in *Non fu mai* the canto attains a'' on the word "vento" ("wind").[77]

3. The words "alto e pomposo" ("high and glorious") cause the canto to attain g'' in *Lasso dicea*[78] [ex. 46].

4. The River Po is emphasized by f'' in the canto, g' in the tenor, in *Corran di puro latte;*[79] in *Lieti, verdi, fiorite*, the canto attains f'' on "questo signor" ("this man").[80]

Unusually low notes may express physical depths ("hell," "earth," "death," "concealment," etc.) or abstract qualities such as humility, in *Ohimè, il bel viso*, where the canto descends to e' on "humile" ("humble"), having previously risen to g'' on "altiero" ("haughty").[81]

Cadences on unusually high or low notes have the same function as unusual pitches *per se*. In authentic modes, cadences on the upper octave have a specifically expressive function (cadences at the lower octave being more usual): at the final cadence of *Madonna mia*[82] the Canto cadences on g'' to represent "Paradiso"; likewise, at the end of *Mentre il ciel*, the "acuti strilli" or "shrill crying" of grasshoppers is represented by a final cadence on d'' in the canto.[83] In plagal modes, upper-fifth cadences are rare (lower-fifth cadences being more common): in *Due rose* the canto cadences on d'' to represent "sol" ("sun").[84] Cadences may fall outside the modally prescribed octave altogether, in which case they are altogether irregular: in *Affliger chi per voi* the canto cadences on c' to represent "chino" ("incline").[85]

An extension of the use of unusually high or low notes is the device known as *mixtio tonorum*,[86] whereby one or more voices move from their authentic to their plagal registers, or *vice versa*, thereby extending the register up or down a fourth or fifth. If the *mixtio* involves ascent, it may represent the same concepts as unusually high notes; if descent, the same as low notes. In *Valli riposte*, mode 11 replaces mode 12 on two occasions: very briefly while the alto descends *c'* - *g* on "valli riposte" ("hidden valleys"),[87] and more extensively in the last line, when the canto, quinto, sesto, and tenor descend abruptly from plagal to authentic range to represent "sepolta" ("buried").[88] In *Scendi dal paradiso* mode 11 replaces mode 12 in all the voices at the opening, the unusually high range representing the heavenly regions from which Venus and Cupid are descending.[89]

Little need be said here of irregular cadences (apart from those already discussed), or of *commixtio tonorum*, the ancestor of modulation. Modally irregular cadences—also called "clausulae peregrinae" or "cadenze fuori di tono"[90]—may have a syntactical or an expressive function: to indicate the relatively low syntactical value of a phrase or clause, or in order to draw attention to the meaning of the words at the end of a phrase or clause. Irregular cadences with the latter function negate the listener's expectations by substituting for a more regular cadence. This negative quality allows them to express not only negative statements, but any deviation from the norm: yielding, falling, excess, pathos, change, extreme height or depth. A similar duality of purpose—syntactical and expressive—underlies the device known as *commixtio tonorum*,[91] i.e. the introduction of melodic material and cadences characteristic of a foreign mode. Like the irregular cadence, *commixtio* may be either syntactical or expressive in function; however, it is very different in effect. Whereas an irregular cadence comes as a surprising twist at the end of an otherwise modally regular phrase, with *commixtio* the new modality extends back to include the whole preceding phrase, the final cadence merely clinching the change of mode instead of coming as a surprise. *Commixtio* may extend over whole sections and movements, and therefore has structural implications which fall outside the scope of this chapter.

Summary

The preference for five- and six-voice combinations over the traditional four-voice sound corresponds with the urge towards individualism and idiosyncratic expression in the late Renaissance. Of particular importance is the position of the quinto and sesto: the greater the concentration of the extra voices in the lower register, the more sombre the composition. Mensuration, too, is dependent on the tempo, and hence on the mood and character of a composition. The normal indication, C , is sometimes replaced by ₵ , indicating a more serious mood and a more archaic, uniform rhythmic flow.

Marenzio makes full use of Glareanus' twelve-mode system, choosing the mode according to the same criterion as that used for choosing the voice combination and mensuration, namely the mood he wishes to convey, and the poetic content. The choice of clefs follows from the choice of mode. Not only the choice of mode, but also the way that the mode is used (or avoided) has expressive significance. The mode may be asserted through characteristic progressions and melodies, or contravened through excessively high or low pitches, irregular cadences, and *commixtio tonorum.*

The Treatment of the Individual Word

Introduction

The individual word is the point of departure in the setting of poetry to music in Marenzio's early period. There is a close correspondence between the words and the melodic motives to which are set; indeed, in its capacity to underscore the denotative meaning of individual words, music begins to assume some of the qualities of language itself.

Such a process was by no means new in Marenzio's music; throughout the last two thirds of the sixteenth century, the subordination of music to the words was an idea close to the hearts of theorists and composers. Zarlino's common-sense attitude is fully representative of contemporary attitudes.[1] However, Marenzio, with his attention to detail, carries Zarlino's instructions to an extreme which Zarlino himself would probably not have approved and certainly could not have foreseen. Other writers reflect Marenzio's practice more closely: for example, Alessandro Guarini, who in the dedication of Luzzaschi's *VI a 5* (1596) implies the importance that contrast has for the virtuoso madrigal.[2] A year later Morley, though heavily reliant on Zarlino,[3] is evidently aware of modern developments when he writes:

> [. . .] the parts of a *Madrigal* either of five or sixe parts go somtimes full, sometimes very single, sometimes iumping together, and somtime quite contrarie waies, like unto the passion which they expresse, for as you schollers say that love is ful of hopes and feares, so is the Madrigall or lovers musicke full of diversitie of passions and ayres.[4]

Problems of Classification

Such is the wealth of musical images, with motives and harmonic progressions assuming exact and unvarying meanings from one composition to another, that it is possible to compile a "dictionary" of these musical devices with an explanation of their "meanings."

A useful point of departure is provided by Artusi's *Arte del contraponto* (1598), in which four types of melodic motion are described. Though Artusi assigns no specific expressive significance to any of them, nevertheless they do acquire certain "meanings" in the music of Marenzio. By adding to Artusi's list other melodic and harmonic motives used by Marenzio, we can build a whole "vocabulary," indeed, a complete "language" of musical gestures.[5]

Artusi[6] divides melodic writing into four categories: *conducimento* (direct motion), subdivisible into *rettitudine* (ascent) and *ritorno* (descent) and *circoito* (circular or turning motion); *complicamento,* defined as a "scambievole positione de intervalli" ("a variable placement of intervals"), meaning unpredictable, haphazard melodic writing; *gioco,* a "reiterata percussione fatta spesse volte" ("a group of notes[7] reiterated many times"); *fermezza,* a "continoata statione di voce" ("a note held continuously in one voice").[8] To Artusi's list we may add other techniques governing word underlay, melody, and rhythm;[9] these tend to depict the physical world either for its own sake, or as symbols of an inner emotion ("laughing," "singing," "crying," etc.), or as metaphor (as when love is represented as a "flame," "snare," or "dart"). Other techniques—chromaticism, dissonance, etc.[10]—or reduction of vocal texture[11] are often used to depict the darker emotions. In the later madrigals, these techniques become more highly developed, the depiction of purely external phenomena receding as the inner emotions are expressed more intensely.[12]

Classifications

1. Direct Motion (Ascending or Descending)

Direct motion, whether ascending or descending, may represent any kind of motion: e.g., flight, evasion, or pursuit [ex. 48]. In example 48(a), imitation at a minim's distance suggests both flight and pursuit.[13] In example 49, the ideas of flight and pursuit are conveyed through ascending and descending motion. Contrary motion may convey proximity if the two voices are converging,[14] separation if diverging [ex. 50]. Contrasted high and low pitches convey high and low regions [ex. 51].

2. Ascending Motion

This may denote a) literal motion such as ascent; b) hope, joy, or renewal:
   a) Ascent or a high place is represented by ascending motion, as in the phrase "Godere il paradiso" ("enjoy Paradise");[15] so also are the concepts, "coming out" [ex. 52] and "departure" [ex. 53].
   b) Ascending motion can represent joy and hope, as at the opening of all three parts of the wedding madrigal, *Bianchi cigni,(RISM* 1583[10]).[16] Dawn (the rising sun) and spring (the upward thrust of plants), both symbols of hope and renewal, are treated likewise [ex. 54].

3. Descending Motion

Descending motion may represent a) literal descent or b) any negative emotion:

a) Literal descent takes place at the openings of *Scendi dal paradiso,* ("Descend from Paradise")[17] and *Giunto a la tomba* ("Having reached the tomb").[18]

b) Descending motion may represent "jealousy," "disdain" or the rejection of love, often in the form of a descending triad [ex. 55].Comparable is the way Marenzio depicts deserted hills, the Petrarchan symbol of loneliness and unreciprocated love [ex. 56]. Descending, syncopated figures may represent the torments of the oppressed lover: "languishing," "swooning," etc. [ex. 57].

4. Turning Motion

Turning motion may represent a) literal "turning," "returning," etc; b) circular objects; c) the concept of ornament; d) happiness; e) profane love; f) benediction. In most of these varied cases, different types of turning motion are used:

a) Returning to a previously heard note symbolizes a return or a repeated action [ex. 58]. A different kind of turning motion may represent "wandering" [ex. 59]

b) Words like "crown," "flower," "garland," or "arc" are symbolized by melodies describing a circular motion [ex. 60].

c) Ornament [ex. 61] or graceful, decorative scenes or objects [ex. 62] may receive turning motion.

d) One particular motive (*b*-flat *a b*-flat *c d*) is commonly used to represent a happy state of affairs.[19] The opening of one madrigal is entirely dominated by it [ex. 63].

e) The same motive, when combined with lively rhythms and a slowly descending bassline, often represents the pleasures and tyrannies of profane love [ex. 64].

f) Undulating motives suggest "fecundity" or benediction at the hand of God or Providence [ex. 65].

5. Complicamento

Deliberately angular melodic patterns may represent a) extreme anguish; b) savagery or error; c) distance:

a) Both Marenzio and G.M. Nanino use a highly "variable placement of intervals" at the same point in *Dolorosi martir* [ex. 66]; such angularity however is generally confined to Marenzio's later style, especially the *IX a 5* (1599).[20]

b) *Complicamento* is once used to depict a "savage man"[21] and "straying from the truth" [ex. 67].

c) "Distance" is represented by wide leaps: e.g. "di lontano" ("from afar")[22] or "lunge" ("far").[23]

6. Gioco

Gioco may be used a) to conjure up scenes of merriment; b) to denote "echo"; c) when combined with *complicamento,* to suggest "abandonment," "scattering," etc.:

a) As a device for setting a joyful, "lascivious" mood, especially in the early madrigals,[24] it imparts a highly characteristic sound, found also in the madrigals of Macque.[25] The words "gioco" ("joke" or "play") and "scherzando" ("playing") are always treated in this way [ex. 68]; other composers soon copied Marenzio [ex. 69].

b) The element of antiphonic repetition makes *gioco* suitable for conveying the concepts "echo" [ex. 70] and "competition" [ex. 71].

c) *Gioco* and *complicamento* together represent joyful abandon [ex. 72], or "sprinkling," "scattering" [ex. 73].

7. Fermezza

Notes sustained or repeated for the duration of more than a semibreve represent a) absence of motion, b) immutability, c) have the function of emphasizing proper names or adjectives conveying some emotional quality.

a) Absence of motion is depicted in the phrase "stando in terra" ("staying on earth");[26] twice Marenzio depicts the quieting of the wind through the combination of *fermezza* and *melismata* (see below, classification 8) [ex. 74].

b) Repeated notes represent immutability [ex. 75] and hence constancy [ex. 76].

c) Occasionally, the accentuated syllable of important adjectives is held for longer than is required from the standpoint of strict declamation, for rhetorical emphasis. Such words are "pietosa" ("pitying"),[27] "bella,"[28] "dolce" ("sweet"),[29] "honeste," and "soavi" ("sweet") [ex. 77]. Further emphasis is often obtained through the use of an accidental.[30]

8. Melismata

In Marenzio's music this is always subordinated to expressive aims. The frequent quaver runs (usually found in groups of four, in direct motion) form an integral part of the music's fabric rather than a mechanical ornament. *Melismata* may represent a) natural phenomena; b) motion; c) beauty, joy, happiness; d) the torments of love; e) may occasionally accompany unimportant words for special reasons:

a) Natural phenomena may be subdivided into i) the sights and ii) the sounds of Nature.

i) Melismas on the words "flowers," "trees," "birds," "hills," "wind," "waves," and "rivers" are so commonplace that they need not be illustrated in detail. "Onde" ("waves") is assigned particularly long melismas;[31] so also are the names of rivers.[32] Flowers and garlands are sometimes represented by the rhythmic motive of a dotted crotchet and two semiquavers [ex. 78].

ii) The sounds of nature are represented through melismatic trill-like sounds,[33] or, on the word "murmur," through voice-crossing [ex. 79].

b) Words of motion are commonly represented by *melismata;* e.g. "fly," "run," "scatter." In *Quando vostra beltà (IV a 5,* 1584, no. 10), Ariosto describes his imagination soaring at the thought of his beloved. At the word "volo" ("flight" or "wing")[34] Marenzio uses long melismas of between eight and sixteen quavers. As may be seen from settings of Tasso's poetry, metaphors are particularly suited to *melismata.* Just as the poet seeks to render the spiritual world visible and tangible, so the musician seeks to bring poetical imagery before the ear, and as if before the eye, of the performer and listener.

c) Words of joy, happiness, or beauty may be subdivided into i) words associated in a general sense with these qualities; ii) words describing female beauty; iii) "singing" or "laughter."

i) Words like "felice," "lieto" ("happy"), "vago" ("pretty"), and "gioia" frequently occur with *melismata.* It is enough to illustrate "gioia" and "felice" with reference to two strikingly similar passages drawn from different pieces [ex. 80].[35] Two other "parallel passages" illustrate the parallelism of the physical and spiritual realms: the first alludes to the four elements as symbol of the Creation [ex. 81], the second to "beautiful, divine thoughts" [ex. 82].

ii) The use of *melismata* to depict female beauty is illustrated in *Occhi lucenti e belli,* where the quaver melismas form an effective contrast to the semibreve "eyes" in the canto.[36]

iii) "Singing" may be literal or metaphorical (in the sense of a poet's "song"). One sonnet opens with an unfurling motive symbolizing both "singing" in this sense, and "freedom" [ex. 83]. "Laughter," whether literal or figurative, is represented by a trill-like motive [ex. 84].

d) Metaphors describing the torments of love ("darts," "chains," "flames," etc.) receive stereotyped descending melismatic figures. Thus the "snares" in one piece are identical with the "fetters" or "chains" in another [ex. 85]. The dragging suspensions used to depict the "chains" and "yoke" of love resemble motives previously discussed [ex. 86].[37]

e) *Melismata* may occasionally appear on unimportant words. This happens when a melisma is transferred from a word generally depicted by a melisma to an inconsequential one nearby.[38] Another reason for their use is to build up to a cadence through a melismatic ascending scale: e.g. *II a 5* (1581), no. 9, b.71 ff; *III a 5* (1582), no. 7, b.42 ff; *V a 5* (1585), no. 1, b.51 ff.

9. Triadic Motives

Melodies outlining the triad may express a) "triumph" or "joy"; b) "war," "hunting"; c) "Fate" or "power":

a) "Triumph" and "joy" are frequently conveyed by triadic outlines, whether melismatic[39] or otherwise [ex. 87].

b) Reminiscences of trumpet fanfares and the sound of hunting horns, common in the aristocratic world of the Renaissance, often accompany metaphors of battle or the hunt [ex. 88].

c) Fate is portrayed by a portentious-sounding descending triad [ex. 89]; love as a paradoxical yet powerful force in human affairs is conveyed through a similar motive [ex. 90]. The powerful threefold reiteration of the dominant foreshadows Beethoven's Fifth Symphony, whose principal motive, so it is said, represents Fate "knocking at the door."

10. Declamation in Quavers

The normal rule governing declamation, whereby each syllable must be assigned an individual duration of at least a crotchet (or minim in the *misura di breve*[40]) is occasionally suspended to allow one syllable per quaver. Rhythmic diminution may represent a) the miraculous, b) brevity, speed, c) life, happiness, or d) may be diminutive, or represent a large number:

a) The phrase "Sarà certo miracolo d'amore" ("It will certainly be a miracle of love")[41] is treated with quavers on the word "miracolo" and begins with the repeated notes which indicate power (of Love).[42]

b) In the descriptions of temporal durations, shorter passages of time are represented by shorter note values [ex. 91].

c) Marenzio follows Zarlino's recommendation to use fast music for cheerful emotions, slow for mournful;[43] it is therefore natural that, at the end of *O voi che sospirate,* the word "lieto" ("happy") prompts the use of crotchets in the context of the *misura di breve.*[44]

d) Quavers may be diminutive [ex. 92] or may represent a large number ("mille," meaning "a thousand") [ex. 93].

11. Rhythmic Motives

Certain rhythmic motives have a precise denotative function. They are a) the sequence, dotted crotchet - quaver - crotchet; b) minim - crotchet - crotchet (and its diminished form, crotchet - quaver - quaver); c) quaver - quaver - crotchet:

a) The sequence, dotted crotchet - quaver - crotchet may represent i) life, spirit, breath [ex. 94]; ii) trembling, fear [ex. 95]; iii) flashing, burning [ex. 96]; iv) violent or sudden action such as wounding, snatching, or breaking [ex. 97]; v) the carefree, natural existence of shepherds. In *I a 4* (1585), nos. 9 and 16, the use of this motive is encouraged by the *versi sdruccioli* with their dactylic endings. The same rhythm also appears in other places [ex. 98].

b) The sequence, minim - crotchet - crotchet[45] or its diminution, convey (among other things) heroism or resolution [ex. 99].[46]

c) The reverse sequence, quaver - quaver - crotchet, conveys the reverse qualities: fickleness, caprice, volatility [ex. 100]

12. Triple Time

Triple time may occur a) within the *tempus imperfectum* (cross rhythms) or b) after a change of mensuration (this involves also a change of speed):

a) Cross rhythms where a triple-time feeling is evident convey happiness. This applies equally to groups of three minims as to those of three crotchets [ex. 101]. In example 101 (a) Marenzio copies Ingegneri by using chromaticism for "misero" then cross rhythms for "perduto bene" ("lost happiness").

b) Outright triple time is conveyed through a variety of notation signs,[47] and also through coloration, or blackening of notes that would normally appear white.[48] It may convey i) happiness [ex. 102]; ii) dancing, singing, festivities [ex. 103]; and iii) change [ex. 104].

13. The Emotional Significance of Intervals

Not only rhythmic, but also intervallic proportions play a large expressive role, whether they are vertically combined as harmony or used melodically. Pathos may be achieved by using a) the minor second, b) the minor third, c) the diminished fourth, d) the diminished fifth and the tritone or e) the diminished seventh:

a) The minor second used melodically is often used (especially in mode-3 compositions) to denote weeping [ex. 105]. A semitonal descent, often repeated at a higher pitch, represents weeping [ex. 106].

b) The minor third plays an elegiac role when used melodically [ex. 107].[49]

c) The melodic diminished fourth is never used directly in Marenzio's madrigals before 1593, though examples of its indirect use (i.e. with at least one note intervening) are to be found [ex. 108].

d) Indirect diminished fifths occur on the word "morte" ("death") in two settings of two stanzas from Petrarch's sestina *Mia benigna fortuna* [ex. 109]. Marenzio's technique of building major chords on two notes a tritone apart appears to be derived from A. Gabrieli [ex. 110].

e) The harmonic diminished seventh is treated as an ordinary dissonance, and is often introduced to convey "falsehood": the diminished seventh in example 111 did not escape the notice of G.M. Artusi.[50]

14. The Expressive Function of Cadences

Cadences may have an expressive or a syntactical function; here we are concerned with the former.[51] Cadences are expressive of the meaning of the words if they fall on an unexpected degree of the modal scale;[52] the more regular types of cadence may also assume great expressive power, in the following ways:

a) Perfect cadences may be adorned with a diminished fourth (or augmented fifth) resolving to a six-four. Always it is the heavily accented penultimate syllable of the line (or phrase) that is affected [ex. 112].

b) A cadence on *re* may be approached through a flatted (phrygian) second degree in order to create a poignant accent, not unlike the Neapolitan sixth [ex. 113]. Such cadences are particularly elegiac when left incomplete, i.e. "hanging" on the dominant [ex. 114].

c) "Phrygian" cadences (the *clausula in mi*)[53] have a poignant effect by virtue of the seven-six suspension [ex. 115]. The combination of *fauxbourdon*[54] with the phrygian cadence often recalls moments of Rore's music [ex. 116].

d) Cadences where the bass assumes the role of *tenorizans*—drops from supertonic to tonic instead of dominant to tonic—are often, like phrygian cadences, characterized by dissonance, especially when the descent *re - ut* in the bass is doubled at the upper third or tenth *(fa - mi)* [ex. 117].

e) The interrupted cadence, whereby one or all of the voices are deflected to an unexpected scale degree where one would normally expect a perfect resolution, can be very poignant. This is especially the case when the bass drops a tone (5 - 4) instead of a fifth (5 - 1), as in two settings from Petrarch's sestina (*Canzoniere, 322*) on the rhyme word "pianto" ("weeping") [ex. 118]. In one madrigal from the *I a 4,5,6,* an expected resolution to *d* is deflected to *e* minor (first inversion) to depict aimless wandering [ex. 119].

15. Chromaticism

The word "chromatic" derives from the Greek *kroma* meaning "color," and it is this original sense of which we are reminded by Marenzio's madrigals. However, the bewildering harmonic juxtapositions of a Lassus or a Vicentino[55] are as foreign to Marenzio's style as Gesualdo's more extreme experiments. Instead, we find chromaticism being used to temper or color diatonic passages, and, conversely, diatonic progressions directing and stabilizing remote modulations. Lowinsky has pointed out that chromaticism may actually aid tonal feeling;[56] this is the case with Marenzio, in whose madrigals the most remote progressions have a logical basis and an expressive justification, and where, at the other extreme, the slightest chromatic touch can have an almost cataclysmic effect.[57]

By "chromaticism" we mean one of five processes: a) the use of single accidentals, b) indirect chromaticism, c) direct chromaticism moving through a major second, d) direct chromaticism through intervals exceeding a major second, e) modulation through a chain of fifths:

a) Isolated accidentals may either i) raise the scale degree by one semitone or ii) flat it by one semitone.

i) The introduction of a sharp or natural may transform a triad that would normally be minor into major. Thus *d* major replaces *d* minor (*f*-sharp instead of *f*-natural) in the phrase "sentirò di dolcezza all' hor bearmi" ("I will feel blessed with sweetness").[58] The same technique can also have a poignant effect: in the opening bars of *Dolorosi martir,* as set by Nanino and Marenzio, the "major" sonorities act as a negative preparation for the "minor" (phrygian) ones that follow [ex. 120].

ii) An extraneous flat sometimes pinpoints an important adjective;[59] if it occurs near a cadence it can lend it an expressive coloring it would otherwise lack. Thus the flatting of the sixth degree in mode 1 transposed can result in a IV - V - I cadence on *b*-flat [ex. 121], or, in mode 2 transposed, in a VI - V - I cadence on *g* [ex. 122].[60]

b) Indirect chromaticism may be defined as the alternating occurrence of a scale degree in its natural then altered form (or *vice versa)*, the two notes being separated by one (or sometimes more) neighbouring note or chord occupying a diatonic relationship with both. The phenomenon may occur in passages which are i) polyphonic or ii) homophonic.

i) Indirectly chromatic lines in a polyphonic (or semipolyphonic) context occur frequently in Marenzio's music [ex. 123].

ii) In example 124[61] the unexpected *d*-cadence (deflected to IV) is preceded by a tritone leap in the bass and a sequence *b*-flat ... *b*-natural in the canto. More common than indirect chromaticism in the same voice is the appearance of a natural then a chromatic version (or *vice versa)* of the same degree in two different voices, resulting in a false unison or octave. Words of endearment and references to sweetness are so treated, the two falsely related chords being connected by an intervening chord diatonically related to both.[62] The warm, sensuous harmonies often recall earlier Venetian composers [ex. 125].

c) Direct chromaticism through a major second may likewise occur in i) a polyphonic or ii) a homophonic context. The first occurrence is extremely rare [ex. 126]; more common is chromatic ascent through a major second homophonically accompanied by a descending minor third or ascending major third in the bass. It is this highly characteristic use of direct chromaticism which sets Marenzio's harmonic style apart from that of Gabrieli and Merulo. Typical occasions for its use are weeping, sighing, dying, extreme cold, endearment, and change [ex. 127].

d) Direct chromaticism through intervals exceeding a major second is rare in Marenzio's earlier works, even if isolated examples do occasionally foreshadow its more frequent use in the homophonic madrigals of the *VII* and *VIII a 5* (1595 and 1598) [ex. 128]. That Marenzio associates such chromatic melodic lines with "modernity" may be seen from the setting of the words "O rara e nuova legge" ("O rare new law") near the opening of the *seconda parte* of *E questo il legno*.[63] Marenzio would have been familiar with the experiments of Rore, Lassus, Vicentino, Ignegneri, and possibly Caimo. Caimo uses descending chromatic lines in his *Piangete valli*;[64] Marenzio however uses only ascending chromatic lines.[65]

e) Modulations where the bass moves through a series of descending fifths (or ascending fourths) may have the function of emphasizing a particular word by introducing an extraneous flat at the extreme "flat"end of the progression [ex. 129]. In two sestina settings by Petrarch and Sannazaro,[66] Marenzio introduces very remote modulations for a symbolic purpose. The two lines in question are obviously related, Sannazaro's being based on Petrarch's: thus Petrarch writes "Muti una volta quel suo antico stile,"[67] Sannazaro, "E tu, Fortuna, muta il crudo stile."[68] In his Sannazaro setting, Marenzio conveys the concept of changed Fortune by modulating through a cycle of descending fifths, arriving at d-flat, a tritone away from a dorian final, g.[69] Later on in the same piece there is a further modulation through a, d and g.[70] The Petrarch setting, though earlier, is bolder and conciser in its chromaticism. The piece starts with an unusual modulation through a, e and b (such modulations through *ascending* fifths are rarely found).[71] Later, when setting the line quoted earlier, Marenzio moves through almost the entire enharmonic cycle: g, c, f, b-flat, e-flat, a-flat, d-flat, g-flat (equals f-sharp), b ... e, a.[72] By introducing enharmonically related chords Marenzio forces us to regard d-flat as equivalent to c-sharp, g-flat as equivalent to f-sharp etc. There can be no more ingenious or succinct method of symbolizing a change in

Death's former ways while at the same time alluding to the "ancient style"[73] of the Greek enharmonic *genus*.

16. Dissonance

In the early madrigals Marenzio prefers softer, less extreme dissonances than in the works after 1594. This is consistent with his more sensuous approach to vocal color and less angular melodic style. The softest dissonance of all (if it can be called a dissonance) is the six-four, which occupies a halfway house between pure consonance and pure dissonance.

a) The ambiguity of the six-four (theoretically it is a consonance but in practice it is treated more like a dissonance) is demonstrated by one particular mannerism: the rhythm of minim-semibreve-minim in which the middle note is a six-four reached on a weak beat, sustained for the duration of the next strong beat, and then resolved like any dissonance. The effect is always melancholy or gently elegiac [ex. 130]. In later years the same rhythmic device is extended to the harsher dissonance of the major seventh [ex. 131].

b) Dissonances pure and simple may be primary (i.e. prepared, suspended, and resolved) or secondary (passing).[74] The latter are frequently found in slow passages in minims in the six-voice madrigals, the rich texture often giving rise to chords of four or five notes [ex. 132]. At the end of *Deh, rinforzate (I a 6,* 1581, no. 12) both primary and secondary dissonances are piled on with greater intensity to convey the words "a dramma a dramma" ("drop by drop").[75]

c) With primary dissonances the standard practice is to prepare, suspend, and resolve within the duration of three minims. Marenzio however freely uses the *sincope minima*[76] (with a duration of three crotchets) to convey distress or excitement. In these cases, the resolution of one dissonance acts as the preparation of the next.[77] The *sincope maggiore*[78] (where the *sincope* or suspension lasts a whole semibreve) is usually reserved for pieces in the *misura di breve*[79] but can appear in the *misura comune;*[80] the dissonance in question is always the ambiguous, gentle-sounding six-four.

d) Despite what was said previously about the softness of Marenzio's earlier style with regard to dissonance, there are a few usages which foreshadow the asperity of the books after 1593. A surprising effect is obtained by the entry of a voice to form a dissonance with a suspended voice.[81] While such a procedure is never specifically outlawed by theorists, it is clear that Marenzio has advanced far beyond the position of Zarlino, for whom dissonance had mainly an architectonic, nonexpressive function.[82] The same applies to Marenzio's use of the double suspension, rare in the earlier works except in conjunction with the six-four [ex. 134].

e) The expressive role of the dissonance is especially apparent at cadences,[83] especially where an affective word occurs near the end of a line or phrase.[84] Cadences on *re* or *la* (in the "minor keys") are characterized by semitone clashes between the second and third degrees above the cadence note [ex. 135].[85] Other types of dissonance are caused by the movement of the bass. The most common pattern is a basic 5 - 1 descent with an ornamental descent to 4, making 5 - 4 - 5 - 1. The pattern 5 - 4 - 5 is meanwhile inverted in one of the upper voices to create 7 - 8 - 7 [ex. 136]. The essential factor here is the dissonance on the first weak beat created by the ascent from the leading note to the tonic (7 to 8). When the occasion demands, this dissonant element can be intensified by the movement of the other voices [ex. 137].

f) Dissonances can become more frequent and intense at the approach of cadences. Therefore dissonances (including the six-four) can be used to create the expectation of a cadence even where the cadence is avoided or concealed. The continual refusal to resolve all tensions through postponement of the cadence, is a powerful way of conveying the "unceasing death" of the characters of *Il pastor fido* whose laments Marenzio sets in the books after 1593; similar passages are sometimes found in the early books [ex. 138].

17. The Symbolic Purpose of Vocal Reductions

Reductions in the total number of singing voices may have an expressive or symbolic purpose. This may be seen in a) reductions from six to four voices, b) from five to three voices, c) from six to three voices, d) from five or four to two voices, e) reductions expressing other specific concepts, and f) symbolic of numbers:

a) Many six-voice madrigals begin *a 4* if they are gently elegiac,[86] amorous,[87] or overtly sensuous.[88] The reduced texture is more intimate and introspective than the full six-voice complement, yet still full enough to sound sensuous.

b) Reduction from five to three voices often has the melancholy sound of *fauxbourdon* (parallel six-three chords). Outright *fauxbourdon* is used with restraint—a reflection perhaps of Zarlino's discouragement of this device.[89] Characteristic is the statement of a phrase in parallel six-threes followed by various restatements during which the *fauxbourdon* element gradually dissolves.[90] An important variation of *fauxbourdon* is a device later given the name of *congeries*,[91] or a succession of alternating five-threes and six-threes in conjunct ascending or descending motion. It is usually associated with ritualistic or conventional expressions of grief [ex. 139]. Other examples of three-voice writing are much freer but still steeped in pathos [ex. 140]. The *VI a 5* (1594) contains some striking examples.[92]

c)The reduction from six to three voices rarely serves a symbolic purpose. Noteworthy however are the similar openings of two Tasso settings, both with pastoral, idyllic overtones: *In un bel bosco* and *In un lucido rio.*[93]

d) Two-voice writing is used in some of the four-voice and five-voice madrigals to portray rusticity. In the tripartite *Vienne Montan (I a 4,* 1585, no. 21) the dialogue is allotted to two choirs of two voices each; Tasso's pastoral monologue, *Al lume de le stelle* is introduced with a descriptive passage scored for two voices.[94]

e) Sparse vocal scoring may represent exposure,[95] drought,[96] abandonment,[97] or extinction.[98]

f) The number of voices used may represent a numeral in the text.[99] Finally, a voice or group of voices may distinguish two characters of different age[100] or sex.[101]

18. The Expressive Role of Silence

Silence may be introduced a) as rests in mid-phrase (or even in the middle of a word), to convey "sighing," "sobbing," etc; b) at the ends of phrases, where one would expect the cadence; c) to separate an incomplete cadence from the beginning of the phrase that follows:

a) Rests are introduced in the middle of a phrase to represent that essential ingredient of "lovers musicke," the sigh [ex. 142]; they may also be used, together with jerking, tortured rhythms, to suggest choked sobbing [ex. 143]. Syncopation and rests often go together to express exclamations such as "ahimè" or "ohimè."[102] For these words Marenzio uses the rhythmic motive of a syncopated semibreve and minim (or a syncopated minim and crotchet) preceded by a rest. This rhythm is used thematically at the opening of *O voi che sospirate* [ex. 144].

b) One striking way in which silence is used is in the noncompletion of cadences. Thus in *Dolorosi martir,* on the word "lamenti" the canto, tenor, and bass abandon the other two voices, who alone are left to complete the cadence on a bare fifth.[103] Incomplete cadences may represent separation and disjunction,[104] negation, deprivation, or swooning [ex. 145]. At the end of the *Seconda parte* of *Deggio dunque* (*II a 5,* 1581, no. 1), the cadence on the word "spento" ("extinguished") remains incomplete until the beginning of the *terza parte,* the dominant and its tonic resolution being separated by a semibreve rest and a reiterated dominant [ex. 146].[105]

c) A further stage of refinement is reached when, after an incomplete cadence, all the voices rest and begin the next phrase on a chord other than the expected resolution chord. The device is particularly effective with spontaneous outbursts of grief [ex. 149].

The Aesthetic Implications of Marenzio's Approach to Word-Painting

Our discussion of silence almost completes out survey of the means used by Marenzio to represent the meaning of individual words. From it we may draw the following final conclusions:

First, the urge towards expression invades every dimension of the music: melodic-rhythmic (classifications 1-12), melodic-harmonic (classifications 13-16) and textural (classifications 17-18).

Second, as stated before, certain motives, progressions, and textural combinations assume specific meanings from one composition to another. This has an important consequence: just as certain words or expressions achieve recognized meaning only through habitual and repeated usage, so musical motives will achieve meaning only through repeated use—whether within one composer's *oeuvre* or that of a whole group of composers. In other words, the whole question of *musica poetica* is indissolubly linked with those of parody (one composer paying homage to another by borrowing from him) and self-borrowing. The examples show that many of Marenzio's *topoi* are borrowed from those of older composers (Rore, Gabrieli, Merulo, Striggio), while younger composers in their turn borrowed from Marenzio.

Third, from the second flows the third conclusion: that in order to appreciate any one madrigal to the full, a knowledge of the entire madrigal genre is necessary; there is pleasure in recognition. That the madrigal genre is destined primarily for those "in the know" is supported by two aspects of word-painting: allusion to musical terminology and eye-music." The first type is illustrated in the chromaticism of *E questo il legno*[106] and in the use of dactylic, *sdrucciole* rhythm (dotted crotchet, quaver, minim) on the word "sdrucciola" ("slips") in the *terza parte* of *Passando con pensier.*[107] The second is also one which could appeal only to the musically educated with a part-book in front of them: "eye-music." Marenzio uses this to express a number of concepts, such as color,[108] light or whiteness, darkness or blackness [ex. 150], and eyes (through the use of semibreves peering out at the reader from the page).[109] As a final example of both "eye-music" and reference to musical terminology, we may mention the use of a ligature to represent the sacred knot of marriage.[110] Common to all these examples is the fact that the sound of the music plays no part in illustrating the meaning of the words.

Fourth, the question of "eye-music" raises an issue which was already hotly debated in the sixteenth century, namely, the propriety or appropriateness of certain types of word-painting. "Eye-music" in particular is open to the charge that it is not perceptible by the listener who lacks the aid of a score or part-book. However, appeal to the intellect of the cultivated performer is an element so deeply embedded in the Italian madrigal that even the new virtuoso style of the 1580's could not eradicate this type of witticism. Besides, there is no instrinsic reason why visual pleasure should not be derived from a musical score. Even the most ungenerous critic is compelled to admit that if "eye-music" adds nothing to the aural pleasure of music, neither does it necessarily detract from it.[111]

Fifth, a more important issue is raised by the allusions to musical terminology, for such references show that Marenzio often saw in a word a meaning not intended by the poet, and of no relevance to the poetic argument.[112] A similar objection is that, even when the denotative meaning of a word is recognized and illustrated according to the meaning intended by the poet, its connotative meaning is often not conveyed in the music.[113] A comparison of two settings of a Petrarch sonnet, one by Marenzio and one by Monteverdi, illustrate that Marenzio's shortcomings are to some extent those of the age he lived in and the style he inherited and perfected. In the line "Ma'l vento ne portava le parole,"[114] the last of the sonnet *Ohimè'l bel viso,*[115] Petrarch seeks to capture the scattering, disruptive effect of Death, who has already claimed Laura. This symbolism is perfectly understood by Monteverdi who captures the rapacity of Death with an abrupt leap introducing "vento" ("wind") followed by a descent into nothingness.[116] With Marenzio, however, the emotional connotations of this line are ignored: a quaver motive (b. 142 ff) depicts the rushing gust of wind, but the elegiac implications are, to say the least, very muted.

Having discussed the question of propriety, we may turn briefly to the objections of Mei, Galilei, Bardi, Caccini, and G.B. Doni against word-painting and indeed polyphony itself. The reasons for these objections are, broadly speaking, twofold: failure to stir the emotions of the listener,[117] and maltreatment of the poetic text.[118] The conventional madrigalisms which Galilei ridicules in his *Dialogo* (1581)[119] continue unabated and are exaggerated even further by Marenzio and the other *virtuosi* of the subsequent two decades. Where, however, Galilei finds the contradictory and mutually self-cancelling textures and emotions merely contemptible, the maturer if less original Morley, as we have seen, justifies these very features with reference to the contradictory and vaccilating figure of the Petrarchan lover.[120] The truth about Marenzio's music perhaps lies between these two extremes. Where the variety of some madrigals may be more apparent than real, and the expression mechanical and sterile (viz. *VI a 5,* 1584, nos. 11 and 12), other compositions use the same contrasts with greater success.[121] In general, the higher the quality of the poetry, the better the music. This is demonstrated by one setting from the *I a 4,5,6* (1588) of a poem which is nothing but a hotchpotch of works by other poets.[122] The banality of one particular line is all too faithfully reflected in Marenzio's mechanical setting, with its entirely unconvincing turning motive on "giri" ("turns").[123]

Objections about the maltreatment of the poetic text varied from Mei's complaint about the incompleteness of the text in the individual voices,[124] to the objection that polyphony rendered the words inaudible[125] and "cut the poetry to bits."[126] Textual incompleteness is an essential feature of Marenzio's madrigals and indeed can have an expressive function; in other words, it is part and parcel of the polyphonic style which Galilei attacked in 1581 and which Marenzio brought to a peak of refinement. Word audibility is another area in which Marenzio often puts expression and symbolism before clarity. Without undertaking a scientific test, it can be tentatively stated that Marenzio's words are potentially more audible than in a good deal of the vocal music of the time, but that he often falls short of the standards of A. Gabrieli and Wert.[127] It is difficult to know how exactly to interpret Doni's observation that Marenzio, Caccini and others

> hanno cominciato a fare cantare con bella grazia le parti, e fare intendere alquanto meglio le parole.[128]

How much was Doni specifically thinking of Marenzio? Was he not perhaps thinking of the *VII* and *VIII a 5* (1595 and 1598), where the words are indeed declaimed much more clearly than before?

It is beyond the scope of this chapter to establish whether or not Marenzio is guilty of "lacerating the poetry." To answer this question we must now turn to the higher structural units: the line or phrase, section, and movement.

6

The Treatment of the Line or Phrase

With the exception of the twelve-syllable *verso sdrucciolo,* all the lines set by Marenzio are of seven or eleven syllables, that is, heptasyllabic or hendeca-syllabic.[1] Flexibility and rhythmic variety are obtained through elisions and the introduction of vowel combinations within the same word which count either as one or two syllables, depending on the context.[2]

The translation of the seven or eleven syllables of the single line is subject to rigid rules which reveal a respect for the metre. Thus if a vowel combination must be taken as two syllables in order to make up the full complement of seven or eleven syllables, then it is treated accordingly [ex. 151]. Similarly, vowel combinations acting as one syllable are treated as one syllable [ex. 152]. But Marenzio often places a rest between two words which otherwise would have been elided; in these cases, we end up with extra syllables [ex. 153]. Elisions cannot occur between the end of one line and the beginning of another [ex. 154].

How the Line is Divided

Highly characteristic of Marenzio are the ingeniously varied means of dividing the line into two or more musical units. These comprise the division of the hendecasyllabic into two nearly equal parts, the isolation of the first two or three syllables from the rest of the line, and the subdivision of the line into three or more fragments.[3]

Division of the hendecasyllabic into two nearly equal parts (*a maiore* if the first part is longer than the second, *a minore* if shorter), is a technique that Marenzio possibly derived from Lassus.[4] Common to both composers is the rhythmic differentiation between the slower first fragment and the faster second fragment. This allows the two fragments to be clearly distinguished when they are combined in double counterpoint. There is every reason to believe that, just as Lassus influenced Marenzio, so the latter in his turn influenced his contemporaries. The opening section of *Perchè adoprar catene* (*RISM* 1583[12]) has already been compared with a similar passage by G.M.

Nanino;[5] moreover, one of Marenzio's most popular and most widely imitated pieces, *Liquide perle* (*I a 5*, 1580, no. 1) begins with a typical division *a maiore*.[6] It is interesting to draw comparisons with Macque and Felice Anerio, both of whom aped Marenzio's contrapuntal style frequently and successfully in the 1580's [ex. 155].[7]

It is difficult to find a precedent for the division of the line after the first two or three syllables. This often occurs at openings and has a number of functions. Marenzio grasps the listener's attention through an elemental harmonic progression (usually I - V, sometimes I - IV - V or I - VI - I) declaimed in semibreves and followed by faster motion. Vocatives and exclamations are thus treated [ex. 157]. Sometimes the first word is repeated [ex. 158].

The division of a line into three, four, or even five fragments occurs most frequently when Marenzio wishes to isolate each separate word for the purpose of tone painting. Once again, Marenzio and Macque can be shown to be very much akin [ex. 159]. Marenzio's *Baci amorosi e cari* (*V a 5*, 1591, no. 12) is something of a showcase in the matter of line fragmentation. Not only is the repeated word "Baci" ("kisses") isolated by a I - V progresion, but sighing is vividly suggested by multiple rests [ex. 160]. In example 160 (b) the central word "sospir" ("sighing") represents an axis of symmetry around which are placed the antiphonically treated words "baci, morsi" ("kisses, bites") and "sguardi, parole" ("glances, words").

The rhythmic treatment of the line or phrase

Just as the meaning of individual words is translated into an equivalent musical symbol, so Marenzio is at pains to find a suitable rhythmic motive for each line or phrase. Certain stereotyped rhythmic formulae appear so frequently that they can be easily identified and classified (table 5). Variations of the basic formulae are also frequent: notes or groups of notes may be augmented or diminished, *melismata* may be introduced, and dotted rhythms (♩♪) may replace even notes (♩♩).[8] Augmentation and *melismata* often affect the penultimate note of a line or phrase, emphasizing it in much the same way as dissonances just before a cadence. First and last syllables are likewise freely elongated [ex. 161].[9] thus the beginnings and ends of lines and phrases are clearly articulated.

Practical Application of the *Rhythmic Formulae*

In rhythm 1 (a) [this and following rhythm notations refer to table 5], the simplest of all possible rhythms, the downbeat crotchets usually coincide with the accented, even-numbered syllables [ex. 162]. The same rhythm sometimes

Table 5.   Rhythmic Formulae Used by Marenzio

Poetic accents of line or phrase	Rhythmic formula
1. Accents on second, fourth, and sixth syllables	(a) ♩ ♩ ♩ ♩ ♩ ♩ ♩ (b) ♩ ♩ ♩. ♪ ♩ ♩ ♩
2. Accents on third and sixth syllables (with types b, c, and d, an accent may additionally occur on the first syllable)	(a) ♪ ♪ ♪ ♪ ♪ ♪ (b) ♩ ♩ ♩ ♪ ♪♪ (c) ♩ ♩ ♩. ♪ ♩ ♩ (d) ♩. ♪ ♩ ♩ ♩
3. Accents on fourth and sixth syllables (with option of additional accent on first syllable; in type d, a secondary accent may occur on the second syllable, in which case the first important accent occurs on the fourth syllable)	(a) ♩. ♪ ♩ ♩ ♩ (b) ♩ ♪ ♩ ♩ ♩ (c) ♩ ♪ ♪ ♩ ♩ (d) ♩ ♩. ♪ ♩ ♩
4. Accents on first, fourth, and seventh syllables	♩. ♪ ♩ ♩. ♪ ♩ ♩. ♪ ♩

occurs also on lines which begin irregularly [ex. 163]. Variations can be obtained through dotted rhythm, augmentation, [ex. 164] or diminution [ex. 165]. Augmentation of the even-numbered notes results in triple-time cross rhythms [ex. 166].

Rhythm 1 (b) is the same as 1 (a) except for the substitution of a dotted rhythm for an even rhythm. The effect is to modify the even-paced neutrality of 1 (a) in a more lively, exhilarating direction, and to articulate through accentuation the beginning of a group of four crotchets. It is no coincidence that this rhythm occurs most frequently in lighter, hedonistic pieces [ex. 167]. In *III a 5* (1582), no. 6, the rhythm is reiterated in three successive lines to induce a strong sense of pulse,[10] after which there comes a striking rhythmic displacement.[11]

Rhythm 2 (a), characterized by anapaestic rhythm, is often varied through elongation of the first syllable [ex. 168]. In example 169, augmentation emphasizes "sassi" ("rocks") through white notation.[12]

Rhythm 2 (b) is similar to 2 (c), but with the first two notes augmented [ex. 170]. Rhythm 2 (c) resembles 2 (b), but with the replacement of ♩ ♩ ♪ by ♩. ♪ ♩ (notes three to five) [ex. 171]. This formula is also found when a secondary accent occurs on the second syllable, without however detracting from the accent on the third [ex. 172].

Rhythm 2 (d) is marked by a strong musical accent on the first syllable; however, the same rhythm may occur whether or not the first syllable is heavily accented [ex. 173]. In example 174, augmentation causes an incidental distortion of "fera" (treated as though the accent were on the second rather than the first syllable); the real reason for augmentation here is to introduce a slow rhythm for the words "fera cagion" ("cruel cause").[13]

Rhythm 3 (a) is musically identical to 2 (d); however, the poetic rhythm is no different, for now the accents are on the fourth and six syllables, not the third and sixth [ex. 175]. As in 2 (d), first syllables can receive much more stress than they deserve [ex. 176]. In the last example Marenzio incorporates a dotted rhythm to represent "arse" ("burnt"),[14] even though this distorts the rhythm of the line.

Rhythm 3 (b) may be interpreted as a variation of 3 (a). The two may indeed appear together [ex. 177].

In rhythm 3 (c) the first three notes of 3 (a) and (b) are changed from ♩. ♪ ♩ to ♩ ♪ ♪ [ex. 178]. Here the line, "Al mio bel sol adorno" is treated as though the first syllable were more heavily accented than the third. Thus Marenzio sacrifices strict rhythmic declamation for the purely musical effect of repetition. Example 179 illustrates the same rhythm with the last three notes augmented. Presumably the white notes are supposed to convey the meaning "pearls."[15] In 3 (c) the first note is often elongated for exclamations or at moments of pathos [ex. 180]. This exaggerated emotionalism already foreshadows similar exclamations from Baroque music [ex. 181].

Rhythm 3 (d) bears a musical resemblance to 1 (b), with the difference that the second syllable is at most a secondary accent [ex. 182]. In the above example the introduction of a dotted rhythm for "vivaci" ("lively")[16] once again shows that expression of the meaning of a word means more to Marenzio than immaculately precise declamation. In lines where the first syllable is accented, extension of the first note is common [ex. 183]. Occasionally however the first note remains shorter than the second, even where the first syllable receives a greater stress than the second [ex. 184].

In the fourth and last group, the accents are spaced at regular intervals to allow triple time cross-rhythms [ex. 185].

Triple Time

So far, the examples have all been drawn from passages notated in duple time, even though ternary rhythmic groupings occur in 1 (a), 3 (b), and 4. The real distinction between duple and triple time is one of tempo than of rhythm or metre.[17] Thus the rhythmic formulae described above are as applicable to passages in triple time as to passages in duple time [ex. 186].

Combinations

In most of the examples so far discussed, only the first six notes of a line or phrase have been given. In practice, however, phrases are often longer, especially where hendecasyllabic lines are concerned. In these longer phrases, Marenzio joins together the first few notes of two rhythmic formulae [ex. 187].

Conclusion

We have already seen, in chapter 5, how rhythmic motives fulfil an expressive function. In this chapter we have seen how the same rhythms have the more elementary purpose of reflecting the poetic rhythm. Thus, for example, the rhythm ♩ . ♪ ♩ may occur whenever the first of the three notes (or the first and the third) are accentuated; it also has the function of representing a whole series of ideas: life, violent motion, flames, etc.[18]

It therefore need not surprise us if a conflict of priorities sometimes occurs, whereby a rhythmic formula is selected in order to convey the meaning of a word at the expense of the rhythm of the phrase as a whole. We have already come across such poetic licences,[19] and more examples could be found. Only occasionally do rhythmic distortions seem ugly and out of place. Why for instance, in *III a 6*, 1585, no. 9, are the line "E ti rech' ad offesa" and "Che di te la mia lingua" treated with rhythm 3 (b) instead of the more correct 2 (d) [ex. 188]? On the whole, however, rhythmic inexactness is defensible according to the aesthetic criteria of the time. Mannerist painters such as Parmigianino obtained great expressivity by distorting the limbs of the human body, while Borghini advised along similar lines: "Give your figures small heads and long limbs, and they will have the required elegance."[20]

The conflicting priorities from declamation (rhythmic exactness versus expressive licence) parallel the dilemma, set out in the previous chapter, between word audibility and coherence, and expression of the meaning of individual words. The two problems are linked, in that correct declamation is essential if the words are to be made comprehensible to the listener. This contradiction is an essential element in Marenzio's style and approach to composition until 1594. After that date, the musical rhythm seeks to reproduce speech rhythm as exactly as possible, rather than taking speech rhythm as a mere point of departure for the selection of rhythmic formulae. There is no more musical accentuation of unaccented syllables, nor are equivalent durations assigned to primary and secondary accents. These developments parallel the gradual elimination of individual word-painting where this might obstruct textural continuity or dissipate the mood of the whole poem. This distinction between the earlier and later styles, essential for the delimitation of this study, will be elaborated in the last chapter.

7

The Treatment of the Section

The section mediates between the line or phrase and the total form. As a unit it is variable and relative rather than fixed and absolute. It is not always easy to see where the divisions come. For instance, in narrative poems, where continuity is of the essence, the division into sections is much less clearcut than usual (e.g. *Tirsi morir volea* and the *seconda parte* of *Con dolce sguardo*).[1] Moreover, some caesuras mark a clearer break than others. This is particularly so with *ottava* and sonnet settings where a primary caesura separates the two quatrains, and a secondary division occurs between the first and second line of each quatrain.

Poetically, a section is equivalent to one statement, thought, or sentence;[2] musically, we may define a section as the gap between two principal cadences—in other words, two cadences that stand out of their context. With this tentative definition in mind, we will discuss three aspects of sectional structure: contrapuntal technique, repetition of lines, phrases, or sections, and cadence structure.

Contrapuntal Technique

Marenzio is rightly famous for his sophisticated contrapuntal technique.[3] The success of such pieces as *Dissi a l'amata*[4] must have stemmed largely from the dexterous manipulation of motives in polyphonic combination without any loss of grace or lightness. "Bell'aria"[5] prevails in even the most complicated of passages.

A passage may be homophonic, polyphonic or intermediate between the two. Often the music fluctuates between the two extremes of homophony and polyphony, its exact course being determined by the expressive requirements of the moment.[6] Even in the most declamatory composition, polyphony is liable to break out at the appearance of a suggestive word, as happens in *Amatemi ben mio*[7] and in *Se tu mi lasci* (*RISM* 1583[11]) with its imitated cries of "misero" and "misera."[8] It is important to distinguish between these highly sensitive examples of declamation and the more relaxed, popular style of such pieces as *Filli tu sei* (*V a 5*, 1585, no. 11). In the former, greater attention is paid to the emotional implications of individual words, and variability of texture is therefore by no means to be excluded. Many passages occupy a no-man's-land between homophony and contrapuntal texture: one voice will surge ahead, others will lag behind to create suspensions and passing dissonances. At the opening of *Chi vol udir* (*I a 4*, 1585, no. 10) the canto exists in a state of tension *vis-à-vis* the three lower voices, at first in the lead of them, then dragging behind.[9] Such passages are already plentiful in the middle of Marenzio's career and become even more so after 1594. A possible influence is Wert, who was much given to isolating one voice (usually the canto) and raising it to soloistic status. In this respect it is remarkable how close to Wert Marenzio is at the opening of *Ecco che un altra volta* (*I a 4, 5, 6*, 1588, no. 10), where the tenor anticipates the other voice in much the same way as in Wert's setting of the same poem, published less than a month later.[10]

Even in the more rigidly imitative passages, contrapuntal technique is generally subservient to overall sonority, which in turn is governed by expressive aims. This is particularly the case when Marenzio suspends the normal rules concerning imitation in order to depict the words' meaning. Thus the normal semibreve lapse between two voices of a *fuga* (assuming the use of the *misura comune*) may contract to a minim or even a crotchet to depict certain concepts: e.g. "following,"[11] "happiness,"[12] violent motion,[13] and "narrowness" or "squeezing" [ex. 189].

Equally characteristic is the departure from the standard practice of imitation at the perfect fifth. Marenzio was perfectly capable of following the standard practice of introducing clusters of two or three voices in imitation at the fifth and octave. A classic example is the opening of *Nova angeletta* (*I a 4*, 1585), which may be compared to Macque's setting of another Petrarch setting [ex. 190]. At other times imitations occur at only the unison and octave, with the result that the harmony changes very little or remains only on one chord or two alternating chords. This often occurs near the end of a piece to reassert the prevailing mode. A case in point is the ending of one piece apparently modeled on a passage from Rore's *Amor, ben mi credevo* [ex. 191]. In *Hor pien d'altro desio* (*RISM* 1582[4]) the opening twin motives are introduced exclusively on *g* (the final) and then on *d* (the dominant), in order to depict the concept of "change";[14] the sound is different and more modern than the hovering effect of the opening of a madrigal by Merulo which employs similar themes imitated at the lower fifth [ex. 192]. The more limited the available number of pitches for imitation, the greater are the opportunities for exploring effects of mass and color. This preoccupation with sonority underlies the use of two half-choirs of the same pitch in *Donò Cinthia* [ex. 193]. Imitations at the unison and octave usually have a cheerful effect and are connected with the device of *gioco*.[15] Imitations at the interval of a sixth and a third are also to be found, though they lack any special expressive significance.[16] They can be very strict (e.g. the double canonic opening of *II a 6*, 1584, no. 10); more usually, however, motives are adapted during the course of a section according to criteria overruling the need for exact recall. Tonal answers are common though by no means predominant: at the opening of *I a 4, 5, 6* (1588), no. 14, the sesto outlines the diapente of mode 1 transposed (*g' - d"*), the quinto, the diatessaron (*d' - g'*). However, in *IV a 5* (1584), no. 2 (mode 1 untransposed), the opening descending fifth in the tenor (*a - d*) is answered exactly at the lower fifth *(d - G)* in the bass. In modes 3 and 8 one finds a special kind of exact imitation: *mi - fa - mi* becomes *re - fa - mi* when imitated at the lower fifth [ex. 194]. The effect of inexact imitation is often to impart a feeling of uncertainty or instability; it is associated with shifting tonality and a texture intermediate between polyphony and homophony. A passage from the *III a 5* (1582), no. 9 presents at first sight a seemingly random collection of notes in three voices [ex. 195]. There is however a consistent pattern: where the quinto has ascending fourths, the canto has ascending seconds, and *vice versa;* descending intervals are the same in both voices. The alto, restricted to major and minor seconds, follows the quinto and then the canto in parallel thirds. Equally sensitive is the treatment of the opening line of *O voi che sospirate,* where the fragments are imitated but never exactly duplicated by all five voices. Marenzio instead prefers to recall only the essential expressive features of each fragment: long notes on "O voi che . . . ," "sighing" rhythms for "sospirate" and a rising leap (of variable pitch) for "a miglior note."[17] As if in compensation, Marenzio unites the opening two lines motivically through the persistence of the "sighing" rhythm[18] and the steady progression from *a* to *b* in ascending fifths.[19]

Other techniques of inexact imitation are partial inversion and partial transposition. Partial inversion occurs when some but not all of the motive is imitated in inverted form [ex. 196]; partial transposition occurs when different fragments of the motive appear at different transpositions[20] [ex. 197]. Another technique is to present two slightly different versions of the same motive on two alternating pitches. *Sola angioletta* (*V a 5*, 1585, no. 1) opens with two variants presented as a pair in the canto and alto (with entries on *d"* and *g'*); the same pair is then imitated by the tenor and bass (on *d'* and *g*).

Genuine bithematicism and polythematicism exist in many forms. Bithematicism is present whenever the same textual fragment is presented in slow, even notes combined with a faster theme [ex. 198]. More common are paired motives—i.e. two motives presented simultaneously or in close overlap, and which reappear with the same vertical alignment. The two voices normally diverge from one of the perfect intervals (octave, fifth, or unison) and then continue in parallel thirds or sixths. This stereotyped procedure results in many similar-sounding passages [ex. 199]. Marenzio's concern for clarity may be seen in the way the voices are paired together in order to reduce their scope for individual polyphonic development. Thus voice pairs moving in thirds and tenths in a six-voice madrigal reduce the number of separate strands from six to three [ex. 200]. In the four-voice madrigals the simple opposition of the top two and bottom two voices is often favored. More elaborate is the pairing of the canto and bass, quinto and tenor, with the alto acting as an axis of symmetry, as happens in *Hor pien d'altro desio*.[21]

The simultaneous combination of two or more successive fragments of text (double or multiple counterpoint) is the crowning glory of Marenzio the polyphonist. The devices pioneered by Rore and Lassus assume, with Marenzio, a refinement unsurpassed until the ensembles of Mozart's operas. By uniting diverse strands of thought into a polyphonic continuum Marenzio is able to explore ramifications scarcely hinted at in the poetic text. A case in point is the contrapuntal drama which is the first section of *V a 6* (1591) no. 1, composed for the marriage of Flavia Peretti and Virginio Orsini. The first two lines are typical of the whole poem, full of the *luoghi comuni* of pastoral allegory:

1.   2.

Leggiadrissima / eterna Primavera

3.   4.

Vive / scherzand'a questi colli intorno[22]

Marenzio assigns a different motive to each of the four fragments of text [ex. 201][23] introducing and developing them with mounting rhythmic and textural intensity. Towards the end there is an ever-increasing emphasis on tonic and dominant (chords of *g* and *d*) and an increasing number of cadences on the final, *g*. Gradually the first three motives are phased out, leaving the incisive and rhythmical fourth motive. The effect is of a wedding procession drawing gradually closer.

Other examples could be cited to show that even during the most intricate of contrapuntal passages, Marenzio never loses sight of his expressive aims. This is particularly true of the opening section of the Petrarch setting, *I a 4* (1585), no. 17 [ex. 202]. This is divided into three contrapuntal segments:

1.   2.   3.

Tutto'l dì piango, / e poi la notte, / quando

Prendon riposo i miseri mortali[24]

The first fragment is presented in two versions, the first an ascending and descending semitone, the second expanding the ascending semitone to a minor third. The second fragment[25] expands the ascending interval further to a major third in order to convey the extension of weeping ("piango") into night as well as day. These two fragments are distributed among the four voices in a symmetrical pattern, the axis of which falls in bar 6 (see table 6). Meanwhile the canto enters with the third fragment (b. 4 ff; notice the omission of the final word, "mortali"), set to an angular theme differing both in length and character from the first two themes. The third theme is not heard again until b. 11, when the tenor sings the first four notes in inversion before continuing with free material. The bass is the next to enter (b. 12), reproducing the entire phrase to the accompaniment of free material in the upper voices (cf. bb. 4-8 and 12-15). The section ends with a distinct *rallentando* on the previously withheld word "mortali" (b. 16 ff). The way in which the voices converge upon the final two words is a measure of Marenzio's ability to combine a seemingly rigid symmetrical scheme with emotional emphasis.

Table 6.   Disposition of Vocal Entries for First Two
Contrapuntal Fragments of *Tutto il dì piango*

	ALTO (b. 6)	
TENOR (b. 5)		TENOR (b. 7)
ALTO (b. 4)		ALTO (b. 8)
BASS (b. 4)		BASS (b. 8)
CANTO (b. 3)		CANTO (b. 8)
TENOR (b. 2)		TENOR (b. 9)
BASS (b. 1)		BASS (b. 10)
		ALTO (b. 10)
		CANTO (b. 11)

Repetition of Lines, Phrases, and Sections

The contrapuntal deployment of motives is but one way of sustaining the length of a section. Another is repetition of the section or of some of its component parts (lines and phrases). This may be a rhetorical device, or may simply serve to built up a section to the required length. The latter objective is predominent at the ends of many madrigals or movements, where purely architectural criteria take over from expressive criteria. The maximum number of repeated lines at the end of a composition is five;[26] at the other extreme, the repetition may affect only a small fragment. Endings normally fall into one of three formal categories: the final unit may be stated twice (A A₁),[27] or three times (A A₁ A₂), or may be subdivided into two smaller units through an extra repetition of the final fragment (A B A₁ B₁ B₂). The three types appear at the endings of thirteen of the eighteen separate *parti* which make up the fourteen pieces of the *I a 5* (1580).[28] Rhythmic augmentation is commonly applied to the last statement of the last fragment.

Varied repetitions are more common than straightforward ones. Transpositions occur at the fifth or fourth, or melodic material is exchanged between two equal voices or is freely transposed and assigned to a higher or lower voice. Exceptionally, contrapuntal elaborations not present in the original statement appear in the restatement. This happens in many of the pieces from that treasure trove of contrapuntal dexterity, the *I a 4, 5, 6* (1588).[29] Particularly instructive are the two statements of the last line of no. 5, a hendecasyllabic *a minore,* in which the two fragments are set successively, then combined.

A few examples will demonstrate both why and how repetition is used. The first, *Madonna poi ch'uccider (III a 5,* 1582, no. 1) has already been mentioned in connection with Baccusi,[30] whom Marenzio surpasses in the eloquent use of repetition. The piece falls into three sections with the forms A B B₁ B₂ (bb. 1-12), A A₁ B (bb. 12-29) and A A₁ B A B₁ B₂ C (bb. 29-49). The repetitions are always justified, whether they convey joyful affirmation (b. 6 ff: "Non nego di morire"),[31] emphasize an affective word ("dolci"[32] or "moia"[33]) or help to create an expansive ending (bb. 29-49). Especially striking is the reintroduction of the word "moia" on a *b*-flat chord where one would expect an *f* chord (cf. bb. 34 and 38). The technique of partial transposition of a phrase is analogous to the way polyphonic motives often undergo partial transposition or inversion. The objective is to isolate a particular word or phrase through an unexpected twist in the tonal orientation. A case in point is the treatment of the word "lasso" at the opening of *II a 5* (1581), no. 1. Here the delayed cadence on *d* in bars 10-11 intensifies the effect of the *g* cadence in bars 5-6.

Another important intensifying device is the redistribution of vocal lines in different voices on repetition, whether or not the process involves a transposition. In *V a 5* (1585), no. 12, b. 76 ff, the tenor theme is transferred to the canto at the upper octave, while the quinto theme appears in the bass at the lower twelfth. Where the bassline is involved in the process of interchange or transposition, the harmonic implications of a phrase can be strikingly transformed, as frequently happens in the later works [ex. 203]. The unmistakeable ingenuity of such passages is equalled only by certain passages in Gesualdo's madrigals.[34]

The Structural Function of the Cadence

Besides having certain expressive functions,[35] cadences serve a syntactical function in nearly all late sixteenth-century vocal music. Cadences are the punctuation marks of music,[36] and it is doubtful whether any composer before

Marenzio had succeeded in matching so closely all the diverse shades of syntactical division. This is one of many ways in which Marenzio's music aspires to the condition of language.

The analysis of the structural function of the cadence in sixteenth-century music is still in its infancy.[37] A useful approach is Bernhard Meier's dual classification of cadences according to their textural-contrapuntal properties, and according to their position within the modal hierarchy.[38] The first type of classification has to do with the extent to which each cadence is clearcut, i.e. easily discernible by the listener. In the second classification, the position of the cadence in the modal hierarchy is decided by the scale degree on which it falls in each particular mode; a cadence may be normal and characteristic for that mode, or may be uncharacteristic, i.e. irregular *(clausula peregrina)*. In general, the higher the syntactical value of a cadence, the more clearcut and regular will be this cadence, the most clearcut and regular ones of all being those which occur at the ends of sections. However, this rule, as we shall see, is riddled with exceptions.

Textural-Contrapuntal

Turning now to the first type of classification, textural-contrapuntal, let us enumerate those factors which make a cadence strong or weak, clearcut or indistinct:

1. The preparation of the cadence (the *antipenultima* and, especially, the *penultima*).
2. The present or absence of a suspension before the sounding of the leading note.
3. The duration of the *penultima*.
4. The duration of the resolution.
5. The extent to which phrases overlap at the cadence.
6. The extent to which the cadence is left incomplete.
7. The extent to which the resolution is delayed.
8. The extent to which the cadence is subject to interruption.

The last four factors may be distinguished from the first four in that they imply concealment or avoidance, rather than mere weakening, of the cadence. It was precisely this concealment or avoidance which theorists found to be artistically desirable; cadences of this type were called "cadenze fuggite."[39]

Preparation of the cadence. It is not necessary to rehearse the various stages through which cadence patterns evolved before the end of the sixteenth century.[40] It is sufficient to observe three standard patterns: those where the bass drops a perfect fifth or ascends a perfect fourth ("perfect"[41] cadence); those where the bass drops a major second ("inverted" cadence),[42] and where the bass drops a perfect fourth or ascends a perfect fifth (plagal). Of these, the first is the strongest and most assertive, the most suited to stand at the end of a section or movement. The inverted cadence occupies a lower syntatical function, presumably because the bassline is melodically rather than harmonically motivated. Thus it may connect two statements of the same line or phrase [ex. 204], introduce speech,[43] separate two adjective phrases ("pien di stupore, / fisso"),[44] connect an adjective with a comparative clause ("più proterva / ch'a Pan non fu colei"),[45] or a verb with its object ("e teco guida / i pargoletti Amor").[46] A plagal cadence may, like an inverted cadence, introduce speech.[47] Generally, however, it carries a higher syntactical value than the inverted cadence, often appearing at the ends of the movements of multi-movement madrigals. It is less assertive however than the perfect cadence, usually appearing when the tonality has already been asserted through emphasis of the V - I relationship of dominant and tonic, or by some other means.[48]

The presence or absence of a suspension before the sounding of the leading note. Cadences where the tonic note is suspended, then resolved to the leading note, will be stonger than those preceded by a succession of bland consonances.[49] Therefore nearly all principal cadences are prepared by a dissonant antepenultimate chord, usually a six-four or a four-three. Where dissonance occurs, the *penultima* is usually lengthened to accommodate it and the resolution (see below, next point). The importance of dissonance is shown by the repetitions of the phrase "s'io resto vivo" ("if I remain alive")[50] where the repeated *d* cadences are weaker than the dissonant *b*-flat cadence.

The duration of the "penultima." A cadence whose *penultima* lasts a minim will tend to be weaker than one with a longer penultima:

> Il suo vago e gioioso e lieto manto
> All'hor feconda rivestè la terra[51]

Here the cadences on "manto" (with minim preparation) are weaker than those for "terra" (semibreve preparation with dissonance), as one would expect from the syntax.

The duration of the resolution. The shorter the duration of the final tonic, the weaker the cadence:

> Dagli lor tu, che, se mai gl'occhi gira
> L'anima bella a le sue belle spoglie[52]

Here, the cadence on "gira" (whose final chord lasts only a crotchet) is weaker than that on "spoglie," as required by the syntax: the first cadence connects a verb with its object, the second delimits the end of the clause.

Cadential overlap. Cadences where the final statement of one line overlaps with the initial statement of the next, represent perhaps the most common type of *clausula fuggita.* They may occur within the section, or (more rarely) at the junction of two sections. Within the section they have the function of welding together either successive statements of the same phrase or statements of successive phrases to form a polyphonic continuum. Some sections rely more heavily on this device than others: for example, the *prima parte* of *Bianchi cigni* (*RISM* 1583[10])[53] is particularly impressive in this respect. The first line is heard in overlap with itself,[54] after which the second and third lines appear as a contrapuntal unity thanks to a series of overlapping phrases.[55] Later on in the movement there occurs a cadential overlap between two sections: at b. 56 the sesto cuts through the other voices with a totally new theme before the other voices have completed the *c* cadence. Though the cadence is definitely a *clausula fuggita,* it feels strong owing to the extent of the dominant preparation (b. 57) and the preceding *c*-major sonority (bb. 55-56). Other instances of sectional overlap reveal similar contrasts between the melodic material of the old and new sections: for example, the final section of *V a 5* (1585), no. 4, b. 45 ff, where the change from homophonic to polyphonic texture ensures sufficient differentiation between the end of the preceding section and the beginning of the next.

An important by-product of contrapuntal overlap is the change in harmonic direction which results from the introduction of a new motive in the lowest voice. Thus an expected resolution of V to I may be diverted to IV or VI. The former occurs near the opening of *Quando i vostri* where a cadence on *d* is completed over a chord of *g* (first inversion).[56] From this type of cadence, the interrupted cadence (see below, point on interruption) probably owes its derivation.

The extent to which the cadence is left incomplete. The noncompletion of a cadence represents a still higher degree of avoidance than mere overlap, and is thus potentially more expressive.[57] It occurs when some or all of the voices fall silent before the final chord is reached. This procedure often occurs at the overlap of two phrases; often a momentary reduction in texture is enough to distinguish two phrases [ex. 205].

The extent to which the resolution is delayed. The delayed cadence is the type of *clausula fuggita* which Marenzio handles with the most originality. Here, the full resolution is postponed until after the conclusion of the line or phrase—in other words, until the beginning, middle, or end of the succeeding phrase. By thus allowing a harmonic progression to overlap with the phrase ending, Marenzio succeeds in tying together distinct phrases which depend on their context for their grammatical sense. As a form of musical punctuation a delayed resolution may be weaker even than a comma in written language. The device often coincides with the poetic device of enjambement, whereby a phrase flows from the end of one line over to the beginning of the next.

Delayed resolutions occur most frequently with the following progressions:

1. I - V - I (major or minor)
2. IV - V - I (major or minor)
3. VI - V - I (major or minor)
4. III - V - I (minor)
5. VII - V - I (minor)

Of all these, the second is the most common, with IV often appearing in first inversion. The fourth and fifth are special and rare occurrences, involving a chromatic approach to the leading note which is expressive as well as syntactical in function [ex. 206].[58]

The first three progressions appear to be interchangeable. The following are some of their functions:

a) to connect two statements of the same phrase: e.g. *II a 5* (1581), no. 13, b. 62, phrase ends with I - V; on second statement, phrase ends with I - V - I (b. 70);

b) to connect adjective and noun [ex. 207];

c) to connect subject and verb: ". . . e'l mormorar de l'onde / S'accorderanno . . . ;[59]

d) to introduce speech: "Gli disse: 'ohimè ben mio . . .' ";[60] "dice: 'Amor...' ";[61]

e) to connect adverb phrase and verb: "E nel suo lume santo/ Scherzan gl'honesti amori";[62]

f) to connect two phrases or short clauses of equal syntactical value: ". . . di verd'herbette / E di novelli fior";[63] "Vissi di spem' / hor vivo pur di pianto";[64]

g) to connect a subordinate with main clause, or *vice versa:* "Ohimè, se tanto amate Di sentir dir 'ohimè,' / deh, perchè fate Chi dice 'ohimè,' morire?"[65]

This list of syntactical functions is by no means complete.

The extent to which a cadence is subject to interruption. The "interrupted" or "deceptive" cadence, whereby an expected V - I pattern is deflected to V - IV or V - VI, has became a stock device for ensuring continuity of musical thought. Its use in the sixteenth century probably derives from the unexpected harmonic patterns arising from contrapuntal overlap. In a homophonic context, it is particularly common for the bass to drop a tone (V - IV) to indicate continuity of poetic thought. The situations in which this pattern occurs are similar to those already described in connection with delayed cadences. Thus an interrupted cadence:

a) can connect two statements of the same phrase: e.g. *I a 5* (1580), no. 9, b. 63, phrase ends with V - IV; on second statement, phrase ends with V - I (b. 66);

b) can connect subject and verb: " . . . ma il core / Si resterà . . .";[66]

c) can indicate continuity of speech [ex. 209].

Equally common is the occurence of cadences which are delayed and interrupted at the same time [ex. 210]. A particularly fine example is the cadence near the opening of *Amor, io non potrei* [ex. 211].

Intervallic Relationship

Turning now to the second way of classifying cadences, according to their intervallic relationship with the modal final, we may for the sake of convenience divide all cadences into three basic categories:

1. Terminal (occurring at the ends of movements and compositions);
2. Principal (occurring at the ends of sections);
3. Transitory (occurring within sections).

Cadences in groups 1 and 2 are usually distinguishable from those in group 3 by virtue of the textural-contrapuntal properties already discussed. The second and more important distinguishing factor is that of pitch, for the higher the structural function of the cadence, the more limited is the number of scale degrees on which cadences are permitted. Thus transitory cadences fall on a greater variety of degrees than principal cadences, which in turn embrace a wider variety of degrees than terminal cadences. At the apex of the pyramid is the final cadence of the final movement of every composition: this invariably falls on the modal final.[67] Terminal and principal cadences are divisible into two types: regular and irregular.[68] The purpose of the latter is to draw attention to the words at the moment of the cadence. If there is usually no doubt as to *why* an irregular cadence occurs,[69] we still have to establish *how* they are introduced. It is important to know whether in fact there is a hard-and-fast distinction between regular and irregular cadences, and, if so, to discover a criterion for telling them apart. The statistical method is not sufficient to solve these problems because, though it can be shown that some cadences appear more frequently than others, it still requires analysis of particular passages in each of the modes to discover why certain cadences occur and how they affect the listener. Taking each modal pair in turn (authentic and plagal), it is in fact possible to show that, if a cadence fulfills the listener's expectations, it is regular, and if it denies them, irregular. It is not enough to show that certain cadences appear more frequently than others; also important is the method of introduction in a given context.

In the dorian and hypodorian pieces selected for analysis,[70] principal cadences appear on degrees 1, 3, 5, 4, and 7. Cadences on the fourth degree sometimes occur as substitutions for an expected third-degree cadence. In example 212, a passage employing *g* and *b*-flat harmonies characteristic of mode 2 transposed, terminates in a *c* cadence in order to depict a negative concept. A more lighthearted application of this technique takes place in *V a 5* (1585), no. 9 (mode 1 untransposed), b. 30, in which, after a series of *f* cadences for "riso" ("laughter"), the word "gioco" ("play") is illustrated by a witty deflection to the fourth degree, *g*. Similar surprising effects are apt to occur on seventh-degree cadences. For instance in *V a 5* (1585), no. 8 (mode 1 untransposed), b. 44, an expected IV - V - I cadence on *f* is deflected to *c*, the dominant of *f*, to depict the words "Chiaro e divino" ("bright and divine").[71] The unusual nature of the cadence is enhanced by augmented note values and *melismata*, which together draw the cadence out to twice its usual length. By a process of elimination we arrive at cadences on degrees 1, 3, and 5. These are the regular cadences for both modes 1 and 2. Third-degree cadences belong to a lower structural level than fifth-degree cadences, for the former are never used as a terminal cadences.

In the phrygian and hypophrygian modes Marenzio shows considerable daring in the matter of irregular cadences. Principal cadences occur (in order of frequency) on degrees 4, 6, 3, 5 (perfect)[72] and 7, while in *I a 5* (1580), no. 6 (mode 3 untransposed), Marenzio goes as far as to conclude with a perfect cadence on the first degree in place of the usual half cadence on the fourth. Here Marenzio exceeds the normal bounds of the mode by sharping the second and seventh degrees in order to illustrate the words "oltr'ogni assentio amara."[73] Marenzio goes further afield in the opening section of *O voi che sospirate* (*II a 5*, 1581, mode 3 untransposed) in which a perfect *b* (fifth-degree) cadence is arrived at through the cycle of fifths (*a* and *e:* bb. 6 and 9). Quartal and quintal relationships play an important role in the derivation of cadences on the third and seventh degrees. In *II a 5* (1581), no. 14 (mode 4 transposed), b. 26, an expected *f* cadence (sixth-degree) is replaced by one on *c* (third-degree).[74] Third-degree cadences may also substitute for fourth-degree cadences. In example 213, the negative attributes mentioned in the text are portrayed by the avoidance of a regular *a* (fourth-degree) cadence for the sake of one on *g,* the major second below. Principal cadences on the seventh degree are rarer: there is a tentative instance in *V a 5* (1585), no. 17 (mode 3 transposed down a major second), b. 84, where the antithesis "amara . . . dolce" ("bitter . . . sweet") is expressed by two incomplete cadences on *g* and *c,* the fourth degree, and its subdominant, the seventh. We are left with the fourth and sixth degrees as regular for principal cadences in modes 3 and 4. The fourth degree occupies a higher structural level than the sixth, since the latter never appears as a terminal cadence.

The lydian and hypolydian pieces in our survey providing no examples of principal cadences which fall outside the first or fifth degrees, we move now to the mixolydian and hypomixolydian, where principal cadences fall on degrees 4, 1, 5, 2, 6, (perfect) and 7. The perfect cadence on the sixth degree (*IV a 5* 1584, no. 10, b. 48) is outlandish in the manner of the final cadence of *Dolorosi martir* (see above).[75] The second-degree cadence in *I a 5* (1580), no. 1 (mode 7 untransposed), b. 17 depicts "ardore" ("boldness") and is a major second higher than expected (on *a* instead of *g*). The seventh-degree cadence (*f*) in *V a 5* (1585), no. 1 (mode 7 untransposed), b. 82, demonstrates once again the derivation of irregular cadences through the cycle of fifths: the phrase "Dal sorger prim'al dipartir del sole"[76] is stated three times with cadences on *g, c,* and *f*; the first two are transitory, the third an irregular principal cadence. By a process of elimination we arrive at the first, fourth, and fifth degrees as regular for modes 7 and 8. Both degrees are used for terminal cadences.

In the aeolian and hypoaeolian, principal cadences fall on degrees 1, 3, 4, 6, and 7. Degrees 6 and 7 occupy a quartal and quintal relationship respectively with the third degree (the *repercussio* of mode 10). Sixth-degree cadences have a disturbing effect: in *Sento squarciar*[77] the changed color of the sky is dramatically conveyed by the deflection of an expected *c* (third-degree) cadence to its subdominant, *f* (sixth-degree)[ex. 214]. The same Good Friday scene is depicted in another *spirituale, Il dì che di pallor,* where the words "Il sol converse il bel carro lucente"[78] lead to a cadence on *c* (seventh-degree)— instead of *f* (third-degree). The fourth degree is ambiguous, sometimes behaving like a regular cadence degree, sometimes not. In example 215, the music appears to be heading for a regular third-degree cadence on *f*, only to be deflected to an inverted cadence on *g*, the fourth degree. At the terminal level, however, the fourth degree appears to occupy a higher rank than the third: thus the *prima parte* of *IV a 5* (1584), no. 7 (mode 9 untransposed) cadences on *d*, not *a* or *c*.[79] The third degree is never used for terminal cadences in modes 9 or 10, though it is perfectly regular at the principal-cadence level. We conclude that at the terminal-cadence level, the first and sixth degrees are regular; at the principal-cadence level, the first and third are regular.

The principal cadences in the ionian and hypoionian modes comprise two on which major triads may be formed (1 and 5), and two in which minor triads (disregarding the *tierce de Picardie*) may be formed (2 and 6). Contrast of major and minor underlies the setting of the antithetical line "E desteriasi Amor là dove dorme" ("And Love will awake where now he sleeps").[80] A passage near the end of *I a 4,5,6* (1588), no. 12 (mode 12 untransposed) illustrates the now familiar procedure of arriving at a *clausula peregrina* through the cycle of fifths.[81] The phrase "In part'ove io non voglia"[82] is repeated with cadences on *c, g* and *d* (degrees 1, 5 and 2), the last, irregular, cadence being left "hanging" before an abrupt return to *c*-major sonorities. Sometimes descending thirds cause a change of harmonic direction culminating in a *clausula peregrina*. Thus in *III a 5* (1582), no. 4 (mode 12 untransposed), b. 42, at the words "ogn'huom vil gagliardo,"[83] an irregular principal cadence is reached through a series of tertially related cadences (*c, a, f* and *d*).[84] Once again, our conclusions are clearcut: regular principal cadences occur on the first and fifth degrees, irregular, on the second and sixth.

We may conclude that, in all the modes, irregular principal cadences are generally reached in one of three ways: through the cycle of fifths (ascending or descending), through taking the scale degree immediately above or below the one expected, or through descent in thirds.

We may summarize principal cadences as follows (figures in parentheses represent scale degrees not used for terminal cadences; brackets indicate that the fourth degree in modes 9 and 10 is regular for terminal cadences, irregular for principal cadences):[85]

	Regular	*Irregular*
Modes 1 and 2	1, (3), 5	4, 7
Modes 3 and 4	4, (6)	1 (perf.) 3, 5 (perf), 7
Modes 5 and 6	1, 5	—
Modes 7 and 8	1, 4, 5	2, 6, 7
Modes 9 and 10	1, (3), [4]	[4], 6, 7
Modes 11 and 12	1, 5	2, 6

Marenzio's use of cadences departs but little from contemporary modal theory in its most evolved form. Particularly significant is Pietro Pontio's three-fold division into "cadenze proprie, et principali" . . . "quasi [. . .] principali" and those to be used "per transito et con diligenza";[86] the first two categories correspond closely with what I have called "terminal" and "principal" cadences, while "per transito" means "transitory," and "con diligenza" implies that certain cadences should be used only for special reasons and introduced carefully, i.e. for expressive reasons and in order to make a special effect.

Pontio however supports the older, eight-mode system.[87] Among the theorists who treat of the modal system in its twelve-mode form, Marenzio approaches Eucharius Hofmann most closely.[88] It is strange that Orazio Vecchi's knowledge of Marenzio's works does not prevent him from adopting an all-too-rigid scheme in which all cadences in all modes are assigned to the first, third, and fifth degrees.[89] For it is the essence of the modal system that the cadence pattern for each mode is distinguishable from all the others.

Transitory Cadences[90]

On the level of transitory cadences, a much wider variety of cadence patterns is permitted. In the case of sections with distant modulations, this freedom extends, in theory if not in practice, to all twelve degrees of the chromatic scale. It has already been stated that the higher the syntactical value of a cadence, the stronger and more regular it will tend to be. Conversely, the more intimate a syntactical connection, the weaker the cadence; the weaker the cadence, the likelier it is to be harmonically remote from the modal final. Most *cadenze fuggite* are at the same time transitory cadences and thus will display their low syntactical status not only texturally and contrapuntally, but also harmonically, through their remoteness from the final.

One hesitates, however, to call these remote transitory cadences "irregular," for they do not have the same effect as such cadences at the terminal and principal levels. Whereas irregular cadences are calculated to surprise the listener, transitory cadences may pass by unobtrusively, for they are usually no more than the outward symptom of a harmonic progression encompassing an entire section. It must be realized, too, that transitory cadences do not *have* to be harmonically remote from the mode; on the contrary, at the opening and close of a movement or section, they are much more likely to fall on the same pitches as regular principal and terminal cadences, if not on the final itself.

Only occasionally do transitory cadences have an expressive function comparable to that of irregular cadences. Thus the words "Interdette speranze e van desio" ("Forbidden hopes and vain desires") are depicted through the use of a cadence upon the scale degree below the final (*f*), the section as a whole cadencing regularly on *c*.[91] More obviously dramatic is the opening of *IV a 5* (1584), no. 6 (mode 9 untransposed) where an expected exordial cadence on *d* is deflected to *b*-flat in order to depict "acerbo caso."[92]

Generally transitory cadences have exactly the same syntactical functions as *cadenze fuggite*—indeed, they usually are *cadenze fuggite*. As we have already discussed the reasons for the use of *cadenze fuggite,* a separate discussion of the reasons for using irregular cadences is unnecessary. Let us turn straightaway to the *method* by which they are introduced.

It has already been stated that transitory cadences are usually no more than the outward sympton of a harmonic progression encompassing an entire section. Nowhere is this more apparent than when a modulation through the cycle of fifths occurs. The most simple form of modulation through fifths occurs with two or more successive statements of a line or phrase. Some of these modulations have been mentioned already;[93] other examples are appended to show how cadences a fifth apart may occur with metronomic regularity, thus giving metrical as well as harmonic form to the passage [ex. 216]. In one *Spirituale* Marenzio conveys the idea of instability by means of a fifths cycle which is disrupted by an interpolation of two extra cadences [ex. 217].

The cycle of fifths may play an important part even when other elements are also present. These more complex progressions often occur at the ends of compositions as a means of affirming the tonal supremacy of the modal final. For instance, the final section of *III a 5* (1582), no. 7 (mode 3 untransposed) consists of two lines (bb. 40-60), the first of which is set as two fragments with transitory cadences on g and d (bb. 42 and 44). These two cadences, both irregular for mode 3, take us up to the end of a conditional clause. The main clause which follows cadences regularly on c (bb. 47 and 49), then at the lower fifth, on f,(b. 51). Both the f cadence and the d cadence which follows (b. 54) are subordinate in function to the third and last c cadence (b. 55) which in turn acts as a support for the final half cadence on a. The assertion of the final cadence on a (I - V) rests entirely on the function of c (the sixth degree) as a structural mainstay.[94]

So far we have considered passages which exhibit at least some degree of verbal repetition. Transitory cadences are equally suited to joining consecutive phrases and clauses within a section. The more involuted the syntax, the greater the tendency for the cadences to depart from and then return to the mode—a process comparable to the curve of an arch or the swing of a pendulum. A favorite pattern, especially at openings, is the progression I - V - I, as may be seen in two examples for six voices [ex. 218]. Other examples abound: the opening movement of the sestina, *Sola angioletta,* has cadences alternately on g and d, the latter occupying a syntactically lower rank than the former.[95]

Two final examples will illustrate the role played by transitory cadences during syntactically complex sections. Let us consider the opening of *I a 5* (1580), no. 12 (mode 2 transposed), where a noun phrase ("Questa . . . vaga e gentil ghirlanda")[96] encloses a qualifying adjective phrase ("di verd'herbette / E di novelli fior tessuta hora").[97] Here the interdependence of the two phrases is made clear by the f cadence after "hora" (b. 12), which acts as a dominant preparation for the all-important noun phrase (b. 13 ff), declaimed on the chord of b-flat, the note of repercussion.

Harmonically remote cadences play an important part in clarifying the syntax in the second and central section of *Ben mi credeva, lasso.*[98] After the first section closes regularly on *d* (b. 17), the text and cadence structure are as follows:[99]

(1) Chè non è sterpo o sasso	*f*
(2) Ch'almen tardi o per tempo	*d*
(3) Vendendo le mie piaghe aperte e nude	*g*
(4) E ciò che l'alma chiude	*g*
(5) A pietà non si mova	*f*
(6) Del mio doglioso stato	*d*

Lines 1 - 2 and 5 - 6 together form the main clause; lines 3 - 4 are a participle phrase. Not surprisingly, the more remote cadences occur at the ends of line 3 - 4, the syntactically inferior participle phrase.[100] The *g* cadence in line 3 (b. 28) is approached in such a way that the listener expects the more regular *f* (note especially the six-four suspension in b. 27); the *c* cadence (b. 31) is also heard against a background of *f* (bb. 29 - 30 and b. 32 ff). No *f* cadence however occurs before the main clause resumes in line 5 (bb. 37 - 38).[101] Sometimes, therefore, transitory cadences resemble irregular cadences in that they can be heard as deviations within a regular modal framework. Whereas however irregular principal cadences have the function of underlining the meaning of the words, irregular transitory cadences normally underline only their syntactical position; through avoidance of the most obvious or harmonious resolution, they indicate that the poetic (and hence musical) thought is not yet complete, and there is more to follow.

Before summarizing and concluding our analysis of cadences, we must mention certain exceptions to the rule that strong cadences correspond with the most important syntactical divisions, weak (or avoided) cadences with the weaker divisions. Sometimes expressive considerations require that a phrase be given more or less emphasis than the syntax would lead us to expect; thus we are confronted with a familiar case of conflicting priorities: clarity and propriety versus imagination and poetic license.

Cadences which are stronger than the syntax alone would require may be called "prominent"; those which are weaker, "receding." "Prominent" cadences are a deviant form of transitory cadence: though they may have the syntactical function of transitory cadences, they bear all the outward signs of principal cadences in that they are strong and occur on the same pitches as regular principal cadences.[102] "Receding" cadences are a weakened form of principal (or, rarely, terminal) cadence: they occur at the ends of sections (or movements), but superficially resemble transitory cadences in being weak or concealed.

The emphatic function of "prominent" cadences is confirmed by the frequent use of *melismata* or some other word-painting device during the preparation. For example, the phrase, "I suoi bei raggi d'oro / Volge"("turns her golden shafts"),[103] is interrupted by a "prominent" *c* cadence after "oro" ("gold"), which had previously been illustrated by a melisma. In *I a 5* (1580), no. 6, "prominent" cadences cause some serious distortions of syntax: in b. 22, after "momenti" ("moments"), in b. 34, after "urli e lamenti" ("cries and lamenting"; note the melisma on "urli" and the slowing-down at "lamenti"), and especially in b. 42, after "sempiterne pene" ("everlasting torment"), where the long dominant preparation indeed seems to last for eternity. This final example illustrates very clearly the conflicting claims of the syntax and of the individual word, for there is no doubt that the syntax would have been better served if the cadence had fallen after "cibo"(b. 42), The wholesale repetition of the last two lines ("Son'il mio cibo . . .")[104] merely emphasizes the distortion of a kind frequently found in early Marenzio.[105]

A special type of "prominent" cadence is that which occurs near the opening to establish the mode of the composition.[106] Examples of exordial cadences are not hard to find. They usually occur on the final, less often on the *repercussio,* upper fifth or some other degree reserved for regular cadences. An exordial cadence need not be the first of the piece, but invariably constitutes the first strong musical caesura. Two examples will suffice: *IV a 5* (1584), no. 11 (mode 7 untransposed), b. 15 ("Accompagnaste / con pietosi accenti"),[107] perfect cadence on *g*; *V a 5* (1585), no. 16 (mode 2 transposed), b. 9 ("e colte in Paradiso, / L'altr'hier nascendo . . ."),[108] perfect cadence on b-flat.

The "receding" cadence is the opposite of the "prominent" cadence: it is weak where the syntax would generally lead one to expect a strong cadence. "Inverted" cadences are a type of weak cadence which often appears with poignant effect at the ends of sections;[109] sometimes an inverted cadence closes a movement in order to convey "descent."[110] An imaginative use of a half cadence replacing an expected perfect cadence occurs in the passage "Sarà certo miracolo d'amore; / Ma tale è'l mio tormento . . ."[111] here the musical elision heightens the tonal and rhythmic contrast between the two lines better than any caesura. Cadences with a weak *penultima* may express lightness,[112] discreet murmuring,[113] or any other concept for which a weak, "throwaway" cadence is suitable.[114]

Summary of Cadential Functions

We may summarize the syntactical and expressive role of cadences as follows:

1. *Terminal* (occur at ends of movements)
   a) Regular ("proprie, et principali"); usually strong; rarely weak

("receding") for expressive reasons.

    b) irregular, to be used "con diligenza"; extremely rare.

2. *Principal* (occur at ends of sections)

    a) Regular ("quasi principali"); usually strong, but often "receding" when meaning of words require it.

    b) Irregular, to be used "con diligenza" to depict the meaning of words.

3. *Transitory* ("per transito"; occur within sections)

No clearcut distinction between "regular" and "irregular"; less likely to be remote harmonically at opening and close of section or movement; only rarely have an expressive function like those in 2 (b); may be strong ("prominent") for emphasis or when exordial; "prominent" cadences are not to be confused with regular principal cadences, even though they usually cadence on "regular" pitches.

Conclusion

We have now completed our survey of sectional structure in Marenzio's madrigals. Of the three elements discussed—repetition, contrapuntal structure, and harmonic structure as manifested through cadence structure—it is the last which is the most original and which has therefore required the most analysis. From the preceding summary we may once again discern two sets of criteria working side by side: those concerning the translation of the syntactical structure into music, and those concerned with the meaning of individual words. Often the two elements appear to be in conflict; in reality, both are necessary if the music is to avoid chaos on the one hand and dullness on the other. Nevertheless, it requires a thorough knowledge of contemporary musical conventions to savor the full significance of each cadence and each harmonic progression. Even the smallest unexpected twist and turn has a basis in some rule or convention, however esoteric.

No clearer illustration of this fact exists than an important structural element about which more needs to be said: *commixtio tonorum,* or the temporary departure from the prevailing mode in favor of another. Whether long or short, passages using *commixtio tonorum* add a complicating factor to the above analysis, for it is obvious that a cadence which is irregular with respect to the prevailing mode may be regular in the context of the *tonus commixtus,* and *vice versa.* Given the structural implications of *commixtio tonorum* on a large scale, it is appropriate to begin our next chapter with an examination of this phenomenon.

8

The Total Form

Our discussion of whole compositions will be divided into three sections: first, an analysis of *commixtio tonorum;* second, a discussion in general terms of the relationship between poetic form and musical form; and third, an analysis of the musical treatment of specific poetic forms.

Commixtio Tonorum

Commixtio tonorum is discussed by Aiguino in his *Tesoro illuminato* (1581).[1] It occurs whenever the individual voices outline the diapente or diatessaron species of a mode other than that prevailing in the composition as a whole. Its use (says Aiguino) is compulsory whenever the meaning of the verbal text requires it; additionally it may be introduced simply for the sake of variety. The new mode is made audible not only through characteristic melodic patterns but also through a series of cadences proper to that mode.[2]

Aiguino's guidelines correspond closely with Marenzio's practice. The originality of Marenzio's approach lies in the number of structural levels at which *commixtio* may operate. At one extreme, the reference to a foreign modality may be very fleeting, posing no challenge to the prevailing mode. At the other extreme, *commixtio* may affect entire sections or cut across sections and movements.

At its most fleeting, *commixtio* has a transitory effect similar to harmonically remote transitory cadences; indeed, the line between the two is very thin, for both are merely the outward symptoms of the harmonic progression of which the section is constructed. Thus the melisma on "ridon" ("laugh") in *II a 5* (1581), no. 5, b.9 ff, outlines a mode-7 scale in the context of a mode-9 composition; harmonically this phenomenon is easily explained as part of a cycle of fiths, *a - d - g - c* (bb. 1-14), the purpose of the mixolydian scale being to illustrate the concept "laugh" not only through *melismata,* but through the temporary replacement of "minor" by "major" sonorities.

One specific way in which *commixtio tonorum* is comparable to the irregular transitory cadence is that both may have a syntactical function.[3]

Thus, the lower the syntactical value of a phrase or clause, the more remote the modality is likely to be at that moment. This point is illustrated in the following examples:

"Che con le sue caprette" ("who with her goats"):[4] mode 7 transposed replaces 2 transposed for adverbial phrase at start of relative clause.

". . . poi ch'uccider mi volete" (". . . since you desire to kill me"):[5] mode 2 untransposed replaces mode 12 untransposed for subordinate clause.

"Ch'a laura il vago e biondo capel chiuda" ("that protected the lovely fair hair from the breeze"):[6] mode 9 untransposed replaces mode 12 untransposed.

Despite these instances, *commixtio tonorum* is more likely to fulfil a role similar to irregular principal cadences, namely the expression of concepts such as distance, change, or novelty:

"Come potrò giammai alontanarmi / E'n vita restar poi?" ("How ever will I be able to go away and then remain alive?"):[7] mode 8 transposed replaces 1 transposed.

"Non fia mai ch'io per voi cangi desire" ("Never allow me to change my desire for you"):[8] mode 8 transposed replaces 1 transposed.

"Con nove foggie e disusate tempre" ("Of a new form and unusual quality"):[9] mode 10 untransposed replaces mode 4 transposed.[10]

Negative emotions or a darkening of mood are often brought about by the replacement of a mode with a major third above the final by one with a minor third. A highly suggestive example is the evocation of "pallor" in example 219, where mode 12 transposed is superseded by mode 2 transposed (the "relative minor"). Conversely, a "major" in place of a "minor" mode will result in a brightening of mood:

"Porto delle miserie" ("Harbour of refuge from all misery"): mode 5 untransposed replaces 3 untransposed.[11]

"Ma tu del cielo eterno alto motore" ("But you, eternal, great mover of the heavens"): mode 11 untransposed replaces 3 untransposed [ex. 220].

"Tanto sollevamento" ("Such relief"):[12] mode 8 transposed replaces 1 transposed.

A curious use of *commixtio* affects two compositions which introduce musical and textual quotation. Here the introduction of the new modality coincides with the quotation in such a way that the quoted passage stands out like a canvas set in a frame: *Donò Cinthia a Damone*[13] begins regularly with cadences on *f* and *d*. At the words "Che parea rosa"[14] Marenzio quotes the opening of his own setting of Petrarch's *Due rose fresche,*[15] at the same time slipping naturally into the hypodorian mode used for that piece. Thus *g* replaces *d* as modal final, and cadences occur on *g, b*-flat and *d*. Much the same procedure occurs in *La dipartita è amara* (*IV a 6,* 1587, no. 3) which quotes Striggio's *Nasce la pena* (mode 1) in the middle of a mode-10 piece, with the result that *g* once again replaces *d* as modal final [ex. 221].[16]

The usual funtion of *commixtio* is to highlight a certain phrase or sentence. Occasionally, however, the reverse happens: the prevailing modality is withheld until the very last bars, its reintroduction serving to emphasize the last line or phrase. For instance, in *I a 5* (1580), no. 4 (mode 9 untransposed), the aeolian mode is only very briefly suggested by the canto's opening rising phrase, after which it disappears, only to resurface in the last two lines (b.50 ff):

Così morendo vivo e con quell'arme
Onde uccidete voi potete aitarme.[17]

This paradoxical conclusion is emphasized through affirmation of the "correct," aeolian mode. The whole of the preceding music is hypoionian, with principal cadences on *c* and *g* (bb. 15, 39, and 50), and transitory cadences on *c, g,* and *d.*[18]

Variety for its own sake may sometimes be a sufficient reason for modal change, especially in the all-purpose dorian and hypodorian, with their wide emotional and expressive range. An early experiment is the popular *Che fa hoggi il mio sole*[19] which starts with a series of unanswered questions. This fact would justify the bewildering cadence pattern (*a, f, d*)[20] which conceals the modality till the end of the third line. Nevertheless, it is difficult to find a textual justification for the introduction of mode 8 untransposed for the subsequent lines: "Hor queste mie viole / E questi fior gli dono."[21] Other dorian and hypodorian pieces are similarly affected:

II a 5 (1581), no. 9 (mode 1 untransposed), bb. 1-38, *commixtio* of mode 10 untransposed (note the principal cadences on *c,* the third degree of the new mode, in bb. 21 and 44).

Spirituali (1584), no. 3 (mode 1 untransposed), bb. 11-64, *commixtio* of mode 12 untransposed.

I a 4 (1585), no. 10 (mode 2 untransposed), bb. 56-63, *commixtio* of mode 7 untransposed; bb. 64-82, *commixtio* of mode 12 untransposed.

In compositions of more than one movement the need to attain variety through *commixtio tonorum* is greater. However, length is not the only criterion; if it were, then the two sestina settings of the early part of Marenzio's career would be more heavily impregnated with this device than is in fact the case. Profundity and concentration of poetic thought seem to be the characteristics which draw from Marenzio his most ambitious essays in *commixtio*. This is especially clear from Marenzio's treatment of that most serious of poetic forms, the sonnet: in no less than ten sonnet settings, *commixtio* occurs at the end of the *prima parte* and often continues well into the *seconda parte* (table 7). Four out of ten sonnets (nos. 1, 2, 3, and 5) modulate to the upper fifth, one (no. 7) to the lower fifth. In others the new final occupies a tertial relationship to the old one: in no. 4, where the introduction of the phrygian is highly effective in depicting the decrepitude of old age; in no. 8, where the hypoaeolian ("relative minor") symbolizes the

Table 7.   Commixtio Tonorum in Sonnet Settings

1.   *Affliger chi per voi* (*I a 4*, 1585, no. 4): mode 1 untransp. replaced by 10 untransp. in bb. 44-69 (lines 8-10); *prima parte* cadences on *a*, the final of the *tonus commixtus* (b. 55).

2.   *L'aura serena* (*I a 6*, 1581, no. 17): mode 1 transp. replaced by 10 transp. in bb. 63-97 (lines 8-10); *prima parte* cadences on *d*, the final of the *tonus commixtus* (b. 68).

3.   *Zefiro torna* (*I a 4*, 1585, no. 18): mode 1 transp. replaced by 10 transp. in bb. 66-80 (lines 8-9); *prima parte* cadences on *d*, the final of the *tonus commixtus* (b. 73).

4.   *La rete fu* (*V a 5*, 1585, no. 6): mode 3 untransp. replaced by 1 untransp. in bb. 56-85 (lines 8-10); *prima parte* cadences on *d* (I - V), the final of the *tonus commixtus* (b. 70); mode 3 untransp. replaced by 8 untransp. in bb. 93-138 (lines 11-14).

5.   *Ecco che un altra* (*I a 4, 5, 6*, 1588, no. 10): mode 7 transp. replaced by 2 transp. in bb. 24-80 (lines 5-11); *prima parte* cadences on *g*, the final of the *tonus commixtus* (b. 58); mode 2 transp. replaced by 9 transp. in bb. 81-92 (lines 12-13).

6.   *Se la mia vita* (*I a 4, 5, 6*, 1588, no. 2): mode 8 untransp. replaced by 3 untransp. in bb. 30-55 (lines 5-8); *prima parte* cadences on *a* (I - V), terminal cadence for mode 3 (b. 55).

7.   *Su'l carro della mente* (*I a 4*, 1585, no. 19): mode 8 transp. replaced by 11 transp. in bb. 73-107 (lines 9-12); *prima parte* cadences on *f*, the final of the *tonus commixtus*.

8.   *In un bel bosco* (*II a 6*, 1584, no. 9): mode 11 untransp. replaced by 10 untransp. in bb. 34-116 (lines 5-12); *prima parte* cadences on *a* (I - V), the final of the *tonus commixtus* (b. 73).

9.   *Ohimè il bel viso* (*III a 5*, 1582, no. 4): mode 2 untransp. replaced by 12 untransp. in bb. 65-99 (lines 7-8); *prima parte* cadences on *d*, the final of the *tonus commixtus* (b. 90).

10.   *E' questo il legno* (*Spirituali*, 1584, no. 9): mode 9 untransp. replaced by 12 untransp. in bb. 75-115 (lines 8-9); *prima parte* cadences on *a* (IV - V), the final of the *tonus commixtus*.

"fallace traccia" ("false trail") mentioned in the text;[22] and in no. 10, where the aeolian (again, "relative minor") portrays the more poignant aspects of Christ's Passion.

Marenzio's adventurous treatment of the modes attracted the attention of Michael Praetorius[23] and G.B. Doni, who specifically mentions *O voi che sospirate* (*II a 5,* 1581, no. 10) for its "tuono ambulatorio, o incerto."[24] More interesting is the same writer's analysis of *Tirsi morir volea* (*I a 5,* 1580, no. 5).[25] Doni discerns two modes being used alongside the basic phrygian mode (which he calls "dorian"): ionian and dorian (which he calls "lydian" and "phrygian" respectively).[26] The ionian appears with the *c*-cadence in b. 15 and is syntactical in function: it continues for the length of the participle clause beginning "Gl'occhi mirando. . . " and the relative clause beginning "Ond'ella . . .";[27] with the resumption of the narrative ("Gli disse . . .")[28] comes the return of the phrygian. The dorian *commixtio* lasts the entire length of the *seconda parte,* and is most clearly audible with the descending scales in bb. 79 ff and 90 ff.

The Relationship Between Poetic and Musical Form

In setting entire poems, the composer has the choice between basing his treatment upon the metrical form or allowing himself to be guided purely by the inner content. A number of poems set by Marenzio display a tension between their metrical form and their internal structure; in particular, the poems of Strozzi, Della Casa and Torquato Tasso are very free with such devices as enjambement, mid-line caesuras, and accentual displacement. In the *cinquecento* madrigal, the external form is merely the incidental outcome of its structure.

Marenzio's settings are the continuation of this liberating process by musical means. It is true that sixteenth-century composers had long been used to paying more attention to the meaning of the words contained in the poem than to its rhyme scheme; it is equally true that Marenzio was more keenly aware than any of his precedessors of the great divide between two sharply defined musical styles: the villanella-aria tradition, where the composer submits completely to the external poetic form, and the "academic,"*riservata* tradition characterized by through composition, where content and syntax are the only guidelines.[29] The latter style predominates in Marenzio's madrigal publications. The only consistent concession to metrical form is the correspondence of musical divisions with the poetry's strophic form: canzoni, sestine, and *ottave* are always divided into separate movements according to the succession of stanzas; sonnets are invariably divided into octave and sestet even where the sense flows across the two parts.[30]

Compositions reflecting the villanella-aria tradition may be counted literally on the fingers of one hand (see table 8). In all of these the poetic lines may be grouped according to their rhyme scheme: those with a similar or identical rhyme scheme are set to the same music, like the individual strophes of a villanella. It is difficult not to interpret the relative lack of formal sophistication in these pieces as a nostalgic allusion to a more primitive musical style, and by implication, the simpler lifestyle of Arcadia. Indeed, the first two pieces are settings of Sannazaro's *Arcadia*. Also significant is the predominance of modes 11 and 12, symbolizing the humble and rustic.

This primitivism, however, is only superficial. This is evident from the fact that musical repetitions are rarely due to the rhyme alone. Thus *IV a 5* no. 9 and *III a 6,* no. 6, lines 1 and 5 (the beginning of the two "A" sections) have similar openings: "Ecco l'aurora. . . Ecco la notte. . ."[31] and "Qual per ombrose. . . Qual verde prato. . . ."[32] The same applies to the first two and last two lines of *V a 5,* no. 11: "Filli. . . Filli. . . Io. . . Io. . ." paired musically as well as poetically.[33] Thus word repetition and syntactical parallelism prompt musical repetition. Casting our net wider, we may easily find poems where recurring lines lead naturally to repeated music.[34] Thus we have turned full

Table 8.   Madrigals with Interdependent Metrical and Musical Form

II a 5 (1581), no. 8	*Terza rima*	Metre:	ABA BCB CDC
		Music:	A A_1 B
I a 4 (1585), no. 21, *3a.p.*	*Terza rima*	Metre:	ABA BCB etc.
		Music:	A A_1 etc.
IV a 5 (1584), no. 9	*Ottava rima*	Metre:	ABAB ABCC
		Music:	A A_1
III a 6 (1585), no. 6, *1a.p.*	Sonnet octave	Metre:	ABBA ABBA . . .
		Music:	A A_1
III a 6 (1585), no. 6, *2a.p.*	Sonnet sestet	Metre:	. . . CDE CDE
		Music:	. . . B
V a 5 (1585), no. 11, *1a.p.*	Canzone (irregular)	Stanzas	1 - 2
		Music:	A A_1
V a 5 (1585), no. 11, *2a.p.*	Canzone (irregular)	Stanzas	3 - 4, envoy
		Music:	B B_1 C

circle: it is the inner patterns created by verbal content that are reflected in the music; the metrical scheme taken by itself plays scarcely any role.

A knowledge of the way verbal patterns are conveyed musically will provide the key to the understanding of the total form. Previous chapters were concerned with the treatment of individual words, phrases, clauses, and sentences; now we must investigate the relationship between these components in any one poem or composition.

Repetition, antithesis, exclamations, rhetorical questions, and the cumulative effect of total form, are the common preoccupation of the orator, poet, and musician in the sixteenth century.[35] Music came to be associated less with the Quadrivium and more with the Trivium;[36] in other words, music was now seen to require originality and genius, not merely knowledge and technique. This change of attitude may be seen in Burmeister's remarkable analysis of a motet by Lassus using the terminology of rhetoric;[37] the same technique could be and indeed has been applied to Marenzio's madrigals.[38]

The most numerous and conspicuous examples of musical rhetoric involve repetition. This may be prompted by a corresponding repetition in the poetic text, or may exist independently from it. There exist examples both of immediate repetition and of thematic recall in a later section.

The most conventional use of repetition is found in the echo poem, of which three examples are set by Marenzio.[39] The function of the echo is to repeat the last two syllables of the rhyme word in such a way as to change their meaning, a device borrowed from Ovid by Poliziano, the first to use it in vernacular poetry.[40] In the echo compositions which conclude the *I a 5* and *I a 6*, the words of the protagonist and Echo's reply are assigned to two separate choirs. In *O verdi selve (VI a 6)*, Tasso's double echo " 'chi può dar fin'a si crudel fortuna?' 'Una.' 'Dunque sol una . . . ' " is amplified to become a triple echo [ex. 222]. The appearance of an extra repetition not found in the poetic text shows how the added dimension of music may exaggerate or extend the rhetorical devices of poetry. There are further instances of this in other settings: for example, the lines "Fuggi, speme mia, fuggi, E fuggi per non far mai più ritorno" encourage further repetitions of "fuggi" in the top three voices[41] [ex. 223].

Musical repetition is capable of bringing into association phrases already related through their sound, syntax, or meaning. It is common to repeat the same music for rhymed heptasyllabic couplets. Thus varied repetition and antiphony may symbolize two opposed types of female beauty [ex. 224]. Repetitions may also connect the end of one line with the beginning of the next [ex. 225] or two fragments of a single line [ex. 226]. Occasionally a repeated motive may appear without any syntactical or semantic justification [ex. 227].

Repeated musical material may underline phrases which open identically (*anaphora*)[42] or in a similar but not identical fashion (*disiunctio*).[43] Anaphora occurs in the lines: *"Maraviglia è di* me che resti in vita, / *Maraviglia è di* voi ch'aura pietosa. . . "[44] where the first four words of each line are set to the same descending motive. *Disiunctio* is illustrated in the first and sixth lines of *V a 5* (1585), no. 14: *"Basciami* mille volte. . . *stringemi* tosto . . .,"[45] where the motive for line one reappears in varied form in line 6. Parallel chord progressions open a number of madrigals. In *V a 6* (1591), no. 7, a motive used twice at the opening ("Nel dolce seno. . . / Ne languidetti rai. . .") is extended to other phrases which bear no specific resemblance to the opening—yet another example of the way in which musical repetitions originally dependent on the poetry may be extended to parts of the text where repetition is absent [ex. 228].[46]

Cadences, too, play their part in underlining parallelism between two successive lines. The final two lines of *I a 5* (1580), no. 3, are set to the same cadential motive a scale degree apart, thus underlining the similar sounding "Paradiso" and "Primavera."[47] In *I a 4,5,6* (1588), no. 13, the rhymes "voglie" ("wishes") and "doglie" ("torments")[48] are set to two cadences a scale degree apart with an effect of intensification: the inverted cadence on g becomes a phrygian cadence on *a* through transposition.[49]

Related musical material may occur with related words and ideas however extensive the intervening sections or movements. Usually this takes the form of a motive with well defined rhythmic properties such as the one associated with death (i.e. sexual excitement) near the end of the first and second parts of *Tirsi morir* [ex. 229]. In *IV a 5*, no. 3, the same rhythmic motive as occurs on "Qual predator" ("like a predator") is repeated on "preda dipredatore" ("prey of a predator");[50] in *I a 5* (1580), no. 9, the words "Et io, prendendo ardire" ("And I, becoming bold") share a rising fourth with the words "ed ardi" ("and burn").[51] Recurring chromatic progressions may depict associated ideas [ex. 230]. Occasionally a related procedure or technique is enough to connect two associated phrases. Thus, in *II a 5* (1584), no. 9, melodic sequences become associated with the ideas of searching and concealment [ex. 231]. As an additional refinement Marenzio foreshadows the motive used for line 13 [ex. 231b] at the opening of the *seconda parte* [ex. 232]. Such thematic recurrences are more frequent in longer compositions when they do not necessarily result from textual repetitions.

The types of repetition so far discussed are based on repeated words, sounds or ideas found in the poetry itself. However it is obvious that a word not repeated by the poet may nevertheless be repeated in the course of musical setting with an intensifying effect. Ideas which lie half concealed or only mechanically conveyed in the text are thus brought into the open and take on a dramatic force. This is especially so when each repetition is higher than the preceding [ex. 233]. Marenzio's powers of suggestion are evident from the transformation of a fragment of monologue into an implied dialogue through antiphonic exchanges. Thus the phrase "anch'io" in *Tirsi morir*[52] sounds as though it is being antiphonically exchanged between the two protagonists, even though in the poem only one character is speaking. The loss in literal meaning is no sacrifice for the gain in expressive power.

Just as words related in meaning receive related treatment, so contrasting words are set to contrasting music. The devices of antithesis and oxymoron are conveyed by rhythmic, contrapuntal, or harmonic means. Rhythmic contrasts underline the contrasts in *V a 5* (1585), no. 7: "Dolor, tant'è la gioia ... che'l mio dolor mi fa beata," both phrases being set to a slow then a fast fragment.[53] A more compelling musical equivalent of antithesis and oxymoron is the simultaneous (rather than successive) combination of two opposed phrases,[54] as used in the richly rhetorical setting of Tasso's *Giunto a la tomba* [ex. 234]. Harmonic contrasts may be illustrated from the final line of Petrarch's *Del cibo (II a 6,* 1584), where Laura, physically dead but alive in Paradise and in Petrarch's dreams, addresses the poet with the words: "C'hor fostu vivo com'io non son morta."[55] Cadences occur after "vivo" and "morta" on scale degrees whose triads are alternately minor and major:

Bar	Word	Cadence
184	vivo	d
189	morta	F
193	vivo/morta	g
198	vivo/morta	B-flat
201	morta	d (I-V)
204	vivo	F
210	morta	d (I-V)

In the first two cadences, "vivo" appears with minor, "morta" with major cadences. Later, the relationship is reversed in order to symbolize the ambiguous meaning of life and death: Petrarch is physically alive but spiritually dead, whereas Laura is physically dead but spiritually alive.

Among many other rhetorical devices one could mention, the most important are *exclamatio* and *interrogatorio*. Exclamations are characterized by sustained or repeated interjections such as "ahi" or "ahimè" as well as by melodic descent in the top voice and alternate descending fourths and ascending seconds in the bass, often in the pattern 1 - 5 - 6 - 3 [ex. 235]. Similar treatment is given to the device of *sententia*—a maxim containing some universal philosophical truth[56]—and to commands and entreaties [ex. 236]. Rhetorical questions *(interrogatorio)* often receive equally pronounced treatment. The most salient characteristic is an ascending major-second rise in the canto at the cadence in imitation of the speech inflexion at the end of a question.[57] [ex. 237]. It was in this form that Monteverdi was later to set questions [ex. 238].

A comparison of music with rhetoric will allow us to appreciate the effect that overall form is designed to produce in the listener. Orations were traditionally divided into four parts: *exordium, narratio, argumentatio,* and *peroratio.*[58] Each section fulfilled a different function, so that it was always possible for a listener to relate the part to the whole. The influence of these divisions is clearly discernible in the vast majority of Marenzio's madrigals— yet another proof of the interpenetration of music and rhetoric in the sixteenth century.[59] The *exordium,* the object of which is generally defined as obtaining the sympathy of the listener, in Marenzio's madrigals has the function of establishing the composition's mode and mood. This is done by means of the exordial cadence and modally characteristic melodies and harmonic progressions; cadences tend to be more regular in the opening than in the ensuing sections. Sometimes an introductory feeling is obtained through the withholding of the complete ensemble until the beginning of the next section. The ensuing sections[60] are tonally more adventurous, with more irregular cadences and *commixtio tonorum.* The ending *(peroratio)* in some ways marks a return to the exordial situation: the basic mode returns if it has been absent, and regular cadences once again become frequent. In addition the *peroratio* must be the climax or focal point, lending weight and emphasis to the final line or lines. This is why greater time is taken over the final section of the poem than any other. This expansive treatment is obtained through greater and more systematic use of repeated phrases, as well as of double and multiple counterpoint. Harmonically, too, the *peroratio* may be set apart from the remainder of the composition: a memorable progression sometimes emphasizes *exclamatio* or *sententia;*[61] more commonly, an expansive ending is achieved through a series of descending notes of even value combined with a number of faster motives [ex. 239]. The lengths to which Marenzio is prepared to go to build up the ending to an impressive climax is seen in many of the later madrigals: in *VI a 5* (1594), no. 13, the final section[62] consists of a combination of five fragments of text over a descending bass. Such a degree of contrapuntal complexity within an elemental harmonic framework is already Baroque, foreshadowing the age of the figured bass. Within the history of the madrigal itself, such passages must have exerted a tremendous influence: one wonders whether Wilbye, when composing the final section of *Lady, when I behold (a 6),* was thinking of a passage near the end of Marenzio's *O che soave* (cf. ex. 239b and 240).

The interpenetration of music and rhetoric provides the key to many of the problems relating to overall structure. This is shown by an analysis of two compositions. The first is by a poet steeped in the classical tradition: it is the seventh stanza of Petrarch's double sestina *Mia benigna fortuna:*

1. Nessun visse giamai più di me lieto,
2. Nessun vive più tristo e giorni e notti;
3. E doppiando'l dolor doppia lo stile
4. Che trahe del cor sì lagrimose rime;
5. Vissi di speme, hor vivo pur di pianto,
6. Nè contra morte spero altro che morte.[63]

The rhetorical devices favoured by Petrarch are anaphora ("Nessun visse... /Nessun vive ...," lines 1-2; "Vissi... / vivo...," line 5), *paronomasia* ("...morte /...morte," line 6),[64] and antithesis (combined with anaphora in lines 1-2 and line 5; also between lines 5 and 6: "Vissi... /vivo... ...morte /... morte"). The repetitions between lines 1 and 2 underline the contrast between the poet's past and former state. Marenzio uses the same harmonic progression (*a* major, *d* major, *g* major and *c* major),[65] continuing, in line 2, with slower, more dissonant material to underline the opposition of "lieto" and "tristo" ("happy" and "sad").[66] The setting of line 3, with its echo ("doppiando...doppia"), contains a number of appropriate duplications: polyphonic imitation, doubling at the third, and the fact that both segments of the line are set to the same descending fifth. Moreover, the whole line is repeated at the unusual interval of the lower third, with the addition of highly poignant dissonance.[67] Line 4, a new section, recapitulates the antithetical opening lines in the space of one line (b. 52 ff). The opposition "speme"/"pianto" ("hope"/"weeping") is conveyed by the use of root triads a tone apart (ascending on "speme," descending on "pianto"[68] in accordance with the opposed emotional connotations of ascending and descending motion). The *cadenza fuggita* for "pianto" (*a* replaced by *d*) is slightly reminiscent of the *cadenza fuggita* on "trista" in b.13; just as line 5 is a more concentrated form of lines 1-2, so the second cadence is more striking and pathetic than the first.[69] Thus Marenzio reflects in his music all the repetition devices of the poetry. In addition he introduces one of his own: a dissonance of a major second, *c*/ *d* in five prominent places, the first and last being accompanied by *f* in the bass.[70] Finally, it should be noted that both the *exordium* and *peroratio* are distinguishable through certain features: the *exordium* (bb. 1-4) is scored for the reduced texture of four, then three voices, the words being declaimed in a dry, *staccato* fashion found nowhere else in the piece.[71] The *peroratio* (b. 61 ff)[72] is distinguishable for exactly the opposite reason: it is the most polyphonic and sustained passage of the whole piece; particularly remarkable are the melismas on the key word "morte" (bb. 69 ff, 79 ff, 80 ff and 88 ff).

The above example may be regarded as a textbook example of the translation of rhetorical devices from poetry into music. Other examples are not lacking: particularly instructive is an *ottava* stanza[73] by Bernardo Tasso (father of Torquato) which, as the poet himself states in a letter, was written with musical setting in mind.[74] It is not necessary to mention in detail the rhetorical devices which appear in *Ohimè, dov'è 'l mio ben* nor Marenzio's treatment of them (anaphora in line 1, lines 3-5 and line 7; *interrogatorio* in lines 1-2, 3-4 and 5-6; *exclamatio* in lines 1 and 7). It is enough to note the use of a recurring motive, $g''(-f'')-e''$ in the canto[75] and the prominence with which the *exordium* and *peroratio* are established through repetition of the first and last lines. Noteworthy is the absence of cadences on *c* (the final) during the middle sections (bb. 20-58), and their frequency at the opening and conclusion.

The Treatment of Specific Forms

Having illustrated the relationship between poetic and musical structure in general terms, we are now in a positon to complete our survey of overall form by examining stylistic traits particular to the poetic forms chosen most commonly by Marenzio. We start with single-movement compositions and progress through the two-movement forms to those in many movements.

The single-movement madrigal is better described as a poetic type than a poetic form: content, tone, and rhythm take precedence over the purely incidental metrical scheme. This is explained by the concentration of rhetorical figures crammed together within the space of a very few lines.

The stimulus provided by echo and antithesis is evident from the musical treatment given to the poetic device frequently (but not exclusively) found in the madrigal, the *parola-chiave*.[76] The "key word" not only defines the subject matter but also provides a key to tonal unity. Examples include the repetition of "misero"/"misera" in *Se tu mi lasci* (*RISM* 1583[11])[77] and the word-pair "v'amerò"/"morirò" in *V a 6* (1591), no. 9.[78] To these we may add Guarini's madrigal *O che soave* (IV a 6, 1587, no. 14) with its key word "rapina" and its derivatives, to which Marenzio sets a suitable "snatching" rhythm [ex. 242];[79] nor is this motive restricted to the *parola-chiave,* for Marenzio extends its use to other words in accordance with the principle of extending repetitive devices beyond the point required by the poetic text [ex. 243]. Another Guarini setting is remarkable in that it has been emended to include a *parola-chiave.* The first line of *Lasso, perchè mi fuggi* is emended to *Crudel, perchè mi fuggi* in order to allow Marenzio to repeat a two-note rising motive in short succession [ex. 244]. In line 5 the rising motive is dramatically inverted to underline the contrast between the preceding questions and the exclamation which follows [ex. 245].

Exclamatio plays a prominent role in those madrigals which end with an epigrammatic point. Epigrammatic madrigals often fall into three sections: an exordial, expository statement; a second statement contradicting or modifying the first; and a concluding exclamation which sums up the contradictory, antithetical element implied in the first two sections.[80] This tripartite division is displayed in two apparently dissimilar compositions: *Liquide perle* and *Donne il celeste lume.*[81] The modifying function of the middle sections is expressed through *commixtio tonorum* in both compositions, a "minor" mode replacing a "major" one: in *Liquide perle,* mode 2 untransposed replaces mode 7,[82] while in *Donne il celeste* mode 3 replaces mode 8.[83] In both pieces the beginning of the final section coincides with the return to the prevailing mode. This takes the form of *exclamatio,*[84] conveyed in *Liquide perle* by sustained note on "Ahi" followed by a descending phrase, and in *Donne il celeste,* by an emphatic triadic motive. Though the final sections of both pieces differ greatly in mood, they both fulfill the structural function of *peroratio* in that they are very expansively treated.[85]

Marenzio's treatment of the melic madrigal, in which euphony and lyricism predominate over wit and ingenuity, is less easy to define. A few madrigals evoke an idyllic atmosphere through an opening description of a pastoral setting followed by a brief lament. Here the interest lies in the contrast between the introductory description and the pathos of the ensuing monologue. In two madrigals by Tasso, *In un lucido rio* and *Al lume de le stelle,*[86] the opening description is scored for a reduced vocal combination, after which the *exclamatio* at the opening of the lament provides an important focal point. Strozzi's elegiac *Piangea Filli*[87] explores a similar vein. Here the monologue is reduced to the cry of "O Tirsi, o Tirsi!" uttered first by the shepherdess, then echoed, with an almost brutal insistence, by the sea, the wind, and the flowers and shrubs. The impact of the repeated cries (bb. 14, 21, 27, and 34 ff) is reinforced by the ever stranger harmonic juxtapositions which introduce them. The phrases before the fourfold occurrence of "O Tirsi..." cadence in a cycle of fifths: *d* (I - V), *g* (IV - V; incomplete), *c* (perfect), and *f* (perfect).[88] On each occasion, regardless of what point has been reached in the harmonic cycle, the lament bursts forth with the same unrelenting progression: *d*-minor, *a*-major, *d*-minor, assertive of mode 3 transposed.

G.B. Strozzi provides us with another excellent example of the melic madrigal. The poem *Dai bei labri*[89] is almost a musical composition in its own right, a song without notes. In his setting Marenzio translates the repetitions and assonances into musical motives with economy and ease, at the same time extending the technique of repetition to words which are not repeated. Thus in line 1 the ascending motive used for the first fragment[90] is also used for the second fragment in rhythmically varied form.[91] In line 2 the dotted rhythm for "Aura" (Strozzi's *parola-chiave)* is an echo from line 1[92] and is even carried over to line 3 (b. 12 ff). The sound pattern created by "*Aura soav'hor movi*" is cunningly depicted through transpositions of the same root major chord for each of the three accented syllables (on *d* and *f* in b. 9, on *e*-flat in b. 10). The assonance "t'instilla Mille e mille" (lines 3-4) is not directly reflected in the music, but the two lines are brought into association through the use of antiphonic repetitions (bb. 11-22).

The opening section having closed conventionally on an f-cadence,[93] the middle section begins with two lines (5 and 6) connected by anaphora ("Dolce spirando piovi, / Dolce spirando fiocca"). Marenzio sets the two lines to the same phrase, replacing mode 12 with mode 2 in order to obtain variety. Part of line 7 and line 8 are also connected through anaphora ("... ond'io sospiro, / Ond'io respiro solo"); here, as one would expect, the words "sospiro" and "respiro" are treated as though identical (bb. 35 ff). At this point, there are signs that the inspiration is flagging: the middle section ends on a rather unconvincing c-cadence (b. 39); in the final section expressive considerations are swept aside, the isolated melisma on "involo" sounding somewhat perfunctory. The final section is in the familiar form A B A_1 B_1 B_2.

Next to the madrigal, the favorite one-movement form is the *ottava stanza*. The rhyme scheme is such that poetic and musical sections tend to coincide with each pair of lines. These sections are often connected through anaphora ("Dunque ha potuto sol desio d'honore... / Dunque ha potuto in me ...";[94] "Ecco l'aurora... / Ecco la notte ..."[95]) or *disiunctio*. The latter device is illustrated most clearly in *Satiati Amor*, in which the first, third and fifth lines begin: "Satiati Amor... / Ridi fortuna .../ Godete donna."[96] In each case Marenzio returns to the chord of g-major (followed by a c chord) with a play on the intervals $d'' - b'$ and $g'' - e''$.[97] A juxtaposition of the motives used by Marenzio and by Monte in his setting of two years earlier, suggests an unusual interest in Monte's setting, which may well have been the younger composer's model [ex. 246]. At other times, Marenzio is less strict: in *Piango che Amor*[98] the *disiunctio* of "Piango... Sospiro... Doglio" (lines 1, 3, and 5)[99] results not in motivic repetition but in the use of "special effects": homophony at the opening, chromaticism in line 3, and canonic entries in line 5. The final line sums up the preceding seven lines with the words "Al lamento, ai sospiri, al duro pianto,"[100] thus recapitulating the sequence "Piango"-"Sospiro"-"Doglio" in reverse. Not only does Marenzio emphasize each of the three fragments of line 8 with rests after each one, but the chromatism for "sospiri" recalls the chromaticism for "Sospiro" in line 3.[101]

The sonnet and the bipartite madrigal pose structural problems not found in the shorter, single-movement forms. The problem of variety is solved partly as we have seen, through recourse to *commixtio tonorum* at the end of the *prima parte* and beginning of the *seconda parte*. Even where there is no *commixtio tonorum*, the *prima parte* invariably cadences on a degree different from that of the final.

Cohesion is provided through thematic recall which may or may not be prompted by repeated words or ideas. Both poet and musician introduce recurring words and motives at the most strategic points, such as the beginning of the quatrain or tercet of a sonnet, or at the end of the *prima* and *seconda parti*. Thus in the sonnet setting *Là 've l'Aurora,* where the *prima* and *seconda parti* open with references to the poem's apostrophee, Laura, the same motive is used [ex. 247]. The same motive is used in the *prima parte* at the opening of the second quatrain and in the *seconda parte* at the opening of the second tercet [ex. 248]. The *seconda parte* of bipartite compositions often opens with a reminiscence of the opening of the *prima parte*. This need not necessarily correspond to a repeated word or idea; it may simply serve to refresh the listener's memory or provide symmetry and cohesion [ex. 249]. Equally, the two *parti* may conclude with similar melodic material [ex. 250].

In the sonnet an emotional climax is often reached in the final tercet, isolated from the rest of the poem by the use of *sententia, exclamatio,* command or entreaty, or *confutatio*. *Sententia* appears in the final tercet of Della Casa's *Affliger chi per voi,* where Marenzio introduces progressions of unprecedented boldness [ex. 251]. A command concludes Petrarch's *Apollo, s'ancor vive,* treated by Marenzio with a motive frequently used for similar passages elsewhere.[102]

Confutatio appears in the final tercet of Sannazaro's *Ecco che un altra volta*[103] a setting the complex organization of which merits close analysis. The first part is a lament addressed to the natural universe (the bare hills, the sea, the wind), reaching its climax in the second part with the words "vero Amor."[104] In the second tercet the poet refutes the notion that Nature can in fact console him: to what avail is all this lamenting if the beloved one remains unmoved?

The emotional development of the poem is sustained by anaphora ("Udrete... / Udrete... / Udrai").[105] This device is not directly reflected in the music; instead, Marenzio achieves an intensifying effect by repeating the same motive at the beginning of two successive lines ("Udrete selve... / E'l tristo suon").[106] The first emotional climax is reached in b. 24 when the canto reaches the unprecedented high note d'', the upper fifth in the scale of mode 2 transposed which now replaces the mode 8 transposed. The new mode becomes firmly entrenched in the second quatrain through motives outlining the diapente (bb. 28 ff and 49 ff) and through cadences on g, d, and b-flat (bb. 48, 53, 58, 62, 64, and 71). Mode 2 transposed continues to prevail up to the middle of the second line of the *seconda parte*. Then, from b. 74 (entry of the canto), it gradually becomes clear that mode 2 is being supplanted by mode 9 transposed as the composition approaches its climax. The new mode is confirmed by the cadence on d, the final, in b. 80, and by the melodic material with which the second tercet opens (b. 81 ff). This final tercet refutes the idea of consolation implied in the whole of the rest of the poem (*confutatio*) and is therefore an appropriate point at which to introduce a further *commixtio tonorum*. Particularly strong is the delayed d cadence between the thirteenth and fourteenth lines (bb. 92-93). The final line, with its tortuous return to mode 8, is the emotional climax. The eighth mode becomes entrenched only after the *c*-cadence in b. 103, at the appearance of the word "fede" ("faith"),— the last word in the poem—and a positive concept requiring modal affirmation. But the line as a whole is negative in meaning: the poet's tears have failed to acquire the longed for "fede." Therefore the final line, even up to the last few bars, is filled with angular melodic lines and lacks a clear tonal orientation. So ends Marenzio's most successful essay in sonnet composition before 1594; it is remarkable that only the first twenty-four and the last eight bars[107] do not use a *tonus commixtus.*

Three madrigals in three movements all belong to the early part of Marenzio's career. The first, *Tirsi morir (I a 5,* 1580, no. 5), has already been discussed in connection with *commixtio tonorum.* Also employing *commixtio* is *Bianchi cigni e canori (RISM* 1583[10]), where the *seconda* and *terza parti* are linked through the replacement of the hypoionian by the mixolydian. In fact the beginnings and ends of all three movements are linked in that the last line of the preceding movement becomes the same as the succeeding, while the *terza parte* concludes by recapitulating the opening. The musical motives are all ascending, as befits the optimistic, joyful messsage[108] of the wedding madrigal [ex. 252]. No less successful is *Deggio dunque partire (II a 5,* 1581, no. 1), which should be compared to the last five-voice piece in the *I a 5 (Partirò dunque).* The two compositions are in related modes: *Partirò dunque* is in mode 2 transposed, *Deggio dunque* in mode 1; they display verbal and musical similarities at their openings. The greater maturity and intensity of the later composition is evident from the more imaginative use of dissonance and rhythm, typified by the dramatic gesture of the half-cadence on "spento" ("extinguished") at the end of the *seconda parte.*

The remaining multi-movement compositions before 1593 comprise one in four movements (*ottava rima*), one in five (canzone), one in six and one in seven (both sestine). The two latter are with texts by Sannazaro and were both published within a year of each other: *Non fu mai cervo* and *Sola angioletta.*[109] Though published in 1584, *Non fu mai* was probably written as early as 1583, for in 1584 Leonhard Lechner published in Nuremberg a parody mass based on it.[110] That the madrigal was obviously written for a *virtuoso* ensemble is apparent from the frequent *melismata* and flurries of quaver motion. The use of diminution is inspired by the idea of the brevity of life, depicted by a series of metaphors in the first stanza. In the following stanzas the poet compares his sinful state to a wood in which he is condemned to wander, buffeted by the evil forces of Nature (wind and rain), and pierced by hostile darts (presumably those of Cupid). In the last stanza the poet prays that he may be pierced by a finer dart ("più bello strale") and his soul directed towards God by means of a devout and holy rain ("devot' e santa pioggia"). The commiato, set as a separate movement, recapitulates in three lines the rhyme words and the description of the poet's hopeless state.

In none of the sestina settings is any attempt made to reflect musically the recurrence of rhyme words in different stanzas. Nevertheless, in *Non fu mai* melodic cells recur with remarkable frequency in order to reinforce the ideas of the speed, instability and transience of mortal existence. The most important of these consists of descending or ascending quavers spanning a perfect fifth. Most of these are too obvious to need illustrating; some however can be singled out as they resemble each other in more specific ways. Thus a motive of four quavers used twice in the *prima parte* becomes inverted to express the negative concepts of life's brevity and danger [ex. 253]. Likewise the idea of interrupted motion prompts a melodic resemblance [ex. 254]. Even where quavers are absent the fifth plays an important part in the shaping of melodic structures [ex. 255]. Contrasting with the generally fast motives is the slow meditation on the word "vita" ("life") which closes both the first stanza and the commiato. Marenzio's second sestina, *Sola angioletta* (also with text by Sannazaro) opens the *V a 5* (1585) just as *Non fu mai* had closed the *Spirituali*. The later piece shows some signs of reaction against the floridity of the first. Despite Einstein's charge that it is "almost neutral in its expression,"[111] it is much less mechanical and more varied than *Non fu mai*. It is the shortest of Marenzio's three sestina settings,[112] and the commiato is set as the end of the *sesta ed ultima parte* rather than forming, as in the other two *sestine*, a distinct movement. The emphasis on compactness is balanced by the clarity of the tonal design: terminal cadences fall on *g, d, c, g, d* (I - V), and *g,* all regular for mode 7 untransposed. A fine consideration for structural equilibrium leads Marenzio to link the second and third, and the fifth and sixth stanzas through a *commixtio* of mode 2 untransposed.[113] The melodies are florid and delicate and undulating as the hill ("colle") mentioned in each stanza. *Melismata* is rare:[114] it use is almost entirely reserved for the rhyme word "ombra" ("shade").[115] Whole lines often appear set to music as a continuous phrase, a procedure uncharacteristic of Marenzio's generally more fragmented melodic style. Many of these long phrases are however constructed out of small motivic fragments duplicated for successive words [ex. 256]. The sustained melodies, often imitated in classical manner at the fifth, are offset by the occasional introduction of more modern-sounding rhythms and textures. Lightness, grace, and constant variety do much to compensate for the feeble conventionality of Sannazaro's text.

Wedged in time between the two faintly archaic Sannazaro *sestine, Giunto a la tomba,* the four *ottava* stanzas from Tasso's *Gerusalemme*, opens the *IV a 5* (1584) on a note of almost startling modernity. With hindsight we may say that Marenzio is taking a leap into the future, anticipating by ten years the nervously fluctuating vocal lines found in the more expressionistic of the *Pastor fido* settings. The repetition of words not repeated in the text, together with the breaking up of the lines into many fragments,[116] result in sound patterns totally unlike the sustained equanimity characteristic of the two Sannazaro settings. Melodic recall occurs frequently and is sometimes prompted by verbal repetitions, sometimes not. The most striking of these is the similarity of procedure at the openings of all four *parti,* where a note is sounded in two voices at the same time, serving as the point of departure for contrary motion [ex. 257]. Moreover, two stanzas (nos. 2 and 3) end with similar themes. Noteworthy is the recurring idea "amate...amando" ("beloved...loving")[117] and the rhythmic diminution at the end of the third stanza to depict the word "vissi" ("I lived") [ex. 258]. Apart from repetition, other prominent rhetorical devices include *exclamatio*[118] and antithesis, the latter, as we have seen, taking the form of opposition between life and death.

The higher degree of musical rhetoric with respect to the two Sannazaro settings is a reflection of the nature of Tasso's poetry: gloomy, grandiloquent, and highly rhetorical. These qualities are reflected in the approach to modality, often murky and ambiguous. Though the terminal cadences are all regular for mode 3 untransposed (*a, c, a* and *a:* I - V), powerful effects are achieved by the abrupt change from one mode to another or the ambiguous vacillation between two modes. The most clearcut example of *commixtio tonorum* occurs at the opening of the *seconda parte,* where the replacement of mode 3 by mode 6 is designed to have a consoling effect.[119] The hypolydian mode is established through the emphasis on the note of repercussion, *á,* in the canto,[120] and through the frequent cadences on *f,* the final (bb. 57, 71, and 81). However, the picture is considerably confused by a number of events: the *a*-cadence in b. 65, which is more typical of mode 3 than mode 6, the chromaticism of bb. 65 - 69, and the unusually wide range of the voices after b. 71. Though the mood changes abruptly with the outburst of b. 71, the hypoionian is not finally shaken off until after the emotionally charged *f*-cadence in b. 81.[121]

The setting of Guarini's *Canzon de' baci*[122] is an equally modern if less ambitious work than the Tasso setting. We encounter the same use of repetition and the same fragmentation of the poetic line, harnessed, however, to a different emotional content: heroic solemnity has given way to the more typically madrigalian theme of love making. It is interesting to note that the canzone setting seems to have provided material for a much shorter composition published two years later, *Bascia e ribascia* (*RISM* 1593³).[123] That the later piece is a "spin-off" from the earlier one is clear from a few comparisons. The compositions share similar subject matter and are both in mode 1 transposed. Both make thematic use of a chord progression (usually *g:* I - V) to underline important concepts at the beginnings of lines. In the *Canzon* this idea usually coincides with the repetition of "Baci" (see below); in the later piece, it occurs on the words "Bascia" and "Mira" in lines 1 and 2 [ex. 259]. Also striking is the similarity between the end of the *prima parte* of the *Canzon* and the final phrase of the later piece [ex. 260].

The *Canzon* is not only much longer but also more ambitious in the way that it reflects the emotional progress of Guarini's text. The adjectives in the first line of each stanza set the mood and indicate a gradual *crescendo* towards the climactic third stanza and sudden falling away in the fourth: "Baci soavi e cari/... amorosi e belli/...affammati e'ngordi/...cortesi e grati...."[124] A new emotional height—this time of anguish instead of joy—is reached in the fifth and last stanza, with its reflection on the passage of time and a very slight hint of impending separation: "Baci, ohimè, non mirate...Come l'hore se'n van fugaci e lieve...Ma la speranza è frale il temp'è breve." Guarini ends his *Canzon* on a chill but muted note. Marenzio however appends a further poem, a madrigal of uncertain authorship, in which the hinted separation actually takes place: "Vivrò dunque lontano/ Da voi...."[125] That the two compositions are in fact one is suggested by their similar openings. The final madrigal brings the cycle, which reached a joyous climax in the third stanza, to a second, anguished climax in its sustained final section. It was probably the wide emotional range of the entire cycle (canzone-plus-madrigal) that determined the use of the bitter-sweet dorian mode transposed.

As the music flows towards its two climaxes (one in the third stanza, the other in the madrigal), so the treatment of the words becomes more expansive [table 9]. The intentionality of the design is suggested by the fact that stanzas 1 and 4 are exactly the same length. Expansion affects individual cells as much as entire movements. Two musical ideas in particular tend to expand on each recurrence: descending motives and the already mentioned chord progression, I-V. Passages employing the polyphonic imitation of a descending motive occur near the openings of the first, second, third, and fifth stanzas.[126] The longest of these passages, both texturally and musically, is the climactic

Table 9.   Time Taken Over the Setting of *Baci soavi e cari* and *Vivrò dunque*

Movement	No. of semibreves		
Stanza 1	69(5.3)		
Stanza 2		81(6.2)	
Stanza 3 (first climax)			91(7)
Stanza 4	69(5.3)		
Stanza 5		75(5.76)	
Commiato			24(8)
Madrigal (second climax)			79(11.3)

Note—Figures in parentheses denote approximate time taken over words expressed as a number of semibreves in movement divided by number of lines.

opening section of the *terza parte* (bb. 156-179). In it Marenzio combines four fragments in contrapuntal combination, of which the descending theme appears as the second (bb. 158 ff, sesto and bass). In b. 163 the same theme appears in diminution in the canto and quinto; these two voices vie with each other for superiority of pitch, with canonic descents from f'' (bb. 163 and 164 ff), then g'' (bb. 166 and 167 ff), and finally, a'' (bb. 169-170). The climax of the *Canzon* coincides with a *commixtio tonorum* (mode 10 transposed replacing mode 1 transposed) which lasts from bars 151-199.[127]

Progressive expansion also underlies the treatment of the word "Baci" at the beginning of each stanza. Here Marenzio invariably uses a I - V progression in g (the final) or d (the upper fifth). On each recurrence the word is more expansively treated and repeated more extensively. In the *quinta parte,* where the whole first line is repeated with partial transposition, the kisses are less passionate but longer and more tender. The above mentioned motive (or one very similar) is also to be found during the course of each movement, in order to draw attention to the openings of new sections: in line 4 (the beginning of the second piede), line 7 (the beginning of the sirma), and line 11. The word "baci" (or "bacia"), if used in the middle of a movement, tends to recall the I - V progression at the beginning of each movement [ex. 261]. The same motive appears in modified form to accommodate groups of three syllables [ex. 262]; another form of modification is the repetition of the tonic (I) in place of the dominant (V), resulting in the repetition of the same chord. The repeated-chord motive is then repeated antiphonically, sometimes in transposition [ex. 263].

The *Canzon de' baci* is an outstanding example of the "vibrant modernity"[128] more characteristic of the six-voice than of the five-voice madrigals. This is clear from the virtuosic manipulaion of texture, with its rapid changes, the handling of multiple counterpoint, antiphonic repetitions, the division of lines, and, in one place, a word, into its component fragments.[129] Though none of these characteristics is new in itself, it is nevertheless possible to detect a more deeply personal way of interpreting the text than hitherto. Whereas previously Marenzio strove to find an exact, conventionally agreed equivalent for each poetic idea (albeit with great originality), it is now the musician whose independent voice is clearly felt through the selection and treatment of the poetry. Thus in the last stanza of the *Canzon*, Marenzio allows the word "Baciate" (line 4) to coincide with an echo of the previous section "fugaci e lieve,"[130] thus implying a comment on the transient nature of love and love making which Guarini did not intend. In his choice of texts, too, Marenzio seems to be guided by personal criteria, as is shown by the unification of the final madrigal with the *Canzon*. Such musical and literary echoes crop up already in the *I a 4,5,6* (1588),[131] and were to lend a personal stamp to the *VI a 5* (1594).[132] With *Canzon de' baci* and its madrigal epilogue, Marenzio has finally exhausted that purely hedonistic vein for which he had been (and was to remain) justly famous. The *Pastor fido* and eclogue settings of the ensuing books are the sequel to the anguished *partenza* which concludes the *V a 5.*

9

The Developing Composer

The interval of three years between the $V a 6$ (1591) and the $VI a 6$ (1594) is the clearest dividing line in Marenzio's career. This is indicated not only by the quality of the later works but also by external evidence: the years 1589-93 are relatively unproductive and there is a further gap from 1596 to 1597 during Marenzio's sojourn in Poland; moreover, few madrigals from the later period ever found their way into anthologies. The continued popularity of the earlier madrigals, many of which were reprinted in the Netherlands (by Phalèse), in Germany (by Kauffmann others), and in England (by Yonge, Watson, and Morley), suggests that, whatever his achievements during the 1590's, Marenzio's reputation with his contemporaries continued to rest mainly on works written by 1591.

If Marenzio had died before 1593, we would still have to consider him the most influential (and in many ways the most original) madrigal composer of the second half of the sixteenth century. The existence of the later works adds a totally new dimension to an already varied and complex picture: from 1594 Marenzio's style begins to grow and develop[1] at a faster rate than hitherto—a process stilled by his death at the end of the decade.

The stylistic development during the preceding decade presents a less clear picture. Elsewhere I have attempted to trace a pattern extending throughout the whole of Marenzio's career by analysing his choice of literary texts;[2] I have since come to the conclusion that if the later style is a linear development (albeit an exceedingly rapid one), the earlier style is best described as a network of multiple developments, a complex system of small, often minute, shifts of emphasis from one book to another. Each book displays a slightly different emphasis: for instance, the $I a 5$ (1580) and $I a 6$ (1581) contain an unusually large number of small poems without literary merit, the $IV a 5$ (1584), of occasional pieces;[3] the year 1585 is noteworthy for the appearance of a number of madrigals in which the poetic and musical forms are interdependent.[4] But none of these tendencies (and one could mention more) leads to further developments in any systematic way.

An exceptionally pronounced shift of emphasis comes with the *I a 4, 5, 6* (1588). This book contains a number of self-conscious echoes and allusions[5] all indicating that Marenzio wishes to discard his "amoroso stile"[6] and "soar with other wings," leaving behind a more "solid reputation."[7] By 1587 at the latest, therefore, Marenzio already felt trapped by and dissatisfied with the graceful "new manner" which he had inherited and standardized, and which was finally discarded in the books published after 1593. The 1588 print is primarily a change of attitude rather than of compositional technique.[8] There is nothing new about compositions using the *misura di breve;* what is unprecedented is the crowding together of fifteen of them into one book, with all the attendant risks of monotony and commercial failure. In fact the *I a 4, 5, 6* is the only collection never to have been reprinted during his lifetime.

That Marenzio was capable of reversion to his earlier style is shown in the *V a 6* (1591), which honors Virginio Orsini and his young bride. The centerpiece of this book is the *Canzon de baci,* which resembles *Bascia e ribascia,* published as late as 1593.[9]

The period 1577-93 is therefore, despite occasional glimpses of things to come, a unified period in which Marenzio's style is consolidated without actually growing or developing very rapidly. The same stylistic premises apply for the *V a 6* (1591) as for the *I a 5* (1580); even the first book displays his mastery of a fully fledged musical language not susceptible of further development without being transformed.

Before considering the later period in more detail, let us make some concluding observations about the earlier style and its influence. The key to this lies in the subordination of virtuosic techniques to the conventional expression of literary ideas; this expression rests in turn on the response of the composer to every level of poetic thought. The meaning of individual words, the rhythmic structure of lines and phrases, the syntactical structure of clauses and sentences, and the disposition of the ideas according to the devices of rhetoric, all require reflections in the musical setting. The skill of the composer lies in doing justice to all these elements so that they are reflected as faithfully as possible. At the same time, a certain amount of poetic license is admitted and is necessary in order to avoid dullness or overconventionality; however, too much license will lead to solecisms or even chaos.

Such a style rests inevitably on a number of agreed conventions: melodic and rhythmic formulae, certain standard imitative procedures and harmonic progressions, and certain rhetorical devices whose meaning or function is unvaried from one madrigal to another and—to a large extent—from one composer to another.

Just because Marenzio's style rests largely on the standardization and conventionalization of the mannerisms of previous composers, so Marenzio's contemporaries and successors had no trouble seizing on the external features of Marenzio's style and copying them in their own works. The emergence of Marenzio in the late 1570's to a large extent determined the course of the virtuoso madrigal of the 1580's and its dissemination outside Italy.

It can be no coincidence that the Italian madrigal underwent a rapid change just after 1580, the year of Marenzio's first book. This change may be seen in the works of older composers like Ingegneri, A. Gabrieli, Lassus, Monte, and Striggio. In all these composers we see the sudden upsurge of rapid declamation and *melismata,* and the development of more brilliant textures—especially the use of two sopranos of equal pitch. How much of this change is due directly to Marenzio is uncertain: the *rapprochement* between Monte and Marenzio implied by Newcomb[10] is certainly plausible, given the similarity of the two composers' settings of *Satiati Amor;*[11] a more precise indication is Ingegneri's resetting of *Due rose fresche,* in which he copies Marenzio's themes.[12]

Turning to the younger composers active in the 1580's, it is difficult to avoid Einstein's conclusion that the structural techniques used by Marenzio were widely imitated but not always perfectly harnessed to expressive needs.[13] Thus Nanino's skilful assimilation of Marenzio's use of double counterpoint lacks the younger composer's textural finesse.[14] More successful is the second of his two resettings of *Dolorosi martir,* both of which belong to the same "family" (modally, and in the choice of clefs) as those of Ingegneri and Marenzio.[15] The brighter side of Marenzio's personality is reflected most clearly in Nanino's pupil, Felice Anerio, whose *II a 5* (1585), dedicated to Marcantonio Serlupi just a few months after Marenzio dedicated his *I a 4* to the same patron,[16] is so close to Marenzio as to suggest mutual acquaintance. His indebtedness is evident above all from the way hendecasyllabic lines are divided into two contrasted segments.[17] Later, in the Roman anthology of 1589,[18] he takes over melismatic themes used by Marenzio in his *Rive, fontane e fiume,* published in the same anthology [ex. 264].

The further one moves from Italy, the more selective the dissemination of Marenzio's madrigals; however, space does not permit an analysis of the way different countries absorbed the Italian style, even though it would be interesting to compare, for instance, the relatively wide and serious choice of German publishers with the narrower, Anglicized, selection of the English editors (based almost entirely on what had been published in Antwerp). The *I a 5* (1580) served as a quarry both for Phalèse in Antwerp[19] and Lindner in Nuremberg.[20] The extent of Marenzio's popularity abroad near the end of the decade may be gauged from the preponderance of his works in Lindner's two anthologies and in Watson's *First sett of Italian madrigals englished.*[21] Nor must we forget the uses to which Marenzio's music was put in the form of *canzonette spirituali*[22] and *contrafacta,* i.e. the replacement of the secular Italian text by a spiritual Latin (or, in some cases, German) text. This enterprising attempt to propagate the Faith by seeking spiritual parallels to the original secular subject matter is a little-studied but fascinating manifestation of Counter-Reformation religious zeal. The fitting of Latin texts to madrigals of Marenzio by Nenninger (Padua, 1606),[23] Berg (Munich, 1609),[24] and Molinaio (Venice, 1610),[25] is instructive in this respect.

Returning to the secular madrigal, we may trace Marenzio's influence through four outstanding composers spread over a large geographical area: Hassler in South Germany, Sweelinck in the Low Countries, and Weelkes and Wilbye in England. Sweelinck's *Rimes françoises et italiennes* (1612) contains two resettings of madrigals already reprinted by Phalèse in 1583: *Liquide perle* and *Qual vive Salamandra*,[26] both of which deploy Marenzio's themes in a three-voice rearrangement. The German and English composers set translated versions of texts set by Marenzio, drawing liberally on the Italian composer's music. Thus Hassler's *Falsch Lieb* is a translation of Guarini's *Crudel, perchè mi fuggi*,[27] while *Ich scheid von dir mit leyde* actually quotes the opening of *Parto da voi*,[28] an English translation of which was later set by Thomas East.[29] Meanwhile, Watson had already translated Marenzio's *Crudel* as *Unkind, o stay thy flying* (*RISM* 1590[29]); in 1598, Wilbye's resetting of this translated version is certainly reminiscent of Marenzio's.[30]

The two greatest English madrigalists, Weelkes and Wilbye, recall different facets of Marenzio's musical personality according to their fundamentally opposed musical personalities. For the more extrovert Weelkes, full-blooded word-painting and chromaticism are the two characteristics which best reflect Marenzio's influence: both may be found in *Thule, the period of cosmography,* the first line of which is divided after the first word[31] and set in double counterpoint. Another technique favoured by Weelkes is *gioco*, which Brown calls "pseudo-antiphony";[32] in many places, Weelkes' use of it resembles Marenzio's. The influence on Wilbye is at times less obvious, though no less profound. In the opening of *Adieu, sweet Amarillis*[33] the word "Adieu" is echoed from one voice to another without, however, any noticeable lapse into straightforward antiphony;[34] the poignancy is achieved through a juxtaposition of tonic major and minor of an emotional ambivalence and harmonic breadth which rivals, if it does not surpass, Marenzio. Harmonically, Wilbye paints on at least as broad a canvas as Marenzio, as may be seen in the aptitude of both composers for constructing root triads on descending or ascending scales in the bass [ex. 265].[35]

Those composers who followed Marenzio's earlier style were mostly unable or unwilling to explore the territories visited by Marenzio in the years after 1593. In the *VI a 5* (1594) Marenzio's style begins to change as if before our very eyes: there are still enough links with the past for one to be able to perceive this change as a continuation rather than an abrupt departure. Dissonance still tends to be soft; the distinction between the *misura comune* and the *misura di breve* still holds,[36] and examples of "eye music" and esoteric forms of word-painting are still to be found.[37] The differences however outweigh the similarities. The most important of these is the book's literary content: the choice of passages from Guarini's new and controversial *Pastor fido*[38] is a sure sign that Marenzio was deliberately attempting to break new ground. Previously Marenzio had set poems in Guarini's most teasing, ironic or hedonistic vein. Now in the *Pastor fido* and some of the madrigals selected in the later period, intensity is the keynote: audacious use of antithesis, a dramatic but calculated use of interjections, and other rhetorical figures. Ironically, it was precisely the play's lyrical qualities, condemned by the pedantic Summo as inappropriate in the theatre,[39] that commended it to composers of the time. The confusion between poetry and drama (a confusion between the boundaries of genres typical of the Late Renaissance generally) is evident on the one hand from the lyricism of such speeches as Mirtillo's in Act III (*Ah dolente partita*)[40] and, on the other, those madrigals which conjure up a theatrical illusion, such as *Crudel, perchè mi fuggi*[41] and *Parto o non parto.*[42] Recollected theatrical situations are even more obviously found in the work of a younger poet to whom Marenzio, among many other composers, turned at this time: the Genoese, Livio Celiano. His *Rimanti in pace*[43] is a kind of mini-tragedy from an imagined pastoral drama, the most blatently theatrical *partenza* Marenzio set in his later years. Another sonnet, *Ahi chi t'insidia,*[44] in which a shepherd attempts to rescue his nymph from a lustful satyr, is perhaps suggested by an episode in Tasso's pastoral drama *Aminta* (1573);[45] the bipartite madrigal, *Il vago e bello Armillo*[46] could be a scene from a piscatory drama.

The pastoral characters of Guarini, Celiano, and of the eclogues of Tasso,[47] are constantly faced with the immediate threat of death, separation, deception, or rape. These extreme situations require extreme musical means—a radical approach to melody, texture, harmony, and form. Angular vocal writing, together with the frequent use of such intervals as the diminished fourth and tritone, becomes the norm where previously it had been the exception. Rapid juxtapositions of *tessitura* are matched by nervously fluctuating rhythms which betray the fears, frustrations, and hesitations of overwrought shepherds and shepherdesses; frequent exclamations become the most effective expressive outlet, the last resort in a seemingly hopeless situation. The chief vehicle of expression is now the canto, whose supremacy is unrivalled by the quinto, now invariably assigned to the tenor pitch. The normal texture is often homophonic, animated by brief echoes between the voices. Tension is provided by the occasional deviation of one of the voices from the homophonic norm to create dissonances and syncopations before closing ranks again with the other voices on an important word or at the cadence. This technique is not new,[48] but the emotional urgency is already apparent at the opening of *S'io parto* (*VI a 5,* no. 1). Together with more frequent use of homophony in the *VI, VII,* and *VIII a 5* comes greater reliance on harmonic means of expression: all-pervasive chromaticism, and constant interplay between major and minor tonalities. Both these characteristics are seen at the opening of a madrigal from the *VII a 5* where alternate hypoionian (major) and phrygian (minor) sonorities convey the oxymoron, "O *dolcezze amarissime* d'Amore" [ex. 266].

Before describing the steady development of the stylistic elements outlined above, we must draw attention to the increasing role played by texture in determining form. In the later madrigals there is an increasing emphasis on mass as a structural element. A number of madrigals are built around the contrast between alternate "solo" and "tutti" sections, the two types of texture intermingling only in the very final section. A simple example of this is provided in the initial antiphonic exchanges of *Hor chi Clori beata,* the contrast between high and low groups dissolving only in the final line.[49] These concerto-like contrasts—a sure sign that the Baroque is only just around the corner—are often found in madrigals whose sections are proportional in length. Particularly instructive is the final madrigal of the *VII a 5* (1595): the wedding madrigal, *Ombrose e care selve*[50] consists of three sections, the first and third of which are almost equal in length (bb. 1-31; bb. 57-86). Each new section is articulated by a change of texture (tutti replaced by solo) and mensuration (duple changing to triple time). In the final section the changes become more frequent as the structure splinters into smaller, mosaic-like fragments. Other examples are not lacking: e.g. *Laura, se pur,* the two parts of which consist of two equal sections of sustained polyphony flanking a relatively disjointed middle section.[51]

This new formal mastery is evident above all in the book immediately succeeding the *VI a 5:* the *VI a 6* (1595) is dominated by two large-scale settings from Petrarch and Tansillo, the latter being Marenzio's longest work. Apart from their length and their sombre scoring,[52] the two works are sharply contrasted.

In the first and presumably earlier work, the section, *Giovane donna,*[53] Marenzio prosecutes the elegant but taut polyphonic style of his previous sestina, *Sola angioletta* (*V a 5,* 1585, no. 1), but combines it with an adventurous tonal structure recalling earlier sonnet settings—in particular, *Se la mia vita,*[54] which, like *Giovane donna,* uses the eighth tone with *commixtio* of the third.[55] Marenzio also draws on the experience of the *Canzon de' baci* by developing further the idea of expanding successive units. Thus each stanza is longer than the last, the climax coming in the envoy, a polyphonic continuum which provides the perfect reflection of Petrarch's quasi-polyphonic recapitulation of six rhyme words in three lines.[56]

If *Giovane donna* is backward looking, *Se quel dolor* looks forward to the last three books *a 5* in its exaggerated emotionalism and emphasis on the expressive moment rather than the continuously unfolding thought. Abrupt rhythmic contrasts, "forbidden" intervals (such as the augmented fifth and diminished fourth near the opening),[57] and the strangely twisted chromatic lines already foreshadow the *IX a 5* (1599).

In the *VII* and *VIII a 5*, Marenzio continues further down the avenue opened up by the *VI a 5* and the six-voice Tansillo cycle. The *VII a 5* (1595) is the bleakest of Marenzio's works to date, drawing for the most part on the more tragic speeches of Mirtillo and Amarilli, the two main characters in the *Pastor fido*. The sombre atmosphere is reinforced by a more oblique approach to modality caused by a still more liberal use of chromaticism; the strain being put on the modal system may be seen in the way a piece may start "fuori di tuono" through the introduction of extraneous accidentals: thus *O Mirtillo* (no. 12) begins on a *c*-minor chord, as though the piece were in mode 2 transposed down a tone; subsequent events however prove the mode to be the eighth transposed [ex. 267]; similarly, *Tirsi mio* (no. 16) begins as though in mode 3 transposed down a tone, but turns out to be in mode 9 transposed [ex. 268]. In the same way, phrygian compositions can sometimes end on perfect cadences on the final, as though aeolian [ex. 269].[58]

The *VIII a 5*, published after a gap of three years, finds Marenzio in a less gloomy frame of mind. The only two settings from the *Pastor fido* are both taken from sub-plots in which the comedy predominates over tragedy (nos. 10 and 15). Comedy is evident, too, in the light, aria-like settings from Celiano and Grillo (nos. 5, 11, and 13) and in some of the passages from Tasso's eclogue, *Il convito de'pastori* (nos. 1, 3, and 14), whose plot is modeled quite clearly on Guarini's *Pastor fido*. However, the dissipation of the tragic atmosphere of the previous book is only partial: there is the same resignation accompanied often by a still more acute sense of emotional crisis and impending catastrophe: examples are two passages from the *Convito* (nos. 2 and 4), and the hyperbolic madrigal by Celiano, *Care lagrime mie* (no. 12). In this book, too, there is still greater refinement in the declamatory technique. The almost entirely homophonic texture is characterized by the repetition of minute fragments which ensure cohesion even where there is no corresponding repetition in the poem [ex. 270]. Nor are syntax and rhetoric neglected: questions consistently appear with triple-time cross-rhythms and often with a rising scale-degree at the end [ex. 271]; exclamations are more audaciously treated than before [ex. 272].

In the *IX a 5* (1599) the anguish of the previous year turns to asperity, making this the most controversial and widely discussed of Marenzio's later books. Just as the literary choice of a previous book, the *I a 4, 5, 6* (1588) self-consciously reflects a change of artistic attitude, so Marenzio does not hesitate to begin his last book with a statement of his intentions:

Così nel mio parlar vogl'io esser aspro.[59]

This is the first line of Dante's third poem "per la Donna di Pietra" ("for the woman of stone"), comparable in blunt hardness to the passage from Petrarch's *Trionfo d'Amore* which begins "Dura legge d'amor" (no. 3). The modally anomalous accidentals at the beginning of both madrigals [ex. 273] are merely the first of a number of audacities, including false relations, dissonances, incomplete cadences with quavers hurtling towards nothingness, and dense webs of severe counterpoint. Even the final item, an innocuous madrigal by Guarini entitled "Mano stretta"[60] in the original print, is set as a rigorous canon. Polyphony has again triumphed in this last publication of Marenzio, but it is rougher and more angular than in his earlier style. The rapid changes of *tessitura* and unpredictable interval structure—in other words, those characteristics which had affected only the canto in the *VI, VII,* and *VIII a 5*—now permeate all the voices. One passage near the end of the bass part of *Chiaro segno Amor* (no. 4) is particularly remarkable in this respect, not only because of its melodic contour, but in the way a complete line is derived from a small motivic cell [ex. 274].[61] This passage was quote by Cerone, who complained that it was "mas para mirar [. . .] que para cantar y goçar."[62] The same writer also took exception to the severe dissonances which, for the first time in Marenzio's works, consistently transgress the established rules for preparation and resolution.[63]

From the preceding summary of his development, it will now be clear how rapidly Marenzio's style continued to evolve right up to the moment of his death. The symptoms of this change are all to apparent, the causes less so. Let us enumerate these possible causes and influences:

1. Events in Marenzio's life.
2. The Counter-Reformation.
3. The Florentine Camerata.
4. The artistic ideals of antiquity in a broader sense.
5. Musical developments in the 1580's—especially of the madrigal at Ferrara.
6. Marenzio's own development as a composer.

The first possibility is the "romantic" explanation; it rests on very frail evidence, since we know little about Marenzio's private life from 1586 till 1595 (or after). There exist only two clues, neither of them conclusive. The first is Peacham's allegation of a love-affair with a "kinswoman" of the Pope, which is supposed to have led to Marenzio's having been sent to Poland.[64] While there is no evidence for this, we may be certain that the change in Marenzio's music stemmed at least partly from a change in his nature.[65] That this change may be due to some unhappy event is faintly suggested in the dedication to Virginio Orsini of the *V a 6* in 1591: there he speaks of his patron as his "felicissima ombra in ogni mio ascide[n]te."[66] However, the *V a 6* lies well within the bounds of Marenzio's earlier style; three years were to elapse before the appearance of the epoch-making *VI a 5*. Marenzio's private life, if it plays any part at all, is insufficient as an explanation of his stylistic development.

Scarcely less so is the theory that Marenzio fell under the influence of the movement to reform the Roman Catholic Church. While this might account for the appearance of the *Spirituali* in 1584 and perhaps even the new serious, didactic tone of the *I a 4, 5, 6* (1588),[67] it would leave unexplained the failure to produce any spiritual or didactic madrigals in the 1590's. Unlike Palestrina, Marenzio never seems to have repented of his secular vein. On the contrary, like many poets and composers of the day, he simply ignores sensitive political and religious issues likely to provoke the wrath of the newly militant church, focussing attention on a narrower range of subject matter.

Much more plausible is the third theory: that Marenzio was affected by the ideas of the musicians and thinkers surrounding Count Giovanni Bardi in Florence in the 1570's and early 1580's. Marenzio would have had the opportunity to meet the members of the former Camerata—Caccini and his protector Bardi, and perhaps also the ageing Galilei—during his work on the Florentine *intermedi* in 1588-89. Further contact may have been possible after Bardi, accompanied perhaps by Caccini, moved to Rome in 1592.[68] It is a matter of debate how far Caccini succeeded in his avowed intention of "moving the affect of the soul":[69] his concern for "grazia" and "sprezzatura"[70] point backwards in time—to Castiglione and Vasari—rather than forward to the Baroque. Nevertheless it is distinctly possible that the new singing style left its mark on Marenzio, who frequently uses exclamatory figures used and annotated by Caccini himself [ex. 275].[71] In this respect, Doni's coupling together of Marenzio and Caccini is significant,[72] while a passage in Severo Bonini's *Discorsi* (quoted at the end of this chapter) further reveals Marenzio's importance for the Florentines of the next generation.

In a broad sense the declamatory madrigals strike a compromise between the earlier polyphonic style and the ideas of the antipolyphonists, Mei, Bardi, and Galilei. By allowing the words to be more clearly enunciated, and by exploiting the expressive possibilities of pitch changes in the canto, Marenzio moves a large step in the direction of Mei's demands for a return to the unencumbered directness which he ascribes to ancient Greek music.[73] How deeply Marenzio was affected by Galilei's extreme views on word-painting and counterpoint it is difficult to say. Certainly the *VI, VII*, and *VIII a 5* go some way down the path indicated in the *Dialogo* in the gradual disappearance of detailed text delineation. However, more than a decade separates the publication of the *Dialogo* of 1581 from the *VI a 5* of 1594; moreover, Galilei's views on counterpoint appear to have mellowed: one of his last works is the *Discorso intorno all'uso delle dissonaze,* part of an unpublished treatise on counterpoint.[74] Galilei's liberal ideas on dissonance often foreshadow the practice of Marenzio in his *IX a 5;*[75] it is worth observing that the opening number, *Così nel mio parlar,* had been set by Galilei himself a few years before, albeit in a very different style.[76]

The chief motivation behind the speculations and experiments of the Florentines was a dissatisfaction with contemporary music and a desire to return to the ideals of antiquity. However, as Pirrotta has pointed out, interest in the monodic sounds ascribed to antiquity was not restricted to the Florentine Camerata.[77] The quest for archaic sounds led to the chromatic and enharmonic experiments of Vicentino, Lassus, and Rore, whose declamatory madrigals were so admired by Bardi.[78] The later descriptions we have of theatre music tend to confirm the seriousness with which composers sought to emulate Greek music. Thus Gabriele Bombasi, in his description of music for *L'Alidoro* (performed in Reggio before the Duchess of Ferrara in 1568), speaks of the "maniera tenuta ne' chori, essendo ella non più veduta nè usata, almeno a' tempi nostri."[79] Among the characteristics noted by Bombasi are the use of alternating solo voices (soprano and accompanying instruments), the use of chromaticism with no verbal repetition, an attempt to express the "affetti dell'anime,"[80] and a capacity to move the listener not only through song, but through facial expressions and gestures.[81] In addition we should mention two musical documents. The first is Striggio's setting of *Fuggi, speme mia* for Francesco d'Ambra's *Confanaria* which, so we are told by Grazzini, greatly moved the audience.[82] The other is Andrea Gabrieli's music for the performance of the translated version of Sophocles' *Oedipus* in Vicenza, 1585.[83] The choruses are composed according to the wishes of the director, Angelo Ingegneri: homophonically, with enough chromaticism and false relations to convey the doleful atmosphere of the Tragedy.[84] By 1594 Marenzio may well have come to the conclusion that a similar homophonic technique was required for the dramatic and quasi-dramatic texts of Guarini, Tasso, and Celiano. Negative evidence of this is provided in the re-emergence of polyphony for the settings of the nontheatrical Petrarchan lyrics of the *IX a 5.*

If the revival of antique ideals in the theatre influenced Marenzio and if, as is well known, one of the most important centers of this theatrical activity proved to be the Ferrarese court, it would be reasonable to expect the activities of madrigal composers attached to that court to have had some bearing on the development of Marenzio's later style. Ferrara, as we have seen, plays a crucial role in the history of the virtuoso madrigal of the 1580's. Virtuosity (whether it emanates from the composer, the performer, or both) presupposes an audience, and the history of the Ferrarese madrigal at this time is centered increasingly on the giving of pleasure to the listener rather than to the performer. Vocal pyrotechnics are merely one way of satisfying the audience's demand for virtuosity; other ways include clear enunciation of the words through homophonic texture, and greater emphasis on harmonic rather than visual means of expression. It is precisely these features which may be found in theatre music and which are reflected in Marenzio's more declamatory madrigals; even Giustiniani's description of the facial expressions and gestures of Ferrarese and Mantuan singers resembles Bombasi's description of the music for *Alidoro*.[85]

Among the crucial composers active in Ferrara during the 1580's we have already mentioned one: Wert, *maestro di cappella* of Santa Barbara, Mantua, who frequently visited Ferrara from 1583 to 1589.[86] His *Giunto a la tomba* sets a challenge in terms of emotional directness which Marenzio was able to meet only partly in his resetting of 1584;[87] otherwise we have to wait several years before finding more explicit echoes of Wert's style. It is almost as if the death of Lassus in 1594 and Wert in 1596 had released in Marenzio a desire to explore similar emotional terrain in the form of spate of resettings. The opening of Marenzio's *Solo e pensoso* resembles the settings of Lassus and Wert[88] in a general sense, in that the four lower voices have wide-ranging, rugged descending themes; more specifically, Marenzio's opening chromatic line, with its melodic contour $g' \ldots a'' \ldots d''$, is a veiled reference to Wert's opening theme, with its descending conjunct fifths, and to a later passage, where the canto ascends and then descends diatonically in the same range [ex. 276]. In other places, Marenzio copies Wert more openly: one example shows the impact of Wert's *Giunto a la tomba* to be as vivid in 1599 as it had been in 1584 [ex. 277]. It is also worth remarking that by 1581 Wert had already acquired the habit of treating homophony as a normal rather than exceptional texture. As a matter of course, he sets two subsequent settings of Tasso's *Gerusalemme* in a declamatory style infused with great dramatic vigor.[89]

Wert's *VII a 5* (1581), which contains both *Giunto a la tomba* and *Solo e pensoso,* is therefore something of a time bomb where Marenzio is concerned: its full impact only becomes apparent more than a decade later. Meanwhile, other developments were beginning to affect musical fashion in Ferrara— developments for which Marenzio himself was partly responsible. A measure of Marenzio's reputation at Ferrara may be seen from his prominence in the Peperara anthologies of 1582-83. Later, his *Filli mia bella, a dio*[90] served as the model for the Ferrarese compositions of *I lieti amanti* (*RISM* 1586[10]);[91] remarkable is the contrast between Marenzio's lightness and the overladen pathos of some of the pieces of the 1586 anthology. Fiorino's opening, with its minor sonorities, injects a conventional pastoral scene with a new dramatic urgency achieved by harmonic means [ex. 278]. The same tendency is exaggerated further in the wide-ranging harmonies of the many farewell scenes of Marenzio's *VI a 5* (1594). The opening piece, *S'io parto,* based on a text by the Reggian poet Arlotti, was in fact reset in 1595 by a prominent Ferrarese, Luzzaschi; nor did the opening progression of Marenzio's setting escape the notice of Artusi, a shrewd if conservative observer of the Ferrarese musical scene.[92]

It is thanks to Artusi that we know of the extent of Monteverdi's popularity among Ferrarese musical circles before 1600.[93] It is surprising that little attention has yet been paid to the extent of Marenzio's influence on the young Monteverdi; less surprising, therefore, that no attempt has yet been made to show what reciprocal effect Monteverdi may have had on Marenzio's transformation in the 1590's. When Monteverdi arrived in Mantua in 1590 he was already the author of two madrigal books containing a number of resettings of texts previously set by Marenzio. Monteverdi's indebtedness is most obvious when he is copying Marenzio's declamatory technique, as in one passage from a Tasso setting [ex. 279], or in the resetting of Guarini's *Crudel, perchè mi fuggi* with Marenzio's alteration of the first word left intact.[94] If Monteverdi was fascinated by that side of Marenzio's temperament which tended towards declamation and exclamation, the more decorative side of Marenzio's early style left him relatively cold. Thus in his resetting of *A che tormi'l ben mio*[95] he piles on the intensity more evenly and more boldly, overloading an unpretentious text with anguished dissonances, augmented chords, and false relations. The same rhetorical power is more successfully exploited in *Rimanti in pace,* the exaggeratedly pathetic *partenza* by Celiano set two years later by Marenzio. Are the resemblances between the two settings due to borrowing on Marenzio's part or coincidence of aims and temperament [ex. 280]?[96]

That Monteverdi's and Marenzio's madrigals were performed alongside each other in Ferrara during the 1590's is practically certain: when in 1600 Artusi mounted his attack on the new music he had recently heard in that city,[97] he chose Monteverdi as his butt rather than risk a dispute with the more established figures of Marenzio and Luzzaschi, let alone the aristocrats Gesualdo and Fontanelli. Three years later, however, he seeks to bolster his original attack with reference to Rore, Wert, and Marenzio, all three of whom had had links with the Ferrarese court.[98] In the case of Marenzio, the attack is three-pronged: it involves the use of false relations, modally extraneous accidentals, and the unprepared seventh. The arguments put forward by Artusi's opponent, "L'Ottuso," in favor of greater freedom in the name of expression, provide a revealing record of contemporary thinking even after Artusi has proceeded to demolish them. For instance, "L'Ottuso" defends

Marenzio's use of the unprepared seventh by likening it to a metaphor.[99] This argument, though of course it failed to convince Artusi, has the ring of authenticity, demonstrating once again the rhetorical aspirations of sixteenth-century composers.

At the heart of the controversy surrounding the conflicting claims of the *prima* and *seconda prattica* was the question: how far was it permitted to stretch or distort existing musical language in the pursuit of expression? In the course of the heated dispute between Artusi and G. C. Monteverdi the issues inevitably became distorted by both sides. While the former mistakenly assigns absolute value to rules govening dissonance and harmony, failing to perceive their relative nature, the latter oversimplifies when he claims that there is a hard-and-fast distinction between two types of music, one in which "l'armonia" prevails over "l'oratione," the other, where the reverse relation exists;[100] for it was a central tenet of sixteenth-century aesthetics that the music should follow the "oration"; the only question was how.[101]

The madrigals Marenzio published in the early 1580's are an attempt to settle this question through focussing inventive capacity primarily on the meaning of the individual word. Never before had such an elaborate system of musical "vocabulary" been required to serve as the basis of an entire musical language. However, it is a basis only: line and phrase structure, syntactical and rhetorical considerations all play their part. It is not altogether surprising if all these diverse elements come into conflict or get in each others' way, as when the normal rules governing rhythmic declamation or cadence structure are reversed because some individual word clamours for attention. It is true that such anomalies and conflicts can be a source of fascination if confronted with verve, ingenuity, and elegance, qualities which Marenzio rarely lacks. But it is also true that such qualities may in the end exhaust themselves, or can be renewed only with a change in artistic orientation. This brings us to the sixth and last possible cause of Marenzio's transformation: that the awareness that he had exhausted a certain vein of expression, coupled with an awareness of certain musical currents of the 1580's, gradually led Marenzio to abandon a somewhat complicated and over-ambitious system for something more direct, more capable of "moving the affect of the soul."

The principal symptom of this dismantling process is the reduction of the role played by word-painting: the imitation of the meaning of words becomes discretionary instead of obligatory. This is well illustrated in the setting of a lament from the *Pastor fido, Cruda Amarilli*,[102] where musical imitation of individual words is admitted only when it reinforces the central mood of pathos. This inevitably means that such poetic images as the "white jasmine" in the *prima parte*, or the "valleys," "hills," "streams," and "winds" in the *seconda parte*, receive little or no attention.[103] The same concentration on psychology at the expense of the physical world is still apparent in the more polyphonic *IX a 5:* in *Solo e pensoso* the tortured, rugged lines are symbolic, as elsewhere, of the contours of the poet's mind, not merely descriptive of the hills in which he is forced to roam. At the beginning of the *seconda parte,* the plains and mountains are very lightly sketched in by two voices,[104] the climax being reserved for the surprising harmonic and melodic twist on the word "selvaggie" ("savage").[105]

Together with a clearer sense of priorities comes a greater subordination of detail to the larger structural units of phrase, sentence and movement; each of these becomes so heavily imbued with drama and pathos that the "neutrality"[106] of which Einstein complains in the earlier style completely disappears. There is a fusion of syntax, rhetoric, and affective expression: each avoided cadence carries a sense of unrequited love, each repetition an emotional crescendo; each *exordium* coincides with an arresting exclamation, and each *peroratio* a shattering or magical climax. The Age of the Lament has arrived.

The new sensitivity is not restricted to nor does it end with Marenzio. Even before pieces like *Cruda Amarilli* began to affect other composers, the 1590's saw an abrupt change of direction in the madrigalian genre: the outpourings of Monteverdi, Luzzaschi, Gesualdo, Fontanelli, Macque, and Pallavicino bear this out. The Ninth and last surviving book[107] sees Marenzio attempting to come to grips with these newer currents—expecially the melodic angularity and crabbed invertible counterpoint of Gesualdo. Whatever precise course Marenzio's music would have taken after 1599, we may be sure that he would have continued to absorb the new into the old.

The last word will be left with a Florentine priest-composer who, writing more than three hundred years ago, provides a precedent for dividing Marenzio's life into two unequal parts. Bonini speaks of three styles ("ordini") in the history of vocal music. In the first period, predating Palestrina, composers neglected the meaning and correct accentuation of the words; in the second (post-Tridentine) period, represented by Palestrina, Lassus, Willaert, Monte, Wert, Vecchi, and Marenzio, the balance between words and music is restored; the third period is represented by Gesualdo, Nenna, Monteverdi, Gagliano—and Marenzio.[108] As Bonini explains:[109]

Luca Marentio [. . .] era stato il più universale compositore di cantilene di tutti gl'altri "poichè ha composto negli ambidui stili del secondo e del terzo: del secondo come in quella muta a cinque voci, dove sono quelle parole: *Liquide perle amore* e *Tirsi morir volea;* del terzo come in quelli medesime a cinque voci: *S'io parto io moro,* in quelli della nona muta: *Così nel mio cantar voglio essere aspro,* tanto artifizziosi, in quelli a sei voci: *Se bramate ch'io mora* e in quelli: *Lucida perla.* Si odono in queste dette opere concetti doppi, crudezze ben intese e ben risolute e dolcezze divine, havendo usato gl'affetti secondo le parole."[110]

We may disagree with Bonini's implied point of division, for there is nothing terribly novel about the *IV a 6* of 1587; in other respects, however, his distinction seems as helpful today as it seemed valid in his own time. No full-length study of Marenzio's later madrigals would do well to ignore it.

Notes

Chapter 1

1. Guerrini, *Dolce cigno;* Ledbetter, *Marenzio* (unpublished thesis), pp. 2 and 103 ff, and app. 1. The first part of this chapter is no more than a brief résumé of the known facts of Marenzio's life, most of which are recorded in Ledbetter, op. cit., Engel, *Marenzio,* and other works later cited.

2. Sartori, in *MGG,* ii, cols 279-283.

3. Contino was active at Brescia from 1551 - 1558 and 1565 - 1566: see Guerrini, "Contino," *NA,* i (1924), 135-136 and 140; Ledbetter, *Marenzio,* p. 4 ff.

4. Both of whom, as Marenzio, were active at Ferrara: *La Musica (Dizionario),* i. 201 and ii. 1430 (arts. "Bertani" and "Virchi").

5. See appendix II, note to *RISM* 1588[17], and appendix IV, note to Martinengo.

6. Madruzzo died at Tivoli on 5 July 1578: Ledbetter, "Marenzio's early career," *JAMS,* xxxii (1979), 313-314.

7. Engel, *Marenzio,* pp. 16-17 and p. 214: cf. Ledbetter, *Marenzio,* p. 19 ff.

8. See Marenzio's letter addressed to the Cardinal dated 18 June 1584 (Ledbetter, *Marenzio,* App. 40).

9. Ledbetter, *Marenzio,* p. 69 ff.

10. Ledbetter, *Marenzio,* pp. 43-58.

11. For a facsimile reprint of the dedication, together with a translation, see *Secular Works,* vii (ed. Ledbetter), pp. xv-xvi.

12. Reproduced in Walker, *Intermèdes,* pp. 36-76. For further details about Marenzio's part in them, see Engel, *Marenzio,* p. 40 ff and "Intermedien," in *Festschrift Schneider,* pp. 71-86; Ledbetter, *Marenzio,* pp. 114-123.

13. Marenzio's dedication, signed in Rome on 1 January 1591, refers to the compositions as being "nate, e nudrite in casa sua" ("born and nourished in your house"). In Gardano's 1595 reprint the same dedication has been updated to 5 January 1595, presumably as a sign of continuing good relations.

14. Einstein, *Madrigal,* ii. 667.

15. Cinzio Aldobrandini (1551-1610) was the son of Aurelio Passeri and Elisabetta Aldobran-

dini; his uncle, Ippolito Aldobrandini, conferred his own name on him shortly before being named pope in 1592. For further details, see E. Guarini, in *DBI*, ii. 102-104.

16. Madrigal books were dedicated to him by Croce (*NV*, no. 676) and Curzio Mancini (*NV*, no. 1562). Literary works include Tasso's *Gerusalemme conquista* (the revised version of the *Gerusalemme liberata* published in 1593) and Grillo's *Rime*, Venice: G. B. Ciotti, 1599.

17. A document published in 1839 the original copy of which is now lost refers to Marenzio as *maestro di cappella* (see Ledbetter, *Marenzio*, p. 137, note 12, and app. 106).

18. See Chomiński, *Słownik Muzyków Polskich*, i. 220, col. 1 ff.

19. This event was recorded in the *avvisi di Roma* (transcribed in Ledbetter, *Marenzio*, p. 139), surely an unusual occurrence for sixteenth-century composers and a sign of the high esteem in which he was held.

20. St. Philip spent his last years (1583-1595) at Santa Maria in Vallicella, a few minutes' walk from via Parione. Many of Marenzio's colleagues provided music for the Oratorio's exercises, e.g. G. F. Anerio (*Teatro armonico*, 1619) and Giovanni Animuccia: see Damilano, *Ancina;* Ponnelle and Bordet, *Neri.*

21. See Giazotto, *Quattro secoli*, p. v ff and ibid, "Storia dell'Accademia Nazionale di S. Cecilia," *SM*, i (1972), no. 2, pp. 237-284.

22. *RISM* 1589[7].

23. *RISM* 1585[29].

24. Pastor, *Popes*, xix. 26. Rota's dedication is reproduced in Gaspari, *Catalogo*, iii. 164.

25. Dedication reproduced in Gaspari, *Catalogo*, iii. 158. Raval also mentions a "Sig. Cavaliere del liuto," Scipione Dentice, and Scipione Stella. Michele Montalto Peretti was brother of Flavia Peretti, nephew of Felice Peretti (Sixtus V, d. 1590).

26. To Scipione Gonzaga Marenzio dedicated the *Motectorum pro festis totius anni* (1585), reproduced in *Opera*, ii (ed. Jackson). For further information on Scipione Gonzaga, see Princivalli, *Tasso nella vita*, pp. 223-238.

27. See appendix IV, note to Strozzi.

28. See especially the madrigal cycle by Giovanni Animuccia of 1565 (*NV*, i, no. 85) and its resetting in Dragoni's *II a 5* (1575). The interest in Strozzi on the part of Roman composers may be due to the presence there of Ferdinando de' Medici, who moved there in 1563.

29. *RISM* 1586[11]; cf. *IV a 5* (1584), no. 7.

30. But see Butchart, *The madrigal in Florence* (unpublished thesis).

31. "Luxuriant" is the epithet used by Newcomb in *Musica secreta* (unpublished thesis).

32. The *concerto delle donne* was never made up of the three singing ladies mentioned by Solerti (*Ferrara e la corte*, pp. 129-140) and Einstein (*Madrigal*, ii. 825 ff). There is however undeniable evidence of a trio forming within the *concerto:* Girolamo Merenda in his chronicle of 1596 mentions Laura Peperara, Livia d'Arco and Anna Guarini (see Newcomb, *Musica secreta*, p. 7 ff). This is corroborated by Piccioli, *Prose tiberine* (1597), p. 146, who mentions the three ladies under their married names: "la dolcissima Laura Turca, la celeste Livia Bevilacqua, & la rubiconda Anna Trotta." (The canzonet they sing is on p. 147 of the *Prose*.)

33. Newcomb, *Musica secreta,* p. 175.

34. Published in Ferrara by Vittorio Baldini, the ducal publisher (*RISM* 1582⁵ and 1583³).

35. Newcomb, "Three anthologies . . . ," *RIDM* x (1975), 334 ff.

36. Hence the pun "Laura"/"lauro" in the titles of the two collections.

37. Newcomb, art. cit., p. 366 ff.

38. In 1581 Marenzio had already dedicated his *II a 5* to the Duke of Ferrara shortly after his visit to that city; also dating from that year is the *I a 6,* dedicated to the Duke's sister.

39. The title is perhaps derived from the passage in Sannazaro's *Arcadia* beginning "I lieti amanti e le fanciulle tenere": cf. Marenzio, *I a 4,* (1585), no. 16.

40. Marenzio's piece falls in eighth position *(Falsa credenza havete).*

41. *II a 6* (1584), no 12: *Opera,* iv (ed. Meier), 190-194. One of the Ferrarese, Alberto L'Occa, goes as far as paraphrasing the first 4 lines of Marenzio's text: cf. Marenzio: " 'Filli mia bella, a Dio;'/'Caro mio Tirsi, a Dio, poichè 'l ciel vuole,'/Dicea sovr'Arno all'apparir del sole/Pastor afflitto, afflitta pastorella' with L'Occa: " ' A Dio, mio dolce Aminta;'/'Bella mia Silvia, a Dio,'/Disse sovra un bel rio/Pastor afflitto, afflitta pastorella."

42. The dedication is signed by the Ferrarese composer Nicoletti on 29 February 1592.

43. See Tinto, *Verona,* pp. 389-90, quoted by Lockwood, *Counter-Reformation,* p. 68, and Ledbetter, in Marenzio, *Secular Works,* vii, pp. xiv-xv.

44. Turrini, *Accademia,* p. 262.

45. ". . . inasmuch as I have aimed, through the imitation of the words and the propriety of the style, at a sombre gravity (so to speak), which will perhaps be far more pleasing to connoisseurs like you and to your most virtuoso ensemble." Translation quoted from Marenzio, *Secular Works,* vii (ed. Ledbetter), introduction, p. xvi.

46. Duke Alfonso d'Este married Margherita, daughter of Duke Gugliemo Gonzaga, in 1579. For details of music written by Marenzio for Margherita, see appendix II,notes to *VI a 6* (1599), nos. 1, 4, and 5.

47. Ledbetter, *Marenzio,* p. 52.

48. The *Spirituali* (1584) and the *I a 5* (1585) were first printed in Rome by Alessandro Gardano.

49. *Donna bella e crudele,* a madrigal with a text by Nannini, then a resident of Venice. There are some important variants from the published version in Nannini's *Rime* (1547); we may conclude that Marenzio was working from a manuscript of Venetian provenance.

50. The organization of the *Musica spirituale* is noteworthy: almost the whole collection is devoted to two strophic poems, each composer contributing one strophe of each. The earlier strophes are set by older composers, the later ones by younger; Marenzio is in eleventh place out of fifteen composers mainly from the Veneto.

51. The patron (and bridegroom) is the Venetian, Leonardo Sanudo, whose bride is apostrophized at the end of each poem with the words "Viva la bella Dori." Doris is the wife of the sea God Nereus, a maritime symbol appropriate for a Venetian patron. (*Kleiner Pauly,* ii. 144.) The anthology is transcribed in Powley, *Dori* (unpublished thesis).

52. Chater, 'Fonti', *RIDM,* xiii (1978), 61-62; see also appendix II, note to *I a 5* (1580), no. 1, and appendix IV, note to Pasqualino.

53. To whom Marenzio dedicated the *IV a 5* (1584), *V a 6* (1591) and *VIII a 5* (1598).

54. As in appendix II, note to *V a 6* (1591), No. 6.

55. E.g. *I a 6* (1581), no. 1 (an acrostic).

56. E.g. *I a 4, 5, 6* (1588), no. 11 and the pieces mentioned in Chater, 'Fonti', *RIDM* xiii (1978), 65-66.

Chapter 2

1. Bianconi, " 'Ah dolente partita': espressione ed artificio," *SM,* iii (1974), 105-130. This article compares settings of G. B. Guarini's *Pastor fido,* iii. 3 (lines 498-505). See appendix II, note to *VI a 5* (1594), no. 7.

2. Haar, "Self-consciousness in 16th-century music," *SM,* iii (1974), 219-232.

3. See above, chapter 1, note 45.

4. Nos. 4 and 7.

5. No. 4, b. 141 ff and no. 7, b. 45.

6. G. C. Monteverdi's *Declaratione,* published with his brother's *Scherzi musicali* (1607), includes Marenzio's name along with those of Rore, Ingegneri, Wert, Luzzaschi, Peri, and Caccini as belonging to the Seconda Prattica, where the "oration" is mistress of the "harmony." For a facsimile reproduction, see Monteverdi, *Opere,* x. 70; tr. in Strunk, *Source readings,* p. 408.

7. Cf. Rore, *Opere,* iv. 80-81 and Marenzio, *IX a 5* (1599), no. 13: *Ten madrigals,* ed. Arnold, pp. 72-79.

8. See for example appendix II, notes to *I a 4* (1585), no. 13.

9. Nuernberger, *Rore* (unpublished thesis), p. 207 ff. and Meier, in Rore, *Opera* iv, introduction, p. iii.

10. Marenzio's model in Ex. 3(b) is a piece which exists also with an attribution to Ingegneri: see Meier, in Rore, *Opera,* v, introduction, p. x.

11. My observations are based solely on an examination of Contino's *I a 5* (1560) and the pieces found in *RISM* 1569[20].

12. See appendix II, note to *V a 5* (1585), no. 13.

13. Ingegneri was in Cremona from 1568 at the latest and became *maestro di cappella* at the cathedral in 1581. See Engel, in *MGG,* vi. col. 1210.

14. *Dolorosi martir,* set by Ingegneri in his *III a 5* (1580); modern repr. by G. Cesari in IMAMI, vi. 127-130. Marenzio's resetting is no. 6 of the *I a 5* (1580).

15. The date on which Ingegneri signed the dedication of his *III a 5* was 25 February 1580; Marenzio's dedication dates from 8 August of the same year.

16. For details of this and other settings, see appendix II, note to *I a 5* (1580), no. 6. The poem survives only in a Neapolitan MS; Monte, who was probably active in Naples in 1542-1554, must have obtained a copy of the poem during his stay there. (See Nuten, in *MGG,* ix. col. 489.)

17. Cf. Ingegneri, b.11 ff, quinto and bass, with Marenzio, b.9 (quinto) and b.11 (tenor).

18. Bars 15-18.

19. Cf. Ingegneri, b.24 ff. Both composers here use chromaticism and triple time at this point.

20. Cf. Einstein, *Madrigal*, ii.477.

21. I-Bc, *S-309*. The single part-book carries Marenzio's signature; reproduced in *Werke*, ii.

22. Both Lassus and Marenzio had a predilection for setting the separate stanzas of Petrarch's sestina, *Mia benigna fortuna*. Thus Lassus sets the first 2 stanzas separately in his *I a 5*. The eleventh stanza, *Se sì alto pon gir* (Lassus, *III a 5*, 1563), was reset by Marenzio in the *IX a 5* (1599), while both composers' settings of the seventh stanza, *Nessun visse giammai*, date from 1584; see appendix II, note to *II a 6* (1584), no. 2.

23. *II a 5* (1581), no. 10; 12th stanza of Petrarch's sestina, *Mia benigna fortuna*.

24. The text of the composition by Lassus is the sixth stanza of the *Canzoniere*, no. 214 (*Sestina VI*).

25. See below, note 50, and cf. note 46.

26. This figure is based on a count of the *capoversi* listed in *NV*, i, nos. 733-806 and my own researches.

27. *Madrigal*, ii.503.

28. Ibid, ii.510

29. Chapter 8, ex. 246.

30. Reproduced in *Works*, vii.32-37; cf. appendix II, note to Marenzio, *XI a 5* (1599), no. 8.

31. Cf. Wert, *Works*, vii.38-43 and Marenzio, *IV a 5* (1584), no. 1.

32. Mode 3 untransp.; barred C and the combination $C_1C_3C_4C_4F_4$.

33. "O sasso amato tanto, amaro tanto" ("O stone, at once so loved and yet so bitter"); cf. Wert, bb. 26-28 and Marenzio, bb. 38-40.

34. "Di color, di calor, di moto privo" ("Deprived of color, warmth and movement"): Wert, bb.8-10 and Marenzio, bb.12-15.

35. E.g. "Deh prendi questi piant'e questi baci" ("O take these tears and kisses"): bb. 14-16, 17-19. Cf. the false relations in bb. 17, 20, 24, and 27.

36. E.g.: "Ohimè," bb.35-36; "prendi," bb.75-77.

37. In Wert's *seconda parte* the *f*-chord near the opening is by contrast warm and hopeful sounding.

38. Though published only in 1587, the dialogue is first mentioned in Tasso's letters in 1585: see Pirrotta, "Note" in *Festschrift Ronga*, p. 557.

39. Tasso, *Opere*, ed. Maier, v.150.

40. Reprinted in Monte, *Opera*, x, musical supplement, pp. 1-10.

41. Marenzio, *IV a 6* (1587), no. 3.

42. Perhaps in Florence in 1588-1589 during the preparation of the *intermedi* of 1589.

43. See below, note 46.

44. *Introduction*, p. 180.

45. Quoted in Strunk, *Source readings*, p. 335.

46. "In a short space of time musical tastes changed and there appeared the compositions of Luca Marenzio and Ruggiero Giovanelli, of a new and delightful inventiveness ... the excellence of which consisted in a new melodic style pleasing to the ear, with some easy fugues lacking in unusual artifice." From Giustiniani's *Discorso* (1628), as reprinted in Solerti, *Origine*, p. 106. The word "aria" may be translated as "air," "melody," or else "manner," "style"; we may assume both meanings are implied. For further discussion of the word "aria" see Pirrotta, "Early opera and aria," in *Festschrift Grout*, p. 57 ff and the *Harvard Dictionary*, article "Aria," pp. 51-52.

47. G.B. Doni, *Lyra Barberina*, ii.17 (reprinted in Solerti, *Origine*, pp. 211-212), and ii.24.

48. This passage has been quoted and commented on by Ledbetter, *Marenzio*, p. 107 ff; Cavicchi, in Luzzaschi, *Madrigali*, introduction, p. 20 ff; Degrada, "Dante e la musica," *Chigiana*, xxii (1965), 268 ff.

49. Della Valle praises *Liquide perle* for "certe sue grazie" ("certain graceful touches"); see *Della musica dell'età nostra* as reprinted in Solerti, *Origini*, p. 170.

50. See passage by Giustiniani quoted above, note 46.

51. The text of which is quoted in Einstein, ii.615. Pallavicino's madrigal is actually a resetting of a madrigal set twice previously. For more details, see appendix II, note to *I a 5* (1580), no. 1.

52. See chapter 5, ex. 123 ff.

53. See chapter 5, ex. 110.

54. First printed in *RISM* 1577[7], also the first anthology to contain a composition by Marenzio; reprinted in Torchi, *Arte musicale*, i.387-392.

55 In *Di Cipriano* [Rore] et Annibale [Padovano] Madregali a quatro; reprinted in Torchi, *Arte musicale*, i.367-370.

56. See chapter 5, para. 6.

57. Similar texts were set by Marenzio: *Se bramate chio mora (IV a 6*, 1587, no. 1) and *Voi bramate chio mora (VI a 5*, 1594, no. 14).

58. Reproduced in Hol, *Vecchi*, Musical App., p. 12, first system, b.2 ff. For the IV-V-I progression, cf. Marenzio, *III a 5* (1582), no.4, b.26 ff; the reiterated cries for "vendetta" ("vengeance") also reappear in Marenzio [ex. 14].

59. Einstein, *Madrigal*, ii.593-606.

60. The phrase means: "My heart nearly died." Palestrina's music quotes the opening phrase of Wert's *Chi salirà per me* ("Who will ascend for me"). Cf. Palestrina, *Opere*, xxxi.44 and Wert, *Works*, xv.62.

61. *RISM* 1574[4]; reproduced in Torchi, *Arte musicale*, i.293-298.

62. Cf. Marenzio, *II a 5* (1581), no. 12.

63. In this respect Macque anticipates what Newcomb (*Madrigal, passim)* calls the "luxuriant" style prevalent at the Ferrarese court in the early 1580's. Indeed, the presence of the three outstanding Roman madrigalists, Macque, Marenzio, and Giovanelli in both the Ferrarese anthologies *RISM* 1582[5] and 1583[10], clearly demonstrates the broadly common aims shared by the Roman and Ferrarese composers at this time.

64. The original ode is edited and translated into English by J. Michie in *The odes of Horace,* pp. 170-173. For further details, see appendix II, note to *RISM* 1582⁴. Movements by Macque and Marenzio transcribed in volume II of this study.

65. Cf. Marenzio b.43 ff and Macque, b.57 ff. Alamanni's paraphrase of lines 4-5 of the fourth stanza reads: "Per cui por l'alma, e'l core/ Bramo ad ogni hor, ma me n'ha privo Amore" ("For whom I long to give my soul and my heart; but Love has deprived me of them"). Macque's alteration, though it damages Alamanni's verse structure, restores Horace's meaning: "Pro quo bis patiar mori,/Si parcent puero fata superstiti" ("For whom I would gladly suffer death twice, if Fate would spare my darling boy"). Its meaning echoes that of the final couplet of the previous stanza.

66. Einstein, *Madrigal,* ii.608 ff.

67. The author is Alessandro Guarini, son of the author of *Il pastor fido.* The letter is printed in A. Guarini, *Prose* (1611), p. 142, together with a letter to Luzzaschi, and reprinted by Cavicchi in Luzzaschi, *Madrigali,* introduction, pp. 12-13. The quotations made below are from the slightly different version in Luzzaschi's *VI a 5* (1596), the only copy of which came to light after Cavicchi's publication.

68. Haar, "Self-consciousness in 16th-century music," p. 225 ff.

69. "...new techniques and a new inventiveness sweeter and more graceful than the accustomed ... from which they have formed a new manner which, not only for its novelty, but also for its exquisite artifice, is capable of pleasing, and drawing universal acclaim."

70. The emphasis on novelty in the above passage foreshadows Giustiniani's *Discorso,* referred to above.

71. "[The musician] weeps, if the verse weeps, laughs, if it laughs, if it runs, stands still, prays, denies, shouts, is silent, lives, dies, all these affects and effects are expressed by him with such vivacity ..."

72. The virtuoso singing style is almost totally absent from the *I a 4,5,6* of 1588; it returns briefly in the *V a 6* (1591), then is gradually transformed in the 1590's.

73. Some of these are described in Newcomb's historical survey in *Musica secreta,* chapter 4 (see especially p. 130 ff).

74. See Chater, "Castelletti," *SM,* viii (1979), 85-148.

75. Published a year before Marenzio's setting (and a year before the first published edition of Castelletti's comedy), in the *I a 5* (1586); it is scored for eight voices.

76. See above, notes 46 and 49.

77. But probably written by 1587: see appendix II, note to *V a 6* (1591), no. 9.

78. The three compositions are transcribed by H.B. Lincoln in his edition of this anthology on pp. 8-13 (Bertani), 26-33 (Giovanelli), and 56-63 (Marenzio).

79. The poem, a madrigal by the Brescian soldier and statesman Antonio Martinengo, describes Hero's attempt to swim the Hellespont in order to reach Leander.

80. Double and triple counterpoint also characterize the endings of the settings by Morsolino (p. 120, b.63 ff) and Virchi (p. 82, b.54 ff).

Chapter 3

1. *Madrigal,* ii. 608-688. The alphabetical list in Engel, *Marenzio,* pp. 225-234, has nothing new to contribute except further errors. A more accurate list appears appended to the article on Marenzio by Jackson and Ledbetter in the new *Grove.* The chronological list of Marenzio's madrigals in this study (see appendix II) is an expanded version of the one in Chater, "Fonti poetiche," *RIDM,* xiii (1978), 84-103.

2. In his *Prose della volgar lingua* (1525); Bembo's explorations in the field of word sounds and their affective significance influenced the development of the early madrigal, according to Mace, "Bembo," *MQ,* lv(1969), 65-86.

3. For further bibliographical references, see appendix IV, note to Petrarch.

4. Morley, *Introduction,* p. 180.

5. Wilkins, *The makings of the Canzoniere.*

6. The traditional dividing line is between nos. 266 and 267. However Wilkins, *The makings,* p. 190 ff, maintains that Petrarch's original intention was to begin the second part with the canzone, *I'vo pensando* (no. 264).

7. It has been pointed out that Petrarch's symmetrical phrase structures and rhythms follow closely the recommendation of the ancient rhetoricians, especially Cicero (Friedrich, *Epochen,* p. 177).

8. Quadrio, *Storia,* ii.422, admires the poem "quando per variazione di formola, e quando per mutazion di concetti" ("as much for its varied formulae as for its transformed conceits").

9. I.e. modes with the minor third above the final. The phrygian is used in *O voi che sospirate, Ov'è condotto, Amor i ho,* and *Crudele acerba.*

10. For bibliography of Petrarchism, see appendix IV, note to Petrarch.

11. *Introduction,* p. 172.

12. Ibid, pp. 172 and 180. (For further comment, see Chater, "Castelletti," p. 115, note 86.)

13. For further details, see appendix II, notes to *II a 5* (1581), no.15 and *IV a 5* (1584), no. 9.

14. See chapter 2.

15. *I a 4* (1585), no. 13.

16. In the ensuing discussion, capital letters stand for rhymes at the end of hendescasyllabic lines, lower-case letters for lines of 7 syllables (*settenari).* This is the system used in Elwert, *Versificazione* and elsewhere.

17. Pelaez, in *EISLA,* viii.812-813.

18. As in the ballata; in the second *piede,* the order in which the rhymes of the first *piede* are to be recapitulated is free, while the order of line lengths must follow that of the first *piede.*

19. *I a 4,5,6* (1588), no. 8, with text by Sannazaro.

20. Set by Marenzio in the *II a 5* (1581), no. 16.

21. E.g. *V a 6* (1591), no.12, and *I a 4,5,6* (1588), nos. 8 and 12.

22. *Spirituali* (1584), no 12, and *V a 5* (1585), no. 1; *VI a 6* (1595), no. 2.

23. Wilkins, *The invention of the sonnet,* p. 38.

24. But see *V a 5* (1585), no. 10.

25. E.g. cde/cde and cdc/dcd, both frequently found in Petrarch. The form cde/edc is found in *I a 4,5,6* (1588), no 4 (Della Casa), *I a 4* (1585), no. 19 (Tasso) and *IV a 6* (1587), no. 11 (also by Tasso).

26. Regarding the use of rhetoric in the sonnet, see Friedrich, *Epochen,* p. 167 ff and Mönch, *Sonett,* p. 63 ff.

27. *I a 4,5,6* (1588), no. 2

28. *IX a 5* (1599), no. 6; text by Petrarch.

29. *I a 6* (1581), no. 17 and *IX a 5* (1599), no. 8; texts by Petrarch.

30. *I a 4,5,6* (1588), no. 4

31. See below, note 105.

32. "It is a harsh and wicked costume for a fair lady to arm herself with scorn and break another's life midway through its course, like a hard rock."

33. From one of which Marenzio selected the passage set in the *IX a 5* (1599), no. 3.

34. Elwert, *Versificazione,* p. 144.

35. *VI a 6* (1595), no. 3.

36. Elwert, *Versificazione* p. 134 ff. The three madrigals set by Marenzio are *Hor vedi, Amor* (ABB/ABB/BCC), *Nova angeletta* (ABC/ABC/DD) and *Non al suo amante* (ABA/BCB/CC)—nos. 5,6 and 8.

37. See appendix II, note to *II a 6* (1584), no. 15.

38. Elwert, *Versificazione,* p. 145 ff.

39. See *II a 5* (1581), no 11; *II a 6* (1584), no. 1; *I a 4,5,6* (1588), no. 3.

40. Printed in the poetic anthology, *Domenichi,* i (1546), 195-203; see *I a 6* (1581), nos. 5 and 10; *IV a 5* (1584), no. 9.

41. *III a 6* (1585), no 15; text by Molza.

42. Thus anticipating Guarini's *Pastor fido,* iii.2-3, where Mirtillo disguises himself as a girl in order to steal a kiss from Amarilli.

43. *RISM* 1593[3]; Marenzio contributes the twelfth stanza.

44. Cf. *II a 6* (1584), no. 14 (Tasso) with rhyme scheme aBa/bAb/cC; *I a 6* (1581), no. 16 with scheme aB/aB/CddE and *II a 6,* no. 5 (Cini) with scheme àB/aB/bcC.

45. aB/*Ba*/cC, dE/eD/fF, gH/hG/iI. Italic letters represent deviations from regular patterns.

46. *IV a 6* (1587), no. 9.

47. *V a 5* (1585), no. 11. The four stanzas have the form aa/bB/cC; the *commiato* introduces new rhymes: yyzZ.

48. Cf. Petrarch, *S'i'l dissi mai (Canzoniere,* no. 206) and the *Vergine* canzone (no. 366) and Guarini's *Canzon de' baci (V a 6,* 1591, no. 12).

49. *RISM* 1582[4]. There are six stanzas altogether; the one set by Marenzio is the third. For transcription, see volume II of this study.

50. Except the fifth, which has the form aBb*A*A.

51. Many of these are contained in Federzoni, *Orazio*.

52. Tasso's description of his odes in the dedication of his *Rime* (1560) could apply equally to Alamanni: "fatti ad imitatione de buoni Poeti Greci, e Latini, non quanto al verso [...] ma ne l'inventione, ne l'ordine, e ne le figure del parlare" ("Made an imitation of good Greek and Latin poets, not so much as regards the line ... but the invention, disposition and figures of speech").

53. See Cardamone, "Forme musicali," *RIDM* xii (1977), 72.

54. Making aBB/cDD/eFF: see *V a 5* (1585), no. 14.

55. E.g. *I a 5* (1580), no. 7 (abC/abC) and *VII a 5* (1595), no. 8 (aBB/aCC).

56. Cf. Luzzaschi, *VI a 5* (1596), dedication: "[il] Madriale, che solo per la Musica par trovato ..." ("[the] madrigal, which seems to have been invented only for music").

57. A similar conclusion was reached by Harran, "Verse types," *MQ,* xxii (1969), 27-53, and Schulz-Buschhaus, *Madrigal.*

58. *I a 4* (1585), no. 8.

59. *I a 5* (1580), no. 4.

60. The rhyme scheme of *Nova angeletta* is widespread: *III a 5* (1582), no. 2 (ABc/abc/dD), *III a 6* (1585), no. 4 and *VII a 5* (1595), no. 5 (abC/abC/dD). The two last are both by Tasso, who also imitates the rhyme scheme of *Hor vedi Amor (Canzoniere*, no. 121) in *Io vidi già (II a 6,* 1584, no. 13): Abb/Acc/Cdd. Other madrigals reflect the tercet structure of the *Trecento* in a more general sense: *II a 6* (1584), no. 14 (aBa/bAb/cC), *V a 6* (1591), no. 9 (abB cdD ceE), and *IX a 5* (1599), no. 11 (aBB/cDD/cEE). Also found are truncated forms: abC/abC in *I a 5* (1580), no.7; aBB/aCC in *VII a 5* (1595), no.8 (cf Harran, op.cit., p. 37 ff and p. 40).

61. Other irregular canzone stanzas using three rhymes and six lines include *I a 5* (1580), no. 8, *I a 6* (1581), nos. 3, 8 and 13, *II a 5* (1581), no. 14 and *IV a 6* (1587), no. 12. In appendix II such texts have been classed as madrigals.

62. *I a 6* (1581), no. 7 (Ab/*bA*/aCC) and no. 15 (AB/*bA*/aCC), *III a 6* (1585), no. 12 (Ab/*aB*/bcDeE) and no. 16 (AB/*bA*/acC).

63. *II a 5* (1581), no. 3; text by Ariosto.

64. Schulz-Buschhaus, *Madrigal*, p. 59 ff.

65. In whose *Diporti* (1550) the madrigal and *strambotto* are described as "vago d'arguzia e di invenzione, sì come apunto vuole apparire il motto" ("adorned with wit and invention, exactly as an epigram should seem"). Quoted from edition of G. Gigli and F. Nicolini, p. 177.

66. "Love scattered crystal pearls from my eyes as the first-fruits of my ardour; but my heart, alas, burnt with a stronger flame. Ah, see how only the first burning pain sufficed to kill me." The poem on which it is based is no. 55 of the *Canzoniere (Quel foco ch'i' pensai che fosse spento).*

67. For further details, see Chater, "Castelletti," *SM,* viii(1979), 104.

68. "Ah happy fate, to live in a flame and not to perish." Like *Liquide perle, Qual vive Salamandra* appears to be an abbreviated version of a pre-existing poem, a sonnet by Giusto de' Conti (see app.II, note to *I a 6* (1584), no. 4).

69. The distinction between "melic" and "epigrammatic" is made by Schulz-Buschhaus, *Madrigal,* chapters 4 and 5.

70. "From the sweet rose lips blow still breath, now sweet breath, and with Love instill for yourself a thousand diverse and new pleasures; shower sweetly breathing, exhale sweetly breathing from the angelic mouth whence I sigh, whence I alone breath; and if you do not give them to me, I will steal them." *III a 6,* (1585), no. 12. Transcribed in volume II of this study.

71. For further details, see Sorrento's edition of the *Rime,* p. 24, note 2.

72. *III a 6* (1585), no 14; *VI a 5* (1594), nos. 10 and 12.

73. *I a 6* (1581), no. 2.

74. *VI a 5,* no. 13.

75. *IV a 5,* no. 16.

76. First complete edition 1504: see Mauro, in his edition of the *Opere volgari,* "Nota sul testo," p. 427.

77. Ibid, p. 451.

78. Ibid, p. 427.

79. Borghini, *Umanista,* p. 209.

80. Leopold, "Madrigali sulle egloghe," *RIDM,* xiv (1979), 83 ff, points out the interest in Sannazaro on the part of musicians active in Rome, and, more particularly, the Accademia di Santa Cecilia. The author has appended a list of all settings of the poetry and the *Arcadia* of Sannazaro: see art.cit., pp. 102-127.

81. A point made by Einstein, *Madrigal,* ii.614, with reference to Domenichi's translation of Polybius.

82. Both the Sannazaro and the Petrarch were set by Marenzio: see appendix II, notes to *I a 4* (1585), nos. 5 and 15.

83. *II a 5* (1581), *III a 5* (1582), *I a 4* (1585), and the *I a 4,5,6* (1588).

84. *Tirrhenia mia (Arcadia,* II, 109-116) set in Rinaldo del Mel's *II a 5* (1584); reproduced in CEMF, xxi (facsimile reproduction of *RISM* 1585[19]). Del Mel arrived in Rome c. 1580 and remained there until 1584.

85. Also at the opening of the *ottava* setting, *Strider faceva (II a 5,* 1581, no. 11).

86. Reflecting the seniority of Elenco, the "bifolco antico" ("old rustic") to Ofelia, the "caprar novello" ("young goatherd"); Cf Arcadia ix, lines 1 and 4.

87. No. 2, 9 and 12. The poems in question are nos. 95, 96 and 94 of the second part of the *Rime.*

88. It is notable that Marenzio sets two sonnets by Sannazaro as fragments (*V a 5,* 1585, no. 10 and *I a 4,5,6,* 1588, no. 13), whereas Petrarch's sonnets are always set complete.

89. Cf. *I a 5* (1580), no. 4 and *RISM* 1582[4].

90. Cf. the Petrarchan sonnet, *Del cibo* (set in the *II a 6,* 1584, no 11) and the canzone, *Quando il soave,* of which Marenzio set the commiato *(II a 5,* 1581, no. 12).

91. *I a 4* (1585), no. 8: see chapter 7, ex. 190 (b).

92. *III a 5* (1581), no. 10 (text by Petrarch) and *I a 4,5,6* (1588), no 14 (text by Sannazaro).

93. Chater, "Fonti poetiche," *RIDM* xiii (1978), p. 72 ff.

94. "Evidently little interest." See Pirrotta, "Note," in *Festschrift Ronga,* p. 567.

95. Einstein, *Madrigal,* i.219 ff. and ii.663.

96. Pirrotta, "Note," pp. 557 ff. and 563-564; cf. Ledbetter, *Marenzio,* p. 130 ff. and Marenzio, *Secular Works,* vii (ed. Ledbetter), introduction, p.xvii ff.

97. Fiesco, *Musica nova* (*NV,* i, no. 985); Wert, *VI a 5 (Works,* vi); Isnardi, *II a 5.*

98. The poetry addressed to these two ladies is contained in the *Rime,* ed. Solerti, i, nos. 1-129 (Bendidio) and 130-204 (Peperara).

99. *Padre del cielo* (*Spirituali,* 1584, no. 5), *Su l'ampia fronte (III a 6,* 1585, no. 7) and *Arsi gran tempo (IV a 6,* 1587, no. 11).

100. For Manuzio's misattributions see *I a 5* (1580), no. 5 and *V a 5* (1591), no. 12 (both by Guarini) and *I a 6* (1587), no. 11 (by Strozzi).

101. *Sul carro de la mente (I a 4,* 1585, no. 19).

102. *Nel dolce seno* (no. 8) and *Amatemi ben mio* (no. 9).

103. *Se tu mi lasci RISM* 1583[11]), *Io vidi già* and *Vita de la mia vita (II a 6,* 1584, nos. 13 and 14.)

104. "Tasso's poetry tends towards light as towards music." Fubini, *Rinascimento,* p. 265.

105. In the early part of the dialogue Tasso compares a sonnet by Della Casa with one by Coppetta, in which Tasso prefers the former (*Opere,* ed. Maier, v.90-98).

106. Di Benedetto, *Tasso, minori e minimi,* p. 77 ff, points out that the metaphor of death is so vivid that for a long time it was taken literally. For further references, see appendix II, note to *V a 6* (1591), no. 8.

107. E.G. *Arsi gran tempo (IV a 6,* 1587, no. 11): canto, f-sharp f'', alto, f to b'-flat; quinto, f to b'-flat; tenor, B-flat to g'; sesto, c-g' bass, D-c'.

108. Einstein, "Narrative rhythm," *MQ,* xxix (1943), 475-484, The "narrative rhythm" is used by Marenzio to suggest resolution or vigorous activity and often appears at the opening of brisk and cheerful madrigals where the narrative or descriptive elements exceed the discursive (e.g. *I a 6,* 1581, nos. 6, 8 and 16; *II a 5,* 1581, nos. 8 and 9; *II a 6,* 1584, no. 7; *IV a 5,* 1584, nos. 9 - 12; *VI a 5,* 1594, no. 13.).

109. The setting may in fact be Marenzio's earliest surviving madrigal. In his edition of the *Rime,* iii, note to no. 553, Solerti dates the poem 1576, the year Leonora Sanvitale left Rome for Ferrara, where she died in 1581. Marenzio could have obtained the poem from Baldini's *Scielta delle rime* or Marenzio's *Seconda parte delle rime,* both printed in 1582, but for two striking variants: "tua" and "tuo" have replaced "sua" and "suo" (lines 11 and 12). This direct apostrophization suggests that Marenzio composed the sonnet while Sanvitale was still alive—perhaps in 1576, the year of her departure from Rome.

110. See reproduction by Engel, *Lied,* p. 31, 2nd system, bb.2-3, and 3rd system, bb.1-2; p. 32, 1st system, bb.1-4; comparable are the repeated notes on the equally emotive word "perfido" ("faithless") on p. 31, 1st system, b.3.

111. But see appendix II, note to *IV a 5* (1585), no. 1.

112. *RISM* 1583[10] (see appendix II).

113. See especially *Quel lauro che fu* (*RISM* 1582[5]) and *Cantai già lieto (II a 6*, 1584, no. 10).

114. Rossi, *Guarini*, pp. 17-18.

115. Ibid, p. 21.

116. See note 97, above.

117. Rossi, *op.cit.*, p. 52 ff.

118. It should be remembered that the *Pastor fido* settings, too, are scored *a 5*.

119. Tasso's misgivings are voiced in *La Cavaletta:* "Dunque il nostro poeta [...] si guarderà di non cadere ne le arguzie de' sofisti, le quali hanno ripiene molte composizioni che piacciono al mondo." ("So our poet ... must beware of lapsing into sophistical ingenuity of which many fashionable compositions are full.") Quoted from Tasso, *Opere*, ed. Maier, v., 151.

120. Highly revealing is a letter to Cornelio Bentivoglio (25 January 1582) in which Guarini describes his position as court poet in succession to Tasso and compares himself to an actor who is obliged to pretend to feel emotions he does not actually feel (*Lettere*, ed. A. Michele, Venice: G.B. Ciotti 1603, p. 96).

121. Later shoretened to *O che soave bacio:* for further details, see appendix II, note to *IV a 6* (1587), no. 14.

122. Here the use of the mournful phrygian is combined with lively rhythms and textures uncharacteristic of that mode, indicating that the dying is figurative, not literal (cf. the first line, which means "Thyrsis desired to die").

123. "Then said the shepherd, with a sigh of love..."

124. Marenzio varies from the 1598 edition in lines 3, 8, 9, 10, 12, 16, 17, and 18. The settings by Caimo, A. Gabrieli, Malvezzi, Monte, and Wert are all of versions slightly different from Marenzio's. Of all the settings consulted, only Castro's and Pallavicino's are based on exactly the same text as Marenzio. Meldert's text differs from Marenzio's in only two places (lines 10 and 18). It is remarkable that the last three lines (the epigrammatic point) remain unchanged in all the versions consulted.

125. Meldert, *I a 5* (1578).

126. Pallavicino, *I a 5* (1581).

127. *VIII a 5* (1598), nos. 7 and 8; *IX a 5* (1599), nos. 11, 12 and 14.

128. "Lady, you believe you have taken my heart away" (*Opere*, ed. Guglielminetti, p. 294). Mention should also be made of *O, come vaneggiate*, set by Wert in 1588, probably the version intermediate between the one used by Marenzio and the definitive version (MacClintock, *Wert*, p. 61). In particular, lines 6-7 of *O, come vaneggiate* resemble Marenzio's line 6: "D'esser tanto più vivo/Quanto di voi son privo" ("To be more alive the more I am deprived of you").

129. "Lady, you believe falsely if you think that I am no longer alive because I do not love you anymore. On the contrary, I will die if I love you, because I am alive as long as I am not in love with you; and if bearing you love was always and is the reason for others' death, dead is he who loves you and lives in a harsh predicament, for he certainly cannot be alive who loves death."

130. Guarini, *Opere*, ed. Guglielminetti, p. 294; cf Tasso's reply, *Ardi e gela* in Solerti's editon of the *Rime*, ii, no. 418. Equally scornful is Tasso's sonnet, *Arsi gran tempo (IV a 6*, 1587, no. 11).

Chapter 4

1. See Carapetyan, "Imitazione," *JRBM,* (1946), 59-60.

2. This statement is not directly verifiable according to 16th-century aesthetics, but may be easily inferred, for, as Carapetyan writes (art.cit., p. 59): "When Glareanus wrote of 'Ars perfecta, cui ut nihil addi potest,' he was appropriately referring to Josquin's work, and his concept of *ars perfecta* included *Vierstimmigkeit* as one characteristic of it." Later composers did "add" to this "perfect art," but their aesthetic aims changed in the process.

3. The same natural order which in Renaissance architecture is expressed through proportional devices such as the Golden Section (Wölfflin, *Renaissance and Baroque,* p. 65 ff).

4. *III a 6* (1585), no. 14: transcribed in volume II of this study.

5. *Madrigal,* ii.617; cf. bb. 4-6, 11-12, 79-82.

6. Bars 1 ff and 13 ff.

7. Bars 9-12 and 30-35.

8. In the ensuing discussion, "double canto," "double tenor," etc. indicate that the two voices share the same clef (and hence the same range). The extra voices are normally designated "quinto" and "sesto."

9. E.g. *I a 6* (1581), no. 13; II a 6 (1584), no. 12; *V a 6* (1591), nos. 1 and 4.

10. Nos. 11 and 12.

11. Nos. 1, 2, 4, 5, 6, 10, 11, 12 and 13.

12. Dragoni in his *IV a 5* (1594) frequently uses double and triple canto.

13. Marenzio never combines the two mensuration signs in one piece; it is therefore hard to believe that the barred-C notation represented an exact proportional equivalent vis-à-vis the normal mensuration. A similar conclusion is reached by Bennett in *Marenzio* (unpublished thesis) p. 127. In fact the minim in $\mathcal{C}$ is perhaps too fast if considered as equivalent to the crotchet in C , as theoretically it ought to be. The Dutch theorist Ban (in the *Zangh-Bloemzel,* introduction, p.vi) suggests that the note values in $\mathcal{C}$ should equal two-thirds (not half) the values in C . For practical purposes this is a useful if rough guide, not to be adhered to rigidly. For further references, see Bennett, loc.cit.

14. Glareanus, *Dodecachordon* (1547), bk.ii, chapter 6.

15. *Istitutioni,* bk.iv, chapter 10 ff (p. 379 ff).

16. Meier, *Tonarten,* pp. 22 ff, 64 ff, 69 ff.

17. *Il tesoro illuminato.* Aiguino's defence of the eight-tone system is on f.9^V ff.

18. D-Rp, MS *A.R. 774.* The two pieces transcribed by Raselius are *Occhi sereni e chiari (II a 6,* 1581, no. 11) and *Liquide perle (I a 5,* 1580, no. 1). They are used as illustrations of the mixolydian mode. (See Debes, *Merulo,* p. 97).

19. I-Bc, MS *C.30.*

20. "Of mingled cheerfulness and gravity," Vecchi, *Mostra delli tuoni* cit., p. 2.

21. See appendix II, note to *V a 6* (1591), no. 9.

22. E.g. the opening of *I a 5* (1580), no 11 and *IV a 5* (1584), no 2.

23. The significance of undulating themes is further discussed in chapter 5.

24. "...much in use because it is appropriate for sorrowful, plaintive words" (*Mostra*, p. 12).

25. "...apt for any kind of sombre-sounding words" (ibid., p. 12).

26. The term "perfect" is used in its modern sense, not that in which Zarlino uses it. See chapter 7, note 41.

27. *II a 6* (1584), no. 6: *Opera*, iv (ed. Meier), p. 140, b.6 (between alto and quinto) and b.13 (between alto and bass); cf *I a 5* (1580), no. 6, b.10, where a striking *e/f* clash is caused by interrupted cadences.

28. Zarlino, *Istitutioni*, bk.iv, chapters 22-23 (p. 401 ff) and chapter 30 (p. 415 ff). Cf. Meier, *Tonarten*, p. 90 ff.

29. *III a 5* (1582), no. 2 (mode 9 untransposed). Exclamations are a characteristic shared between phrygian, aeolian and hypoaeolian pieces [ex. 37].

30. "...apt for plaintive words, and ones threatening revenge" Vecchi, *Mostra* p. 21.

31. *I a 5* (1580), no. 8.

32. *I a 4,5,6* (1588), no. 3: *Secular Works*, vii (ed. Ledbetter), 12-15.

33. *RISM* 1586[10]; see above, chapter 3, note 128.

34. Printed as a separate piece in *Spirituali* (1584), no. 11; reprinted in *Ten madrigals*, ed. Arnold, pp. 64-71.

35. "...apt for modesty and for the comforting of troubled spirits" (op.cit., p.15).

36. "... very apt for lascivious compositions, as may be seen in Marenzio's madrigal *Spuntavan già"* (*I a 5*, 1580, no. 3) (op.cit., p. 17).

37. "suave, sweet, and also grave subjects" (op.cit., p. 18).

38. *III a 5* (1582), no. 5 (mode 7 untransposed).

39. *I a 4* (1585), no. 16 (mode 8 untransposed).

40. "Tanto più peggiora quanto più invetera" (*Arcadia*, vi, line 111).

41. "with words which could break stones" (b.26 ff).

42. "...apt for dancing and playful subjects" (*Mostra*, p. 22).

43. "...apt for triumph" (ibid, p. 23).

44. Nos. 4 and 5; cf. *Leggiadre ninfe (V a 6*, 1591, no. 2) and *Uscite, uscite Ninfe (RISM* 1591[23]), both in mode 12 transposed.

45. *RISM* 1583[10] (mode 12 untransposed); *prima parte* transcribed in volume II of this study.

46. *I a 4* (1585), no. 16 (mode 8 untransposed); see below, chapter 5.

47. *II a 5* (1581), no. 11 (mode 11 untransposed).

48. *III a 5* (1582), no. 14 (mode 12 transposed).

49. "A peasant lay" (b.29 ff).

50. Similarly, Alban Berg, in act II of *Wozzeck,* symbolizes the prosaic counting of money with a held *c*-major chord (Reich, *Berg*, p. 125).

51.　*Syntagma musicum,* iii.36.

52.　*V a 5* (1585), no. 7 (mode 6 untransposed).

53.　Bars 2 ff, 12 ff, 28 ff, 37 ff, 47 ff, and 53 ff.

54.　*II a 5* (1581), no. 6 (mode 12 untransposed).

55.　"Stubborn" (b.34).

56.　"Tremulous" (b.44).

57.　*IV a 5* (1584), no. 12 (mode 11 transposed), bb.12-18.

58.　Cf. the opening of *Al vago del mio sole,* quoted in ex. 39.

59.　*III a 6* (1585), no. 14 (mode 3 transposed), with *chiavette:* transcribed in volume II of this study.

60.　*IV a 5* (1584), no. 1 (mode 3 untransposed), with *chiavi naturali.*

61.　This conclusion is reached after some discussion in Bennett, *Marenzio,* p. 137 ff. It is now generally thought that the downward transpostion applied only in the case of church music, and that madrigals written in the *chiavette* were never intended for transposition. Morley's exhortation that composers should relate the choice of pitch to the mood of the text (*Introduction,* p. 166), is consistent with this supposition.

62.　The use of C₄ in the bass becomes less and less frequent, disappearing completely from the *V a 6* (1591) and after.

63.　Used only in *V a 5* (1585), no. 17. The key signature is with two flats, the final, *d.*

64.　*Mostra,* p. 24 ff.

65.　*Syntagma musicum,* iii.36.

66.　*I a 6* (1581), no. 6.

67.　Meier, *Tonarten,* p. 30.

68.　Similarly, modes 3 and 10 share similar ranges: $e'-e''$ and $e-e'$ $(a'-a''$ and $a-a'$ if transposed).

69.　Cf. ex. 32.

70.　For the purposes of analysis only the canto and tenor voices were consulted. This does not mean that irregularities do not occur in the other voices and for the same reasons.

71.　*I a 4,5,6* (1588), no. 5 (mode 2 transposed).

72.　*Secular Works,* vii (ed. Ledbetter), p. 28, b.33; p. 30, b.51.

73.　*II a 5* (1581), no. 10 (mode 3 untransposed), b.43.

74.　*III a 6* (1585), no. 14 (mode 3 transposed): transcribed in Vol.ii, pp. 27-33.

75.　*IV a 5* (1584), no. 1 (mode 3 untransposed).

76.　*III a 5* (1582), no. 4 (mode 12 untransposed), b.143.

77.　*Spirituali* (1584), no. 1 (mode 11 transposed): in Lechner, *Werke,* viii.170, b.38.

78.　*I a 5* (1585), no. 2 (mode 10 transposed).

79.　*IV a 5* (1585), no. 5 (mode 12 transposed), bb. 8 and 10.

80. *V a 5* (1585), no. 15 (mode 12 transposed), b.67. The high note here may also be connected with "gridar" ("shouting").

81. *III a 5* (1582), no. 4 (mode 12 untransposed), bb. 19 and 31.

82. *I a 5* (1580), no. 10 (mode 1 transposed).

83. *IV a 5* (1584), no. 2 (mode 1 untransposed).

84. *V a 5* (1585), no. 16 (mode 2 transposed), b.67.

85. *I a 4,5,6* (1588), no. 4 (mode 1 untransposed), *Secular Works,* vii (ed. Ledbetter), p. 18, b.37.

86. See Meier, *Tonarten,* p. 270 ff, 273 ff, and 276 ff.

87. *I a 4,5,6* (1588), no. 12 (mode 12 untransposed): *Secular Works,* vii (ed. Ledbetter), p. 93, b.4.

88. *I a 4,5,6* (1588), no. 12 (mode 12 untransposed): *Secular Works,* vii (ed. Ledbetter), pp. 100-101, b.54 ff.

89. *IV a 5* (1584), no. 4 (mode 12 transposed).

90. "Cadence outside the mode." See Meier, *Tonarten,* p. 233 ff. For more detailed discussion of irregular cadences, see below, chapter 7.

91. For a fuller discussion, see chapter 8.

Chapter 5

1.   *Istitutioni,* bk.iv, chapter 32 (p. 415 ff), tr. in Strunk, *Source readings,* p. 255 ff; cf. Morley's similar pronouncements, *Introduction,* pp. 177-178. Both passages are quoted in Bennett, *Marenzio* (unpublished thesis), pp. 41-42.

2.   See chapter 2, note 71.

3.   See above, note 1.

4.   Morley, *Introduction,* p. 172.

5.   It is not always easy to define the extent to which this "language" is of Marenzio's own making and how much of it is inherited from other composers. In the ensuing discussion, implicit comparisons with Marenzio's contemporaries will be made through inclusion of examples by other composers which resemble those by Marenzio. The reader is invited also to reflect on the similarity of some of the examples to those quoted from a much wider range of sources by Cooke in *The language of music,* 6th edn., London, 1968, chapter 3 ("Some basic terms of musical vocabulary") and on the highly developed system of pictorial representation also found in the music of J.S. Bach (see Schweitzer, *Bach,* ii, chapters 21-22: "Word and tone in Bach" and "The musical language of the cantatas").

6.   *Arte del contraponto,* p. 23 ff.

7.   The meaning "group of notes" can be inferred from Artusi's own example [ex. 47].

8.   See below, classifications 1-7.

9.   Classifications 8-12.

10. Classifications 13-16.

11. Classifications 17-18.

12. However, one cannot in reality draw a sharp distinction between the "inner" and "outer" worlds. Thus the descent into the tomb at the opening of *Giunto a la tomba (IV a 5*, 1584, no. 1), represented by a descending melody, has sombre emotional as well as purely physical connotations.

13. Cf. *VI a 6* (1595), no. 2, (*Giovane donna,* ed. Arnold, b.171 ff): "Seguirò l'ombra di quel dolce Lauro" ("I will follow the shadow of that sweet laurel").

14. E.g. *III a 5* (1582), no. 15: "Sì presso a voi, mio foco" ("So near to you, my flame").

15. *I a 5* (1580), no. 10, b.30 ff.

16. See chapter 8, ex. 252.

17. *IV a 5* (1584), no. 4.

18. *IV a 5* (1584), no. 1 (especially bass).

19. Particularly in modes 1 and 2: cf. chapter 4, exx. 32-33.

20. See chapter 9, ex. 274.

21. "Un huom selvaggio": *V a 5* (1585), no. 16, b.40 ff, bass.

22. *I a 5* (1580), no. 9, b.27: tenor and bass ascend an octave.

23. *III a 5* (1582), no. 6, b.1 ff: bass descends an octave.

24. E.g. *I a 5*, b.1 ff; ibid, no. 3, b.1 ff; ibid, no. 5, b.108 ff; *II a 5* (1581), nos. 3 and 4, b.1 ff.

25. See chapter 2, ex. 17.

26. *I a 5* (1580), no. 10, b.25 ff.

27. *III a 5* (1582), no. 15, b.53.

28. *IV a 5* (1584), no. 1, b.97.

29. *IV a 5* (1584), no. 2, b.21.

30. See classification 15, a,ii.

31. *III a 5* (1582), no. 8, b.41 ff; *V a 5* (1585), no. 2, b.16 ff.

32. E.g. on "Arno" in *II a 6* (1584), no. 10: *Opere,* iv, (ed. Meier), p. 191, b.17 ff.

33. *III a 5* (1582), no. 14, b.55 ff ("cicada"); *IV a 5* (1584), no. 2, b.12 ff ("grilli," meaning "grasshoppers").

34. See b.35 ff: "amore/Mi leva a volo" ("Love lifts me up on his wings").

35. Ex. 80(b) is in fact an example of a "transferred" melisma: see below section (e).

36. *III a 5* (1582), no. 12: "Occhi lucenti e belli ("transferred" melisma) ... Lieti, vaghi, superbi ..." ("Bright, beautiful eyes ... happy, fair, proud ...")

37. Cf. ex. 57.

38. As in notes 35 and 36 above.

39. When melismatic, they may resemble the examples quoted in classifications 8, c,i.

40. Zarlino, *Istitutioni,* bk.iv, chapter 33, rule 4 (p. 422), translated in Strunk, *Source readings,* p. 260.

41. *II a 5* (1581), no. 1, b.91 ff.

42. Cf. the phrase "Stravaganza d'Amore" [ex. 90].

43. *Istitutioni*, bk.iv, chapter 32 (p. 420), transcribed in Strunk, *Source readings*, p. 258.

44. *II a 5* (1581), no. 10, b.48 ff.

45. The "narrative rhythm." Cf. chapter 3, note 108.

46. In ex. 99(c), the "resolution" rhythm is immediately contrasted with the dotted rhythm symbolizing fear.

47. These have been listed in Bennett, *Marenzio*, p. 130; Bennett concludes that the overwhelming evidence is for a consistent transcription of all "tripla" passages in a "reduced sesquialtera," i.e. that notes in triple time lose a third of their value.

48. Here again, blackened notes lose a third of their value (Apel, *Notation*, p. 126 ff). For the expressive function of coloration, see third conclusion at the end of this chapter.

49. Vicentino, *Antica musica*, ff 33^V-34^r, distinguishes between the sadness of the minor third and the relatively cheerful major third.

50. *Considerationi musicali* (appended to the *Seconda parte dell'Artusi*), p. 30.

51. The syntactical function of cadences is discussed in chapter 7.

52. The so-called *clausulae peregrinae*.

53. Meier, *Tonarten*, p. 81 ff.

54. See below, classification 17, b.

55. Lowinsky, *Tonality*, p. 39 ff.

56. *Tonality*, p. 43 ff.

57. As for instance on the words "Il Mar s'acqueta" ("the sea becomes calm") in *II a 5* (1581), no. 15, b.30.

58. *V a 5* (1585), no. 7, b.28 ff, quoted in ex. 102.

59. See above, classification 7, c.

60. In both examples the use of naturals would have led to a breach in the *mi-contra-fa* rule; however, this does not mean that the accidentals are not endowed with an expressive function.

61. Quoted also in Steele, *Studies in Music*, iii (1969), 23.

62. As happens with the "Neapolitan" progression.

63. *Spirituali* (1584), no. 9; quoted in Arnold, *Marenzio*, p. 14. The prototype for this imitation of the chromatically ascending tetrachord is no doubt Rore's motet, *Calami sonum ferentes*, the opening of which is quoted in Kroyer, *Chromatik*, p. 67.

64. Caimo, *I a 4* (1564); reproduced by Einstein, *Italian madrigal*, iii.216-218 and Roche, *Penguin Book of Madrigals*, pp. 117-120.

65. Except in *Solo e pensoso* (*IX a 5*, 1599, no. 8), where an ascending chromatic line is followed by a chromatic descent. See Torchi, *Arte musicale*, ii.228.

66. *II a 5* (1581), no. 10 and *I a 4,5,6* (1588), no. 14.

67.   "May he (Death) for once change his former ways."

68.   "And you, O Fortune, change your cruel ways."

69.   *Secular Works*, vii (ed. Ledbetter), pp. 110-111, bb.7-19. The use of the cycle of fifths to symbolize the wheel of Fortune may be seen in Greiter's *Passibus ambiguis Fortuna*, a four-voice composition containing a cycle of descending fifths *f* ... *f*-flat: see Lowinsky, "Greiter," *MQ*, xlii (1956), 503 ff.

70.   *Secular Works*, vii, pp 113-116, bb.33-50.

71.   Bars 4, 9, and 15.

72.   Bars 35-41. This passage has been variously quoted and commented on, notably by Winterfeld, *J. Gabrieli*, p. 87 ff; Kroyer, *Chromatik*, p. 135 ff; Lowinsky, "Echoes,) in *Festschrift Strunk*, pp. 194-196. Cf. the dissenting opinions in Fétis, *Traité*, p. 164 ff; Tanaka, "Stimmung," *VJM*, vi (1890), 70-71. For further comment and bibliography, see Zimmerman, *Madrigals* (unpublished thesis), p. 29 ff.

73.   The words "antico stile" can be taken to mean "ancient style," i.e. the style of music in ancient times, as well as "former ways," the meaning intended by Petrarch.

74.   The terms "primary" and "secondary" are those used in Jeppesen, *Palestrina*, p. 85 ff.

75.   Passage quoted in Einstein, *Madrigal*, ii.619 and Arnold, *Marenzio*, p. 18.

76.   Vicentino, *Antica musica*, bk.ii, f.29^V.

77.   *II a 5* (1581), no. 3, b.52 ff: "Già presso a venir manco" ("Already near to fainting").

78.   Vicentino, op.cit., f.29^V.

79.   E.g. in *I a 4,5,6* (1588), no. 4 (*Secular Works*, vii, ed. Ledbetter, p. 16, b.3); ibid, no. 7 (*Secular Works*, vii, p. 44, b.16).

80.   Vicentino, op.cit., f.29^V.

81.   Cf. Engel, *Marenzio*, p. 120 ff: ex. 133.

82.   "... as a conscious proposal ... in aesthetically accentuated contradistinction to consonance" (Jeppesen, *Palestrina*, p. 207). Cf. Zarlino, *Istitutioni*, bk.iii, chapter 27 (p. 200-201), transcribed Strunk, *Source readings*, p. 231 ff.

83.   Cf. classification 14, c and d.

84.   The penultimate syllable of a line phrase is often stressed through dissonance (Zimmerman, *Madrigal*, p. 67 ff).

85.   In ex. 135(c) the antithesis "amato"/"amaro" ("beloved"/"bitter") is conveyed by upward, positive motion on the first word, and downward, negative motion on the second (cf. classification 2, b, and 3 , b).

86.   *III a 6* (1584), no. 14 (transcribed in vol.ii of this study); *IV a 6* (1587), nos. 9 and 10 [ex. 218(a)].

87.   *V a 6* (1591), no. 9 [ex. 218(b)].

88.   *III a 6* (1585), no. 15 [ex. 125(g)]; *V a 6* (1591), no. 8 [ex. 125(f)].

89.   See examples in Arnold, *Marenzio*, pp. 22 and 24. Cf. Zarlino, *Istitutioni*, bk.iii, chapter 61 (pp. 291-292), transcribed Marco and Palisca, p. 195.

90.   E.g. *V a 5* (1585), no. 5, b.57 ff.

91.   By Burmeister in *Hypomnematum Musicae poeticae* (1599): see Brandes, *Figurenlehre*, p. 19.

92.   E.g. the opening of no. 6 and the opening of the *seconda parte* of no. 15.

93.   See above, chapter 3, ex. 25-26.

94.   *VII a 5* (1595), no. 5: *Il settimo libro*, ed. Steele, pp. 25-27. Compare the simplicity of the two-voice writing in *II a 5* (1581), b.14 ff: "Il pastorel ..." ("The shepherd ...").

95.   E.G., *II a 6* (1584), no. 10 on the words "Ignude, inerme" ("naked, unarmed"): *Opera*, iv, (ed.Meier) p. 171, b. 63 ff.

96.   E.g. *Mentre l'aura* (*RISM* 1582⁵), at the words "secco ti vedo" ("I find you dry") [ex. 141].

97.   E.g. *Spirituali* (1584), no. 9, line : "Qui 'l signor lasciò *la spoglia e sangue*," ("Here Our Lord left his mortal remains and blood"); the italic words are scored *a 4* in the context of a five-voice passage.

98.   E.g. *IV a 5* (1584), no. 6, bb.156-160: "ogni sua gloria estinse" ("extinguished all its glory"), where the final cadence is scored for two voices.

99.   E.g. *I a 5* (1585), no. 16: "Due rose fresche" ("Two fresh roses"). The choice of mode 2 may also be symbolic.

100.   As in *I a 4* (1585), no. 21, where the older shepherds' words are scored for tenor and bass, the younger, for canto and alto, chapter 3, ex. 22-23).

101.   As in *II a 6* (1584), no. 12, where the shepherd's voice and emotions are scored for lower voices than are those of the shepherdess: *Opera*, iv. (ed. Meier), 190-194.

102.   See *I a 5* (1580), no. 2, b.5 ff; *III a 5* (1582), no. 4, bb. 1 ff, 13 ff and 20 ff; also on the word "lagrime" ("tears") in *III a 5*, no. 2, b.27 ff, and "sospirando" ("sighing") in *IV a 5* (1584), no. 7, b.51 ff.

103.   *I a 5* (1580), no. 6, b.34 ff.

104.   E.g. *I a 4,5,6* (1588), no. 4: *Secular Works*, vii. (ed. Ledbetter), p. 18, b.27.

105.   Incomplete cadences are one of the clearest indications of Marenzio's debt to Rore. Cf. ex. 146 with Rore's representation of "death" at the end of *Non è, lasso, martire* [ex. 147] or "extinction" at the end of *Amor, ben mi credevo* [ex. 148].

106.   See above, classification 15, d, and note 63.

107.   *II a 6* (1584), no. 19: *Opera*, iv (ed. Meier), p. 214, b.124, canto.

108.   E.g. *I a 5* (1580), no. 3, b.17 ff: "Di color mille" ("Of a thousand colors"). The visual means, coloration, results in triple time; the actual sound of the music plays no part in illustrating the meaning of the text.

109.   See especially *III a 5* (1582), no. 12: *Occhi lucenti e belli* ("O bright, beautiful eyes") and cf. the openings of *I a 6* (1581), no. 11 (*Opera*, iv, ed. Meier, p. 56) and *V a 5* (1585), no. 12.

110.   *IV a 5* (1584), no. 4, b.73 ff, canto; ibid, no. 5, b.59 ff, quinto.

111.   Even Einstein, who calls "eye-music" "the most extreme and ... horrible testimony of naturalism" concedes that "a good interpreter might conceivably give some life even to abstract or 'paper' music of this kind." (*Madrigal*, i.234-235).

112. E.g. *III a 5* (1582), no. 11, b.112 ff: "siate seconde" ("be witness"), where the word "seconde" is scored for two voices as though it meant "second." Cf. the play on the meaning of "antico stile" in *O voi che sospirate* (see note 73).

113. Carapetyan, "The concept of 'Imitazione...,' " *JRBM,* i (1946), 53.

114. "But the wind took her words away."

115. Marenzio, *III a 5* (1582), no. 4; Monteverdi, *VI a 5* (1614), reproduced in *Opere,* vi.70-76.

116. *Opere,* vi.76, 1st system, b.5.

117. On this score the opinions of Girolamo Mei, the humanist scholar, are clearly set forth in his first letter to Vincenzo Galilei (1572) and later in the *Discorso sopra la musica antica e moderna* (published in 1602); these opinions are reflected in Count Bardi's *Discorso mandato a Giulio Caccini,* Galilei's *Dialogo* (1581) and Caccini in the preface to his *Nuove musiche* (1602). See Mei, *Letters,* ed. Palisca, p. 89 ff; Palisca, "Mei," *MQ* xl (1954), 9 ff; Strunk, *Source readings,* pp. 294 ff and 312-313; Caccini, *Nuove musiche,* ed. Hitchcock, p. 44 ff.

118. Thus Bardi inveighs against musicians who "think . . . nothing of spoiling [the verse] to pursue their ideas or of cutting it to bits to make nonsense of the words." (Quoted from Strunk, *Source readings,* p. 294). Similar sentiments are expressed in Caccini, *Nuove musiche,* ed.cit., p. 44. See also notes 125 and 128, below.

119. Galilei's attack is translated in Strunk, *Source readings,* pp. 315-317; for further quotation and discussion, see Carapetyan, art.cit., p. 55 ff and Palisca, "Mannerism," *SM,* iii (1974), 320 ff.

120. See above, note 4.

121. E.g., in *IV a 5* (1584), no. 6, b.99 ff, where the black notation for "tenebre" ("darkness") is dramatically superseded by slower tempo for "immortal dolore" ("eternal grief").

122. No. 6, on a text by Troiano (see appendix II).

123. *Secular Works,* vii (ed. Ledbetter), p. 34, b.31.

124. *Letters,* ed. Palisca, pp. 100-101.

125. Complaints about word inaudibility are not restricted to the Florentine Camerata: see Zarlino, *Istitutioni,* bk.ii, chapter 9, transcribed in Einstein, *Madrigal,* ii.837-838. Zarlino's ex-pupil and arch-enemy, Galilei, complains that contrapuntalists aim only "to delight the sense of hearing with the variety of consonances" (quoted from Strunk, *Source readings,* p. 313)—an implied criticism of the inaudibility of words in a contrapuntal setting. Similar complaints and admonitions are contained in Caccini, *Nuove musiche,* ed.cit., preface, p. 44; Della Valle, *Della musica,* reprinted in Solerti, *Origine,* p. 150 ff, and G.B. Doni, *Compendio,* pp. 103-104 and *Lyra Barberina,* ii.28 ff (reprinted in Solerti, *Origine,* p. 220 ff).

126. See above, note 118.

127. In this respect a comparison of the settings of *Due rose fresche* by Gabrieli and Marenzio, and *Giunto a la tomba* by Wert and Marenzio, would be highly instructive (see appendix II, notes to *V a 5,* 1585, no. 16 and *IV a 5,* 1584, no. 1); Gabrieli's setting is reproduced in Einstein, *Madrigal,* iii.182-189, Wert's in ibid., pp. 221-229 and *Works,* vii.38-43.

128. " . . . began to allow the individual voices to sing with beauty and grace and to allow the words to be somewhat better heard." From the *Musica Scena,* printed in *Lyra Barberina* ii.24 and in Solerti, *Origine,* pp. 211-212.

Chapter 6

1. The only two exceptions are the irregular *II a 6* (1584), no. 15 and the final line of the *III a 5* (1582), no. 7.

2. Elwert, *Versificazione*, p. 6 ff.

3. The line as a unity can also be obscured by repeated words or fragments and the fusion of the end of line with the beginning of the succeeding (enjambement).

4. See chapter 2, note 22.

5. See chapter 4, ex. 30.

6. "Liquide perle Amor/da gl'occhi sparse." (More grammatical would have been: "Liquide perle/Amor da gl'occhi sparse").

7. Macque's *Non veggio, ohimè* (*RISM*, 1585[29]: see ex. 155(b)) must have been written by 1582, the date of Moscaglia's letter of dedication (reprinted in *NV*, ii.1211). Macque's opening is very close to Marenzio's *Hor vedi, Amor* (*I a 4*, 1585; see ex. 155(a)) both as regards text and music; as the latter is a setting of a madrigal by Petrarch, we may asssume that it was in fact Macque that was following Marenzio, and not *vice versa*. The piece by Marenzio must therefore have been *written* by 1582 and reached Macque in MS form. Marenzio in his turn derives his opening material from Cambio's much earlier setting [ex. 156].

8. In the musical examples, these variations are shown by square brackets.

9. Free elongation of the first syllable often results in the motive, minim - crotchet - crotchet, or "narrative" rhythm (see chapter 3, note 108); e.g. *II a 5* (1581), no. 8, b.1 ff ("*I*tene a l'ombra . . ."), b. 12 ff ("*Su*'l mezzo giorno . . ."), etc. The accentuation of the first example is correct, that of the second, incorrect (the accent should fall on "*mezzo*").

10. In bb. 2 ff, 11 ff and 13 ff. In the first line the motive is modified by the melisma on the second, third, and fourth notes.

11. In b.18 ff.

12. Cf. ex. 179.

13. Cf. chapter 5, classification 10, c.

14. See chapter 5, classification 11, a, iii.

15. Cf. ex. 169.

16. Cf. chapter 5, ex. 94.

17. A point supported by the example given in Bennett, *Marenzio*, p. 126, where a colored rhythmic motive "is immediately contrasted with the same figure uncolored" with an effect of rhythmic acceleration.

18. See above, Chapter 5, classification 11, a.

19. See above, exx. 174, 176, and 182.

20. Quoted in Blunt, *Artistic theory*, p. 101.

Chapter 7

1. *I a 5* (1580), no. 5 and *III a 6* (1585), no. 15.

2. In a poem with long and involved sentences, a subordinate clause may be treated like a sentence (or section): e.g., *I a 4, 5, 6* (1588), no. 2, lines 1-4, reprinted in *Secular Works* (ed. Ledbetter), vii. 5-7, bb.1-29, where a conditional clause ends with the first clearcut cadence in the piece.

3. This is clear from the transcriptions and analyses in G.B. Martini, *Saggio,* ii. 78-103 and 164-236 (esp. p. 229 ff).

4. *I a 4* (1585), no. 2: reproduced in Roche, *Penguin book,* pp. 136-140, and elsewhere.

5. G.B. Doni's phrase (see above, chapter 2, note 47).

6. Cf. the passage from Morley's *Introduction,* p. 180, in which he describes the madrigal as "wavering like the wind."

7. *V a 6* (1591), no. 9; see chapter 2, ex. 20.

8. See reprint in Engel, *Lied,* p. 31.

9. *Ten madrigals,* ed. Arnold, pp. 5-6, bb.1-14.

10. In the *IX a 5* of 1588. The two dedications are signed 10 December 1587 and 1 January 1588 respectively (but Marenzio's book was not *published* until 1588); cf. the *Secular Works,* vii (ed. Ledbetter), 71 and Wert, *Works,* ix. 5 ff.

11. *II a 5* (1581), no. 13, b.128 ff and no. 9, b.34 ff.

12. *V a 5* (1585), no. 15, b.1 ff.

13. The dotted rhythm representing violent motion is often subjected to imitation at the crotchet (see chapter 5, classification 11).

14. The first line means: "Now full of another desire." Transcribed in volume II of this study.

15. See chapter 5, classification 6.

16. E.g. in *II a 5* (1581), no. 10, b.26 ff, on "delle miserie" ("of miseries"): imitation is in parallel tenths, starting on the notes *e′* and *c, c′* and *a, a′* and *f,* and *d′.* The descending motive is of expressive significance, but the pitches at which it is imitated are not.

17. *II a 5* (1581), no. 10, bb.1 ff, 3 ff, and 5 ff. The first line means "O you that sigh with better notes." Marenzio has amended the final word "notti" ("nights") to "note" ("notes"), perhaps to draw attention to the uncharted musical realms explored in this composition.

18. See chapter 5, classification 18, a.

19. See chapter 5, classification 15, e.

20. The examples also illustrate the phenomenon of *note cavate,* or notes which correspond to solmization syllables which happen to occur in the text. As the various fragments appear in different transpositions, so the solmization syllables alluded to may be those of the soft, natural, or hard hexacords.

21. *RISM* 1582[4]: see volume II of this study.

22. "The most graceful eternal springtime dwells joyously among these hills."

23. But the motive for fragment 2 (first heard in b.3 canto) is also set to fragment 1 (bb.1-2, alto) while the melisma of "Primavera") (b.3, alto) foreshadows the melisma of "Vive" (first heard in b.6, canto).

24. "I weep all day long, then at night, when miserable mortals take rest."

25. First heard in b.3, canto.

26. *IV a 6* (1587), nos. 3 and 10.

27. In the following discussion a different letter is assigned to each repeated unit. The numbers refer to varied repetitions; thus A, A₁, and A₂ constitute three variations of the same phrase.

28. No. 3 (*prima* and *seconda parti*), no. 5 *(terza parte)*, nos. 7, 8 and 9 *(prima parte)* and no. 10 end in A A₁; nos 2 and 5 *(prima parte)* end in A A₁ A₂; nos. 6 and 9 *(seconda parte)* end in A B A₁ B ₁ B₂; no. 11 ends in A B A₁ B ₁ B₂ B₃, no. 12 in A B A₁ B₁ B A₂ B₂ B₂.

29. See especially nos. 3, 5, and 11: *Secular Works,* vii (ed. Ledbetter), pp. 15, 28-30 and 90-92. Also instructive are the final sections of *Perchè adoprar* (*RISM* 1583¹²) and *Coppia di donne* (*RISM* 1592¹⁴).

30. See above, chapter 2, ex. 12.

31. "I do not refuse to die."

32. "Sweet" (bb. 13 and 16).

33. "Die" (bb. 34 and 38).

34. See Watkins, *Gesualdo,* p. 134 ff.

35. See above, chapter 5, classification 14.

36. Cf. Zarlino, *Counterpoint,* tr. Marco and Palisca, p. 142: "The cadence has a value in music equivalent to the period in prose and could well be called the period of musical composition."

37. As indeed is the attempt to link modal theory with what we know of modal practice. The most important exposition of modal theory remains Meier's *Tonarten;* also stimulating is Luoma's "Relationships between music and poetry," *Musica Disciplina,* xxxi (1977), 135-154. I am grateful to Howard Mayer Brown for sending me his as yet unpublished "Words and music: Willaert . . ."

38. *Tonarten,* p. 75 ff.

39. Meier, *Tonarten,* p. 84 ff.

40. Such a survey has already been given in Meier, *Tonarten,* p. 76 ff.

41. The term "perfect" is used here and elsewhere in its modern sense, and not that in which Zarlino uses it (to denote cadences on the octave or unison: see Zarlino, *Counterpoint,* tr. Marco and Palisca, p. 142 ff, and cf. Luoma, "Music and poetry" cit., p. 141 and notes 1 and 2.)

42. See chapter 5, classification 14, d.

43. *IV a 5* (1584), no. 1, b. 38: "disse/ . . ." ("said").

44. "Full of amazement, immobile" (*V a 5,* 1585, no. 8, b. 51).

45. "More obstinate than to Pan was she . . ." (*II a 5,* 1581, no. 6, b. 35).

46. "And lead with you the Cupids" (*IV a 5,* 1584, no. 4, b. 12).

47. "Le ripose il pastore/ . . ." ("The shepherd replied to her . . ."; *I a 5,* 1580, no. 5, b. 108); "dicendo/ . . ." ("saying . . ."; *I a 5,* no. 9, b. 21).

48. E.g. at the end of *I a 5* (1580), no. 2, where the final plagal cadence on *c* merely confirms the tonal feeling already conveyed by the descending triadic motive *g″ - e″ - c″* (canto, b. 59 ff.)

49. Zarlino calls the latter "simple," the former, diminished (*Counterpoint*, p. 142 ff.).

50. *II a 5* (1581), no. 1, bb. 77-82.

51. *V a 5* (1585), no. 3, b. 1 ff ("Then fertile Earth again put on her bright, joyful, and happy cloak").

52. "Convey [my sighs and kisses to the mortal remains], so that, if the beautiful soul ever turns its eyes to its beautiful remains . . ." (*IV a 5*, 1585, no. 1, b. 96 ff).

53. Transcribed in volume II of this study.

54. With cadences in bb. 5, 7 and 10.

55. See bb. 13-28.

56. "Quando i vostri begl'occhi un caro velo/Ombrando copre . . ." ("when your beautiful eyes are covered by a dear, shadowy veil . . ."; *I a 5*, 1580, no. 4, b. 8).

57. See chapter 5, classification 18, b.

58. Cf. chapter 5, classification 15, c, ii.

59. ". . . and the murmuring of the waves will assent" (*II a 5*, 1581, no. 8, bb. 43-44: delayed IV-V-I cadence).

60. "Said to him: 'Ah, my love . . .' " (*I a 5*, 1580, no. 5, bb. 23-24: delayed IV-V-I cadence).

61. Ex. 208.

62. "And in her god-like eyes the honest Cupids play" (*IV a 5*, 1584, no. 14, bb. 26-27: delayed IV-V-I cadence).

63. ". . . of green shrubs and fresh flowers" (*I a 5*, 1580, no. 12, b.5: delayed VI-V-I cadence).

64. "I lived from hope, now I live only from tears" (*II a 6*, 1584, no. 2, reproduced in *Opera*, iv, ed. Meier, p. 119, b. 55: delayed IV-V-I cadence).

65. "Alas, if you love so much to hear [me] say 'Alas,' tell me, why do you make the person who says 'Alas,' die?" (*III a 5*, 1582, no. 7, bb. 10-11: delayed IV-V-I cadence).

66. ". . . but the heart will remain" (*II a 5*, 1581, no. 1, bb. 69-70: deflection of V-I to V-VI).

67. The frequency with which cadences fall on each scale degree is illustrated in appendix I, to which the ensuing discussion refers.

68. But irregular cadences are more common among principal than among terminal cadences.

69. Discussed near the end of chapter 4, above.

70. Listed in appendix I.

71. The final resolution to *f* occurs at the opening of the next section (b. 45).

72. This entails the sharping of the second, fourth, and sixth degrees.

73. "Bitterer than any absinth."

74. The text, "Fin ch'ella di pietà non scaldi il core" ("Until she warms her heart with pity") describes a hypothetical event, a remote possibility; hence the remote cadence.

75. The text reads: "e me di me fa uscire" ("and leads me to be beside myself").

76. "From the rising till the setting of the sun."

77. *Spirituali* (1584), no. 7 (mode 9 transposed).

78. "The sun transformed the bright, luminous chariot." (*Spirituali*, 1584, no. 4; mode 9 transposed).

79. Cf. *VIII a 5* (1598), no. 16 (also in mode 9 untransposed), which also cadences on *d* at the end of its *prima parte*.

80. *II a 5* (1581), no. 16 (mode 12 untransposed), bb. 35-43: major-chord cadences on "Amor," *d*-minor (I-V) cadence on "dorme."

81. Cf. note 76.

82. "In a direction in which I do not want to go": *Secular Works*, vii, (ed. Ledbetter), pp. 99-100, bb. 49, 51, and 54.

83. "Every vile, base man" (bb. 31, 36, 38, and 40).

84. Cf. IV a 6 (1587), no. 2 (mode 10 transposed) where a seventh-degree cadence (*c:* I-V) is reached through a progression *d, b*-flat, *g, e*-flat, *c* (but without cadences on these degrees); see chapter 5, ex. 88(b).

85. A comparison with appendix I will show that the cadence degrees in the left-hand column are not only the most regular, but also (in most cases) the most frequent.

86. "Principal and proper cadences . . . almost principal . . . for transitions and with discrimination." See Pontio, *Ragionamento di musica* (1588), p. 99 ff. Pontio's discussion of cadences is summarized in Meier, *Tonarten*, pp. 88 and 91-92.

87. Moreover he admits and excludes different cadences from the various categories. Thus in mode 5 cadences on *a* occupy a rank equal to those on *f* and *c* ("principali") while *b*-flat occupies a higher rank than *g* and *d;* the reverse is the case in Marenzio. In mode 7, Pontio designates *c* cadences "per transito"; in Marenzio's madrigals, however, they achieve the rank of principal cadences.

88. *Doctrina de tonis* (1582): see summary by Meier in *Tonarten*, pp. 96-97; the main distinctions between Hofmann's theory and Marenzio's practice lie in the low rank assigned by Marenzio to the third degree in modes 5, 6, 11, and 12, and the rarity with which he uses fifth-degree cadences in modes 9 and 10.

89. *Mostra delli tuoni*, p.23 ff; in this he follows Zarlino, who however qualifies his statements regarding the phrygian by allowing *a* as well as *e, g* and *b* (*Istitutioni*, bk. iv, chapter 22, p. 401).

90. Cf. note 86.

91. *I a 4, 5, 6* (1588), no. 13 (mode 7 untransposed): *Secular Works*, vii (ed. Ledbetter), p. 104, bb. 13 and 16.

92. "Cruel accident."

93. E.g. the line by Sannazaro, "Muti una volta quel suo antico stile"; see chapter 5, classification 15; cf. this chapter, notes 76 and 82. The cycle of fifths, whatever its precise form, often represents gradual transformation, motion or movement of any kind: see also exx. 216 and 217, and note 94.

94. It is of interest that the Petrarch setting of which this madrigal is a parody (no. 4 of the same book) also ends with an equally broad progression based on the simpler pattern of fifths: thus, in b. 128 ff, cadences on *c, a, d, g,* and *c* follow at two-bar intervals.

95. *V a 5* (1585), no. 1 (mode 7 transposed), bb. 17, 23, 38, and 53.

96. "This . . . fine and noble garland."

97. "Just recently weaved from green shrubs and fresh flowers."

98. *I a 4, 5, 6* (1588), no. 8 (mode 3 transposed): *Secular Works,* vii (ed. Ledbetter), 58-60. In this composition the principal cadences fall regularly on *d* (bb. 17, 40 and 66); the first cadence (b. 17) is left incomplete in order to convey "crude," meaning cruel: cf. chapter 5, classification 18, b; the final cadence is a half cadence, as one would expect in mode 3.

99. Ibid, bb. 17-40. ("Because there is neither twig nor stone which, soon enough, even if late, seeing my open and naked wounds and that which my soul contains, is not moved to pity for my grievous state." Quoted from ed. cit., p. xxiv).

100. Thus illustrating that harmonically remote transitory cadences are less likely to occur at the opening and close of a section than in the middle.

101. The *f* cadence here is both plagal and delayed. The insistence on *b*-flat (b. 37) illustrates the phrase "non si mova" ("is not moved"): the harmony fails to "move" towards the expected cadence.

102. Their function is to assert or affirm; therefore they must be modally assertive, i.e. have a close harmonic relationship with the final.

103. *I a 5* (1580), no. 8, b. 24.

104. "Are my food . . ." The subject of the verb "son" ("are") is contained in lines 5-6. Thus the repetition of the last two lines on their own results in the dismemberment of a sentence.

105. An equally glaring distortion occurs at the end of *III a 5* (1582), no. 4, where Marenzio repeats the last two lines where it would have been better to repeat the last three or only the last single line (cf. bb. 126 ff and 144 ff.).

106. Meier, *Tonarten,* stresses the importance of the first cadence in establishing the mode (see especially pp. 114 ff, 128 ff, and 142 ff).

107. ". . . accompanied with pitying accents"

108. ". . . and culled in Paradise, having been born the day before yesterday"

109. E.g. *I a 4* (1585), no. 17, b. 34, after "miseri Mortali" (ex. 202); cf. *IV a 6* (1587), no. 15, b. 47 "si nutre e vive" (". . . is nourished and lives"; see Chater, "Castelletti," *SM* viii (1979), p. 137, b. 42 ff.

110. E.g. *III a 5* (1582), no. 4, b. 90, after the line "Se non fussi fra noi scesa sì tardo" ("If only you had not descended among us so late"); cf. *I a 4* (1585), no. 14, cadence at end of *prima parte:* "Et fia sin che la vita al suo fin giunge" ("and may it be, until my life arrives at its end").

111. "It will certainly be a miracle of love; but so great is my torment . . ."; see *II a 5* (1581), no. 1 (mode 2 transposed), b. 94: half cadence on *b*-flat.

112. *I a 5* (1580), no. 2, b. 47, after "Ambitiose e troppo lievi voglie" ("ambitious and too light-headed wishes").

113. *V a 5* (1585), no. 15, b. 92, after "mormorar occolto" ("discreet murmuring").

114. Other cases of the "receding" cadence we have met before: e.g. chapter 5, ex. 146, and this chapter, note 98 ("crude").

Chapter 8

1. On f.31^r ff.

2. Meier, *Tonarten,* p. 276.

3. As far as I know, this particular function is mentioned neither by contemporary theorists nor writers of our own time.

4. *I a 5* (1580), no. 12, bb.27-35.

5. *III a 5* (1582), no. 1, bb.3-6.

6. *I a 4* (1585), no. 5: *Ten madrigals,* ed. Arnold, pp. 27-29, bb.38-49.

7. *V a 5* (1585), no. 13, bb.23-31.

8. *III a 5* (1582), no. 11, bb.98-108.

9. *I a 6* (1581), no. 5, b.84 ff: *Opera,* iv (ed. Meier), 30-31.

10. This is the only case in Marenzio's madrigals where a transposed mode gives way to an untransposed one through the consistent replacement of *b*-flat by *b*-natural.

11. *II a 5* (1581), no. 10, bb.27-32. A "lydian cadence" confirms the lydian modality in b.32. The use of the lydian is consistent with Vecchi's observation that it is "suitable for the comforting of troubled spirits" (see chapter 4, note 35).

12. *II a 5* (1581), no. 3, bb.72-76. (Quoted in Meier, *Tonarten,* p. 401 ff).

13. *III a 6* (1585), no. 10 (mode 9 transposed): *Madrigali a 5, 6,* ed. Mompellio, pp. 13-15.

14. "That appeared like a rose" (b.17 ff).

15. *V a 5* (1585), no. 16 (mode 2 transposed).

16. For further details, see chapter 2, and ex. 7.

17. "Thus dying I live, and with the weapons with which you kill you can save me."

18. In bb. 8, 11, 19, 21, 22, 25, 27, 30, 34, 37, and 45. Cf. *V a 5* (1585), no. 3 (mode 2 untransposed), which starts in mode 12 (cadences are on *c* and *g*) before modulating to mode 2 (b.60 to the end); also, *V a 5* (1585), no. 6, *seconda parte,* in which the phrygian modality is withheld until the last seven bars in order to emphasize the words "o d'altro effetto pio" ("or of some other sign of pity").

19. *I a 5* (1580), no. 7 (mode 1 untransposed).

20. See bb.7 and 12, 17, and 24.

21. "Now I give her these my violets and these flowers" (bb.24-30 and 35-41).

22. The hypoaeolian is introduced at the words "Così il mio cor, c'havea di due gioconde / Luci seguita la fallace traccia . . ." ("Thus my heart, which of two playful eyes had followed the false trail . . ."): *Opera,* iv (ed. Meier), p. 160, b.34 ff.

23. Praetorius mentions Marenzio's "Madrigalia in genere Chromatico" in the *Syntagma Musicum,* ii.35, but does not name any specific madrigal.

24. "Wandering, uncertain tone." See *Compendio,* p. 89.

25. *Annotazioni,* p. 141.

26.   The difference in terminology is explainable through Doni's adherence to the nomenclature used by the ancient Greeks and his rejection of Glareanus' system (*Compendio,* p. 1 ff).

27.   Bars 13-22: "Gazing into the eyes of she who he adores, whence she, who burned no less than he . . ."

28.   ". . . said to him . . ." (bb. 22-24)

29.   This point is brought home by the realization that it was feasible to set prose to music, as did Soriano in his "Prosa del Sannazzaro," published in 1601 with his *I a 4 (NV,* ii, no. 2620).

30.   As in *I a 4, 5, 6* (1588), no. 4 where the main division occurs not after the octave, but after the first tercet: *Secular Works,* vii (ed. Ledbetter), p. 21, b. 73.

31.   "Behold the dawn . . . behold the night."

32.   "For what shadowy . . . for what green field."

33.   Marenzio designates this piece an "Aria."

34.   *Io morirò d'amore* and *Posso cor mio partire* (*III a 6,* 1585, nos. 1 and 8), whose musical and poetic forms are ABA_1; cf. *I a 5* (1580), no. 13, with its similar second and last lines: "Porgimi aita Amore . . . Prestami aiuto Amore" ("Offer me help, O Love . . . Lend me help, O Love"); also, *II a 5* (1581), no. 4, where the lines concluding the *prima* and *seconda parti* are identical.

35.   The relationship between music and rhetoric is the subject of Unger, *Musik und Rhetorik,* and Brandes, *Musikalischen Figurenlehre.*

36.   Cf. Haar, "Self-consciousness . . .," *SM,* iii (1974), 227; Lowinsky, "Genius," *MQ,* 1 (1964), 479 ff.

37.   In his *Musica autoschediastike* (1601) and *Musica poetica* (1606); summarized and illustrated by Palisca in "Musical definition of Mannerism," *SM,* iii (1974), 325 ff.

38.   In Unger, *Musik und Rhetorik,* pp. 134 ff. The analyses by both Burmeister (as reproduced and amplified by Palisca) and Unger raise the issue of terminology when applying rhetorical terms to music. The problem lies in the inconsistency between the terms as used in the writers of antiquity and the various meanings they later accumulated when applied to music. In the ensuing analysis I have adhered to the meanings as defined in Lausberg, *Handbuch der Rhetorik,* unless otherwise stated.

39.   *I a 5* (1580), no. 14 (*a* 8); *I a 6* (1581), no. 18 (*a* 10) and *VI a 6* (1595), no. 5 (*a* 6).

40.   For a comparison of Ovid and Poliziano, see Sternfeld, "Repetition and echo" in the *Festschrift Gardner,* pp. 33-43. For further details on echo, repetition, dialogue, and the lament, see Kroyer, "Dialog," *Jahrbuch Peters,* xvi (1909), 13-32.

41.   The same kind of repetition occurs in *IV a 5* (1584), no. 1, b. 71 ff: "Deh, prendi i miei sospiri e questi baci/ Prendi . . ." ("Oh, take my sighs, and these kisses take"); the last word is twice repeated in all the voices.

42.   Lausberg, *Handbuch,* para. 629 ff.

43.   Ibid, para. 630.

44.   "It is a miracle that I remain alive; it is a miracle that you [do not lend me your] pitying sighs . . ."; *III a 5* (1582), no. 15, b. 40 ff.

45.   "Kiss me a thousand times . . . hug me tightly." Cf. bb. 1 ff and 79 ff.

46. Other examples include the opening of the *seconda parte* of *I a 5* (1580), no. 5 (cf. bb. 59 ff and 76 ff) and the opening of *III a 6* (1585), no. 15: "Con dolce sguardo . . . / Con lagrime" ("With sweet glances . . . with tears").

47. "Paradise" and "spring." Cf. bb. 127 and 135.

48. Lines 3 - 4.

49. *Secular Works* vii (ed. Ledbetter), p. 105, b. 23 and p. 106, b. 31.

50. Cf. bb. 84 ff and 111 ff.

51. Cf. bb. 8 ff and 26 ff.

52. *I a 5* (1580), no. 5, b. 35 ff. The phrase reads: "Deh non morir anchora / Che teco bramo di morir anch'io" ("Ah, do not die yet, because I also long to die with you") and is spoken to Thyrsis by the Nymph.

53. "O Grief, such is the joy . . . that my grief makes me happy" (bb. 1 ff and 48).

54. Einstein, *Madrigal,* ii. 723, points out the use of the same device in Monteverdi's madrigals, where "a *contrapposto* of different parts of the text" acts as "a reflection of the poetic oxymoron"; the same author calls this device "the musical equivalent of the poetic oxymoron" (ibid, ii. 855).

55. "If only you were now alive in the same way as I am not dead": *Opera,* iv (ed. Meier), p. 188, b. 180 ff.

56. The Greek word for *sententia* is given by Lausberg as "gnome" (Handbuch, para. 872 ff); it is presumably from this word that Burmeister derives the term "noema," assigning it a purely musical meaning: homophonic texture designed to stand out from its context (Unger, *Musik and Rhetorik*, p. 82 ff). The meaning given by Burmeister only sometimes overlaps with the original meaning: it is obvious that not all *sententiae* are set homophonically, and that not all homophonic passages contain a *sententia*.

57. Unger, *Musik und Rhetorik*, p. 22, points out the use of a rising scale degree at the end of a question in plainsong.

58. Lausberg, *Handbuch,* para. 260-442.

59. Cf. Burmeister's threefold division of a musical composition into the *exordium, confirmatio*, and *finis* ("ultimus periodus est velut epilogus in oratione"), described by Unger, *Musik und Rhetorik,* p. 47 ff.

60. There is no direct equivalent for *narratio* and *argumentatio* (though the latter is similar in function to the epigrammatic point); the number of sections is determined by the number of sentences in the literary text (see chapter 7).

61. See above, ex. 235-236.

62. Bar 60 ff.

63. "No-one ever lived happier than I; no-one lives sadder both night and day; and, my grief redoubling, the style also redoubles which dragged such doleful rhymes from my heart; I lived for hope, now I live for weeping, nor against Death do I hope for anything but death." *II a 6* (1584), no. 2: *Opera,* iv (ed. Meier), 116-120.

64. The play on words is between Death personified and death as an abstract noun.

65. Cf. bb. 1-3 and bb. 5-10.

66. A similar mixture of repetition and antithesis occurs across a larger time gap in *I a 4* (1585), no. 18: "Zefiro torna . . . Ma per me tornan" [ex. 241]. The two *parti* begin with similar descending motives and three-voice writing to draw attention to the repetition "torna . . . tornan," but differ in mood: while the *prima parte* is joyful at the return of spring, the *seconda parte* is a slower, more mournful depiction of private grief.

67. Cf. bb. 18-27 with bb. 26-37. The words "doppiando . . . doppia" in line 3 refer to the beginning of the second part of the double sestina, whereby the rhyme scheme of stanzas 1-6 is exactly duplicated in stanzas 7-12.

68. Cf bb. 54-55 with 62-63.

69. It is all the more striking for occurring at the end of a section.

70. See bb. 11, first minim, 25, first crotchet, 66, first crotchet, 84, first crotchet, and b. 89, first minim.

71. It will be noted that "exordium" is not quite synonymous with "opening section"; the opening section lasts till the end of line 2 (b. 17), the second section till the end of line 4 (b. 52), the third till the end of line 5 (b. 63), after which begins the fourth and last section.

72. Note that the sesto takes the unusual liberty of omitting the first three words of the last line on the first entry, so as to proceed "hor vivo pur . . . / . . . spero altro" (bb. 57-63); this textual omission is apparently of no expressive significance.

73. *I a 5* (1580), no. 2.

74. Williamson, *B. Tasso*, pp. 47-48; also quoted in Einstein, *Madrigal*, i. 209-210.

75. In bb. 1 ff, 8 ff, 32 ff, 48 ff, 59 ff, 64 ff and 67 ff. The note *e''* is the *repercussio* of mode 12.

76. Duranti, *Sulle rime del Tasso,* p. 64, calls the *parola-chiave* ("key word") the "nucleo inventivo" of a madrigal and compares it with the theme as used in a musical composition.

77. Reproduced by Engel, *Lied,* pp. 31-32.

78. The use of antithetical word-pairs is however more characteristic of Guarini than of Tasso: *Tirso morir volea* (*I a 5,* 1580, no. 5) is built round the antithesis "vivere"/"morire" ("live"/"die"), *Parto o non parto?* (*IX a 5,* 1599, no. 11), round "partire"/"restare" ("depart"/"stay").

79. See Chapter 5, classification 11, a.

80. A point I have already made in Chater, "Castelletti," *SM,* viii (1979), 104 ff. The tripartite division of many madrigals corresponds with Burmeister's division (see note 59).

81. *I a 5* (1580), no. 1 and *IV a 6* (1587), no. 15.

82. See b. 18 ff: "Ma lass'ohimè" ("But woe, alas").

83. See transcription in Chater, art. cit., p. 135 ff, bb. 29-40.

84. Also, in the case of *Donne, il celeste lume,* of antithesis: the heart burns continuously without being consumed.

85. In *Liquide perle* the three sections last 16, 14, and 27 bars; in *Donne, il celeste,* 28, 25, and 60 bars.

86. *III a 6* (1585), no. 4 and *VII a 5* (1595), no. 5. The two madrigals share the same rhyme scheme. The latter is transcribed in *Il settimo libro de madrigali,* ed. Steele, pp. 25-27.

87.   *III a 6* (1585), no. 14: transcribed in volume II of this study.

88.   Bars 13, 20, 25 and 33.

89.   Also from the *III a 6* (no. 12). The text is reproduced in chapter 3; for transcription of the music, see volume II of this study.

90.   Bar 1 ff. canto.

91.   Bar 4 ff, tenor; b. 6 ff, bass.

92.   Cf. b. 6, canto, with b. 9, quinto.

93.   At the end of line 4 (b. 25); the piece is in mode 12 transposed.

94.   "Thus has mere thirst for honour been able . . . thus was more powerful in me . . ." (*I a 5*, 1580, no. 2, lines 3-5: bb. 20 ff and 32 ff).

95.   "Behold the dawn . . . behold the night . . ." (*IV a 5*, 1584, no. 9, lines 1 and 4: bb. 1 ff and 39 ff).

96.   "Be satisfied, O Love . . . laugh, O Fortune . . . rejoice, O my lady . . ."; *II a 6* (1584), no. 1: *Opera,* iv (ed. Meier), pp. 111-113, bb. 1 ff, 22 ff and 37 ff.

97.   The piece is in mode 7 untransposed.

98.   *I a 4, 5, 6* (1588), no. 3: *Secular Works,* vii (ed. Ledbetter), 12-15; the text is from the same poem as *Satiati Amor.*

99.   "I weep . . . I sigh . . . I lament" (bb. 1 ff, 10 ff and 22 ff).

100.   " . . . for my lament, my sighs, my harsh weeping."

101.   Cf. bb. 10 ff and 43 ff.

102.   See above, ex. 236(e).

103.   *I a 4, 5, 6* (1588), no. 10: *Secular Works,* vii (ed. Ledbetter) pp. 71-83.

104.   "True love": line 9.

105.   "You will hear . . .": lines 2, 3 and 5 (bb. 6 ff, 13 ff and 28 ff).

106.   "You woods will hear . . . and the sad sound": lines 3 and 4 (bb. 13-14, alto; b. 20 ff. tenor, quinto, and b. 24, quinto).

107.   Even here the sense of modality is confused by the chromaticism in bb. 104-106.

108.   See chapter 5, classification 2, b.

109.   *Spirituali* (1584), no. 12 (reproduced in Lechner, *Werke,* viii. 156-178); *V a 5* (1585), no. 1.

110.   *Werke,* viii. 31-72.

111.   *Madrigal,* ii. 642.

112.   Of 342 bars as opposed to *Non fu mai* (474 bars) and *Giovane donna* (515 bars).

113.   Bars 106-123 and 265-289.

114.   A fact which would seem to negate Einstein's charge that the piece is "striking only in its use of the high register and . . . neutral ornament." (op. cit., ii. 642).

115.   Bars 7 ff, 134 ff, 201 ff, 315 ff, and 320 ff.

116. E.g. in bb. 28 ff, 71 ff and 106 ff. Cf. chapter 2, note 36.

117. At the end of the *seconda* and *terza parti* (bb. 86 ff and 122).

118. Bar 34 ff, canto, and bb. 71-72, canto (both falling fourths asserting the phrygian mode); also the quotation from Wert (b. 38 ff), and the concluding line (b. 159 ff).

119. Bars 53-82. The text here may be translated: "You are the receptacle not of death, but of living ashes, where Love is concealed; from your coldness I feel the spent fire, which, though less sweet, is no less cold to my heart. Ah! take my sighs, and these kisses take, which I bathe in tearful moisture." The first sentence of this speech is consolatory: Vecchi, *Mostra delli tuoni,* p. 16, mentions the fifth mode as having the power to console; presumably the sixth mode might have been considered to have a similar effect.

120. The note of repercussion is the same as for the prevailing mode 3 and is therefore pivotal in function.

121. Equally ambiguous are the *c*-major sonorities at the opening of the *quarta parte* (bb. 93-106) which act as negative preparation for the bleak phrygian sound of "Perdona il mio fallo" ("Forgive my weakness").

122. *V a 6* (1591), no. 12: transcribed in volume II of this study.

123. But the only source in which it survives complete is *RISM* 1596[10]; I have been unable to consult this source and am indebted to Rosalind Halton for allowing me to quote from her transcription.

124. English transcribed in volume II of this study.

125. Transcribed in volume II of this study.

126. Bars 8-15, 75-86, 156-179, and 326-338.

127. Viewed in this way, the *b*-flat-cadence in b. 156 may be regarded as transitory (rather than a regular mode-1 cadence); the *f*-cadence in b. 179 is a principal third-degree cadence for mode 10 and the *d*-cadence in b. 199 marks the close of the hypoaeolian episode.

128. Pirrotta, "Note," in *Festschrift Ronga,* p. 568.

129. See chapter 5, ex. 160(a).

130. Bar 339 ff.

131. E.g. the occurrence of "pianto" ("weeping") at the ends of nos. 1, 2 and 9 (sestine); nos. 6 and 7 (texts by Troiano and Sannazaro) begin with similar words; no. 6, line 4 ("O fere stelle," meaning "Ah, cruel stars") is echoed at the opening of no. 14 (text by Sannazaro) both as regards words and music: *Secular Works,* vii (ed. Ledbetter), p. 33, b. 21 ff and p. 109, b. 1 ff.

132. See Chater, "Fonti poetiche . . .," *RIDM,* xiii (1978), 76 ff.

Chapter 9

1. The epithet "The Developing Composer" is used in Arnold, *Marenzio,* p. 39.

2. In "Fonti poetiche," *RIDM,* xiii (1978), 60-103.

3. Nos. 4-8; no. 14.

4. *V a 5,* no. 11; *III a 6,* nos. 1, 6 and 8.

5. See chapter 8, note 131.

6. No. 1, line 1; cf. Einstein, *Madrigal,* ii.662 ff.

7. *I a 4, 5, 6,* no. 15 (text by Sannazaro), lines 5 and 8.

8. Arnold, *Marenzio,* p. 23.

9. *RISM* 1593[3].

10. In "Three anthologies," *RIDM,* x (1975), 333.

11. See chapter 8, ex. 246.

12. Cf. Marenzio, *V a 5* (1585), no. 16, and Ingegneri, *V a 5* (1587), reproduced in the *Madrigale,* (*CW,* 115), pp. 11-17; both pieces are in mode 2 transposed and use similar themes at the beginning of the first two quatrains of the *prima parte* (Marenzio, bb. 1 ff and 24 ff; Ingegneri, bb. 1 ff and 9 ff). The two composers' *seconde parti* also begin with similar two-voice material.

13. Einstein, *Madrigal,* ii.855-856.

14. See chapter 4, ex. 30.

15. See chapter 2, and ex. 120.

16. The two books were both printed in Rome by Alessandro Gardano.

17. See chapter 6, ex. 155(c).

18. *RISM* 1589[7].

19. *RISM* 1583[14], 1583[15], and 1585[19].

20. Lindner also draws on the *II a 5* and the *I a 6* (1581).

21. *RISM* 1590[29].

22. Such as *RISM* 1586[3], 1591[13] and 1599[6].

23. *RISM* 1606[6].

24. *RISM* 1609[14] and 1609[15].

25. *RISM* 1610[2].

26. Marenzio *I a 5* (1580), no. 1 (reprint in *RISM* 1583[15]); *I a 6* (1581), no. 4 (reprint in *RISM* 1583[14]; modern reproduction in *Opera,* iv, ed. Meier, 22-25).

27. Cf. Marenzio, *IV a 6* (1587), no. 6 (illustration in ex. 244-245) with Hassler, *Neue teütsche Gesang* (1596), reproduced in *Werke,* ii (= *DTB,* v/2), 122-127.

28. Cf. Marenzio, *III a 6* (1585), no. 5 and Hassler, op. cit., pp. 117-121. Both compositions reproduced and discussed by Hucke in *SM* iii (1974), 255-284.

29. Kerman, *Madrigal,* p. 24.

30. Reproduced in *EMS,* vi.92-96.

31. Reproduced in *EMS,* xii.44. "Thule" is the archaic name for Iceland and is represented by two ice-like semibreves which resemble islands on the top of a map.

32. *Weelkes,* p. 70 ff and note 2.

33. *EMS,* vi.48 ff.

34. As might have been the case had Weelkes been setting it: see Brown, *Wilbye,* p. 21.

35. See also chapter 8, ex. 239.

36. The *misura di breve* is used in nos. 5, 7, 8, 9 and 15; in the subsequent books, it is used only once: in *VII a 5* (1595), no. 4.

37. E.g. the coloration on "Sono il mio sangue" ("are my blood") in no. 11, b. 69 ff; the use of semibreves to depict "pietra" ("rock") in no. 13.

38. First published in Venice, 1590; the first setting known to me is Monte's adaption of the famous lament, *Cruda Amarilli,* published in 1590: see Chater, "Fonti poetiche," *RIDM,* xiii (1978), p. 72, no. 50.

39. See appendix II, note to *IV a 6* (1587), no. 14. Another critic, Pietro Malacreta, attacked several passages for their inappropriately madrigalian character: among others, *Cruda Amarilli, Ah dolente partita* and *Udite lagrimosi,* set by Marenzio in the *VI* and *VII a 5* (1594 and 1595). See Guarini, *Opere* (1737), iv.101 ff.

40. Which has the typically madrigalian form aa/Bc/ddeE: see appendix II, note to *VI a 5* (1594), no. 7.

41. *IV a 6* (1587), no. 6. The dramatic interjections of Marenzio's setting foreshadow the later style: see above, ex. 244-245 and below, note 94.

42. *IX a 5* (1599), no. 11.

43. *VI a 5* (1594), no. 15.

44. *VIII a 5* (1598), no. 6.

45. The episode in act iii.1 narrated by Tirsi, in which Silvia is assailed by Satiro and rescued by her lover, Aminta. Lustful satyrs figure prominently in the *pastorale:* e.g. Giraldi Cintio's *Egle,* first performed in Ferrara, 1545.

46. *IX a 5* (1599), no. 7: Torchi, *Arte musicale,* ii.215-223.

47. For further details see Chater, "Fonti poetiche," *RIDM,* xiii (1978), 72 ff.

48. See chapter 7.

49. *VI a 5* (1594), no. 10; the same technique is already used to contrast the two ladies described in *Coppia di donna altera* (*RISM* 1592[14]).

50. Reproduced in *Il settimo libro,* ed. Steele, facsimile 3, pp. 107-111.

51. *VIII a 5* (1598), no. 16; the *prima parte* has sections of 27, 14 and 28 bars (bb. 1-27; 28-41; 42-69; a ratio of very nearly 2:1:2). The *seconda parte* has sections of 24, 39, and 24 bars (bb. 70-93; 94-132; 133-156; a ratio of nearly 2:3:2).

52. The two works are scored for one canto and double alto and tenor in the *chiavi naturali,* C_1, C_3, C_4, and F_4. The subdued coloring is aided by the use of plagal modes (8 untransposed and 2 transposed).

53. Reprint by Arnold (Penn State Music Series, 8).

54. *I a 4, 5, 6* (1588), no. 2: *Secular Works,* vii (ed. Ledbetter), 7 (bb. 30-55).

55. See above, chapter 8; cf. *Giovane donna,* ed. Arnold, p. 39 ff (bb. 329-420).

56. The lengths of the seven movements are 68, 70, 70, 73, 74, 98, and 62 bars. The final movement consists of three rather than six lines and is therefore proportionately longer than all the others.

57. Quoted in Einstein, *Madrigal,* ii.673 ff and Arnold, *Marenzio,* p. 34.

58. Cf. the perfect cadence on *e* at the end of *I a 5* (1580), no. 6.

59. "Thus wish I to be harsh in my diction." Marenzio's setting is reproduced by Einstein in *AMW,* iii (1921), 412-421.

60. "Squeezed hand." The setting of *La bella man vi stringo* is reproduced in Torchi, *Arte musicale,* ii.224-227.

61. Cf. above, ex. 270.

62. "More for looking at . . . than for singing or enjoyment." *El Melopeo,* p. 678.

63. Ibid., p. 699 ff. Cerone's disapproval is already foreshadowed by Artusi in 1603 (see below). The *IX a 5* was transcribed in 1630 by the Sienese composer, Tommaso Pecci, with the apparent motive of studying Marenzio's dissonance technique: asterisks are placed above the more striking ones. The MS survives as I-Sc, *L.V.34.*

64. Strunk, *Source readings,* p. 335; quoted also in Arnold, *Marenzio,* p. 21.

65. Arnold, *Marenzio,* p. 21.

66. "A most happy shade in my every mishap."

67. Arnold, *Marenzio,* p. 21 ff.

68. Hitchcock, introduction to Caccini, *Nuove musiche,* p. 7.

69. Caccini, preface to *Le nuove musiche,* translated by Hitchcock in edn. cit., p. 45.

70. The English equivalents, "grace" and "negligence," are hardly adequate translations. For further discussion, see edn. cit., p. 43, note 6, and pp. 44-45, note 10.

71. See also chapter 6, ex. 181.

72. See chapter 5, note 128.

73. Particularly significant is Mei's comment on the different emotional effects of high, low, and intermediate pitches (the *netoid, mesoid,* and *hypatoid*); the same expressive range, argues Mei, is not available to composers in the polyphonic style, where all three pitch areas are superimposed and therefore cancel out whatever emotional effect they may possess on their own: see Palisca, "Mei," *MQ,* xl (1954), 10: Mei, *Letters,* ed. Palisca, first letter to Galilei (8th May 1572), p. 48.

74. I-Fn, MS *Ant. Galilei II,* ff. 55^r-136^r; I, ff. 104^r-174^V; I, ff. 148^r-196^V; see Palisca, "Galilei's treatise," *JAMS* ix (1956), 81-95.

75. The possible influence of Galilei is discussed in Arnold, *Marenzio,* p. 35 ff.

76. Reproduced in Palisca, "Camerata," *SM,* i (1972), no. 2, pp. 229-230.

77. See "La meraviglia, ohimè, degli intermedi," in *Li due Orfei,* pp. 200-275, especially p. 222 ff.

78. See the *Discorso mandato a Giulio Caccini,* tr. in Strunk, *Source readings,* p. 295.

79. "The style of the choruses being neither heard nor used, at least in our times." Quoted from Crocioni, *"Alidoro,"* p. 36.

80. "The affects of the soul."

81. Crocioni, op. cit., p. 37.

82. *La Cofanaria* was performed in Florence in 1565; Striggio's music, a homophonic piece for solo voice and four instruments, was reproduced in Galilei's *Fronimo* (2nd edn., 1584) and is now available in Brown, "Psyche's lament," in *Festschrift Merritt*, p. 17. For further details, see appendix II, note to *II a 6* (1584), no. 5.

83. Reproduced in *La représentation d'Edipo Tiranno*, ed. Schrade.

84. Ingegneri makes his views on theatre music plain in his *Poesia rappresentativa* (1598), reproduced in G.B. Guarini, *Opere*, Verona, 1737, iii.494 ff and 536 ff.

85. Quoted in Solerti, *Origine*, pp. 109-110. Further evidence of the importance of "stage presence" among singers is quoted by Newcomb, *Musica secreta* p. 117 ff.

86. MacClintock, *Wert*, p. 44 ff.

87. See chapter 2, p. 18 ff.

88. *IX a 5* (1599), no. 8 (repr. in Torchi, *Arte musicale*, ii.228-237); cf. Lassus, *Werke*, ii.71-75; Wert, *Works*, vii.32-37. All three openings quoted in Engel, *Marenzio*, p. 158.

89. *Misera, non credea* and *Forsennata gridava (VIII a 5*, 1586; *Works*, viii.29-33 and 49-50).

90. *II a 6* (1584), no. 12: *Opera*, iv (ed. Meier), 190-194.

91. See chapter 1, note 41.

92. *Seconda parte dell'Artusi* (1603), p. 18. Artusi presumably refers to the second note in the canto, an extraneous *e*-flat which upsets the listener's sense of mode at the very opening. Other examples are cited: e.g. the *b*-flat which opens *Dura legge (IX a 5*, 1599, no. 3). For a summary of the arguments contained in the *Seconda parte*, see Palisca, "Artusi," in *The Monteverdi Companion* (eds. Arnold and Fortune), pp. 133-166.

93. See below, note 97.

94. Cf. Monteverdi, *II a 5* (1590), (*Opere*, ii.83-86) with Marenzio *IV a 6* (1587), no. 6. The two composers' treatment of the interjection "Ah, non si può morir," repeated by both composers, is very similar: for musical examples, see above, ex. 244-245, and Engel, *Marenzio*, pp. 195-196.

95. Cf. Marenzio, *IV a 5* (1584), no. 15 and Monteverdi, *I a 5* (1587; reproduced in *Opere*, i.8-10).

96. Marenzio may have been influenced by Monteverdi even though his version of the text differs both from Monteverdi's 1592 version and the literary source, *Rime di diversi*, ed. Licino, Bergamo, 1587.

97. In *L'Artusi, ovvero delle imperfezioni . . .* (1600), translated in Strunk, *Source readings*, pp. 393-404; the madrigals discussed by Artusi were performed in the house of Antonio Goretti, a young nobleman and dilettante living in Ferrara. Luzzaschi and Fiorino are mentioned as having been present. (Strunk, op. cit., p. 394).

98. In the *Seconda parte dell'Artusi* (1603), pp. 16-18; later on, in the *Considerationi musicali* (appended to the *Seconda parte*), p. 30, Artusi mentions Marenzio's *Falsa credenza*, written for the Ferrarese anthology, *RISM* 1586[10].

99. *Seconda parte*, p. 36. See also Palisca, "Artusi" cit., pp. 155-156.

100. In his *Declaration*, published with his brother's *Scherzi musicali* (facs. edn. in Monteverdi, *Opere*, x.70); translated in Strunk, *Source readings*, p. 408.

101. The same point is made at the opening of Brown's "Words and music" (unpubl. art.).

102. *VII a 5* (1595), no. 3: *Il settimo libro,* ed. Steele, pp. 11-20; also reproduced as musical supplement in Chater, "Cruda Amarilli," *MT,* cxvi (1975), pp. 231-234.

103. Arnold, *Marenzio,* p. 30 ff; Chater, art. cit. in previous note.

104. Torchi, *Arte musicale* ii.234.

105. Ibid., p. 236, second system, b. 1.

106. See chapter 8, note 111.

107. Marenzio's last book, consisting almost entirely of settings of Grillo's poetry, has not survived: see Einstein, *Madrigal,* ii.688.

108. Marenzio is the only composer whom Bonini places in two categories.

109. In his MS treatise, *Discorsi e regole sopra la musica* (I-Fr, MS *Riccardiana 2218,* f. 95^V). The treatise was written between 1646 and 1663, as Luisi points out in the introduction to his edition (Cremona, 1975). A bilingual edition has been prepared by M.A. Bonino, Provo, Utah, 1979. I have preferred to transcribe directly from the manuscript source.

110. "Luca Marenzio . . . was the greatest of all composers of songs 'because he composed in both the second and the third styles: in the second, as in that book for five voices where there are the words *Liquide perle amore* [*I a 5,* 1580, no. 1] and *Tirsi morir volea* [ibid, no.5]; in the third, as in that madrigal for five voices, *S'io parto io moro* [*VI a 5,* 1594, no. 1], in those of the Ninth Book [*a 5,* 1599] *Così nel mio cantar* [sic] *voglio essere aspro* [no. 1], so ingenious, and in those for six voices: *Se bramate ch'io mora* [*IV a 6,* 1587, no. 1] and *Lucida perla* [*IV a 6,* 1595, no. 1]. In these works one hears double conceits, dissonances skilfully contrived and resolved, and divine sweetness, [Marenzio] having used affects appropriate to the words.' " The speaker in single quotation marks is a friend of Bonini; he implies a distinction between an early period and a more mature period beginning with the *IV a 6* (1587).

Appendix I

Analysis of Cadence Pitches in Each Mode

Note: This analysis is based on the first five madrigal books *a 5*, together with the following extra madrigals: *I a 6* (1581), nos. 2, 5, 8, and 14; *II a 6* (1584), no. 11; *Spirituali* (1584), nos. 4, 10, 11, and 12; *III a 6* (1585), nos. 14 and 15; *I a 4* (1585), nos. 10, 18, and 20; *IV a 6* (1587), nos. 2 and 13; *I a 4, 5, 6* (1588), nos. 9 and 10. The selection is designed to ensure a sufficient coverage of each of the 12 modes; other examples might have been included had further time been available.

Passages in foreign modes *(commixtio tonorum)* have been omitted from consideration. The results have been collected and presented in such a way as to assume no essential difference between the cadence behavior of a mode in its natural and transposed forms. The numerals indicate the scale degree on which the cadences are formed, the order corresponding with their frequency. The same numeral indicates the same pitch (or its octave transposition) in both authentic and plagal forms (for instance, the numeral "4" indicates *c* in both modes 7 and 8 untransposed). A hyphen linking 2 figures indicates that these cadences occur with equal frequency. There has been no general attempt to indicate cadences of different types: i.e. plagal, perfect, inverted, or avoided. However, perfect cadences which entail chromatic alteration of the second degree are given the abbreviation "perf." It should be noted that delayed cadences are counted according to the note of tonic resolution, i.e. that a IV - V - I cadence on *a* is reckoned to be cadence on *a*, not *e*. Phrygian cadences are counted as such only if there is no strong subsequent pull towards the tonic resolution. Thus the cadence in example 281, a cadence on *e-mi* with no resolution to *a*, would be represented: 3 *(mi)*. However, the cadence in example 282 is a delayed IV - V - I cadence and is therefore counted as a perfect cadence on 4 rather than a phrygian cadence on 1. The final cadence of a mode-3 or mode-4 composition is counted as "4."

Mode	Structural value	Scale degree
1	Terminal	1 5
	Principal	1 3 - 5 4 - 7
	Transitory	1 5 4 3 7 2*(mi)*
2	Terminal	1 5
	Principal	1 5 3 4
	Transitory	1 5 4 3 7
3	Terminal	4 1(perf.) 6
	Principal	4 6 3 7 5(perf.)
	Transitory	4 6 7 3 1*(mi)* 1(perf.)

4	Terminal	4
	Principal	4 - 6 3
	Transitory	4 - 6 2 3 7 2 - 1*(mi)*

5	Terminal	1
	Principal	5 1
	Transitory	1 5 2 - 6 4 3*(mi)*

6	Terminal	1
	Principal	1 - 5
	Transitory	1 6 5 2 3 7*(mi)*

7	Terminal	1 4 - 5
	Principal	4 5 1 -2 - 6(perf.) - 7
	Transitory	4 1 5 2(perf.) 7 2*(mi)* - 6(perf.) - 6*(mi)*

8	Terminal	1 4 - 5
	Principal	1 4 5
	Transitory	1 4 2 5 7 6*(mi)* 3*(mi)* - 6(perf.)

9	Terminal	1 4
	Principal	3 1 - 4 - 7 6
	Transitory	3 1(perf.) 4 7 6 5(perf.) 1*(mi)* -5*(mi)*

10	Terminal	1
	Principal	1 3 - 7
	Transitory	1 3 4 7 6 5*(mi)* 1*(mi)*

11	Terminal	1 5 6
	Principal	1 5 6 2
	Transitory	1 5 2 3*(mi)* 6 4 3(perf.)

12	Terminal	1 5
	Principal	5 1 2 6
	Transitory	1 5 6 2 4 3*(mi)* 7

Appendix II

Marenzio

Note: An expanded and corrected version of the list in *RIDM*, xiii (1978), 84-103. Information is given in the following order: mode, literary content, reprints, arrangements, modern reprints, other settings, other information. Modern reprints are listed only if the madrigal does not yet appear in one of the "complete" editions; other settings are referred to only if they have been consulted and their sources listed in appendices III and VI. The lists of early reprints is designed to be as all-inclusive as possible. It should be borne in mind that many of the anthologies referred to have substituted texts in English, German or Latin. (See below, "Anthologies Containing Reprints Only," and the inventories in *VE*, ii).

Individual Publications

Il primo libro de' madrigali a cinque voci (1580)
Dedicated to Cardinal Luigi d'Este, Rome, 8.8.1580. Printed in Venice: A. Gardano (1580, 1582, 1587, 1602); herede di G. Scotto (1585, 1600, 1608); G. Vincenzi and R. Amadino (1586); G. Vincenti (1588); A. Raverij (1608). Most items repr. in *I-V a 5* (1593); all items repr. in *I-IX a 5* (1601). Modern repr. by Einstein, *PÄM*, iv/1, 1-37.

1. *Liquide perle Amor da gl'occhi sparse*

   Mode 7 untransp.

   Text by Pasqualino (madrigal): ascription survives in setting by Pisanelli (1586): "M[olto] R[everendo] Lelio Pasqualino Romano." Subject matter drawn from Petrarch, *Canzoniere*, no. 55 (chapter 3, note 66).

   Repr. in *RISM* 1583[15] (without attribution), 1588[17], 1588[21] and 1606[6]; transcribed in Raselius, *Dodecachordon* (see Debes, *Merulo*, p. 97).

   Instrumental arr. in *Brown* 1582[1], 1584[3], 1591[2], 1599[11], and 1600[5a].

   Set by Pesciolini, *III a 6* (1581); Pisanelli, *I a 5* (1586); Castro, *I a 3* (1588); Sweelinck (1612: *Werke*, viii. 21-22); Capece, *I a 4, 5, 8* (1616). All these settings contain quotations of Marenzio.

   Other quotations are found in: *Liquide perle Amore / Dai ruscelletti fuore* in Tresti, *I a 5* (1585); *Se le lagrime tue* by Vopa, in Pace-Vopa, *I a 5* (1585); *Ridea la donna mia* in Coma, *IV a 5* (1587); *Liquide perle in sì nuova maniera* by G.B. Loccatello, in Cancineo, *I a 4, 5, 6, 8* (1590); *Donna se quel "ohimè,"* set by Giulio Belli in *I a 4, 5, 6* (1589), by Scaletta in *II a 5* (1590) and by Pallavicino in *V a 5* (1593: *Flanders*, no. 173); *Candide perla ch'in fin oro accolta* in Del Mel, *II a 6* (1593). Parodied by Banchieri in "Liquide ferl'Amor . . ." (1601:

Opera, i/2, pp. 42-45); quoted in the Centone concluding Biffi's *Ricreatione di Posilipo* (1606), and the Quodlibet in Zacconi's *Prattica di musica,* ii (1622), 113 ff. Praised by Della Valle, 1640 (Solerti, *Origine,* p. 170).

2. *Ohimè, dov'è 'l mio ben? Dov'è 'l mio core?*

SATTB

Mode 12 untransp.

Text by B. Tasso *(ottava rima);* 5th stanza of *Se ben di nove stelle* ("... sette stelle" in earlier edns.); pr. in poet's *Rime* (1560), iv. 19. Bibl: Williamson, *B. Tasso,* p. 48 ff.

Repr. in *RISM* 1590[29].

Set by Nasco and Ruffo (Einstein, *Madrigal,* i. 464); Moscaglia, *I a 4, 5, 6* (1575); Macque, *I a 6* (1576: transc. in Shindle, *Macque,* ii. 109-118); Monte, *I a 3* (1582: transcr. by Einstein, *SCA,* xxxix); Monteverdi, (1619: *Opere,* vii. 152-159). Often as *seconda parte* of *Vita della mia vita* (4th stanza).

3. *Spuntavan già per far il mondo adorno*
   Quando 'l mio vivo sol . . .

SSATB

Mode 7 untransp.

Sonnet.

Repr. in *RISM* 1588[21], 1590[29], 1591[10], 1609[14].

Model for Demantius, *Magnificat a 5* (Engel, *ZMW,* xvii. 286). Mentioned in Vecchi, *Mostra,* p. 17.

4. *Quando i vostri begl'occhi un caro velo*
   Mode 9 untransp.

SATTB

Sannazaro, no. 38 (madrigal).
Repr. in RISM 1590[29].

Instrumental arr. in *Brown* 1591[2], 1593[7].

Set by Arcadelt, *IV a 5* (1539); Vicentino (1546: *Opera,* pp. 3-5); Cifra, *I a 5* (1605).

Analysed in Unger, *Musik und Rhetorik,* p. 134 ff.

5. *Tirsi morir volea*
   Frenò Tirsi il desio
   Così moriro . . .

SATTB

Mode 3 untransp.

Text by Guarini (madrigal); first pr. in T. Tasso, *Rime,* i, Venice, 1581, p. 144, with attrib. to Tasso; but Tasso's authorship denied in *Rime,* i, Ferrara, 1581, p. 95. Printed in Guarini, *Rime,* Venice, 1598, f. 132[v]. Subject matter similar to *V a 6* (1591), no. 8 with text by Tasso; for comparisons, see Di Benedetto, *Tasso,* pp. 77-78, and Schulz-Buschhaus, *Madrigal,* p. 204 ff; cf. Einstein, *Madrigal,* ii. 541 ff and 547 ff.

Repr. in *RISM* 1583[14], 1584[5], 1588[21], 1588[29], 1606[6].

Instrumental arr. in *Brown* 1584[3], 1591[2], 1592[6], *RISM* 1600[5a], and Philips, in *Fitzwilliam Virginal Book,* ed. Fuller Maitland and Barclay Squire, i. 280-287.

Set by Meldert, *I a 5* (1578); Gabussi, *I a 5* (1580); Pallavicino (1581: *Flanders,* no. 47); Wert (1581: *Works,* vii. 56-63); Malvezzi (1584: transcr. in Butchart, *Madrigal in Florence,* ii. 176-182); Milleville, *II a 5* (1584); Caimo, *IV a 5* (1585); Monte, *IX a 5* (1586: transcr. by Einstein, *SCA,* xlii); A. Gabrieli, *Concerti* (1578); Castro, *I a 3* (1588); Croce, *I a 6* (1590); Gesualdo (1594: *Werke,* i.50-56).

Model for a mass by Luyton, *Magnificat a 8* by Demantius and a five-voice mass by G. Posch (Engel, *ZMW,* xvii.286). Analysed for use of modes in G.B. Doni, *Annotazioni,* p. 141.

6. *Dolorosi martir, fieri tormenti*

SATB

Mode 3 untransp.

Text by Tansillo *(ottava rima);* survives only in MS; pr. in *Canzoniere,* ed. Pèrcopo, p. 152.

Repr. in *RISM* 1588[21] (the copy in D-Mbs is underscored with a sacred text: "Misere mei, o Dei meus . . ."), 1597[24], 1609[14] and 1624[16]. Transcr. in GB-Lbm, *R.M. 24.d.2.).*
Parody mass by Harant (*Opera,* pp. 45-78); *Magnificat a 6* by Praetorius, (*Gesamtausgabe,* xiv. 42-48).

Set by Monte (1558: repr. in Roche, *Penguin Book of Italian Madrigals,* pp. 95-98); Isnardi, *II a 5* (1577); Striggio (*RISM* 1577[7]); Ingegneri (1580: repr. by G. Cesari, *IMAMI,* vi. 127-130); G.M. Nanino, in Nanino-Stabile, *I a 5* (1581) and *III a 5* (1586); Soriano, *II a 5* (1592); Luzzaschi (1594: repr. in Einstein, *Madrigal,* iii. 257-261); Bati (1598: transcr. in Butchart, *Madrigal in Florence,* ii. 247-250).

7. *Che fa hoggi il mio sole?*

SSATB

Mode 1 untransp.

Madrigal.

Repr. in *RISM* 1583[14], 1584[5], 1588[21], 1593[5], 1605[9], 1606[6], 1618[8]; Eng. tr. in *RISM* 1588[29] ("What doth my pretty darling?") reset by East, 1606 (Kerman, *Madrigal,* p. 24).

Vocal arr. *a 2* in Banchieri, *Il principiante* (1625: see Mischiati, *Banchieri,* p. 118). Instrumental arr. in *Brown* 1592[6], *RISM* 1600[5]a.

Reset by Caimo, *IV a 5* (1585); Stabile, *III a 5* (1585); Castro, *I a 3* (1588); Tollius (1597: *Madrigalen,* ed. Seiffert, pp. 71-73).

Parody mass by Gregorio Allegri in I-Rvat, MS *Capp. Sist. 53.*

8. *Lasso, ch'io ardo, e'l mio bel sole ardente*

Mode 10 untransp.

Madrigal; acrostic on "Livia B . . ." (Einstein, *Madrigal,* ii. 617 ff). Cf. Petrarch, "Lasso, ch'i' ardo et altri non mel crede" (*Canzoniere,* no. 203).

Repr. in *RISM* 1589[8], 1606[6]

9. *Venuta era Madonna al mio languire*
   Intanto il sonno . . .

Mode 5 untransp.

Text by Sannazaro, no. 64 (madrigal). The "dream motive" recalls certain poems by Petrarch: see *II a 5* (1581), no. 12 and *II a 6* (1584), no. 11.

Repr. in *RISM* 1590[29] (without *seconda parte*) and 1606[6].

Set by Baccusi, *III a 6* (1579).

Mentioned in Vecchi, *Mostra*, p. 15.

10. *Madonna mia gentil, ringratio Amore*

Mode 1 transp.

Madrigal.

Repr. in *RISM* 1585[19] and 1590[29].

Instrumental arr. in Brown 1584[3], 1591[2], *RISM* 1600[5a].

Set in Castro, *I a 3* (1588).

11. *Cantava la più vaga pastorella*

Mode 1 transp.

Madrigal.

Repr. in *RISM* 1588[21], 1590[29], 1605[9].

12. *Questa di verd'herbette*

Mode 2 transp.

Madrigal.

Repr. in 1590[29], 1606[6].

13. *Partirò dunque: ohimè, mi manca il core*

Mode 2 transp.

Madrigal.

Repr. in *RISM* 1590[29] and 1606[6].

Instr. arr. in *Brown* 1584[3].

Marenzio's second and last lines ("Porgimi aiuta, Amore . . . Prestami aiuta Amore") are quoted in Hassler's *Non vedo hogg'il mio sole* (*DTB*, v. 41-42.)

14. *O tu che fra le selve occulta vivi*

Mode 2 transp.

T. Tasso (?), madrigal ("Dialogo a 8 in risposta d'ecco"). Attribution to Tasso doubted by Solerti (in his edn. of the *Rime*, i. 123) and challenged by Pirrotta in "Note" (*Festschrift Ronga*, p. 564); first pr. posthumously in the *Rime fatti a diversi Prencipi ed huomini*, bound with the *Sonetti fatti a diversi prencipi e huomini e donne illustre compositi dal Sig. Torquato Tasso da lui ult*[imamente] *in Roma e da altri nobili autori*, Venice 1597. The version printed here, addressed to the Countess of Saponara, was repr. in the *Opere*, ed. Rosini, iv. 256. It differs greatly from the one used by Marenzio, which follows exactly the

"Eco d'Incerto" in I-Bu, MS *1171*, f. 108^V. Other MS sources include: I-Fn, *II.IV.16*, f. 48^r. ("O tu, che fra le selve occulta stai"—attrib. to Piero Naccherelli); I-Fn, *Palat. 256*, f. 256^r ("O tu che nelle selve occulta stai"—attrib. to Tasso in a modern hand on f. 256^V). First and last lines quoted from Sannazaro, *Arcadia* xi, lines 13 and 15.

Repr. in *RISM* 1590[11], 1609[15], and Marenzio, *Spirituali e temporali* (1610); omitted from *I-V a 5* (1593).

Set by D. Belli, *Arie* (1616); Anon, I-Rvat, MS *Barb. Lat. 4288*, ff. 2^V-5^V.

Il primo libro de' madrigali a sei voci (1581)
Dedicated to Duke Alfonso II of Ferrara, Venice, 10.4.1581. Printed in Venice: A. Gardano (1581, 1584, 1603); herede di G. Scotto (1596). Most items repr. in *I-V a 6* (1594) and *I-VI a 6* (1608). Modern repr. in *Opera*, iv (ed. Meier), 2-108. Transcr. in Bennett, *Marenzio*, ii. 3-110.

1. *Come inanti de l'alba ruggiadosa*
       Così questa di cui canto . . .

    Mode 12 transp.

    Madrigal; acrostic on "Cleria Cesarini," renowned for her beauty, literary patron, daughter of Cardinal Alessandro Farnese: see Chater, "Castelletti," *SM*, viii (1979), 88 ff. Repr. in Einstein, *Madrigal*, ii. 618.

2. *Potrò viver io più se senza luce*

    Mode 6 transp.

    Madrigal; the constant repetition of "luce" suggests it is one of the "Luce" poems of Strozzi the Elder (cf. *Madrigali*, ed. Ariani, nos. 21-38).

    Repr. in *RISM* 1591[10].

3. *Per duo coralli ardenti*

    Mode 2 transp.

    Madrigal.

    Repr. in *RISM* 1587[14].

4. *Qual vive Salamandra in fiamm' ardente*

    Mode 2 transp.

    Madrigal; cf. sonnet by Giusto de' Conti, *Qual Salamandra in su l'acceso foco*, pr. in Giolito, *Rime scelte*, ii (1565), 563 and Obertello, *Madrigale*, p. 511.

    Repr. in *RISM* 1583[14], 1589[8], 1609[14], 1610[2], and *VE* 1622[A].

    Instrumental arr. in *Brown* 1592[6] and *RISM* 1600[5a].

    Set by Castro, *I a 3* (1588) and Sweelinck (1612: *Werke*, viii. 69-70); both composers quote Marenzio's themes.

5. *Ben mi credetti già d'esser felice*

    Mode 4 transp.

Text by Quirini *(ottava rima);* 7th stanza of *Hor che nell'oceano;* in *Domenichi,* i (1546), 197. Other settings of this poem are *I a 6,* no. 10 and *IV a 5* (1584), no. 9.

6. *Mentre fia caldo il sol, fredda la neve*

   Mode 7 transp.

   Ottava rima.

7. *Al suon de le dolcissime parole*

   Mode 8 untransp.

   Madrigal; repr. in Einstein, *Madrigal,* ii. 754.

   Repr. in *RISM* 1589[9].

   Words and music of last 2 lines quote opening of Rore's *Non mi toglia il ben mio (Opera,* v. 18).

8. *Nel più fiorito Aprile*

   Mode 11 untransp.

   Madrigal.

   Repr. in *RISM* 1589[8], 1609[14].

   Set by A. Ferrabosco, *II a 5* (1587).

9. *O dolorosa sorte*

   Mode 3 untransp.

   Madrigal.

   Set by Pallavicino (1604: *Flanders,* no. 240).

10. *Ahimè, tal fu d'Amore e l'esc'e l'hamo*

    Mode 10 untransp.

    Text by Quirino *(ottava rima):* 6th stanza of *Hor che nell'oceano,* in *Domenichi,* i (1546), 196. (Cf. above, no. 5, and *IV a 5,* 1584, no. 9.)

    Set by A. Gabrieli, *I a 5* (1566).

11. *Occhi sereni e chiari*

    Mode 7 untransp.

    Madrigal; first line from Spanish, "Ojos claros, serenos" by Gutierre de Cetina, in De Castro (ed.), *Biblioteca,* i. 42.

    Repr. in *RISM* 1589[8], 1609[15]; transcr. in Raselius, *Dodecachordon* (Debes, *Merulo,* p. 97).

    Model for *Magnificat a 6* by Demantius (Engel, *ZMW,* vii. 286).

12. *Deh, rinforzate il vostro largo pianto*

    Mode 9 untransp.

    Madrigal.

13. *Cantate Ninfe leggiadrette e belle*

    Mode 12 untransp.

    Madrigal.

    Repr. in *RISM* 1589[8], 1609[14].

14. *Non è questa la mano*
        Ecco c'hor pur si trova

    Mode 5 untransp.

    Text by T. Tasso (madrigal); first pr. in *Rime,* i (Venice, 1581), 47; repr. in the *Rime,* ed. Solerti, ii, no. 47.

    Set by Pallavicino, *I a 4* (1579: *Flanders,* no. 21); Castro, *Rose fresche (1591);* Gesualdo (1594: *Werke,* ii. 41-44).

15. *Strinse Amarilli il vago suo Fileno*

    Mode 10 transp.

    Madrigal.

16. *Mentre sul far del giorno*

    Mode 11 transp.

    Canzone stanza.

17. *L'aura serena, che fra verdi fronde*
        Le quali ella spargea . . .

    Mode 1 transp.

    Text by Petrarch, *Canzoniere,* no. 196 (sonnet).

    Repr. in *RISM* 1589[8].

    Set by Conversi, *I a 6* (1584).

18. *Viene Clori gentil; boschetti e prati*

    Mode 8 untransp.

    Madrigal ('Dialogo a 10'); attrib. to Poliziano in *NV,* ii. 1022, but this echo poem is obviously of the late *Cinquecento.*

    Omitted from the *I-V a 6* (1594).

Il secondo libro de' madrigali a cinque voci (1581)
Dedicated to Lucrezia d'Este, Duchess of Urbino, Rome, 25.10.1581. Printed in Venice: A. Gardano (1581, 1583, 1593, 1606); Vincenzi (1587); herede di G. Scotto (1606); A. Raverij (1608). Most items repr. in *I-V a 5* (1593); all items pr. in *I-IX a 5* (1601). Modern repr. by Einstein in *PÄM* iv/1, 43-88.

1. *Deggio dunque partire*
        Io partirò, ma il core
        Ma voi, caro ben mio

SSATB

Mode 1 transp.

Canzone (irregular in first stanza: see chapter 3, note 45).

Repr. in *RISM* 1588[21] (without *terza parte*), 1588[29] (*seconda parte* only), 1591[10], 1606[6], 1607[20] (*prima parte* only), 1616[8].

Set by Rota, *II a 5* (1589); Pesciolini, *III a 6* (1591).

2.   *Perchè di poggia il ciel non si distille*

SAATB

Mode 5 untransp.

Madrigal.

3.   *Amor io non potrei*
      Deh, fa ch'ella sappia anco

(S)
SMATB

Mode 1 transp.

Text by Ariosto, Madrigal 3 (*Lirica,* ed. Fatini, p. 52).

Repr. in *RISM* 1589[8].

Set by G. Blotagrio, *RISM* 1591[10].

4.   *Amor, poichè non vuole*
      Chi strinse mai . . .

SSATB

Mode 12 untransp.

Text by Parabosco (madrigal); in *Rime,* i (1546), 9.

Repr. in *RISM* 1585[19], 1589[8], 1606[6], 1616[8].

Instrumental arr. in *RISM* 1600[6].

Set by Wert (1561: *Works,* xv. 27-29); Ingegneri, *I a 4* (1578); Castro, *I a 3* (1588).

5.   *Quando sorge l'aurora/Ridon l'herbette e i fiori*

Mode 9 untransp.

Madrigal; cf. A. Gabrieli, *I a 5* (1566): "Quando lieta ver noi sorge l'aurora/Ridon l'aria e la terra."

Repr. in *RISM* 1588[21].

Set by Macque (1599: transcr. in Shindle, *Macque,* ii. 430-38).

6.   *Fillida mia, più che i ligustri bianca*

Mode 12 untransp.

Text by Sannazaro (stanza in form of madrigal): *Arcadia,* ii, lines 101-108, spoken by Montano.

Repr. in *RISM* 1589[8], 1606[6], and 1616[8].

Set by F. Anerio, *I a 3* (1598).

Quoted by Del Mel in *Tirrhenia mia* (*Arcadia,* ii, lines 109-116), *I a 5* (1584: facs. repr. in *CEMF,* xxi: see chapter 3, ex. 21).

7.   *Al vago del mio sole*

SATTB   Mode 7 untransp.

Madrigal.

Repr. in *RISM* 1589[8].

8.   *Itene a l'ombra de gli ameni faggi*

SSATB   Mode 12 untransp.

Text by Sannazaro *(terza rima): Arcadia*, ii, lines 1-9, spoken by Montano.

Repr. in *RISM* 1588[21] and 1609[14].

Instrumental arr. in *RISM* 1600 .

Set by Caccini, who mentions his setting in the Preface to *Euridice* (1600) and *Le nuove musiche* (1601): see *NV*, i. 287-288.

9.   *La bella Ninfa mia, ch'al Tebro infiora*

SATTB   Mode 1 untransp.

Text by F. Molza *(ottava rima):* first stanza of *La Ninfa Tiberina*, in *Stanze*, ed. Dolce, i (1556), 146.

— 10.   *O voi che sospirate a miglior note*

SATTB   Mode 3 untransp.

Text by Petrarch: *Canzoniere*, no. 332, lines 67-72 (sestina stanza); "note" has been emended from "notti."

Transcr. in GB-Lbm, *R.M. 24.d.2*

Set by Micheli Romano (1621: see Lowinsky, "Echoes," in *Festschrift Strunk*, ed. Powers, p. 184 ff).

Bibl: Doni, *Lyra Barberina*, ii.17; for further references, see chapter 5, note 72.

11.   *Strider faceva le zampogne a l'aura*

SAATB   Mode 11 untransp.

Ottava rima: 46th stanza of *O bionde Iddio*, in *Domenichi*, iv (1551), 325. For other settings, see *II a 6* (1584), no. 1; *I a 4, 5, 6* (1588), no. 3.

Repr. in *RISM* 1588[21], 1606[6].

— 12.   *I' piango; ed ella il volto*

Mode 8 transp.

SATTB   Text by Petrarch: *Canzoniere*, no. 359, lines 67-71 (canzone fragment).

Repr. in *RISM* 1609[14].

Set by Ingegneri, Il Martoretta, Sabino (see Einstein, *Madrigal*, ii. 625); Zoilo, *II a 4, 5* (1563); Rore (1566: *Opera*, iv. 4-6); Coma, *I a 5* (1568).

13. *Già Febo il tuo splendor rendeva chiaro*
     Hor tu gli cedi . . .

SATTB

Mode 2 transp.

Sonnet.

14. *Mi fa, lasso, languire*

"

Mode 4 transp.

Madrigal.

+ 15. *Già torna a rallegrar l'aria e la terra*

SSATB

Mode 12 transp.

Ottava rima

repr. in *RISM* 1589[8] ("*Chi* torna . . .") and 1605[9].

Eng. tr., "To former joy" (Second Part of "Zephirus brings the time") set by Cavendish, 1598 (R. Leavis, in Einstein, *Essays,* 1958 edn., p. 148, *n*).

16. *Se'l pensier che mi strugge*

SATB x 2

Mode 12 transp.; scored for 8 voices.

Text by Petrarch: *Canzoniere,* no. 125, lines 1-13 (canzone stanza).

Repr. in *RISM* 1587[14], 1590[11], 1596[8]; omitted from *I-V a 5* (1593).

Set by Palestrina (1586: *Opere,* xxxi. 28-30).

Il terzo libro de' madrigali a cinque voci (1582)
Dedicated to the Academici Filarmonici of Verona, Rome, 1.12.1582. Printed in Venice: A. Gardano (1582, 1595); G. Vincenti (1591). All items repr. in *I-V a 5* (1593) and *I-IX a 5* (1601). Modern repr. by Einstein, *PÄM,* iv/1, 93-132.

– 1. *Madonna, poich'uccider mi volete*

Mode 12 untransp.

SSATB

Canzone (single-stanza); survives without ascription in I-Fn, MS *Palat.256,* f.21[8r]. ("Donna, poi cuccider mi volete").

Repr. in *RISM* 1583[14].

Instrumental arr. in Brown 1594[5].

Set by Striggio, *I a 6* (1560); Wert (1561: *Works,* xv. 60-62); Merulo (1561: in Torchi, *Arte musicale,* i. 367-370); Portinaro, *I a 4* (1563); Baccusi, *II a 6* (1572).

2. *Caro dolce mio ben, chi mi vi toglie?*

Mode 9 untransp.

SATTB

Madrigal.

Repr. in *RISM* 1598[15].

Set by Striggio, *I a 5* (1560); Baccusi, *II a 6* (1572); Bottegari (1574: *Lutebook*, ed. MacClintock, no. 26).

Opening quotes Bellasio's *Caro dolce ben mio, perchè fuggire?* (1578: see chapter 5, ex. 125c).

3. *Rose bianche e vermiglie*

   Mode 12 untransp.

   SSATB

   Madrigal.

   Repr. in *RISM* 1585[19].

4. *Ohimè, il bel viso, ohimè, il soave sguardo*
   Per voi convien ch'io arda . . .

   SSATB

   Mode 12 untransp.

   Text by Petrarch: *Canzoniere*, no. 267 (sonnet).

   Repr. in *RISM* 1605[9].

   Set by Monteverdi (1614: *Opere*, vi. 70-76).

5. *La pastorella mia spietata e rigida*
   Ecco ribomba . . .

   SSATB

   Mode 7 untransp.

   Text by Sannazaro *(terza rima sdrucciola): Arcadia*, i, lines 91-106, spoken by Ergasto.

   Set by Giovanelli, *II a 4* (1589); F. Anerio, *I a 3* (1598); Monteverdi (1607: *Opere*, x. 41-42).

6. *Lunge da voi, mia vita*
   Ma da voi l'altrui voglia

   SATTB

   Mode 8 untransp.

   Madrigal.

7. *Ohimè, se tanto amate*

   Mode 3 untransp.

   fi

   Text by Guarini (madrigal): *Rime*, Venice, 1598, f. 73[r].

   Set by Pallavicino, *VI a 5* (1600: *Flanders*, no. 197); S. Rossi, *I a 5* (1600); Monteverdi (1603: *Opere*, iv. 54-58).

8. *Scherzando con diletto*

   SSATB

   Mode 11 untransp.

   Madrigal.

9. *Se la mia fiamma ardente*

   SATTB

   Mode 8 untransp.

   Madrigal.

10.   *Ecco più che mai bella e vaga l'aura*

SSATB

Mode 1 transp.

Madrigal; possibly for Laura Peperara (cf. Chater, "Fonti poetiche," *RIDM,* xiii (1978), 65 ff and below, no. 11).

11.   *Ridean già per le piagg'herbette e fiori*
     Piagge, herbe, fiori . . .

Mode 1 transp.

Sonnet for Laura Peperara (cf. no. 10). Cf. Petrarch, *Canzoniere,* no. 239, line 31: "Ridon' hor per le piaggie, herbett'e fiori."

Transcr. in I-VEaf, MS *220.*

12.   *Occhi lucenti e belli*

SATTB

Mode 1 transp.

Text by Gambara (madrigal): in *Domenichi,* i (1546), 311 and *Gaspara Stampa e le altre poetesse del cinquecento,* Milan, 1962, p. 71.

Repr. in *RISM* 1589[8].

Set by Vicentino (1572: *Opera,* pp. 110-114).

13.   *Deh, vezzose del Tebro amate Ninfe*

SSATB

Mode 12 transp.

Madrigal.

14.   *Scaldava il sole di mezo giorno l'arco*

Mode 12 transp.

SSATB

Text by Alamanni *(ottava rima):* from the *Favolo di Narciso,* in Dolce, *Stanze,* i (1556), p. 184; repr. in Alamanni, *Versi e prose,* Florence, 1859, p. 84.

15.   *Sì presso a voi, mio foco*

SATTB

Mode 9 transp.

Text by Guarini (madrigal): in *Rime,* Venice, 1598, f. 62[r].

16.   *Togli, dolce ben mio*

SSATB

Mode 2 transp.

Madrigal.

Set by De Marinis in *RISM* 1597[15] (as *seconda parte* of *La mia leggiadra Clori);* Boschetti, *I a 5* (1613).

17.   *O dolce anima mia, dunque è pur vero*

Mode 12 transp.

Text by Guarini (madrigal); in *Rime di diversi celebri poeti* (ed. Licino, 1587), p. 199, and Guarini, *Opere* (Verona, 1737), ii. 130.

Reset by Monte, *XV a 5* (1592); Monteverdi (1592: *Opere*, iii. 19-25); V. Aleotti, *I a 4* (1593).

Analysed in Dürr, "Lingua e musica."

Il secondo libro de' madrigali a sei voci (1584)
Dedicated to the Cardinal de Guise, Rome, 15.4.1584. Printed in Venice: A. Gardano (1584, 1600); herede di G. Scotto (1596). All items repr. in *I-V a 6* (1594) and *I-IV a 6* (1608). Modern repr. in *Opere*, iv (ed. Meier), 111-218. Transcr. in Bennett, *Marenzio*, ii. 111-234.

1. *Satiati Amor, ch'a più doglioso amante*

   Mode 7 untransp.

   Ottava rima: 7th stanza of *O bionde Iddio*, in *Domenichi*, iv (1551), 312. Cf. other settings, in *II a 5* (1581), no. 11 and *I a 4, 5, 6* (1588), no. 3.

   Set by Monte, *I a 3* (1582: transcr. by Einstein, *SCA*, xxxix).

   Marenzio quotes or resembles Monte in several places (see chapter 8, ex. 246.)

2. *Nessun visse giamai più di me lieto*

   Mode 9 untransp.

   Text by Petrarch, *Canzoniere,* 2 no. 332, lines 37-42 (sestina stanza).

   Set by D. Ferrabosco, *I a 4* (1542); Palestrina (1568: *Opere*, ii. 15-16); Lassus (1587: *Werke*, viii. 137-140).

3. *Vaghi e lieti fanciulli*

   Mode 7 untransp.

   Text by Barbati (canzone): from *Porgetemi la lira*, 12th stanza and lines 5-6 of 13th stanza; in Barbati, *Rime* (1712), pp. 32-33; attrib. to G. Mutio in *Domenichi*, ii (1547), 153.

   Repr. in *RISM* 1605[9].

4. *Cedan l'antiche tue chiare vittorie*
        Mentre novella . . .

   Mode 12 untransp.

   Sonnet; the word "Archi" in line 3 suggests Vittoria Archilei, the Roman singer, as the addressee.

   Repr. in *RISM* 1605[9].

5. *Fuggi, speme mia, fuggi*

   Mode 1 untransp.

   Text by G.B. Cini (single-stanza canzone): 5th interlude to *La Cofanaria* by Francesco d'Ambra; cf. Il Lasca (A.F. Grazzini), *Descrizione degl' intermedii rappresentati colla Commedia nelle nozze dell'Illustriss. ed Eccellentiss. Sig. Principe di Firenze e di Siena*, Florence, 1566, p. 12. Music for this event was by Striggio (see below): cf. H. Brown, "Psyche's lament," in *Words and music*, pp. 2-27.

Set by Striggio, pr. in Galilei's *Fronimo* (1584: repr. by Brown, op. cit. p. 17); A. Gabrieli (*IIa 5*, 1570).

6. *Tutte sue squadre di miserie e stenti*

    Mode 3 untransp.

    Madrigal.

7. *Vaghi capelli aurati*

    Mode 10 untransp.

    Madrigal.

8. *E s'io mi doglio, Amore*

    Mode 6 untransp.

    Madrigal.

9. *In un bel bosco di leggiadre fronde*
        O dolce laccio . . .

    Mode 11 untransp.

    Text by T. Tasso (sonnet): first pr. in *Scielta delle rime*, ii (Ferrara, 1582), 62; repr. in *Rime*, ed. Solerti, ii, no. 395.

    Transcr. in F-Pn, MS "Bourdenay" (Mischiati, *RIDM* x, 1975, p. 319).

    Set by Monte, *XI a 5* (1586: transcr. by Einstein, *SCA*, xlii).

10. *Cantai già lieto il mio libero stato*
        Che la mia donna . . .

    Mode 1 transp.

    Sonnet; cf. Petrarch, *Canzoniere*, no 229 ("Cantai, or piango"); T. Tasso, "Cantai già lieto, e ritrovai nel canto," in *Rime*, ed. Solerti, iii, no. 741; P. Barignano's sonnet, "Io già cantando la mia libertade," in *Domenichi*, i (1546), p. 23.

    Repr. in *RISM* 1588[29].

    Model for Praetorius, *Magnificat a 6 (Gesamtausgabe*, xiv. 23-29).

11. *Del cibo, onde il signor mio sempr'abonda*
        Con quella man . . .

    Mode 3 untransp.

    Text by Petrarch, *Canzoniere*, no. 362 (sonnet).

12. *Filli mia bella, a Dio*

    Mode 12 transp.

    Madrigal.

    Repr. in *RISM* 1610[3].

    Reset by Croce, *I a 6* (1590: "A Dio, Filli mia cara").

13.   *Io vidi già sotto l'ardente sole*

Mode 2 transp.

Madrigal.

Text by T. Tasso (madrigal): *Rime et prose,* iv (Venice, 1586), 168; repr. in *Rime,* ed. Solerti, ii, no. 247. Rhyme scheme is same as for Petrarch's *Hor vedi, Amor* (*Canzoniere,* no. 121), but with heptasyllabics: Abb/Acc/Cdd.

14.   *Vita de la mia vita*

Mode 12 transp.

Text by T. Tasso (single-stanza canzone): *Rime et prose,* iv (Venice, 1586), p. 168; *Rime,* ed. Solerti, ii, no. 248.

Repr. in *RISM* 1605[9].

15.   *Passando con pensier per un boschetto*
          Noi starem troppo . . .
          Fuggendo tutte . . .

Mode 2 transp.

Text by Sacchetti (caccia): in *Il libro delle rime,* Bari, 1936, p. 94 ff; pr. without attribution in the *Rime di diversi,* ed. Atanagi, ii (1565), 171[r-v]; repr. in Einstein, *Madrigal,* ii. 634-635; see also Einstein, "Caccia," in *Festschrift Liliencron,* pp. 72-80.

Set by Nicola da Perugia, in the 14th century (ed. Pirrotta in Li Gotti and Pirrotta, *Sacchetti,* pp. 83-89); Philips (1598: *Madrigals,* ed. Steele, pp. 172-202).

Madrigali spirituali . . . a cinque voci (1584)
Dedicated to Lodovico Bianchetti, *Maestro di Camera* to Pope Gregory XIII, Rome 24.4.1584. Printed in Rome: Alessandro Gardano (1584); Venice: herede di G. Scotto (1588, 1606); Antwerp: Phalèse (1610). Most items repr. in *Spirituali e temporali* (1610).

1.   *Gratie renda al signor meco la terra*

Mode 8 untransp.

Text by Guidi (sestina stanza): in *Rime di diversi,* ed. Atanagi, ii (1565), 156[r] (8th stanza of *Padre tu, che volendo il freddo ghiaccio*).

2.   *Le dubbie, spemi, il pianto e 'l van dolore*
          Sì che s'al cominciar . . .

Mode 3 untransp.

Text by Sannazaro, no. 95 (sonnet).

3.   *Qual mormorio soave*

Mode 1 untransp.

Madrigal.

Repr. in *Ten madrigals* (ed. Arnold), pp. 54-63.

SSATB

4. *Il dì che di pallor la faccia tinse*

   Mode 1 transp.

   Text by Castelletti: *Rime spirituali,* f.19^v (first stanza of canzone).

5. *Padre del cielo, hor ch'altra nube il calle*
      Deh, pria che'l verno . . .

   Mode 12 transp.

   Text by T. Tasso (sonnet): first pr. in the *Rime de gli Eterei* (1567), f.71^r and the *Rime,* i (Venice, 1581), 21; repr. in *Poesie,* ed. Flora, p. 925, and Caretti, *Tasso,* p. 171. Tasso's original line reads: "Padre del cielo, hor ch'*atra* nube . . ."

   Set by Monte, *Spirituali* (1589: ed. Nuten, 1958, pp. 8-17).

6. *Quasi vermiglia rosa*

   Mode 2 transp.

   Text by Orsi (madrigal): in *Le piacevoli rime,* ed. Caporali (1582), p. 140.

   Set by D. Belli, *Arie* (1616).

7. *Sento squarciar del vecchio Tempio 'l velo*

   Mode 9 untransp.

   Text by Coppetta *(ottava rima):* in *Rime* (1580), p. 21; repr. in Giudiccioni-Coppetta, *Rime,* Bari, 1912, p. 321. Based on Matthew, xxvii.51.

   Set by Monte, *Spirituali* (1583: transcr. by Einstein, *SCA,* xxxix); G.F. Anerio, *Teatro armonico* (1619).

8. *Vergine saggia e pura*

   Mode 7 untransp.

   Strophe ?

   Omitted from *Spirituali e temporali* (1610).

9. *E questo il legno che del sacro sangue*
      O Pietà somma . . .

   Mode 12 untransp.

   Text by Sannazaro, no. 96 (sonnet).

   Omitted from *Spirituali e temporali* (1610).

10. *Signor, cui già fu pocho*

    Mode 2 untransp.

    Strophe; 1st stanza of poem set in *RISM* 1586^1.

    Reset by A. Gabrieli (*RISM* 1586^1); Monte, *Spirituali* (1589: ed. Nuten, 1958, pp. 77-83); Merulo, *II a 5* (1604).

11.   *Vergine gloriosa e lieta, o quanto*

Mode 4 untransp.

Strophe: 11th stanza of *Vergine ancella, nel cui santo chiostro,* set in *RISM* 1586[1]

Repr. in *RISM* 1586[1].

Modern repr. in *Ten madrigals,* ed. Arnold, pp. 64-71.   *SSATB*

12.   *Non fu mai cervo sì veloce al corso*
          Fallace, incerta . . .
          Se s'acquetasse . . .
          Ma, lasso, io sento . . .
          Tal'hor dal cor si more . . .
          Signor, tu vedi . . .
          Dal dì ch'io presi il corso . . .

Mode 11 transp.

Text by Sannazaro, no. 94 (sestina).

Repr. in *RISM* 1588[21].

Modern repr. in Lechner, *Werke,* viii.156-178.

Parody mass by Lechner (1584: in *Werke,* viii.31-72).

Il quarto libro de' madrigali e cinque voci (1584)
Dedicated to Girolamo Ruis, Venice, 5.5.1584. Printed in Venice: G. Vincenci and R. Amadino (1584); G. Vincenti (1589); A. Gardano (1594); A. Gardano et fratelli (1607). all items repr. in *I-V a 5* (1593) and *I-IX a 5* (1601). Modern repr. by Einstein, *PÄM,* vi.1-42.

1.   *Giunto a la tomba, ov'al suo spirto vivo*
          Non di morte sei tu . . .
SATTB   *Dagli lor tu . . .*
          Et amando morrò

Mode 3 untransp.

Text by T. Tasso, *Gerusalemme,* xii, stanzas 96-99 *(ottava rima).* Marenzio's version differs substantially from most of the published versions, but resembles most closely a pirated version, *Il Goffredo di M. Torq. Tass,* ed. D. Cavalcalupo, Venice: Celio Malaspina, 1580, f.64[r]. The only variants are the replacement of "dagli" by "dalli" in stanza 97, line 7 and stanza 98, line 1, and the substantial one in stanza 96, lines 3-4, in which Marenzio's "Di color, di calor, di motto privo/ Già freddo marmo al marmo il volto affisse" replaces Cavalcalupo's "Pallido, freddo, muto, e quasi privo/ Di movimento, al marmo il volto affisse." Marenzio's retention of this version allows him to express the concept of color by *note nere* (Pirrotta, "Note," in *Festschrift Ronga,* p. 566, note 1). For modern edn. with notes on the variants of all the MSS and printed versions, see *Gerusalemme,* ed. Solerti, iii.78-80.

Marenzio's setting contains a quotation from Wert's of 1581 (see chapter 2, note 33).

Wert's setting (*Works,* vii.38-42) is the first known; others include Cifra, *I a 5* (1605).

2.   *Mentre il ciel è sereno*

Mode 1 untransp.

Madrigal.

3. *Disdegno e gelosia*
        Tal che, lasso, d'intorno

    SAATB

    Mode 12 transp.

    Text by T. Tasso (madrigal): first pr. in the *Rime e prose*, iii, Venice, 1583; repr. in the *Rime*, ed. Solerti, ii, no. 93.

4. *Scendi dal paradiso*

    SSATB

    Mode 12 transp.

    Madrigal.

5. *Corran di puro latte / Del Po superbo onde*

    Mode 12 transp.

    SSATB

    Madrigal; probably destined for wedding at Ferrara.

    Set by Milleville, *II a 5* (1584)

6. *Filli, l'acerbo caso*
        Tu, morendo innocente

    Mode 9 transp.

    Madrigal; set as "*Scipio,* l'acerbo caso" by Monte, *X a 5* (1581: transcr. by Einstein, *SCA*, xlii); Soriano, *I a 5* (1581); Del Mel (1584: see Pirrotta, "Note," in *Festschrift Ronga*, pp. 567-568, note 2); Moscaglia (*III a 5*, 1587); Ingegneri (*V a 5*, 1587). Marenzio's emendation of the first word is ungrammatical: the apostrophee undergoes a sex change in the *seconda parte* (Pirrotta, loc. cit.).

7. *Real natura, angelico intelletto*
        Come due masse d'or . . .

    SATTBar

    Mode 9 untransp.

    Text by G.B. Zuccarini (attribution survives in *RISM* 1586[11]): sonnet in honor of Bianca Cappello, wife of Grand Duke Francesco of Florence. First line same as a sonnet by Petrarch, *Canzoniere* no. 238.

    Repr. in *RISM* 1586[11].

8. *Spirto a cui giova gli anni a buona fine*

    SATTB

    Mode 12 untransp.

    Madrigal.

9. *Ecco l'aurora con l'aurata fronte*

    Mode 12 untransp.

    SATB

    Text by Quirino *(ottava rima):* 24th stanza of *Hor che nell'oceano* (cf. *I a 6*, 1581, nos. 5 and 10), in *Domenichi*, i (1546), 202.

    Other settings by A. Gabrieli (1566: repr. by Einstein, *Golden Age*, pp. 32-39) and Stabile (*I a 5*, 1572).

10.   *Quando vostra beltà, vostro valore*

SATTB

Mode 7 untransp.

Text by Ariosto, Madrigal no. 2 (*Lirica,* ed. Fatini, p. 51: "Quando bellezza, cortesia e valore").

11.   *Vaghi augelletti, che per valli e monti*

SAATB

Mode 7 untransp.

Madrigal.

Repr. in *RISM* 1650⁹.

Set by A. Gabrieli, *II a 5* (1570); Macque, *III a 4* (1610: transcr. in Shindle, *Macque,* ii.612-17).

12.   *Sapete amanti perchè ignudo sia*

Mode 11 transp.

Text by Marcellini (madrigal): in *Rime di diversi,* ed. Atanagi, i (1565), f.191ᵛ; Eng. paraphrase, "Do you not know how Love," set by Morley (1593: ed. Fellowes, *EMS,* i.84-86).

13.   *Senza cor, senza luce*

SATTB

Mode 3 transp.

Madrigal.

14.   *Caddè già di Tarquinio al cieco errore*

Mode 1 transp.

SSATB

Madrigal; possibly intended to celebrate the beauty of Tarquinia del Cavalliero (Einstein, *Madrigal,* ii.640).

15.   *A, che tormi'l ben mio*

SMATB

Mode 11 transp.

Madrigal.

Set by Masenelli (*RISM* 1586³); Monteverdi (1587: *Opere,* i.8-13).

Il quinto libro de' madrigali a cinque voci (1585)
Dedicated to Nicolo Pallavicino, Rome, 15.12.1584. Printed in Venice: herede di G. Scotto (1585, 1588); A. Gardano (1594, 1605). All items repr. in *I-V a 5* (1593) and *I-X a 5* (1601). Modern repr. by Einstein, *PÄM,* vi.47-97.

1.   *Sola angioletta starsi in treccie a l'ombra*
          Lasso, vedrò io mai . . .
          Quando ripenso . . .
SATTB   *O qual gratia sentì . . .*
          Non vide'l mondo . . .
          Ben credo ch'ancor tu . . .

Mode 7 untransp.

Text by Sannazaro, no. 44 (sestina).

Set by Stivorio, *I a 4* (1583).

2. *Consumando mi vo di piagg'in piaggia*

Mode 12 untransp.

Text by Petrarch, *Canzoniere,* no. 237, lines 19-24 (sestina, 4th stanza)

3. *Il suo vago, gioioso e lieto manto*

Mode 2 untransp.

Sestina stanza.

4. *Oimè, l'antica fiamma*

Mode 8 untransp.

Text by Guarini (madrigal): in the *Rime,* Venice, 1598, f. 113^V.

Set by Soriano, *II a 5* (1592) and anon., I-Rvat, *Chigiana Q.IV.4,* ff. 111^V.-115^V. (with *seconda parte,* "E così a poco a poco . . .").

5. *Quella che lieta del mortal mio duolo*
   Ben puote ella . . .

Mode 10 untransp.

Text by Della Casa (sonnet): in *Opere,* ed. Prezzolini, p. 662.

6. *La rete fu di questa fila d'oro*
   Per la dolce cagion . . .

Mode 3 untransp.

Text by Ariosto, sonnet no. 9 (*Lirica,* ed. Fatini, p. 31).

At the words "Io son ferito, io son prigion per loro" (line 5, b. 27 ff), Marenzio quotes the opening of Palestrina's madrigal of that name (Einstein, *Madrigal,* ii.643; see Palestrina, *Opere,* ii.161).

Set by Sabino, *I a 6* (1579).

7. *Dolor, tant'è la gioia che mi dai*

Mode 6 untransp.

Madrigal.

8. *Sotto l'ombra de tuoi pregiati rami*

Mode 1 untransp.

Madrigal.

9. *Chi vuol veder Amore*

Mode 1 untransp.

SSATB

Madrigal.

Reset by Castro, *Rose fresche a 3* (1591).

10.   *L'alto e nobil pensier, che sì sovente*

SAATB

Mode 10 untransp.

Text by Sannazaro, no. 47 (sonnet); Marenzio sets the octave only, which is in the unusual form ABAB/BAAB.

11.   *Filli, tu sei più bella*   *SATTB*
            Io son il più costante

SATTB

Mode 8 transp.

Text by Pavesi: in *Rime di diversi*, ed. Atanagi, ii (1565), f. 168^r. Poem in 4 strophes set in 2 *parti*. Marenzio designates setting "Aria."

Set by Merulo, *I a 5* (1566).

12.   *Occhi miei, che miraste sì bel sole*
            Ma forse non sapete . . .

SSATB

Mode 1 transp.

Sonnet.

Set by Cifra (*I a 5*, 1605).

13.   *Se voi sete cor mio*

Mode 1 transp.

Madrigal.

Set by Contino (*RISM* 1569^{20}).

14.   *Basciami mille volte*

Mode 2 transp.

SATTB

Madrigal.

Opening similar to D. Ferrabosco, *Basciami vita mia* (1554: see Einstein, *Madrigal*, i.310 ff and ii.644 ff).

15.   *Liete, verdi, fiorite e fresche valli*
            Che se'l gridar

Mode 12 transp.

Text by Sannazaro, no. 88 (sonnet).

Set by Dragoni, *III a 5* (1579).

16.   *Due rose fresch' e colte in Paradiso*

SSATB

Mode 2 transp.

Text by Petrarch, *Canzoniere*, no. 245 (sonnet). Opening contains quotation of A. Gabrieli's setting.

Other settings by A. Gabrieli (1566: repr. in Einstein, *Madrigal*, iii.182-189); Ingegneri (1587: *CW*, cxv. 11-17).

17.   *S'io vissi cieco, e grave fall'indegno*
        O fera voglia . . .

SATTB

Mode 3 transp. down a tone.

Text by Della Casa (sonnet): in *Opere*, ed. Prezzolini, p. 647.

Il terzo libro de' madrigali a sei voci (1585)
Dedicated to Bianca Cappello, Rome, 12.2.1585. Printed in Venice: herede di G. Scotto (1585, 1589); A. Gardano (1594). All items repr. in *I-V a 6* (1594) and *I-VI a 6* (1608); transcr. in Bennett, *Marenzio*, ii.235-334.

1.   *Io morirò d'Amore*

Mode 8 untransp.

Madrigal.

Repr. in *RISM* 1588[29].

Modern repr. in *Musica Transalpina*, ed. Harman, London, 1954 ("I will go die for pure love").

2.   *Danzava con maniere sopr'humane*
       "Son presa," disse . . .

Mode 1 untransp.

Text by Pace *(ottava rima):* first 2 stanzas of eclogue in *Domenichi*, i (1546), 253.

Repr. in *RISM* 1605[9].

Set by Monte, *II a 4* (1569: transcr. by Einstein, *SCA*, xxxix).

3.   *Stringeami Galatea*
       Ella che se n'accorse . . .

Mode 3 untransp.

Madrigal.

4.   *In un lucido rio*

Mode 11 untransp.

Text by T. Tasso (madrigal): earliest version in I-Sc, MS *I.XI, 11*, p. 11 (repr. in Tasso, *Madrigali*, ed. Gargani, p. 47); definitive version ("Sovra un lucido rio") in Tasso, *Gioie di rime e prose*, v, vi, Venice, 1587, repr. in *Rime*, ed. Solerti, ii, no. 318. Version set by Marenzio is a slightly emended edition of the Sienese source; repr. in Einstein, *Madrigal*, ii.650). See also Chater, *RIDM* xiii (1978), 67, notes 31-32. In all versions, rhyme scheme follows Petrarch's *Nova angeletta* (*Canzoniere*, no. 106, abC/abC/dD): cf. *I a 4* (1585), no. 8 and *VII a 5* (1595), no. 5.

5. *Parto da voi, mio sole*

    Mode 9 untransp.

    Madrigal.

    Repr. in *RISM* 1588[29] and 1605[9].

    Modern. repr. in Hucke, *SM*, iii (1974), 274-279 and *Musica Transalpina*, ed. Harman, London, 1956 ("Now I must part").

    Set in Ger. tr. by Hassler (1596: *Werke*, ii.117-121; for comparison with Marenzio and additional repr., see Hucke, op. cit., pp. 264-273).

6. *Qual per ombrose e verdeggianti valli*
       Puote agguagliar l'alto piacer . . .

    Mode 12 untransp.

    Text by Gottifredi (sonnet): in *Domenichi*, i (1546), 253.

    Set by Stabile, *I a 5* (1572); Marenzio quotes Stabile's opening phrase at the upper third.

7. *Su l'ampia fronte il cresp'oro lucente*
       Io, che forma . . .

    Mode 2 untransp.

    Text by T. Tasso (sonnet): first pr. in *Rime di diversi*, ed. Atanagi, i (1565), 187 and the *Rime de gli . . . Eterei* (1567) f. 61[r]. (This earlier version also repr. in Caretti, *Tasso*, p. 152). Tasso's definitive version is repr. in the *Rime*, ed. Solerti, ii. no. 3.

8. *Posso, cor mio, partire*

    Mode 2 transp.

    Madrigal.

    Repr. in *RISM* 1593[4].

    Instrumental arr. in *RISM* 1600[5a].

    Set by Macque (*RISM* 1583[11]: transcr. in Shindle, *Macque*, ii.863-9).

9. *Tigre mia, se ti pesa*

    Mode 9 transp.

    Text by Groto (madrigal): in *Rime*, Venice, 1587, p. 86.

    Set by Croce, *I a 5* (1585); Raval, *I a 5* (1593); Monte *IX a 6* (1603: transcr. by Einstein, *SCA*, xxxviii).

10. *Donò Cinthia a Damone*

    Mode 9 transp.

    Text by Guarini (madrigal): in *Rime di diversi*, ed. Licino (1587), p. 196. ("Donò *Licori* a *Bacco*") and *Rime*, Venice, 1598, f.97[r] ("Donò *Licori* a *Batto*").

    Repr. in *RISM* 1610[3].

Modern repr. in *Madrigali a 5, 6*, ed. Mompellio, pp. 13-15.

Set (with different versions of line 1) by Giovanelli, *I a 5* (1586) and Monte, *XII a 5* (1587: transcr., by Einstein, *SCA*, xlii).

11. *Quell'ombra esser vorrei*

Mode 12 transp.

Text by Casone (madrigal): first pr. in *Rime de gli academici affidati* (1565), p. 119; also in Casone's *Rime*, Venice, 1598, f.14^r.

Reset by Monteverdi (1590: *Opere*, ii.49-52).

12. *Dai bei labri di rose aura tranquilla*

Mode 12 transp.

Text by G.B. Strozzi (madrigal): I-Fn, MS *Palat. 242*, no. 37; pr. in the *Venticinque madrigali inediti*, Lucca, 1866, p. 14.

Transcr. in Vol. ii, pp. 21-26.

Set by Feliciani, *I a 5* (1579).

13. *Donna, più d'altr'adorna di beltate*

Mode 1 transp.

Madrigal.

14. *Piangea Filli, e rivolte ambe le luci*

Mode 3 transp.

Text by G.B. Strozzi (madrigal): I-Fn, MS *Palat. 242*, no. 18; repr. in Trucchi, *Poesie italiane*, iv.352; Einstein, *Madrigal*, ii.651; Strozzi, *Madrigali inediti*, ed. Ariani, p. cxxxvii.

Instrumental arr. in *Brown 1592*[6].

Transcr. in volume II of this study.

15. *Con dolce sguardo alquant'acerb'in vista*
       Di lagrime indi . . .

Mode 8 transp.

Text by F.M. Molza *(ottava rima)*: 15th and 16th stanzas of *Quantunque paia meno*, in *Stanze*, ed. Dolce, i (1556), 143.

16. *O quante volte in van, cor mio, ti chiamo*

Mode 1 transp.

Text by Guarini (madrigal): authorship known through dedication of V. Aleotti's *Ghirlanda* (1593), all settings of texts by Guarini (dedication repr. in *NV*, i.30-31).

Set by Luzzaschi, *III a 5* (1582); Aleotti (1593: see above); S. Rossi, *I a 4* (1614).

Madrigali a quatro voci (1585)

Dedicated to Marcantonio Serlupi, Rome, 15.7.1585. Printed in Rome: Alessandro Gardano (1585); Venice: R. Amadino (1587), G. Vincenzi (1587; with dedication by Michael Booth to the publisher, Venice, 8.1.1587), A. Gardano (1592 and 1603) and herede di G. Scotto (1608); Paris: Le Roy and la veufve R. Ballard (1598); Nuremberg: Kauffmann (1603); Antwerp: Phalèse (1607).

1. *Non vidi mai dopo notturna pioggia*

    Mode 2 transp.

    Text by Petrarch (canzone): *Canzoniere,* no. 127, lines 57-65.

    Repr. in *RISM* 1590[29].

    Modern repr. in *Ten madrigals,* ed. Arnold, pp. 14-23.

2. *Dissi a l'amata mia lucida stella*

    Mode 12 transp.

    Text by Moscaglia (madrigal): attribution survives in dedication of Moscaglia's *II a 4* (*RISM* 1585[29]), signed in 1582.

    Printed in *RISM* 1585[29]; repr. in *RISM* 1590[17], 1593[5].

    Instrumental arr. in *Brown* 1591[2] and 1594[5].

    Modern repr. in Hawkins, *History,* ii.432-433; Kiesewetter, *Schicksale,* pp. 43-45; Roche, *Penguin book,* pp. 136-140. Transcr. in Sloan, *Moscaglia,* (unpubl. diss.).

    Set by Castro, *Rose fresche* (1593)

3. *Veggo, dolce mio bene*

    Mode 9 transp.

    Madrigal.

    Repr. in *RISM* 1590[29].

    Instrumental arr. in *Brown* 1594[5].

    Set by Ingegneri, *II a 4* (1579); Luzzaschi, *III a 5* (1582); Castro, *Rose fresche* (1593).

4. *O bella man, che mi distring' il core*
        Candido, leggiadretto e caro . . .

    Mode 12 transp.

    Text by Petrarch, *Canzoniere,* no. 198 (sonnet).

    Set by Castro, *Rose fresche* (1591).

    At the words "Pur questo è furto" ("Even this is theft": line 14, bb. 132-135 and 144-150) Marenzio quotes opening of Rore, *Anchor che col partire (Opera,* iv.31).

5. *Non al suo amante più Diana piacque*

    Mode 12 untransp.

    Text by Petrarch, *Canzoniere,* no. 102 (madrigal).

Repr. in *RISM* 1591[10].

Modern repr. in *Ten madrigals,* ed. Arnold, pp. 24-31.

Set by Jacopo da Bologna (*HAM,* i.52-53); Macque, *I a 4, 5, 6* (1579: transcr. in Shindle, *Macque,* ii.237-42); Giovanelli, *I a 3* (1605).

6.   *Hor vedi, Amor, che giovinetta donna*

Mode 7 untransp.

Text by Petrarch, *Canzoniere,* no. 121 (madrigal). Marenzio omits line 6, presumably because he was using Vellutello's commentary (Venice, 1538, f.11r), which likewise omits the same line.

Marenzio's motive for the first 3 words is the same as Cambio's; in its turn, Marenzio's opening provoked a number of imitations (see above, chapter 6, ex. 155).

Set by Cambio, *II a 5* (1550); Moscaglia, *IV a 5* (1587); Falcone-Raval, *I a 5* (1603); Giovanelli, *I a 3* (1605).

7.   *Apollo, s'ancor vive il bel desio*
       E per virtù . . .

Mode 12 untransp.

Text by Petrarch, *Canzoniere,* no. 304 (sonnet).

8.   *Nova angeletta sovra l'ale accorta*

Mode 7 untransp.

Text by Petrarch, *Canzoniere,* no. 106 (madrigal).

Set by Monte, *I a 4* (1562: transcr. by Einstein, *SCA,* xxxviii); Portinaro, *I a 4* (1563); Pallavicino, *I a 4* (1579: *Flanders,* no. 8); Moscaglia, *II a 5* (1579); Castro, *Rose fresche* (1591); Giovanelli, *I a 3* (1605).

9.   *Vedi le valli e i campi che si smaltano*

Mode 12 untransp.

Text by Sannazaro *(terza rima sdrucciola): Arcadia,* viii, lines 142-147, spoken by Eugenio.

Repr. in *Spirituali e temporali* (1610).

Vocal arr. by Balbi in *RISM* 1589[12] (repr. by Bianconi in Marsolo, *Madrigali,* Introduction, pp. xlv-xlix).

Modern repr. in Marsolo, *Madrigali,* ed. Bianconi, Introduction, pp. xliv-xlviii.

10.   *Chi vol udir i miei sospiri in rime*

Mode 2 untransp.

Text by Sannazaro (sestina, first stanza): *Arcadia,* iv, lines 1-6, spoken by Logisto (cf. *I a 4, 5, 6,* 1588, no. 9).

Repr. in *Ten madrigals,* ed. Arnold, pp. 5-13.

11. *Madonna, sua mercè, pur una sera*

    Mode 10 untransp.

    Text by Sannazaro (sestina, 5th stanza): *Arcadia,* vii, lines 25-30, spoken by Sincero.

    Repr. in *RISM* 1590[29] and 1597[15].

    Instr. arr. in *Brown* 1591[2] and *RISM* 1607[29].

    Modern repr. by Schinelli, *Collana,* iii.96-101.

12. *Vezzosi augelli in fra le verdi fronde*

    Mode 10 untransp.

    Text by T. Tasso *(ottava rima), Gerusalemme* xvi, lines 89-96 (stanza 12).

    Repr. in *RISM* 1590[29], 1597[15].

    Modern repr. in Martini, *Saggio,* ii.95-103; Kiesewetter, *Schicksale,* pp. 46-49; *Madrigali,* ed. Virgili, pp. 9-12; Roche, *Penguin book,* pp. 141-146.

    Set by Wert (1586: *Works,* viii.11-14).

13. *Ahi, dispietata morte, ahi, crudel vita*

    Mode 3 untransp.

    Text by Petrarch (ballata): *Canzoniere,* no. 324, lines 4-12.

    Repr. in *RISM* 1590[29] with Eng. text: "Alas, what a wretched life"; reset in that form by Wilbye (1598: *EMS,* vi.86-92).

    Modern repr. in Martini, *Saggio,* ii.78-82; *Madrigali a 4, 5,* ed. Virgili, pp. 13-15.

    Set by Pesciolini, *III a 6* (1581); often is part of *Amor, quando fioria.*

14. *Dolci son le quadrella onde Amor punge*
          Come doglia fin qui . . .

    Mode 1 untransp.

    Text by Della Casa (sonnet): *Opere* (ed. Prezzolini), p. 643.

15. *Menando un giorno gl'agni presso un fiume*

    Mode 11 untransp.

    Text by Sannazaro *(rime sciolte): Arcadia,* i, lines 61-67, spoken by Ergasto (cf. *III a 5,* 1582, no. 5). This passage is characterized by the *rimalmezzo,* whereby the 4th and 5th syllables of each line rhyme with the 10th and 11th of the preceding (Borghini, *Umanista,* p. 151). Subject matter related to Petrarch's madrigal, *Canzoniere,* no. 102 (see above, no. 5).

16. *I lieti amanti e le fanciulle tenere*

    Mode 8 untransp.

    Text by Sannazaro *(terza rima sdrucciola): Arcadia,* vi, lines 103-111, spoken by Opico.

    Repr. in *RISM* 1590[29].

Modern repr. in Schinelli, *Collana*, iii.92-95.

Set by Pallavicino (1587: *Flanders*, no. 108); Giovanelli, *II a 4* (1589); F. Anerio, *I a 3* (1598); Clemsee (1613: see Schmalzriedt, *Schütz*, p. 86).

17. *Tutto'l dì piango, e poi la notte, quando*
    Lasso, che pur . . .

Mode 3 transp.

Text by Petrarch, *Canzoniere*, no. 216 (sonnet); opening related to Rore's setting (see chapter 5, ex. 105).

Set by Lassus (1567: *Werke*, iv.122-127); Rore (1549: *Opera*, iv.4-6); Monte, *II a 6* (1569: transcr. by Einstein, *SCA*, xxxvii); Bottegari (1574: *Lutebook*, ed. MacClintock, no. 52).

18. *Zefiro torna, e'l bel tempo rimena*
    Ma per me, lasso . . .

Mode 1 transp.

Text by Petrarch, *Canzoniere*, no. 310 (sonnet); analysed in Friedrich, *Epochen*, p. 273 ff.

Repr. in *RISM* 1590[29].

Modern repr. in Martini, *Saggio*, ii.88-95 (with 2 *parti* in reverse order); Schinelli, *Collana*, iii.84-91; *Novello Tonic Sol-fa Series*, no. 2148 (*seconda parte* only); *Madrigali a 4, 5*, ed. Virgili, pp. 1-8.

Set by Monte, *I a 5* (1554: transcr. by Einstein, *SCA*, xl); Baccusi, *II a 6* (1572; octave only); Dragoni, *III a 5* (1579); Conversi, *I a 6* (1584); A. Ferrasbosco, *II a 5* (1587); Tollius (1597: *Madrigalen*, ed. Seiffert, pp. 14-22).

19. *Su'l carro della mente auriga siedi*
    Verdi ch'egli ama . . .

Mode 8 transp.

Text by T. Tasso (sonnet): first pr. in the *Scielta*, ii (Ferrara, 1582). 46; repr. in *Rime*, ed. Solerti, iii, no. 71. Tasso's poem (and perhaps also Marenzio's setting) dates from 1576, and is in honor of Leonora Sanvitale (see above, chapter 3, note 109).

20. *"Lasso," dicea, "perchè venisti, Amore . . ."*

Mode 10 transp.

Text by T. Tasso (*ottava rima*): *Rinaldo* v, stanza 16. The original edn. of *Rinaldo* (1562) is dedicated to Marenzio's patron, Cardinal Luigi d'Este. Marenzio's setting may therefore have been intended as a compliment to his employer.

Reset by Stivorio, in Lauro-Stivorio, *I a 3* (1590).

21. *Vienne, Montan, mentre le nostre tormora*
    Corbo malvaggio . . .
    La santa Pale . . .

Mode 12 transp.

Text by Sannazaro (*terza rima sdrucciola,* then *terza rima piana): Arcadia,* ix, lines 37-75, spoken and sung by Ofelia, Elenco and Montano.

Overlaps with Sabino, "Quando talhor a la stagion novella" (*V a 5-6,* 1586) and Giovanelli, "Dimmi, caprar" (*I a 4,* 1585).

Il quarto libro de madrigali a sei voci (1587)
Dedicated to the Marquis of Pisani (whom Einstein, *Madrigal,* ii. 660, identifies as Jean de Vivonne), Rome, 20.12.1586. Printed in Venice: G. Vincenti (1587); R. Amadino (". . . ristampato, et da molti errori diligentissimamente emendato," 1587); A. Gardano (1593, 1605); herede di G. Scotto, 1603). Most items repr. in *I-V a 6* (1594) and *I-VI a 6* (1608); transcribed by Bennett, *Marenzio,* ii. 335-430.

1. *Se bramate ch'io mora*

    Mode 1 transp.

    Madrigal.

    Repr. in *RISM* 1610[3].

2. *Di nettare amoroso ebro, la mente*
        Sonar le labra . . .

    Mode 10 transp.

    Text by T. Tasso (sonnet); first pr. in the *Rime,* i (Venice, 1581), 2; repr. in *Rime,* ed. Solerti, ii, no. 183.

    Repr. in *RISM* 1590[29], 1597[13].

3. *La dipartita è amara*

    Mode 9 transp.

    Text by Pigna: *Il ben divino,* madrigal no. 79.

    Repr. in *RISM* 1597[13].

    Last line ("Nasce la gioia mia") introduces a quotation of the opening of Striggio's *Nasce la pena mia* (1560: repr. in Monte, *Opera,* x, music suppl., pp. 1-10).

4. *Vattene, anima mia*

    Mode 8 transp.

    Text by Pigna: *Il ben divino,* madrigal no. 76.

5. *Tra l'herbe a piè d'un mirto*
        Per più gradirla . . .

    Mode 12 untransp.

    Text by Gottifredi (sonnet): *Domenichi,* i (1546), 248.

6. *Crudel, perchè mi fuggi*

    Mode 9 untransp.

Text by Guarini (madrigal): *Rime,* Venice, 1598, f.68[r] ("Lasso, perchè mi fuggi").

Repr. in *RISM* 1590[29] ("Unkind, O stay thy flying"); reset in this form by Wilbye, 1598: *EMS,* vi.92-96.

Set as "*Lasso,* perchè mi fuggi" by Giovanelli, *I a 3* (1605) and anon, I-Rvat, *Chigiana Q. IV.4,* ff. 120[V]-123[r]; as "*Crudel,* perchè . . ." by Pallavicino (1587: *Flanders,* no. 106) and Monteverdi (1590: *Opere,* ii. 83-86); as "Ohimé, perché . . ." by Giovanelli, I a 5 (1586); Ger.tr. set by Hassler (1596: *Werke,* ii. 122-127).

7. *Dice la mia bellissima Licori*

    Mode 7 untransp.

    Text by Guarini (madrigal): first pr. in *Rime di diversi,* ed. Licino (1587), p. 191; also in *Rime,* Venice, 1598, f.96[V].

    Repr. in *RISM* 1593[4], 1597[13], 1597[24], 1605[9].   .

    Modern repr. in *Musica Transalpina,* ed. Harman, London, 1956 ("So saith my fair . . .") and *Novello Part-Song Book,* no. 1277 ("So saith my fair . . .").

    Set by Monte, *XII a 5* (1587: transcr. by Einstein, *SCA,* xlii); Lauro, *I a 3* (1590); Castro, *Rose fresche* (1591); Monteverdi (1619; *Opere,* vii.58-63); set in Eng.tr. by Wilbye, 1598 ("Thus saith my Cloris bright," *EMS,* vi.44-47).

8. *Nè fero sdegno mai, Donna, mi mosse*
    Talchè dovunque vò . . .

    Mode 7 untransp.

    Text by Tansillo (sonnet): *Domenichi,* viii (1558), 472 and *Canzoniere,* ed. Percopò, p. 95 ("Nè lungo esilio il cor, Donna, mi mosse").

    Repr. in *RISM* 1590[29], 1591[10], 1605[9], 1609[15].

9. *Caro Aminta, pur vuoi*
    Non può, Filli, più il core

    Mode 3 untransp.

    Madrigal (dialogue with 2 strophes).

10. *Non porta ghiaccio Aprile*

    Mode 1 untransp.

    Text by Pocaterra (madrigal): *Due dialoghi* (1607), no. 43; attrib. to Cesare Cremonini in Frati, *Rime inedite,* p.97; also repr. in Chater, "Fonti," *RIDM* xiii (1978), p.69.

    Set by Monte, *XII a 5* (1587; transcr. by Einstein, *SCA,* xlii); Castro, *Rose fresche* (1591); Banchieri (1622; *Vivezze,* ed. Piattelli, pp.49-53).

11. *Arsi gran tempo, e del mio foco indegno*
    Lasso, e conosco ben . . .

    Mode 2 transp.

    Text by T. Tasso (sonnet): *Rime de gli . . . Eterei* (1567), f.68[V]; *Rime,* i (Venice, 1581), 16; repr. in *Rime,* ed. Solerti, ii, no. 107.

12. *Questa ordì il laccio, questa*

Mode 12 transp.

Text by Strozzi the Elder; attrib. to Tasso in his *Rime,* i (Venice, 1581), p.113; pr. in Strozzi, *Rime* (1593), p.62. Marenzio's version identical to one used by Bertani, *I a 5* (1584).

Repr. in *RISM* 1590[29].

Set by Bertani (see above); Monteverdi (1587: *Opere,* i.46-49).

13. *Vaneggio, od'è pur vero*

Mode 8 transp.

Text by Barignano (madrigal): in *Rime di diversi,* ed. Atanagi, i (1565), f.160[V]; repr. Frati, *Rime inedite,* p.160.

Set by D. Ferrabosco, *I a 4* (1542); Stabile, in G.M. Nanino-Stabile, *I a 5* (1581).

14. *O, che soave e non inteso bacio*

Mode 9 transp.

Text by Guarini (madrigal): in *Rime di diversi,* ed. Licino (1587), p.191 ("O che soave e non *intero* bacio"); *Nova scelta,* ed. Varoli (1590), p.42 (without attrib.), and Guarini, *Opere,* Verona, 1737, ii.81. Shorter version ("O, che soave bacio") in *Rime,* Venice, 1598, f.93[V]. The longer version was later included in the *Pastor fido,* v.8 (lines 1424-1425 and 1442-1450). This incorporation was criticized by Summo in the second of the *Discorsi,* repr. in Guarini, *Opere* (1737), iii.591 and *Opere,* ed. Guglielminetti (1971), p.710.

Repr. in *RISM* 1605[9].

15. *Donne, il celeste lume*

Mode 8 untransp; *a 8,* with 9th voice *ad libitum.*

Text by Castelletti (madrigal): *Le stravaganze d'Amore,* Venice: G.B. Sessa, 1587, f.74[r] (5th and last *intermedio:* see Chater, "Castelletti," *SM,* viii (1979), 85-148).

Repr. in *RISM* 1590[11], 1597[13], and the *Spirituali e temporali* (1610); omitted from *I-V a 6* (1594).

Modern repr. in Chater, op.cit., pp.133-141.

Set by Melfio, *I a 5* (1587).

Il quarto libro delle villanelle a tre voci (1587)
Dedicated by A. Gualtieri to Annibale de' Paulis, Rome, 5.2.1587. Printed in Venice: G. Vincenzi, 1587. Reprints, see *NV,* ii, nos. 1700 ff.

For further details see *V a 6* (1591), no. 9.

Madrigali a quatro, cinque et sei voci, libro primo (1588)
Dedicated to Count Mario Bevilacqua, Venice, 10.12.1587. Printed in Venice: G. Vincenti (1588); most items transcr. by Baldwin in GB-Lbm, *R.M.24.d.2.* Modern repr. in *Secular Works,* vii (ed. Ledbetter).

1. *Ov'è condotto il mio amoroso stile?* (*a 4*)

Mode 3 untransp.

Text by Petrarch, *Canzoniere*, no. 332, lines 13-18 (sestina stanza).

Not transcr. by Baldwin.

Set by Lassus (1560: *Werke*, viii.38-40).

2.   *Se la mia vita da l'aspro tormento*   (*a 4*)
        Pur mi darà . . .

Mode 8 untransp.

Text by Petrarch: *Canzoniere*, no. 12 (sonnet).

Set by Wert (1567: *Works*, iv.8-12).

3.   *Piango che Amor con disusato oltraggio*   (*a 4*)

Mode 10 untransp.

Ottava rima: 5th stanza of *O bionde Iddio*, in *Domenichi*, iv (1551), 312. Cf. *II a 5* (1581), no. 11; *II a 6* (1584), no. 1.

Set by Monte, *I a 3* (1582: transcr. by Einstein, *SCA*, xxxix).

4.   *Affliger chi per voi la vita piagne*   (*a 4*)
        Nulla da voi . . .

Mode 1 untransp.

Text by Della Casa (sonnet): in *Opere*, ed. Prezzolini, p.640.

Opening quotes Rore, *Non è ch'il duol* (*Opera*, iv, 23, b.1 ff).

5.   *Fuggito è'l sonno a le mie crude notte*   (*a 5*)

Mode 2 transp.

Text by Petrarch: *Canzoniere*, no. 332, lines 31-36 (sestina stanza).

6.   *Senza il mio vago sol qual fia il mio stato*   (*a 5*)
        O giorno che per me . . .

Mode 2 transp.

Text by Troiano (sonnet): in *Rime di diversi*, ed. Atanagi (1565), i, 112^r; a hotchpotch of reminiscences and plagiarisms: line 1 recalls the opening of a poem by Sannazaro (see below, no. 7); the first quatrain is reminiscent of Petrarch, *Canzoniere*, no. 359 ("Quando il soave mio fido conforto," etc.). The most unscrupulous "borrowing" occurs in lines 9-12, lifted (with only small variants) from Tansillo's *Se quel dolor*, lines 16-19 (set by Marenzio, *VI a 6*, 1595, no. 3, *terza and quarta parti*). It is probable that Marenzio set this poem not through personal choice, but to please the Veronese academicians, of whom Troiano was (or had been) one (see below, appendix IV, note on Troiano).

7.   *Senza il mio sole, in tenebre e martiri*   (*a 5*)
        Altro che lagrimar . . .

Mode 12 transp.

Text by Sannazaro, no. 60 (sonnet).

Not transcribed by Baldwin.

8. *Ben mi credeva, lasso*   (a 5)

Mode 9 transp.

Text by Sannazaro, no. 53; 2nd stanza of the canzone, *Amor, tu voì ch'io dica;* same metrical structure as Petrarch, *Canzoniere,* no. 125.

Not transcribed by Baldwin.

9. *Fiere silvestre, che per lati campi*   (a 5)

Mode 4 transp.

Text by Sannazaro (sestina, 5th stanza): *Arcadia,* iv, lines 25-30, spoken by Logisto (cf. *I a 4,* 1585, no. 10).

Set by Stivorio, *I a 4* (1583), dedicated to Mario Bevilacqua.

10. *Ecco che un'altra volta, o piagge apriche*   (a 5)
       E se di vero Amor . . .

Mode 7 transp.

Text by Sannazaro, no. 34.

Set by Dragoni, *I a 6* (1584); Monte, *III a 4* (1585: transcr. by Einstein, *SCA,* xxxix); Wert (1588: *Works,* ix.5-9).

11. *Com'ogni Rio che d'acque dolci e chiare*   (a 6)

Mode 9 transp.

Madrigal; alludes to the name of the dedicatee, Mario Bevilacqua (e.g. "Com'ogni *Rio* che d'*acque* dolci e chiare/Porge tributo al *Mare,*" etc.); reminiscent of T. Tasso, "Come ogni Rio l'honor col corso rende/Al Mare . . . ," in F. Caroso, *Nobiltà di Dame,* Venice, 1600, p.2.

12. *Valli riposte e sole*   (a 6)

Mode 12 untransp.

Text by Sannazaro, no. 59: canzone, first stanza; metrical structure same as for Petrarch, *Canzoniere,* no. 126.

13. *Interdette speranze e van desio*   (a 6)

Mode 7 untransp.

Text by Sannazaro, no. 196 (sonnet); Marenzio sets only the first quatrain.

Whole sonnet set by Soriano, *I a 5* (1581); D'India (1607: *Madrigali,* ed. Mompellio, pp.60-71).

14. *O fere stelle, homai datemi pace*   (a 6)

Mode 1 transp.

Text by Sannazaro, no. 33 (3rd stanza of sestina, *Spent'eran nel mio cor*).

15. *Basti fin qui le pen' e i duri affanni (a 10)*

    Mode 8 transp.

    Text by Sannazaro, no. 89, lines 31-38 (from 3rd stanza of canzone, *Sperai gran tempo*); same metrical structure as Petrarch, *Canzoniere*, no. 119.

    Repr. in *RISM* 1589[8], *I-V a 6* (1594) and *Spirituali e temporali* (1610).

Il quinto libro de madrigali a sei voci (1591)
Dedicated to Virginio Orsini, Duke of Bracciano, Rome, 1.1.1591. Printed in Venice: A. Gardano (1591, 1595); herede di G. Scotto (1595); A. Gardano et fratelli (1610). All items repr. in *I-V a 6* (1594) and *I-VI a 6* (1608). Transcribed by Bennett, *Marenzio*, ii.431-544 and Butchart, *A set of madrigals . . .* (unpubl. bachelor's diss.)

1. *Leggiadrissima eterna Primavera*
       Già le Muse . . .

    Mode 2 transp.

    Madrigal honoring wedding of Virginio Orsino and Flavia Peretti.

    Repr. in *RISM* 1609[14].

2. *Leggiadre Ninfe e Pastorelli amanti*

    Mode 12 transp.

    Text by L. Guicciardi, madrigal (author's name in *RISM* 1592[11]).

    Repr. in *RISM* 1592[11], 1605[9], 1609[14], 1610[3], 1612[13], 1613[13], 1619[16], 1624[16].

    Instrumental arr. in *Brown* 1599[11].

    Modern repr. in Harman, *Popular madrigals*, p.73; transcr. in Powley, *Dori* (unpubl. thesis).

    Model of Demantius, *Magnificat a 6* (see Engel, *ZMW*, vii.286).

3. *Candide perle e voi labbra ridenti* (by Antonio Bicci)

    Mode 12 transp.

    Madrigal; has same rhyme scheme as *Liquide perle (I a 5*, 1580, no. 1).

    Repr. in *RISM* 1597[24] with Eng. text: "Dainty white pearl"; reset in this form by East, 1610 (Kerman, *Madrigal*, p.25); also *RISM* 1605[9] (attrib. to Marenzio) and 1610[2].

    Instrumental arr. in *Brown* 1599[11].

    Opening text and music quoted by Carletti, "Candide perl' uscian da tuoi bei lumi," (*RISM* 1601[5]).

4. *Come fuggir per selva ombrosa e folta*

    Mode 12 untransp.

    Text by Della Casa (canzone, 1st stanza): *Opere*, ed. Prezzolini, p.666.

    Repr. in the *Arion Series*, no. 37; *Novello Part-Song Book*, ser.ii, no. 411.

    Parody mass by Hassler (*Werke*, iv.71-88).

5. *Ecco che'l ciel a noi char'e sereno*
    Ecco che mill'augei . . .

    Mode 12 untransp.

    Text by Troiano (sonnet): in *Rime di diversi,* ed. Atanagi, i (1565), 113^V.

    Repr. in *RISM* 1605^9.

6. *Spiri dolce Favonio Arabi odori*
    Tacciano i venti . . .

    Mode 7 untransp.

    Text by Troiano (sonnet): in *Rime di diversi,* ed. Atanagi, i (1565), 112^r. Marenzio substitutes "Tirsi ed Amarilli" in the penultimate line for "Annibale [Gattola] e Lucretia [Cavalcanti]": see Troiano's *Lettera consolatoria,* bound with the *Rime di diversi . . . nella morte della signora Lucretia Cavalcanti de' Gattoli,* Venice, 1568-1569.

    Set by Sabino, *I a 6* (1579).

7. *Giunt'a un bel fonte, il trasmutato in fiore*

    Mode 8 untransp.

    Ottava rima

8. *Nel dolce seno della bella Clori*
    Perchè l'una e l'altr'alma . . .

    Mode 10 untransp.

    Text by T. Tasso (madrigal): first pr. in the *Aggiunta,* 1585; *Rime et prose,* iii (Ferrara, 1589), 60r; repr. in *Rime,* ed. Solerti, ii, no. 174, and Einstein, *Madrigal,* ii.542. Subject matter close to Guarini's *Tirsi morir,* set as *I a 5* (1580), no. 5; comparisons in Di Benedetto, *Tasso,* pp.77-80, and Schulz-Buschhaus, *Madrigal,* p.204 ff.

    Repr. in *RISM* 1624^{16}.

    Set by Pallavicino (1587; *Flanders,* no. 119); Rota, *II a 5* (1589); Casentini, *III a 5* (1607).

9. *Amatemi ben mio*

    Mode 1 untransp.

    Text by T. Tasso (madrigal); first pr. in the *Aggiunta,* Venice, 1585; *Rime et prose,* iii (Ferrara, 1589), 60^r; repr. in the *Rime,* ed. Solerti, ii, no. 288.

    Set by Pallavicino (1585: *Flanders,* no. 94); Bertani, *I a 6* (1585); Giovanelli, *I a 5* (1586); Coma, *IV a 5* (1587); Macque (1589: see Shindle, *Macque,* i. 369); Rota, *II a 5* (1589); Montella, *I a 5* (1595).

    Marenzio's setting was presumably the model for a piece from the *Quarto libro delle villanelle a tre voci* (1587), the first stanza of which reads: "Amatemi ben mio/Che se d'amarmi, dolce vita mia,/Non vi mostrate pia,/ Viverò sconsolato/Sol per amarvi non essendo amato." The last 2 lines of the 4th stanza are almost identical to the last 2 of Tasso's madrigal: "Morirò disperato,/Sol per amarvi non essendo amato." The music for line 1 of each stanza is the same as for the madrigal; so is the music for the penultimate line ("Morirò disperato"). The madrigal presumably was written too late for inclusion in the *IV a 6* (1587).

10.   *Con la sua man la mia*

Mode 8 untransp.

Madrigal; repr. by Einstein, *Madrigal,* ii.668.

11.   *S'a veder voi non vengo, alma mia luce*

Mode 1 transp.

Madrigal.

Repr. in *RISM* 1610³.

12.   *Baci soavi e cari*
         Baci amorosi e belli
         Baci affammati e'ngordi
         Baci cortesi e grati
         Baci, ohimè, non mirate

Mode 1 transp.

Text by Guarini: *Canzon de' baci:* attribution survives in MS version, repr. in Frate, *Rime inedite,* p.142. Poem attrib. also to T. Tasso and Marino: to Tasso in *Rime,* i (Venice, 1581), 128, and *Opere,* iv (Pisa, 1822), 295; authorship of Tasso however denied in the *Rime,* i, ed.cit., (1581), p.95. The traditional attribution to Marino (see Rosini in Tasso, *Opere,* Pisa, 1822, loc.cit.) must stem from the fact that Marino also wrote a *Canzone de'baci* ("O baci avventurosi . . .") closely modeled on Guarini's (repr. in Mirollo, *Marino,* pp.280-285; see also ibid, pp.8-9).

Transcr. in volume II of this study.

Set by Girolamo Belli, *I a 6* (1583); *prima parte,* by Monteverdi (1587: *Opere,* i.14-17); Gesualdo (1594: *Werke,* i.13-16).

13.   *Vivrò dunque lontano*

Mode 1 transp.

Madrigal.

Repr. in *RISM* 1597³, 1610³.

Modern repr. in *Musica Transalpina,* ed. Harman, London, 1956 ("Shall I live . . ."); transcr. in volume II of this study.

Opening is musically the same as opening of no. 12.

Madrigali a cinque voci ridotti in un corpo (1593)
Dedicated by P. Phalèse to Gherardo di Hornes, Antwerp, 8.8.1593. Printed in Antwerp: P. Phalèse and G. Bellère (1593); P. Phalèse al re David, (1609).

I-V a 5 (1580-1585).

Il sesto libro de madrigali a cinque voci (1594)
Dedicated to Cinzio Aldobrandini, Cardinale di San Giorgio, Rome, 1.1.1594. Printed in Venice: A. Gardano (1594, 1603, 1614); all items repr. in *I-IX a 5* (1601) and *VI-IX a 5* (1609); modern repr. by Einstein, *PÄM,* vi.103-141.

1. *S'io parto, i' moro, e pur partir conviene*

   SATTB

   Mode 2 transp.

   Text by Arlotti (madrigal): in Parnaso, ed. Scaiolo (1611), f.101^V.

   Set by Luzzaschi, *V a 5* (1595); Cifra, *I a 5* (1605).

2. *Clori nel mio partire*

   Mode 2 transp.

   Madrigal.

3. *Donna de l'alma mia, de la mia vita*

   Mode 2 transp.

   Text by T. Tasso (*versi sciolti*): *Convito de' pastori*, lines 71-77.

4. *Anima cruda sì, ma però bella*

   Mode 12 transp.

   SATTB

   Text by Guarini (*versi sciolti*): *Pastor fido*, iv.9 (lines 1254-1259, spoken by Dorinda).

   Set as part of *seconda parte* of Monteverdi's *Ecco Silvio* (1605: *Opere*, v.20-23).

5. *Udite, lagrimosi*

   Mode 4 transp.

   Text by Guarini (*versi sciolti*): *Pastor fido*, iii.6 (lines 814-821, spoken by Mirtillo). Criticized in Malacreta, *Considerazioni* (1600), repr. in Guarini, *Opere* (1737), iv.102 ff; anon, in I-Rvat, MS *Chigiana Q.IV.4.*, ff. 98^V-100^V.

   Set by Wert (1595: *Works*, xii.24-27); Monte, *II a 7* (1600); Rossi, *I a 5* (1600); Piccioni, *VI a 5* (1602); Cifra, *I a 5* (1605).

6. *Stillò l'anima in pianto*

   Mode 3 untransp.

   Text by Ongaro (madrigal): *Rime*, Farnese, 1600, p.114.

7. *Ah, dolente partita*

   Mode 10 untransp.

   Text by Guarini: *Pastor fido*, iii.3 (lines 498-505, spoken by Mirtillo). The form is that of a madrigal: aa/Bc/ddeE; censured by Malacreta (see above, no. 5).

   Set by Wert (1595), Monteverdi (1597), Monte (1600), Falcone (1603), Cifra (1605), Rossi (1614); for further details, see Bianconi, ' "Ah dolente partita",' *SM*, iii (1974), especially p.110, note 14, p.111, note 15, and p.112; also Petrobelli, ' "Ah dolente partita" ' in *Claudio Monteverdi e il suo tempo*, pp.361-376. Bianconi does not mention Giovanelli's setting (*I a 3*, 1605). The setting in Bargnani, *Canzonette* (1599), omits the final couplet and adds a further stanza. The anonymous setting in I-Rvat, MS *Chigiana Q.IV.4*, ff.92^V-95^V adds a *seconda parte* with the same metrical structure ("O che dolce ritorno").

8. *Ben ho del caro ogetto i sensi privi*
    Dille, la mia speranza . . .

SMATB   Mode 8 untransp.

Text by Caro (sonnet): *Opere*, Turin, 1974, p.336. Attrib. to Flaminio Orsini in *Rime in vita e morte . . . Liviae Columnae* (1555), f. 50r and to Silvia Piccolomini in *Rime di donne* (1559), p.76 and Trucchi, *Rime inedite*, iii. 208.

Set by Roussel (1559: *Opera*, iii. 56-62); Cifra, *I a 5* (1605).

9. *Amor, se giusto sei*

SATTB   Mode 8 untransp.

Madrigal: in I-Bu, MS *1210*, i, no. 14, with title: "Amante ad Amore."

Set by Monteverdi (1605: *Opere*, v.81-89).

10. *Hor chi Clori beata*

SATTB   Mode 7 untransp.

Text by G.B. Strozzi (madrigal): in *Madrigali* (1593), p.50 ("Hor chi *Filli* beata").

— 11. *Deh Tirsi, Tirsi, anima mia, perdona*
    Che se tu sei . . .

SATTB   Mode 9 untransp.

Text by Guarini (*versi sciolti*): *Pastor fido*, iii.4 (lines 539-547, spoken by Amarilli: "E tu, Mirtillo, anima mia, perdona").

Set by Monte, *II a 7* (1600: "Perdona, anima mia . . ."); Monteverdi (1603: *Opere*, iv.26-34, as "Anima mia, perdona . . .").

12. *Clori mia, Clori dolce, Oh sempre nuovo*

II   Mode 9 untransp.

Text by G.B. Strozzi (madrigal): in *Madrigali* (1593), p.49: "*Filli* mia, *Filli* dolce . . ."

13. *Mentre qual viva pietra*

Mode 12 untransp.

SATTB   Madrigal.

Repr. in *RISM* 1616[8].

Model of Praetorius' *Magnificat a 6* (repr. in *Gesamtausgabe*, xiv.64-71).

14. *Voi bramate ch'io moia*

Mode 1 transp.

SAATB   Madrigal; cf. lines 1-3 with Traiano Bordoni (in *Domenichi*, ix, 1560, p.128; repr. in Mompellio, *Vinci*, p.67): "Voi bramate ch'io mora,/ Et io bramo morire/ . . ." and last line: "Poi che vi piacia almen con la mia morte."

Many poems with similar openings are repr. in the *Gareggiamento* (1611), V.124r ff.

Set by Monte, *XIII a 5* (1588: transcr. by Einstein, *SCA*, xlii).

15. *"Rimanti in pace," a la dolente e bella*
     Ond 'ei, di morte . . .

SATTB

Mode 3 transp.

Text by Celiano (sonnet): in *Rime di diversi*, ed. Licino (1587), p.133; Celiano's "Fillide" is replaced by "Cloride."

Set by Monte, *XV a 5* (1592); Monteverdi (1592: *Opere*, iii.104-113); Rossi, *I a 5* (1600).

16. *Ecco Maggio seren; chi l'ha vestito*

h

Mode 8 transp.

Text by G.B. Strozzi (madrigal): in *Madrigali* (1593), p.89.

17. *Cantiam la bella Clori*

SATB
× 2

Mode 12 transp.

Madrigal; on the possible identity of "Clori" (Flavia Peretti?), see Chater, "Fonti," *RIDM* xiii (1978), 76 ff and note 69.

Madrigali a sei voci in un corpo ridotti (1594)
Dedicated by P. Phalèse to Edouardo, Ferdinando, and Consalvo Ximenez, Antwerp, 26.1.1594. Printed in Antwerp: P. Phalèse and G. Bellère (1594); P. Phalèse al re David (1610). Copy in GB-Lbm, *K.3.f.15*, contains Eng. translations: see inventory in Bennett, *Marenzio*, p. 121.

1594 edn. contains *I-V a 6* (1581-1591), except *I a 6* (1581), no. 18; *IV a 6* (1587), no. 15. Also contains *I a 4, 5, 6* (1588), no. 15. 1610 repr. is as 1594, but with *Bianchi cigni* :(*RISM* 1583[10]) added.

Il sesto libro de madrigali a sei voci (1595)
Dedicated to Margherita Gonzaga d'Este, Duchess of Ferrara, Rome, 30.3.1595. Printed in Venice: A. Gardano (1595), A. Gardano et fratelli (1609); Antwerp: Phalèse (1610). All items repr. in *I-VI a 6* (1608).

1.   *Lucida perla, a cui fu conca il cielo*
     Oda'l ciel questi voti

SMTTB

Mode 12 untransp.

Text by Guarini (eclogue): *Licore, Dafne e Armida*, lines 73-85, in *Opere*, Verona, 1737, ii. 179. The basis of this attribution is not clear: it is not in Guarini's *Rime*, Venice, 1598 and is attributed to Tasso in many sources, among them the *Rime et prose*, iv (Venice, 1586) 159-161. The text, and presumably the music, were written for Margherita's marriage to Alfonso II of Ferrara in 1579. (Ledbetter, *Marenzio*, pp. 31-32.)

Repr. in *RISM* 1597[13], 1601[5].

2.   *Giovane donna sott'un verde lauro*
     All'hor saranno . . .
     Ma, perchè vola il tempo . . .

> *Non fur giamai* . . .
> *I temo di cangiar* . . .
> *Dentro pur foco* . . .
> *L'auro e i topaci* . . .

Mode 8 untransp.

Text by Petrarch, *Canzoniere*, no. 30 (sestina). See Battaglia, *Le rime "pietrose" e la sestina*.

Repr. by D. Arnold, *Penn State Music Series*, xiii.

Set by A. Gabrieli, *Madrigali e ricercari* (1589).

3. *Se quel dolor che va inanzi al morire*
> *Quando si more* . . .
> *Dunque da voi* . . .
> *Dammi, pietosa morte* . . .
> *O Fortuna* . . .
> *Ma quest'oimè, temo* . . .
> *Altr'aurora bisogna* . . .
> *Un tempo io mi credea* . . .
> *Occhi de' miei desiri* . . .
> *Una pur chiederò* . . .

Mode 2 transp.

Text by Tansillo *(capitolo):* first pr. in *Domenichi*, v (1552), 13-17; repr. in Tansillo, *Canzoniere*, ed. Pèrcopo, pp. 179-183.

Quinta parte repr. in Martini, *Saggio*, ii. 229-236.

Set by Wert (1577: *Works*, vi. 68-87). *Prima parte* only set by Donato (1568: see Einstein, *Madrigal*, ii. 673).

4. *Là, dove sono i pargoletti Amori*

Mode 1 transp.

Text by T. Tasso (madrigal): *Rime et prose*, iv (Venice, 1586), 112; repr. in the *Rime*, ed. Solerti, iv, no. 1021. One of a series of madrigals addressed to a dwarf in the service of Margherita Gonzaga (*Rime* cit., iv. nos. 1016-1024).

Repr. in *Madrigali a 5, 6*, ed. Mompellio, pp. 19-23.

5. *O Verdi Selve, o dolci fonti, o rivi*

Mode 1 transp.

Text by T. Tasso (madrigal with echo): in *Rime et prose*, iv (Venice, 1586), 62; repr. in *Rime*, ed. Solerti, ii, no. 309. Cf. longer version, *Diceva un mesto coro: "O dolci fonti . . .,"* where the words "Manto" and "Este" appear in capital letters, alluding to Margherita Gonzaga d'Este (*Rime*, ed. Solerti, iv, no. 990).

Il settimo libro de' madrigali a cinque voci (1595)
Dedicated to Diego de Campo, Chamberlain to the Pope, Rome, 20.10.1595. Printed in Venice: A. Gardano (1595, 1600); A. Gardano et fratelli (1609); herede di G. Scotto (1609). All items repr. in *I-IX a 5* (1601) and *VI-IX a 5* (1609). Transcr. and analysed in Myers, *Il settimo libro . . .* (unpubl. master's diss.); repr. in *Il settimo libro*, ed. Steele, and *Secular Works*, xiv, ed. Myers.

1. *Deh, poi ch'era ne' fati*

   Mode 10 untransp.

   Text by Guarini *(versi sciolti): Pastor fido*, i. 2 (lines 322-327, spoken by Mirtillo: *"Ma* poi ch'era . . .").

2. *Quell'augellin che canta*

   Mode 8 untransp.

   Text by Guarini *(versi sciolti): Pastor fido*, i. 1 (lines 175-186, spoken by Linco); subject matter possibly derived from Tasso's *Sovra le verdi chiome* (*RISM* 1583[10] and *Rime*, ed. Solerti, ii, no. 195); the passage existed independently as a madrigal before incorporation into the *Pastor fido:* appears as "Dolce canor'e garulo augeletto" in *Nova scelta*, ed. Varoli (1590), p. 51 (set by Ingegneri, *VI a 5*, 1607); cf. settings by Macque and Monte, listed below.

   Set by Macque, *III a 5* (1597: "Quel rossignol che plora"); Leoni, *II a 5* (1591); Stivorio, *Madrigali e dialoghi* (1598); Monte, *I a 7* (1599: "Quel augellin che canta Aprile e maggio"); Monteverdi (1603: *Opere*, iv. 66-71).

3. *Cruda Amarilli, che col nome ancora*
   Ma grideran per me . . .

   Mode 3 untransp.

   Text by Guarini *(versi sciolti): Pastor fido*, i. 2 (lines 272-291, spoken by Mirtillo). Censured by Malacreta: cf. *VI a 5* (1594), no. 5.

   Set by Wert (1595: *Works*, xii. 43-48); Pallavicino (1600: repr. in Arnold, *Vier Madrigale*, pp. 17-26); Cifra, *I a 5* (1605); Giovanelli, *I a 3* (1605); Monteverdi (1605: *Opere*, v. 1-4); D'India (1607: *Madrigali*, ed. Mompellio, pp. 13-17; 1609: *Musiche*, ed. Mompellio, pp. 82-85); Anon, GB-Lbm, MS *Add. 31, 440*, f. 33[V] (Willetts, *ML*, xliii. 329-339). Set as "O d'aspido più sorda e più fugace" in Monte, *XIV a 5* (1590).

   For comparisons, see Chater, "Cruda Amarilli," *Musical Times*, cxvi (1975), 231-234.

4. *O disaventurosa acerba sorte*

   Mode: Locrian (with final on *b*).

   Text by Bembo (canzone): *Alma cortese, che dal mondo errante*, lines 74-80; in *Prose et rime*, ed. Dionisotti, p. 625. Written on death of brother Carlo.

5. *Al lume delle stelle*

   Mode 9 untransp.

   Text by Tasso (madrigal): first pr. in the *Rime et prose*, ed. Borgogni, Milan, 1586; repr. in *Rime*, ed. Solerti, ii, no. 246. Shares identical verse form with *III a 6* (1584), no. 4 (also with text by Tasso).

   Set by Monteverdi (1619: *Opere*, vii. 129-136).

6. *Ami, Tirsi, e me'l nieghi*

   Mode 9 untransp.

   Set by Piccioni, *I a 6* (1598).

7. *O dolcezze amarissime d'amore*
   Qui pur vedroll'al suon . . .

   Mode 12 untransp.

   Text by Guarini *(versi sciolti): Pastor fido*, iii. 1 (lines 15-24, 27-28, 30-45, spoken by Mirtillo).

   Set by Rossi, *I a 4* (1614); often set as part of "O Primavera, gioventù dell'anno."

8. *Sospir, nato di foco*

   Mode 4 untransp.

   Madrigal.

9. *Arda pur sempre, o mora*

   Mode 11 transp.

   Text by Guarini *(versi sciolti): Pastor fido*, iii. 6 (lines 894-901, spoken by Mirtillo).

   Set by Gastoldi, *IV a 5* (1602); overlaps with "Questo mi resta solo," set by Monte, *II a 7* (1600).

10. *Questi vaghi concenti*
    Deh, se potessi anch'io

    Mode 1 transp.

    Madrigal (2 stanzas).

    Set by Stivorio, *I a 8* (1598); Monteverdi (1605: *Opere*, v. 104-130).

11. *O fido, o caro Aminta*

    Mode 3 transp.

    Text by Guarini *(versi sciolti): Pastor fido*, i. 2 (lines 462-473, spoken by Ergasto); line 462 originally read: "O fido, o *forte* Aminta"; line 473 emended to "Tal fin'hebber gli sfortunati amanti."

12. *O Mirtillo, Mirtillo, anima mia*

    Mode 8 transp.

    Text by Guarini *(versi sciolti): Pastor fido*, iii. 4 (lines 506-518, spoken by Amarilli).

    Set by Monte, *II a 7* (1600: "Anima mia dolcissima . . ."); Giovanelli, *I a 3* (1605); Monteverdi (1605: *Opere*, v. 5-8); Boschetti, *I a 5* (1613); Rossi, *I a 4* (1614).

13. *Deh, dolce anima mia* (by Antonio Bicci)

    Mode 2 transp.

    Text by Guarini *(versi sciolti): Pastor fido*, iii. 3 (lines 485-491, spoken by Amarilli); emended from: "Partiti; e ti consola / Ch'infinita è la schiera. . . ." In line 489, "Mirtillo" is replaced by "mio core."

    Set by Pallavicino, *VI a 5* (1600: *Flanders*, no. 182).

14.   *Come è dolce il gioire, o vago Tirsi*

Mode 2 transp.

Text by Guarini *(versi sciolti): Pastor fido,* iii. 6 (lines 979-995, spoken by Corisca); last 3 words of line 979 are added.

Set by Piccioni, *VI a 5* (1602: "Come è soave cosa . . ."); Giovanelli, *I a 3* (1605: "Crudele ed amarissima Amarilli,/Com'è soave cosa . . ."); Rossi, *I a 4* (1614).

15.   *Care mie selve, a Dio*
          Così (ch'il crederia?) . . .

Mode 9 transp.

Text by Guarini *(versi sciolti): Pastor fido,* iv. 5 (lines 752-777, spoken by Amarilli).

Set by Schütz (1611: *Werke,* xxii. 103-109) as "Dunque addio, care selve."

16.   *Tirsi mio, caro Tirsi*

Mode 9 transp.

Text by Guarini *(versi sciolti): Pastor fido,* iv. 5 (lines 733-734, 736-742, spoken by Amarilli); line 733 emended from *"Padre mio, caro padre."* Last 3 lines added to original.

Set by Rossi, *I a 5* (1600).

17.   *Ombrose e care selve*

Mode 12 transp.

Text by Guarini *(versi sciolti): Pastor fido,* v. 8 (lines 1337-1344, spoken by Ergasto); line 1337 emended from: "Selve beate/. . . ." In line 1344, the words "De' beati amanti" have been replaced by "D'Amarilli e di Tirsi,/Aventurosi amanti."

Set by Schütz (1611: *Werke,* xxii. 16-23) as "Selve beate . . . ."

L'ottavo libro de' madrigali a cinque voci (1598)
Dedicated to Ferrante Gonzaga, Prince of Molfetta and Lord of Guastalla, Venice, 20.10.1598. Printed in Venice: A. Gardano (1598, 1605); herede di G. Scotto (1609). All items repr. in *I-IX a 5* (1601) and *VI-IX a 5* (1609).

1.   *O occhi del mio core e d'Amor lumi*
          Anima bella . . .

Mode 2 transp.

Text by T. Tasso *(versi sciolti): Convito,* lines 210-229.

2.   *Dunque romper la fè? Dunque deggio io*

Mode 11 transp.

Text by T. Tasso *(versi sciolti): Convito,* lines 111-123.

3.   *Filli, volgendo i lumi al vago Aminta*

Mode 11 transp.

Text by T. Tasso *(versi sciolti): Convito,* lines 78-87; repr. in Einstein, *Madrigal,* ii. 683. Emended from: "Qui tacque. Et ella in lui volgendo i ilumi/Dal profondo del cor. . . ."

Repr. by Steele, music suppl. to article in *Studies in Music, iii (1969), 17-24.*

4. *Vita soave e di dolcezza piena*

    Mode 9 transp.

    Text by T. Tasso *(versi sciolti): Convito,* lines 189-200.

5. *Provate la mia fiamma*

    Mode 8 untransp.

    Text by Celiano (madrigal): in *Rime di diversi,* ed. Licino (1587), p. 131.

    Arr. for 4 voices by Bargnani (*RISM* 1599[12]) with addition of extra stanza sung to same music as the first: "Mirate la mia vita"; designated "aria."

6. *Ahi, chi t'insidia al boscareccio nido?*
        Vieni, deh vieni a me . . .

    Mode 8 untransp.

    Text by Celiano (sonnet): in *Rime di diversi,* ed. Licino (1587), p. 127.

    Set by Bertani, *I a 6* (1585).

7. *Ite amari sospiri*

    Mode 10 untransp.

    Text by Guarini (madrigal): in *Rime,* Venice, 1598, f. 79[r].

    Set by anon. in I-Rvat, MS *Chigiana Q. IV. 4,* ff., 120 - 104.

8. *Pur venisti, cor mio*

    Mode 3 untransp.

    Text by Guarini (madrigal): in *Rime,* Venice, 1598, f. 100[r].

    Set by Rossi, *I a 5* (1600); D'India (1607: *Madrigali,* ed. Mompellio, pp. 56-59).

9. *Quando io miro le rose*

    Mode 1 transp.

    Text by Grillo (Madrigal no. 8): in *Rime,* i (ed. Licino, Bergamo, 1589), 75, and ii (Venice, 1599), 131[V]. Attrib. to Celiano in *Rime di diversi* ed. by the same Licino, 1587, p. 116; attrib. to Angelo Galeotini in the *Ghirlanda* (1609); attrib. to Grillo by Verdonck, 1603 (*NV,* ii, no. 2893).

    Repr. in *Madrigali a 5, 6,* ed. Mompellio, p. 6.

    Set by Coma, *IV a 5* (1587); Verdonck (1603: see above); set as "Son sì belle le rose" by Gesualdo (1594: *Werke,* i. 73-75) and Macque (1610: transcr. in Shindle, *Macque,* ii. 636-40); set as "È si bello il tuo viso" by D'India (1608: see Obertello, *Madrigali,* p. 519). Eng. paraphrase, "Lady, when I behold," set twice by Wilbye (1598: *EMS,* vi. 40-43; 116-123).

➤ 10.   *Deh Tirsi mio gentil, non far più stratio*

Mode 8 transp.

Text by Guarini *(versi sciolti): Pastor fido,* ii. 6 (line 905 emended from "Deh, Satiro gentil, non far più strazio").

Set by Boschetti, *I a 5* (1613).

11.   *Questi leggiadri, odorosetti fiori*

Mode 11 transp.

Text by Celiano (madrigal): in *Rime di diversi,* ed. Licino (1587), p. 116.

Set by Gesualdo (1594: *Werke,* i. 64-67); Boschetti, *I a 5* (1613).

12.   *Care lagrime mie*

Mode 3 transp.

Text by Celiano (madrigal): in *Rime di diversi,* ed. Licino (1587), p. 129.

Set by Coma, *IV a 5* (1587); Rota, *II a 5* (1589); Monte, *XV a 5* (1592); Agazzari, *I a 6* (1596); Hassler (1596: *Werke,* iii. 50-53); Gagliano, *II a 5* (1604); Kapsberger, *I a 5* (1609). Eng. paraphrase, "Weep, O mine eyes", set by Wilbye (1598: *EMS,* vi. 15-18) and Bennet (1599: *EMS,* xxiii. 60-62).

13.   *La mia Clori è brunetta*

Mode 1 transp.

Text by Celiano (madrigal): in *Rime di diversi,* ed. Licino (1587), p. 141.

Arr. for 4 voices by Bargnani (*RISM* 1599[12]).

14.   *"Non sol," dissi, "tu poi, anima fera . . ."*

Mode 7 untransp.

Text by Tasso *(versi sciolti): Arezia, Ninfa,* lines 118-133 (attrib. also to Ferrante Gonzaga, the dedicatee of this book: see below, app. IV, note on T. Tasso).

15.   *Se tu, dolce mio ben, mi saettasti*
        Dorinda, ah, dirò mia . . .
        Ferir quel petto, Silvio . . .

Mode 12 untransp.

Text by Guarini *(versi sciolti): Pastor fido,* iv. 9 (lines 1231-1250, 1260-1267, 1272-1279, 1284-1294 and 1300-1304, spoken by Dorinda and Silvio).

Overlaps with Monteverdi's "Ecco Silvio" (1605: *Opere,* v. 14-38).

16.   *Laura, se pur sei l'aura*
        Perfida, pur potesti

Mode 9 untransp.

Text by Celiano: *Rime di diversi,* ed. Licino (1587), p. 125. Subsequent sources prove that the two madrigals which constitute the two *parti* of Marenzio's setting were printed together by mistake; in reality they are two separate poems. The *prima parte* was repr. in *Fiori di madrigali,* ed. Caraffa (1598) and with attrib. to Tasso in *I nomi delle donne,* ed. Alchino (1621), p. 8. Both poems appear with attrib. to Tasso in *Rime,* iv-v (Genova, 1586), 162.

Set by Scaletta, *II a 5* (1590; *prima parte* only); G.F. Anerio, *I a 5* (1599); Pallavicino, *IV a 5* (1588: *Flanders,* no. 149; *seconda parte* only).

Il nono libro de' madrigali a cinque voci (1599)
Dedicated to Vincenzo Gonzaga, Duke of Mantua, Rome, 10.5.1599. Printed in Venice: A. Gardano (1599, 1601); A. Raverii (1608); A. Gardano et fratelli, (1609); herede di G. Scotto (1609). All items repr. in *I-IX a 5* and *VI-IX a 5* (1609). Transcr. by Tommaso Pecci, 1630: I-Sc, MS *L.V. 34,* ff 1^r-53^v. Nos. 1-4 censured by Artusi in *Seconda parte,* pp. 16-17 and Cerone, *Melopeo,* pp. 669 ff and 677-678.

1.   *Così nel mio parlar voglio esser aspro*
         Et ella ancide . . .

     Mode 10 untransp.

     Text by Dante (canzone): *Rime,* no. 103, lines 1-13 (no. 3 of the *Rime per la donna di pietra*). See Battaglia, *Rime "petrose."*

     Repr. by Einstein, *AMW,* iii (1921), 414-420; see also Degrada, *Chigiana,* xxii (1965), 257-275.

     Set by V. Galilei (repr. by Palisca, *SM,* i. 203: "Così nel mio cantar . . .").

2.   *Amor, i' ho molti e molt'anni pianto*

     Mode 3 untransp.

     Text by Petrarch, *Canzoniere,* no. 332, lines 55-60 (sestina stanza).

3.   *Dura legge d'Amor, ma benchè obliqua*
         E so come in un punto . . .

     Mode 1 untransp.

     Text by Petrarch *(capitolo): Trionfo d'Amore,* iii, lines 148-159.

     Repr. by Steele, musical suppl. to article in *Studies in Music,* iii (1969), pp. 17-24.

4.   *Chiaro segno Amor pose alle mie rime*

     Mode 1 untransp.

     Text by Petrarch, *Canzoniere,* no. 332, lines 25-30 (sestina stanza).

5.   *Se sì alto pon gir mie stanche rime*

     Mode 2 untransp.

     Text by Petrarch, *Canzoniere,* no. 332, lines 61-66.

     Set by Lassus (1563: Werke, iv. 59-61).

6.   *L'aura, ch'el verde lauro e l'aureo crine*
      Sì ch'io non veggia . . .

Mode 9 untransp.

Text by Petrarch, *Canzoniere,* no. 246 (sonnet).

Repr. in Torchi, *Arte musicale,* ii. 238-246.

Opening text and music similar to *VIII a 5* (1598), no. 16: see Chater, "Fonti," *RIDM,* xiii (1978), 81-82.

Set by Vicentino (1572: *Opera,* pp. 96-101).

7.   *Il vago e bello Armillo*
      E dicea: "O beate onde . . ."

Mode 12 untransp.

Text by Celiano (madrigal): in *Rime di diversi,* ed. Licino (1587), p. 131 ("Il vago e bello *Eurillo").*

Repr. in Torchi, *Arte musicale,* ii. 215-223.

8.   *Solo e pensoso i più deserti campi*
      Sì ch'io mi credo . . .

Mode 7 untransp.

Text by Petrarch: *Canzoniere,* no. 35 (sonnet).

Repr. in Schering, *Geschichte,* pp. 174-176; Torchi, *Arte musicale,* ii. 228-237; *Madrigali a 4, 5,* ed. Virgili, pp. 20-27.

Set by Lassus (1555: *Werke,* ii. 71-75); Monte, *II a 4* (1569: transcr. by Einstein, *SCA,* xxxix); Vicentino (1572: *Opera,* pp. 123-124); Anon (*RISM* 1577[8]); Wert (1581: *Works,* vii. 32-37); Conversi, *I a 6* (1584); A. Ferrabosco, *II a 5* (1587); Giovanelli, *I a 3* (1605).

9.   *Vivo in guerra mendico, e son dolente*
      E gl'occhi al cielo . . .

Mode 9 transp.

Text by Ongaro (sonnet): *Rime,* Farnese, 1600, p. 20. First pr. in the *Scelta di rime,* i (ed. Bartoli, 1591), 97.

10.   *Fiume, ch'a l'onde tue ninf'e pastori*
      Ahi, tu me'l nieghi . . .

Mode 12 transp.

Text by Ongaro (sonnet): in *Rime* (1600), p. 13; first pr. in the *Scelta,* i (ed. Bartoli, 1591), 98.

Seconda parte repr. in Martini, *Saggio,* ii. 164-172; Burney, *History,* ii. 168-170.

Set by D'India (1607: *Madrigali,* ed. Mompellio, pp. 26-35).

11.   *Parto o non parto? Ahi, come*

Mode 1 transp.

Text by Guarini (madrigal): in *Rime*, Venice, 1598, f. 102^V.

Repr. in Nef, *Histoire*, pp. 150-152.

12. *Credete voi ch'io viva*

Mode 10 transp.

Text by Guarini (madrigal): in *Rime*, Venice, 1598, f. 102^V.

Repr. in *Madrigali a 5, 6*, ed. Mompellio, pp. 3-5.

13. *Crudele, acerba, inesorabil morte*

Mode 3 transp.

Text by Petrarch, *Canzoniere*, no. 332, lines 7-12.

Repr. in *Ten madrigals*, ed. Arnold, pp. 72-79.

Set by Lassus (1555: *Werke*, ii. 44-46); also as *seconda parte* of *Mia benigna fortuna* by Rore (1557: *Opera*, iv. 80-81) and Wert (1588: *Works*, ix. 38-42).

14. *La bella man vi stringo*

Mode 1 transp. ("Canone alla quarta inferiore").

Text by Guarini (madrigal): in *Rime*, Venice, 1598, f. 88^r; first pr. in *Rime di diversi*, ed. Licino (1587), p. 202.

Repr. in Torchi, *Arte musicale*, ii. 224-227.

Set by Monte, *XVI a 5* (1593).

Madrigalia quinque vocum . . . uno volumine conjunctim excusa, Nuremberg: P. Kauffmann, 1610.

  I-IX a 5 (1580 - 1599)

Madrigali sex vocum . . . uno volumine conjunctim excusa, Nuremberg: P. Kauffmann, 1608.

  I-VI a 6 (1581 - 1595)

Il sesto, settimo, ottavo et nono libro . . . de' madrigali a cinque voci, (1609), printed in Antwerp: P. Phalèse al re David (1609); heredi di P. Phalèse al re David (1632).

  VI-IX a 5 (1594 - 1599)

Madrigali spirituali e temporali . . . a cinque, sei, otto, nove e dieci voci, Nuremberg: P. Kauffmann, 1610.

  Miscellaneous selection of sacred and secular madrigals: see inventory in *NV*, ii, no. 1680.

Anthologies Containing First Editions of Madrigals by Marenzio

RISM 1577[7]: *Il primo fiore della ghirlanda musicale*, ed. G.B. Mosto, Venice: herede di Scotto, 1577.

  Donna e bella e crudel, se sdegn'havete (a 5)

Mode 2 transp.

Text by Remigio Nannini (madrigal): in *Rime,* Florence, 1547, p. 30

RISM 1582[4]: *Dolci affetti . . . de' diversi eccellenti musici di Roma,* ed. by the "Accademico Anomato," Venice: herede di G. Scotto, 1582.

[1] *Hor pien d'altro desio (a 5)*

Mode 1 transp.

Text by Alamanni, tr. from Horace (ode): 3rd stanza of *Mentre ti fui sì grato,* in *Rime di napoletani,* v (1555 edn.), 476. Original ode *(Donec gratus eram tibi)* in *The odes of Horace,* ed. and tr. J. Michie, pp. 170-171 (*Carminum,* iii. 9). For further details, see chapter 2, notes 64-65.

Other stanzas are set by G.M. Nanino, G.B. Moscaglia, Macque, Soriano, Zoilo. Whole ode repr. in *RISM* 1588[21]; first 4 stanzas in *RISM* 1585[19];

Marenzio's stanza repr. in *Spirituali e temporali* (1610).

Stanzas by Marenzio and Macque are transcr. in Vol. ii, pp. 1-13

Whole ode set by A. Ferrabosco, *I a 5* (1587).

[2] *In quel ben nato aventuroso giorno (a 5)*

Mode 8 untransp.

Text by Sannazaro, no. 24 (madrigal).

Repr. in *RISM* 1605[9] and *Spirituali e temporali* (1610).

Set by Vicentino (1546: *Opera,* pp. 5-8); Monte, *III a 4* (1585: transcr. by Einstein, *SCA,* xxxix).

RISM 1582[5]: *Il lauro secco,* Ferrara: V. Baldini, 1582. Preface signed by "I Rinovati" ("The Renewed Ones"). See Newcomb, "Three anthologies" *RIDM,* x (1975), 329-345.

[1] *Mentre l'aura spirò nel verde lauro (a 5)*
      Ma perchè, lasso . . .

Mode 1 transp.

Madrigal.

Repr. in *RISM* 1589[8] and *Spirituali e temporali* (1610)

Transc. in Newcomb, *Madrigal,* ii. 62-71

Set by G.B. Mosto, *I a 6* (1595).

[2] *Quel lauro che fu in me già così verde (a 10)*

Mode 12 transp.

Dialogue in form of madrigal.

RISM 1583[10]: *Il lauro verde,* Ferrara: V. Baldini, 1583. See Newcomb, art. cit. in previous note. References are to the repr., *RISM* 1591[8].

Bianchi Cigni e canori (a 6)
   Alzate il novo Lauro . . .
   Guidate dolci . . .

Mode 12 untransp.

Madrigal; perhaps by Tasso (Newcomb, art. cit., p. 342 ff).

Repr. in *RISM* 1589[8], *I-V a 6* (1610 repr.); *Spirituali e temporali* (1610).

Instrumental arr. in *RISM* 1600[6].

Transcr. in Newcomb, *Madrigal,* ii. 112-135; *prima parte* transcr. in volume II of this study.

RISM 1583[11]: *De'floridi virtuosi d'Italia il primo libro,* ed. A. Barbato, Venice: G. Vincenzi and R. Amadino, 1583.

Se tu mi lasci, perfido, tuo danno (a 5)

Mode 8 transp.

Text by T. Tasso (madrigal): first pr. in *Rime et prose,* iv (Venice, 1586), 185; repr. in *Rime,* ed. Solerti, ii. 467. "Perfido" is emended from "perfida."

Repr. in Engel, *Lied,* pp. 31-32.

Set by Stivorio, in Lauro-Stivorio, *I a 3* (1590); Monteverdi (1590: *Opere,* ii. 65-67).

RISM 1583[12]: *Li amorosi ardori,* ed. C. Corradi, Venice: A. Gardano, 1583.

Perchè adoprar catene (a 5)

Mode 8 untransp.

Text by Manfredi (madrigal): in *Cento donne* (1580), p. 46; for Camilla Tiene, a dancer at the Ferrarese court (Chater, *RIDM,* xiii. 65).

RISM 1585[29]: *Di Gio. Battista Moscaglia il secondo libro de madrigali a quattro voci con alcuni di diversi eccellenti musici di Roma,* Venice: G. Vincenzi and R. Amadino, 1585. Dedication signed 10.9.1582. See Sloan, *Il Secondo Libro de Madrigali a Quattro Voci of Giovanni Battista Moscaglia. Transcription and stylistic study* (Unpubl. Master's diss.)

Dissi a l'amata mia lucida stella (a 4)

See above, note to *I a 4* (1585), no. 2.

RISM 1586[1]: *Musica spirituale,* Venice: A. Gardano, 1586.

[1]   *Signor, che già te stesso (a 5)*

   Mode 4 untransp.

   Strophe: 11th stanza of *Signor, cui già (Spirituali,* 1584, no. 10).

[2]   *Vergine gloriosa e lieta, o quanto (a 5)*

   Mode 4 untransp.

   Strophe; *seconda parte* of [1]: see above, *Spirituali* (1584), no. 11.

RISM 1586[10]: *I lieti amanti,* ed. I. Gianluca, Venice: G. Vincenzi and R. Amadino, 1586.

Falsa credenza havete

Mode 10 untransp.

Madrigal: by Guarini? (chapter 3, note 128).

RISM 1588[17]: *L'amorosa Ero,* ed. A. Morsolino, Brescia: V. Sabbio, 1588. Whole anthology ed. Lincoln (New York, 1968).

Ero così dicea (a 4)

Mode 1 transp.

Text by M.A. Martinengo (madrigal); set by 18 composers, all writing in the same mode.

Spiritual parody, *"Pietro* così dicea," in Rome, Vallicelliana, *Q.V. 23,* a copy of the anthology in which the original words have been overlaid with sacred words by Giovenale Ancina.

Repr. in Lincoln, ed. cit., pp. 56-63.

RISM 1589[7]: *Le gioie . . . di diversi ecce[lentissi]mi musici della compagnia di Roma,* ed. F. Anerio, Venice: R. Amadino, 1589. See Giazotto, *Quattro secoli,* p. 19 ff.

Rivi, fontane e fiumi a l'aur'al cielo (a 5)

Mode 9 untransp.

Sesstina, 4th stanza: lines 19-24 of *Al'hor che lieta l'alba adduce il giorno,* set entire by Monte, *I a 7* (1599).

Repr. in *RISM* 1592[15] as *seconda parte* of Striggio's *Al'hor che lieta* (1st stanza); also pr. in *RISM* 1596[10] and 1605[2].

Transcr. in Newcomb, *Madrigal,* ii. 170-177.

Set by Monte (see above).

RISM 1590[31]: *Selva di varia ricreazione di Horatio Vecchi,* Venice: A. Gardano, 1590.

"O messir . . .," "o Patrù . . ." (a 4)
    "O disgratio . . ."

Mode 12 untransp.

Diversi linguaggi: dialogue *a 4* with 5-voice addition by Vecchi.

Repr. Kirkendale, in *CW,* cxxv. 1-19.

Bibl: Kirkendale, "Franceschina . . .," *Acta Musicologica,* xliv (1972), 181-235.

RISM 1591[23]: *La Ruzina, canzone di Filippo de Monte . . . et altri madrigali de' diversi,* Venice: A. Gardano, 1591.

Uscite, uscite Ninfe (a 6)

Mode 12 transp.

Madrigal: celebrates a wedding.

Repr. in *Spirituali e temporali* (1610).

RISM 1592[14]: *La gloria musicale*, ed. F. Nicoletti, Venice: R. Amadino, 1592.

Coppia di donne altera (a 5)

Mode 12 untransp.

Madrigal: perhaps for two sisters of the Guerrieri family (the 4th line reads: "L'una e l'altr'è guerriera"); the Guerrieri were a Mantuan family known to T. Tasso (see *Rime*, ed. Solerti, iii. 521 and 525).

RISM 1593[3]: *Florinda e Armilla, canzon pastorale*, Venice: R. Amadino, 1593.

Bascia e ribascia, hor sugge (a 5)

Mode 1 transp.

Text by M. Veniero (canzone): 12th stanza of *Poichè più volt'in vano*, in D. Veniero, *Rime* (1750), pp. 159-161; attrib. survives in *Scelta di rime*, ii (ed. Bartoli, 1591), 38-41. Neither version contains the stanza set by Marenzio; however, other versions survive without ascription: in the setting by Cavaccio (see below) and the *Rime*, ed. Caporali, Milan, 1585, pp. 220-224 and in I-Sc, MS *I.XI.11*, ff. 28[r]-30[v].

Repr. in *RISM* 1596[10] and *Spirituali e temporali* (1610).

Set by Cavaccio, *Musica* (1585).

RISM 1596[11]: *Vittoria amorosa*, ed. G. Vaiano, Venice: G. Vincenti, 1596.

Donna, col sguardo tenti (a 5)

Mode 7 untransp.

Madrigal: the whole collection is in honor of a singer whose first name is Vittoria (perhaps Vittoria Archilei). This text, however, does not mention the name "Vittoria."

MS anthology, I-VEaf, no. *220* (c. 1580): "Madrigali a 5 e a 6 voci." See Kenton, "Wreath," in *Festschrift Reese*, pp. 500-518; Newcomb, "Three anthologies," *RIDM*, x (1975), 329-345.

[1] *Ridean già per le piagg'herbette e fiori (a 5)*
     Piagge, herbe, fiori . . .

See app. II, note to *III a 5* (1582), no 11.

[2] *Là 've l'Aurora appar' più chiaro, il giorno (a 5)*

Mode 10 untransp.

Sonnet; cf. Petrarch, *Canzoniere*, no. 239: "Là ver l'aurora che sì dolce l'aura." Marenzio quotes the opening of Striggio's setting of this sestina stanza (chapter 2, ex. 1).

Anthologies Containing Reprints Only

RISM 1583[14]: *Harmonia celeste,* ed. A. Pevernage, Antwerp: P. Phalèse and J. Bellère, 1583. Facs. repr. in *CEMF,* xx.

RISM 1583[15]: *Musica divina,* Antwerp: P. Phalèse, 1583. Facs. repr. in *CEMF,* xix.

RISM 1584[5]: *Spoglia amorosa,* ed. F. Landono, Venice: herede di G. Scotto, 1584.

RISM 1585[19]: *Symphonia angelica,* ed. H. Waelrand, Antwerp: P. Phalèse and G. Bellère, 1585. Facs. repr. in *CEMF,* xxi; cf. repr., *RISM,* 1590[17].

RISM 1586[11]: *Corona de dodici sonetti alla gran Duchessa di Toscana,* ed. G.B. Zuccarini, Venice: A. Gardano, 1586. See *IV a 5* (1584), no. 7.

RISM 1587[14]: *Primus liber suavissimas praestantissimorum,* Erfurt: G. Baumann, 1587.

RISM 1588[21]: *Gemma musicalis . . . liber primus,* ed. F. Lindner, Nuremberg: C. Gerlach, 1588.

RISM 1588[29]: *Musica Transalpina,* ed. N. Yonge, London, T. East, 1588. Facs. repr., Farnborough, 1972. Inventory in Kerman, *Madrigal,* pp. 54-55; Eng. texts repr. in Obertello, *Madrigali,* pp. 212-257. Music repr. in *Musica Transalpina,* ed. Harman.

RISM 1589[8]: *Liber secundus gemmae musicalis,* ed. F. Lindner, Nuremberg: C. Gerlach, 1589.

RISM 1589[12]: *Musicale esercitio di Ludovico Balbi,* Venice, A. Gardano, 1589.

RISM 1590[11]: *Dialoghi musicali,* Venice: A. Gardano, 1590. Facs. repr. in *CEMF,* xxix.

RISM 1590[17]: *Symphonia angelica,* ed. H. Waelrand, Antwerp: P. Phalèse and J. Bellère, 1590. Rev. edn. of *RISM,* 1585[19].

RISM 1590[29]: *The first sett of Italian madrigalls englished.* ed. T. Watson, London: T. East, 1590. See inventory in Kerman, *Madrigal,* p. 59; Eng. texts repr. in Obertello, *Madrigali,* pp. 260-286.

RISM 1591[10]: *Melodia olympica,* ed. P. Philips, Antwerp: P. Phalèse and G. Bellère, 1591. Facs. repr. in *CEMF,* xxi.

RISM 1592[11]: *Il trionfo di Dori,* Venice: A. Gardano, 1592. See Powley, *Il trionfo di Dori: a critical edition* (unpublished thesis).

RISM 1592[15]: *Spoglia amorosa. . .novamente ristampata,* Venice: A. Gardano, 1592.

RISM 1593[4]: *Harmonia celeste,* ed. A. Pevernage, Antwerp: P. Phalèse and J. Bellère, 1593. Rev. edn. of *RISM* 1583[14].

RISM 1596[8]: *Madrigali a otto voci de' diversi,* Antwerp: P. Phalèse, 1596.

RISM 1596[10]: *Il paradiso musicale,* Antwerp: P. Phalèse, 1596. (Not consulted).

RISM 1597[13]: *Fiori del giardino,* Nuremberg: P. Kauffmann, 1597.

RISM 1597[15]: *Il vago alboreto,* Antwerp: P. Phalèse, 1597. Facs. repr. in *CEMF,* xxiii.

RISM 1597[24]: *Musica Transalpina. . .the second booke,* ed. N. Yonge, London: T. East, 1597. Facs. repr., Farnborough, 1972. See inventory in Kerman, *Madrigali,* pp.62-63; Eng. texts repr. in Obertello, *Madrigali,* pp.289-310. Music repr. in *Musica Transalpina,* ed. Harman.

RISM 1598[15]: *Madrigals to five voices celected out of the best approved Italian authors* by Thomas Morley, London, T. East, 1598. See inventory in Kerman, *Madrigal,* pp.68-69; Eng. texts repr. in Obertello, *Madrigali,* pp.314-330.

RISM 1599[12]: *Canzonette, arie et madrigali a tre et a quattro voci di Ottavio Bargnani,* Venice: Ricciardo Amadino, 1599.

RISM 1601[5]: *Ghirlanda di madrigali a sei voci,* Antwerp: P. Phalèse, 1601.

RISM 1605[9]: *Nervi d'Orfeo,* Leyden: H.L. van Haestens, 1605. (Not consulted).

RISM 1606[16]: *Hortus musicalis. . .liber primus,*ed. M. Herrer, Padua: M. Nenninger, 1606. Latin texts.

RISM 1607[20]: *Musica tolta da' madrigali di Claudio Monteverdi e d'altri autori. . .fatta spirituale,* ed. A. Coppini, Milan: A. Tradate, 1607. Latin texts.

RISM 1609[14]: *Hortus musicalis. . .liber II,* ed. M. Herrer, Munich: A. Berg, 1609. Latin texts.

RISM 1609[15]: *Hortus musicalis. . .liber tertius,* ed. M. Herrer, Munich: A. Berg, 1609. Latin texts.

RISM 1610[2]: *Fatiche spirituali. . .libro primo,* ed. S. Molinaro, Venice: R. Amadino, 1610. Latin texts.

RISM 1610[3]: *Fatiche spirituali. . .libro secondo,* ed. S. Molinaro, Venice: R. Amadino, 1610. Latin texts.

RISM 1612[13]: *Musicalische Streitkräntzlein,* ed. J. Lyttich, Nuremberg: A. Wagenmann and D. Kauffmann, 1612. Cf. *RISM,* 1592[11]; Ger. texts.

RISM 1613[13]: *Rest musicalisches Streitkräntzleins,* ed. J. Lyttich, Nuremberg: D. Kauffmann. (Not consulted). Cf. inventory in *VE,* 1613[2]; also *RISM,* 1592[11], 1612[13], 1619[16].

RISM 1616[8]: *Madrigali. . .accommodati per concerti spirituali,* ed. R.F.P.G. Cavaglieri. Latin texts.

RISM 1619[16]: *Triumphi di Dorothea,* ed. M. Rinckhard, Leipzig: B. Voigt, 1619 (Not consulted). Cf.*RISM,* 1592[11], 1612[13], 1613[13].

VE 1622[A]: *Periculum musicum VIII. cum 3 Madrig. Marentii 6 voc.,* ed. J. Dillinger, Wittenberg: Gormann, 1622. (Not consulted) Contains 3 madrigals by Marenzio with Ger. texts, of which Einstein identifies one (*I a 6,* 1584, no. 4).

RISM 1624[16]: *Erster Theil lieblicher welscher Madrigalien,* ed. V. Diezel, Nuremberg: S. Halbmayern, 1624. (Not consulted). Contains 3 items with Ger. sacred texts (see *VE* 1624[1]).

Instrumental and Vocal Arrangements

Brown 1582[1]: *Novae tabulae musicae,* ed. G.C. Barbetta, Strasbourg: B. Jobin, 1582. (Not consulted).

Brown 1584[3]: *Il primo libro de intavolatura da liuto,* ed. G. Fallamero, Venice: herede di G. Scotto, 1584. (Not consulted).

Brown 1591[2]: *Motetti, madrigali et canzoni francese di diversi auttori. . .diminuiti per sonar con ogni sorte di stromenti,* ed. G. Bassano, Venice: G. Vincenti, 1591. (Not consulted).

Brown 1592[6]: *Novum pratum musicum,* ed. E. Adriansen, Antwerp: P. Phalèse and J. Bellère, 1592. (Not consulted).

Brown 1593[7]: *Intavolatura di liutto. . .libro primo,* ed. G.A. Terzi, Venice: R. Amadino, 1593.

Brown 1594[5]: *Florilegium,* ed. A. Denss, Cologne: G. Grevenbruch, 1594. (Not consulted).

Brown 1599[11]: *Il secondo libro de intavolatura di liuto,* ed. A. Terzi, Venice: G. Vincenti, 1599.

RISM 1600[5a]: *Flores musicae,* ed. J. Rudenius, Heidelberg: Voegelin, 1600. (Not consulted: cf. Engel, *Marenzio,* p. 246.)

RISM 1600[6]: *Florum musicae. . .liber secundus,* ed. J. Rudenius, Heidelberg: Voegelin, 1600. (Not consulted: cf. Engel, *Marenzio,* p. 246.)

RISM 1607[29]: *Tabulatur Buch,* ed. B. Schmid, Strasbourg: L. Zetzner, 1607. (Not consulted: cf. Engel, *Marenzio,* p. 246; Sartori, *Musica strumentale,* i.148.)

MS anthology: *The Fitzwilliam Virginal Book,* ed. J. Fuller Maitland and W. Barclay Squire, repr. of 1899 edn., 2 vols., New York, 1963.

Modern Editions Containing Exclusively Madrigals by Marenzio

Note: This list is selective: a more complete list is given by Bennett in *Marenzio,* pp. 186-194 (bibliography). Anthologies, articles, monographs, or theses containing editions of Marenzio's works are listed in appendix VI and marked with an asterisk (*).

Arion collection of madrigals, glees, partsongs etc., London, 1895 ff.

Giovane donna, [*VI a 6* (1595), no. 2], ed. Arnold (Penn State Music Series, 13), University Park and London, 1967.

Madrigale für fünf Stimmen, Buch I-III and *IV-VI,* ed. A. Einstein (*PÄM* iv/1 and vi), Leipzig 1929 and 1931.

Madrigali a cinque e a sei voci, ed. F. Mompellio, (Le Chant du Monde), Milan, 1953.

Madrigali a 4 e 5 voci, ed. L. Virgili (Madrigalisti Italiani, 1), Rome, 1952.

Musica Transalpina, London 1953-1956. Individual editions by R.A. Harman of 10 pieces from *RISM,* 1588[29] and 1597[24].

Novello Part Song Book, second series, London, 1869 ff.

Novello Tonic Sol-fa Series, London, 1876 ff.

Opera Omnia, ed. B. Meier and R. Jackson (*CMM,* 72), n.p., [American Institute of Musicology], 1978 ff (4 vols. to 1979).

Secular Works, The, ed. S. Ledbetter and P. Myers, New York, 1977 ff. So far only vols. vii (ed. S. Ledbetter) and xiv (ed. P.A. Myers) have appeared.

Settimo libro de' madrigali a 5 voci, Il, ed. J. Steele, 3 fascicles, New York, 1975. Vol.vii of a projected *Opera Omnia.*

Ten madrigals for mixed voices, ed. D. Arnold, London, 1966.

Appendix III

Printed Musical Sources Before 1700

Individual Publications

Agazzari, A., *Il primo libro de' madrigali a sei voci,* Venice: A. Gardano, 1596.

Anerio, F., *Madrigali. . .a cinque voci. . .secondo libro,* Rome: Alessandro Gardano, 1585.

———, *Madrigali spirituali. . .a cinque voci. . .libro primo,* Rome: Alessandro Gardano, 1585.

———, *Il primo libro de' madrigali a cinque voci,* Venice: G. Vincenzi, 1587.

———, *Madrigali a tre voci,* Venice: G. Vincenti, 1598.

Anerio, G.F., *Il primo libro de' madrigali a cinque voci,* Venice: R. Amadino, 1599.

———, *Teatro armonico spirituale di madrigali a cinque, sei, sette et otto voci,* Rome: G.B. Robletti, 1619.

Baccusi, I., *Il secondo libro de' madrigali a sei voci,* Venice: G. Scotto, 1572.

———, *Madrigali. . .libro terzo a sei voci,* Venice: A. Gardano, 1579.

Bellasio, P., *Il primo libro de' madrigali a cinque voci,* Venice: herede di G. Scotto, 1578.

Belli, D., *Il primo libro dell'arie a una, e a due voci,* Venice: R. Amadino, 1616.

Belli, Girolamo, *Madrigali a sei voci. . .libro primo,* Ferrara: V. Baldini, 1583.

Belli, Giulio, *Il primo libro de' madrigali a cinque et a sei voci,* Venice: A. Gardano, 1589.

Bertani, L., *Il primo libro de' madrigali a cinque voci,* Brescia: P.M. Marchetti, 1584.

———, *Il primo libro de' madrigali a sei voci,* Venice: A. Gardano, 1585.

Biffi, G., *Della ricreatione di Posilipo,* Naples: G.B. Sottile, 1606.

Boschetti, G.B., *Il primo libro de' madrigali a cinque voci,* Rome: G.B. Robletti, 1613.

Caimo, G., *Il primo libro de' madrigali a quattro voci,* Milan: F. Moscheni, 1564.

———, *Madrigali a cinque voci. . .libro quarto,* Venice: G. Vincenzi and R. Amadino, 1585.

Cambio, Perissone, *Il segondo (sic) libro de' madregali a cinque voci,* Venice: A. Gardane, 1550.

Cancineo, M., *Il primo libro de' madrigali. . .a quattro, cinque sei, et otto voci,* Venice: A. Gardano, 1590.

Casentini, M., *Tirsi e Clori. Terzo libro de' madrigali a cinque voci,* Venice: G. Vincenti, 1607.

Castro, J., *Madrigali. . .a tre voci,* Antwerp: P. Phalèse and G. Bellère, 1588.

———, *Rose fresche. . .a tre voci,* Venice: R. Amadino, 1591.

Cavaccio, G., *Musica a cinque voci. . .sopra le parole di una leggiadrissima Canzon pastorale,* Venice: A. Gardano, 1585.

Cifra, A., *Il primo libro de' madrigali a V. voci,* Rome: L. Zanetti, 1605.

Coma, A., *Il primo libro de' madrigali a cinque voci,* Venice: A. Gardano, 1568.

Coma, A., *Il quarto libro de' madrigali a cinque voci,* Venice: G. Vincenti, 1587.

Contino, G., *Il primo libro de' madrigali a cinque voci,* Venice: G. Scotto, 1560.

Conversi, G., *Il primo libro delle canzoni a cinque voci,* rev. repr. of 1572 edn., Venice: herede di G. Scotto, 1575.

———, *Il primolibro de' madrigali a sei voci . . .novamente vistarupati,* Venice: herede di G. Scotto, 1584.

Croce, Go.*Il primo libro de' madrigali a cinque voci,* Venice: A. Gardano, 1585.

———, *Il primo libro de' madrigali a sei voci,* Venice: G. Vincenti, 1590.

Da Montagnana, R., *Canzone. . .con alcuni madrigali aierosi a quattro voci. Libro primo,* Venice: G. Scotto, 1558.

Dragoni, G.A., *Il primo libro de' madrigali a cinque voci,* Venice: herede di G. Scotto, 1575.

———, *Il secondo libro de' madrigali a cinque voci,* Venice: herede di G. Scotto, 1575.

———, *Il terzo libro delli madrigali a cinque voci,* Venice: herede di G. Scotto, 1579.

———, *Il primo libro de' madrigali a sei voci,* Venice: herede di G. Scotto, 1584.

Falcone, A., and Raval, S., *Alli signori musici di Roma madrigali a cinque voci,* Venice: G. Vincenti, 1603.

Feliciani, A., *Il primo libro de' madrigali a cinque voci,* Venice: A. Gardano, 1579.

Ferrabosco, A., *Il secondo libro de' madrigali a cinque voci,* Venice: A. Gardano, 1587.

Ferrabosco (Ferabosco), D., *Il primo libro de' madrigali a quatro voci,* Venice: A. Gardane, 1542.

Gabrieli, A., *Il primo libro de' madrigali a cinque voci,* repr. of 1566 edn., Venice: figliuoli di A. Gardano, 1572.

———, *Il secondo libro di madrigali a cinque voci,* repr. of 1570 edn., Venice: figliuoli di A. Gardano, 1572.

———, *Madrigali et ricercari. . .a quattro voci,* Venice: A. Gardano, 1589.

Gabrieli, A. and G., *Concerti. . .a 6.7.8.10.12. et 16,* Venice: A. Gardano, 1587.

Gabussi (Gabucci), G.C., *Il primo libro de' madrigali a cinque voci,* Venice: A. Gardano, 1580.

Gagliano, Marco da, *Il secondo libro de' madrigali a cinque voci,* Venice: A. Gardano, 1604.

———, *Il terzo libro de' madrigali a cinque voci,* Venice: A. Gardano, 1605.

Gastoldi, G., *Il quarto libro de' madrigali a cinque voci,* Venice: R. Amadino, 1602.

Giovanelli, R., *Sdruccioli. . .il primo libro de' madrigali a quatro voci,* repr. of 1585 edn., Venice, G. Vincenzi, 1587.

———, *Gli sdruccioli. . .a quatro voci con una Caccia in ultimo,* Venice: A. Gardano, 1585.

———, *Il secondo libro de' madrigali a cinque voci,* Venice: A. Gardano, 1589.

———, *Il terzo libro de' madrigali a cinque voci,* Venice: A. Gardano, 1599.

———, *Il primo libro de' madrigali a cinque voci,* repr. of 1586 edn., Venice: A. Gardano, 1600.

———, *Il primo libro de' madrigali a tre voci,* Venice: A. Gardano, 1605.

Ingegneri, M.A., *Il primo libro de' madrigali a quatro voci, novamente. . .ristampati,* Venice: A. Gardano, 1578.

———, *Il secondo libro de' madrigali. . .a quattro voci,* Venice: A. Gardano, 1579.

———, *Il quinto libro de' madrigali a cinque voci,* Venice: A. Gardano, 1587.

———, *Il sesto libro de' madrigali a cinque voci,* Venice: R. Amadino, 1606.

Kapsberger, J., *Libro primo de' madrigali a cinque voci,* Rome: P. Manelfi, 1609.

Lassus, O., *Il primo libro de' madrigali a cinque voci,* repr. of 1555 edn., Venice: G. Scotto, 1573. Copy in I-Bc (*S.309*) contains Marenzio's signature.

Lauro, D. and Stivorio, F., *Madrigali a tre voci,* Venice: R. Amadino, 1590.

Leoni, L., *Bella Clori. Secondo libro de' madrigali a cinque voci,* Venice: A. Gardano, 1591.

Luzzaschi, L., *Terzo libro de' madrigali a cinque voci,* Venice: A. Gardano, 1582.

———, *Quinto libro de' madrigali a cinque voci,* Ferrara: V. Baldini, 1595.

———, *Sesto libro de' madrigali a cinque voci,* Ferrara: V. Baldini, 1596.

Macque, J. de, *Madrigali a quattro, a cinque et sei voci,* Venice: A. Gardano, 1579.

———, *Il terzo libro de' madrigali a cinque voci,* Ferrara: V. Baldini, 1597.

Mazzocchi, D., *Dialoghi e sonetti,* Rome: F. Zannetti, 1638.

Meldert, L., *Il primo libro de' madrigali a cinque voci,* Venice: G. Scotto, 1578.

Merulo, C., *Il primo libro de' madrigali a cinque voci,* Venice: Claudio [Merulo] da Correggio and F. Betanio, compagni, 1566.

———, *Il secondo libro de' madrigali a cinque voci,* Venice: A. Gardano, 1604.

Milleville, A., *Madrigali. . .libro secondo a cinque voci,* Ferrara: V. Baldini, 1584.

Monte, P. de, *Il decimo libro delli madrigali a cinque voci,* Venice: Girolamo Scotto, 1581.

———, *Il quartodecimo libro delli madrigali a cinque voci,* Venice: A. Gardano, 1590.

———, *Il quintodecimo libro de' madrigali a cinque voci,* Venice: A. Gardano, 1592.

———, *Il sestodecimo libro de' madrigali a cinque voci,* Venice: A. Gardano, 1593.

———, *La Fiammetta, canzone. . .insieme altre canzoni et madrigali vaghissimi a sette voci. . . libro primo,* Venice: A. Gardano, 1599.

———, *Musica sopra il Pastor Fido. . .libro secondo a sette voci,* Venice: A. Gardano, 1600.

Montella, G.D., *Primo libro de' madrigali a cinque voci,* Naples: Stamperia dello Stigliola a Porta Regale, 1595.

Moscaglia, G.B. *Il primo libro de' madrigali a quattro a cinque et a sei voci intitolati gl'Amorosi Gigli,* Venice: A. Gardano, 1575.

———, *Il secondo libro de' madrigali a cinque voci,* Venice: heredi di F. Rampasetto, 1579.

———, *Il terzo libro di madrigali a cinque voci,* Venice: Girolamo Scoto, 1585.

———, *Il quarto libro de' suoi madrigali a cinque voci. . .intitolati Amorosi Fioretti,* Venice: herede di Girolama Scoto, 1587.

Nanino, G.M., *Il primo libro de' madrigali a cinque voci novamente ristampati,* Venice: A. Gardano, 1579.

———, *Il terzo libro de' madrigali a cinque voci,* Venice: A. Gardano, 1586.

Nanino, G.M. and Stabile, A., *Madrigali a cinque voci,* Venice: A. Gardano, 1581.

Pace, G.B. and Vopa, G.D., *Il primo libro de' madrigali a cinque voci,* Venice: A. Gardano, 1585.

Pallavicino, B., *Il primo libro de' madrigali a quattro voci,* Venice: A. Gardano, 1579.

———, *Il quarto libro de' madrigali a cinque voci,* Venice: A. Gardano, 1588.

———, *Il quinto libro de' madrigali a cinque voci,* Venice: G. Vincenti, 1593.

———, *Il sesto libro de' madrigali a cinque voci,* Venice: A. Gardano, 1600.

———, *Il primo libro de' madrigali a cinque voci,* repr. of 1581 edn., Venice: A. Gardano e fratelli, 1606.

Pesciolini, B., *Il terzo libro de' madrigali a sei voci,* Venice: Alessandro Gardane, 1581.

Piccioni, G., *Il primo libro de' madrigali a sei voci,* Venice: A. Gardano, 1598.

———, *Il pastor fido. . .sesto libro di madrigali a cinque voci,* Venice: G. Vincenti, 1602.

Pisanelli, P.P., *Madrigali a cinque voci, libro primo,* Ferrara: V. Baldini, 1586.

Portinaro, F., *Il primo libro de' madrigali a quattro voci,* Venice: Girolamo Scotto, 1563.

Raval, S., *Il primo libro de' madrigali a cinque voci,* Venice: G. Vincenti, 1593.

Rossi, S., *Il primo libro de' madrigali a cinque voci,* Venice: R. Amadino, 1600.

———, *Il primo libro de' madrigali a quattro voci,* Venice: R. Amadino, 1614.

Rota, A., *Il primo libro de' madrigali a cinque voci,* Venice, herede di G. Scotto, 1579.

———, *Il secondo libro de' madrigali a cinque voci,* Venice: A. Gardano, 1589.

Sabino, I., *Madrigali a sei voci. . .libro primo,* Venice: A. Gardano, 1579.

———, *Il quinto libro de' madrigali a cinque et a sei voci,* Venice: G. Vincenzi and R. Amadino, 1586.

Scaletta, O., *Amorosi pensieri, il secondo libro de' madrigaletti a cinque voci,* Venice: herede di G. Scotto, 1590.

Soriano, F., *Il primo libro de' madrigali a cinque voci,* Venice: A. Gardano, 1581.

———, *Il secondo libro de' madrigali a cinque voci,* Rome: F. Coattino, 1592.

Stabile, A., *Il terzo libro de' madrigali a cinque voci,* Venice: herede di Girolamo Scotto, 1581.

———, *Il primo libro de' madrigali a ginque (sic) voci novamente ristampati,* rev. repr. of 1572 edn., Venice: herede di G. Scoto, 1586.

———, see Nanino, G.M.

Stivorio, F., *Il primo libro de' madrigali a quattro voci,* Venice: G. Vincenci and R. Amadino, 1583.

————, *Madrigali e dialoghi a otto voci,* Venice: R. Amadino, 1598.

————, see Lauro, D.

Striggio, A., *Il primo libro de' Madregali a cinque voci. . .con nova giunta ristampato,* repr. of 1560 edn., Venice: A. Gardano, 1569.

————, *Il primo libro de madrigali a sei voci,* repr. of 1560 edn., Venice: A. Gardano, 1565.

Tresti, F., *Il primo libro de' madrigali a cinque voci,* Venice: A. Gardano, 1585.

Zoilo, A., *Libro secondo de' madrigali a quattro et a cinque voci,* Rome: A. Blado, 1563.

Anthologies Not Containing Madrigals by Marenzio

RISM 1559[16]: *Il secondo libro de le Muse a cinque voci,* Venice: A. Gardano, 1559.

RISM 1569[20]: *La eletta di tutta la musica intitolata corona di diversi. . .libro primo,* n.p., 1569 (see *VE* 1569[3a]).

RISM 1574[4]: *Il quarto libro delle Muse a cinque voci,* ed. T. Benigni, Venice: figliuoli di A. Gardano, 1574.

RISM 1577[8]: *Aeri racolti insieme. . .dove si cantano sonetti, stanze e terze rime, nuovamente ristampati,* ed. R. Rodio, Naples: G. Cacchio dell' Aquila, 1577.

RISM 1585[16]: *De' floridi virtuosi d'Italia il secondo libro de' madrigali a cinque voci,* Venice: G. Vincenzi and R. Amadino, 1585.

RISM 1586[3]: *De' floridi virtuosi d'Italia il terzo libro de' madrigali a cinque voci,* Venice: G. Vincenzi and R. Amadino, 1586.

Appendix IV

Literary Sources

Individual Poets

Note: In this section each poet whose works Marenzio set to music is listed in alphabetical order. The first paragraph ("works consulted") lists full titles of books containing works by that author. The second ("bibliography") lists reference works whose full titles are listed in appendix VI.

Alamanni, Luigi (1495-1556)

Works consulted: *Versi e prose,* ed. P. Raffaelli, 2 vols, Florence, 1859.

Bibl: Hauvette, *Alamanni;* Weiss, in *DBI,* i.568-571. See also app. II, note to *III a 5* (1582), no. 14; app. II, note to *RISM* i.e. 1582⁴.

Ariosto, Ludovico (1474-1533)

Works consulted: *Lirica,* ed. G. Fatini (Scrittori d'Italia), Bari, 1924.

Bibl: Sapegno, in *DBI,* ii.172-188.

Arlotti, Ridolfo (1545-1613)

Poems pr. in the *Rime de gli. . .Eterei* (1567) and the *Parnaso* (1611).

Bibl: Newcomb, "Fontanelli," in *Festschrift Mendel,* pp. 50-56; Quadrio, *Storia,* i.85-86, ii.288, vi.678; Tiraboschi, *Bibliografia modenese,* i.109.

Barbati, Petronio (c.1600-1554)

Works consulted: *Rime,* Foligno: Campitelli, 1712.

Bibl: Girardi, in *DBI,* vi.127-128. See also app. II, note to *II a 6* (1584), no. 3.

Barignano, Pietro (d. bef. 1550)

Bibl: Ceserani, in *DBI,* vi.127-128.

Bembo, Pietro (1470-1547)

Works consulted: *Prose e rime,* ed. C. Dionisotti, 2nd rev. edn., Turin, 1966.

Bibl: Dionisotti, in *DBI,* viii.133-151; Mace, "Bembo," *MQ,* lv (1969), 65-86.

Caro, Annibale (1507-1566)

Works consulted: Opere, ed. S. Jacomuzzi, Turin, 1974.

Bibl: Mutini, in *DBI,* xx.497-508.

Casone, Girolamo (d. 1593)

Works consulted: *Rime,* Venice: G.B. Ciotti, 1598. See also the *Rime de gli. . .Affidati* (1565), *Gioie poetiche* (1593) and many other anthologies.

Bibl: Ghilini, *Teatro,* i.116.

Castelletti, Cristoforo (d. 1596)

Works consulted: *Rime spirituali,* Venice: herede di Marchiò Sessa, 1582; *Le stravaganze d'Amore,* Venice: G.B. Sessa e fratelli, 1587.

Bibl: Chater, "Castelletti," *SM,* viii (1979), 85-148; Patrizi in *DBI,* xxi.671-673.

Celiano, Livio

See *Rime di diversi,* ed. Licino, Bergamo, 1587, from which Marenzio appears to have taken all the poems he ever set by this author; also the *Gareggiamento* (1611).

Bibl: Crescimbeni, *Istoria,* v (=*Comentari,* iv, bk.2), p. 69; Quadrio, *Storia,* ii.368, vii.175.

Cini, Giovambattista (d. 1586)

Bibl: Brown, H.M., "Psyche," in *Festschrift Merritt,* pp. 2-27; Lasca, Il, *Descrizione;* Osthoff, *Theatergesang,* p. 342 ff; Pirrotta, *Due Orfei,* p. 207 ff; Winspeare, *Isabella Orsini,* pp. 73 and 147 ff. See app. II., note to *II a 6* (1584), no. 5.

Coppetta (Beccuti, Francesco; 1509-1553)

Works consulted: G. Guidiccione and F. Coppetta Beccuti, *Rime,* ed. E. Chiorboli (Scrittori d'Italia), Bari, 1912.

Bibl: Quadrio, *Storia,* i.90; Rua, in *EISLA,* vi.464-465.

Dante Alighieri (1265-1321)

Works consulted: *Opere,* ed. F. Chiappelli, 2nd edn., Milan 1965.

Bibl: Barbi, in *EISLA,* xii.327-347. See also app. II, note to *IX a 5* (1599), no. 1.

Della Casa, Giovanni (1503-1556)

Works consulted: B. Castiglione and G. della Casa, *Opere,* ed. G. Prezzolini, Milan and Rome, 1937; *Prose,* ed. A. di Benedetto, Turin, 1970; *Rime,* ed. A. Seroni, Florence, 1944.

Bibl: Baldacci, *Petrarchismo,* pp. 181-268.

Gambara, Veronica (1485-1550)

Works consulted: Flora, ed., *Gaspara Stampa e altre poetesse del '500.*

Bibl: Fatini, in *EISLA,* xvi.352-353.

Gottifredi, Bartolomeo (d. c.1600)

Bibl: Mensi, *Dizionario,* p. 216; Quadrio, *Storia,* i.91-92, ii.352.

Grillo, Angelo (1550-1629)

Works consulted: *Parte prima delle rime,* ed. G.B. Licino, Bergamo: C. Ventura, 1589; *Parte seconda. e.g.,* Venice: G.B. Ciotti, 1599.

Bibl: Einstein, "Grillo," in *Essays on music,* pp. 159-177; Novelli, *Grillo.*

Groto, Luigi (Il Cieco d'Adria; 1541-1585)

Works consulted: *Rime,* Venice: F. and A. Zoppini fratelli, 1587 (repr. of 1577 edn.); *Rime. . . parte prima, a cui seguono altre due parti hora di novo date in luce con la vita dell'autore,* Venice: A. Dei, 1610.

Bibl: Ariani, introduction to Strozzi, *Madrigali inediti,* pp.xci-xcvi; Bocci, *Groto;* Chater, in *RIDM,* xiii (1978), 68; Groto, *Groto;* Groto, *Rime* (ed.cit. of 1610); Schulz-Buschhaus, *Madrigal,* p. 170 ff; Turri, *Groto.*

Guarini, Giovambattista (1538-1612)

Works consulted: Lettere, ed. A. Michele, 6th edn., Venice, G.B. Ciotti, 1603; *Opere,* 4 vols., Verona: G.A. Tumermani, 1737-1738 (includes polemics of De Nores, A. Ingegneri, Summo, Malacreta, Beni, and Savio); *Opere,* ed. M. Guglielminetti, Turin, 1971 (rev. enl. version of edn. of L. Fassò, Turin, 1950); *Pastor fido,* Venice: G.B. Bonfadino, 1590 (repr. several times, notably with Guarini's own commentary, Venice: G.B. Ciotti, 1602); ibid, ed. L. Fassò, Turin, 1976 (with line numbers); *Rime,* Venice: G.B. Ciotti, 1598.

Bibl: Abert, in *MGG,* v, cols. 1002-1005; Battaglin, "Linguaggio tragicomico. . .del 'Pastor fido'," in Folena, *Lingua e struttura;* Hartmann, "Guarini and 'Il pastor *fido'," MQ,* xxxix (!953), 415-425; Perella, *"Pastor fido":* Rossi, V., *Guarini ed il "Pastor fido."*

Guicciardi, Lorenzo: see app. II, note to *V a 6* (1591), no. 2.

Guidi, Benedetto (d. 1590)

Bibl: Quadrio, *Storia,* ii.365; T. Tasso, *Lettere,* ed. Guasti, ii.265.

Manfredi, Muzio (d. 1618)

Works consulted: Cento donne cantate, Parma: G.B. Viotto, 1580.

Bibl: Dolci, G., in *EISLA,* xxii.111-112; Ghilini, *Teatro,* i.172; Ginanni, *Memorie,* ii.15; Quadrio, *Storia,* ii.264, iii.316, v.406. See also app. II, note to *RISM* 1583[12].

Marcellini, Valerio

Bibl: Quadrio, *Storia,* ii.367.

Martinengo, Marcantonio, Count of Villachiara (1560-1595)

Bibl: Guerrini, *Celebre famiglia,* pp. 489-492; see above, app. II, note to *RISM* 1588[17].

Molza, Francesco Maria (1489-1543)

Poems in many contemporary anthologies; Quadrio mentions an edn. of the *Rime,* Bologna: Pisarri, 1713. Neither this, nor the *Poesia. . .colla vita dell'autore,* ed. P. Serassi, Milan, 1808, were consulted.

Bibl: Palaez, in *EISLA,* xxiii.592; Quadrio, *Storia,* ii.231; Serassi, in ed.cit. of the *Poesia;* Tiraboschi, *Biblioteca,* iii.230-243.

Moscaglia, Giovambattista (c. 1550-1589)

Works consulted: *RISM* 1585[29] (app. II); musical works listed in app. III. Ledbetter, art. "Moscaglia" in the new *Grove,* xii. 598-599 I-Rvic, San Lorenzo in Damaso, *Matrimonii,* i. 151[V].

Nannini, Remigio (d. 1581)

Works consulted; *Rime di M. Remigio Fiorentino,* Venice: Bindoni and Pasini, 1547.

Bibl: Negri, *Scrittori fiorentini,* p. 481.

Ongaro, Antonio (c. 1560-1598)

Works consulted: *Rime,* ed. T. Palella, Farnese: N. Mariani, 1600.

Bibl: Chater, in *RIDM,* xiii (1978), 76-77; Crescimbeni, *Istoria,* ii (= *Comentari,* ii, Bk. 3), 463-466; Palella, in edn. cit. of *Rime;* Piccioli, *Prose;* Quadrio, *Storia,* ii. 287; Vedova, *Scrittori padovani* ii. 17.

Orsi, Aurelio (fl. in Rome, c. 1585)

Works consulted: *Poemata omnium,* Rome, 1734 (contains only Latin poetry); Tiraboschi mentions editions of Bologna, 1594 and Rome, 1743, but I have been unable to trace these.

Bibl: Crescimbeni, *Istoria,* v (= *Comentari,* iv, Bk. 2), 101; Mandosi, *Bibliotheca romana,* i. 105-106; Quadrio, *Storia,* ii. 525; Tiraboschi, *Storia,* vii. 1436. See also app. II note to *Spirituali* (1584), no. 6.

Pace, Pompeo

Bibl: Quadrio, *Storia,* ii. 365.

Parabosco, Girolamo (1520 or 1524-1557)

Works consulted: *I diporti* (1550), in *Novellieri minori,* ed. Gigli and Nicolini; *La prima parte delle rime,* Venice: T. Botietta, 1546; *La seconda parte. . . ,* Venice: F. and P. Bocca, fratelli, 1555.

Bibl: Bianchini, *Parabosco;* Bussi, *Parabosco;* ibid, in *MGG,* x, cols. 740-742.

Pasqualino, Lelio (1549 or 1548-1611; Bolognese; canon at Santa Maria Maggiore, 1571-1611)

Bibl: Chater, *RIDM,* xiii (1978), 61-62; De Angelis, *Basilicae S. Mariae Maioris descriptio,* xii. 47-48; *Historiae Basilicae Liberianae S. M. Majoris* (MS in I-Rsm), iv. 240ff.

Pavesi (Pavese), Cesare

Bibl: *Rime di diversi,* ed. Atanagi, ii (1565), index: "eccelente poeta, et musico insieme" ("excellent both as a poet and a musician"); T. Tasso, *Rinaldo,* Venice, 1562, Preface; Quadrio, *Storia,* vii. 103.

Petrarch, (Petrarca, Francesco; 1304-1374)

Works consulted: *Canzoniere,* ed. G. Contini, annotated by D. Ponchiroli, Turin, 1974; *Il Canzoniere, Trionfi, e rime varie,* ed. C. Muscetta and D. Ponchiroli, Turin, 1958; *Il Petrarcha con l'espositione d'Alessandro Vellutello,* repr. of 1525 edn., Venice, 1538 (see above, app. II, note to *I a 4,* 1585, no. 6).

Bibl: Baldacci, *Petrarchismo;* De Sanctis, *Petrarcal;* Forster, *Icy fire;* Wilkins, *Life of Petrarch;* ibid, *Making of the "Canzoniere";* ibid, *Studies in the life and works.* See also chapter 3, table 2; app. II, note to *VI a 6* (1595), no. 2.

Pigna (Nicolucci) Giovambattista (1530-1575)

Works consulted: *Il ben divino,* ed. N. Bonifazi, Bologna, 1965.

Bibl: Bonifazi, "Pigna," *Studi Tassiani,* x (1960), 53-71; Di Benedetto, "Due canzonieri" in *Tasso,* pp. 177-187; Nolan, *The "Amori" of G.B. Pigna.*

Pocaterra, Annibale (1559-1593)

Works consulted: *Dui dialoghi della vergogna con alcune prose et rime,* ed. B. Angeli, Reggio: F. and F. Bartholi, 1607.

Appendix IV235

Bibl: Angeli, in edn. cit. of 1607; Di Benedetto, "Due canzonieri," in *Tasso*, pp 187-193.

Quirino (Quirini), Vincenzo (d. 1514)

Bibl: Dionisotti, art. "Bembo," in *DBI* viii. 137; Quadrio, *Storia*, ii. 351 and iii. 262. See also app. II, notes to *I a 6* (1581), nos. 5 and 10; *IV a 5* (1584), no. 9.

Sacchetti, Franco (c. 1330 - c. 1400)

Works consulted: *Il libro delle rime*, ed. A. Chiari, Bari, 1936.

Bibl: Sapegno, in *EISLA*, xxx. 390-391. See also app. II, notes to *II a 6* (1584), no. 15.

Sannazaro, Iacopo (1546-1530)

Works consulted: *Opere*, ed. E. Carrara (Classici Italiani), Turin, 1952 (with annotated edn. of the *Arcadia*); *Opere volgari*, ed. A. Mauri (Scrittori d'Italia, 220), Bari, 1961.

Bibl: Borghini, *Umanista*, Carrara, in *EISLA*, xxx. 737-740; ibid, *Sannazaro;* Leopold, "Egloghe", in *RIDM*, xiv (1979), 75-127.

Strozzi, Giovambattista, The Elder (1504-1571)

Works consulted: Strozzi, *Madrigali*, ed. Lorenzo and Filippo Strozzi, Florence: Sermatelli, 1593; *Madrigali*, ed. L. Sorrento (Bibliotheca Romanica), Strasbourg, 1909 (= repr. of 1593 edn.); *Madrigali inediti*, ed. M. Ariani, Urbino, 1975; *Venticinque madrigali inediti*, ed. G. Sforza and G. Pierotti, Lucca, 1866; T. Tasso, *Cinquanta madrigali inediti. . . alla Granduchessa Bianca Cappello*, ed. G. Gargani, Florence, 1871, pp. 17-33; Trucchi, *Poesie inedite*, iv. 35 ff and 350.

MSS consulted: I-Fl, *Conv. Soppr. 504*, pp. 11-192; I-Fn, *Magl. 327* and *328*, and *Palat. 242;* I-Sc, *I.XI. 8-9*.

Bibl: Ariani, "Strozzi," in *Madrigali inediti* cit., pp. vii-cxlviii; Litta, *Famiglie celebri*, vi, tables 18 and 22; Maylender, *Accademie*, v. 365; Minor and Mitchell, *Renaissance entertainment;* Osthoff, *Theatergesang*, ii. 90.

Tansillo, Luigi (1510-1568)

Works, consulted: *Il Canzoniere edito e inedito*, ed. E. Pèrcopo, Naples, 1926.

Bibl: Guerrieri-Crocetti, in *EISLA*, xxxiii.238-239.

Tasso, Bernardo (1493-1569)

Works consulted: *Rime*, Venice: G. Gioliti, 1560.

Bibl: Williamson, B. Tasso (esp. pp. 74 ff and 77 ff).

Tasso, Torquato (1544-1595)

Arezia, Ninfa: first pr. in the *Rime di diversi*, ed. Licino (1587); repr. in *Opere minori*, iii.409-419; attrib. to Ferrante Gonzaga in I-Bu, MS *1171*.

Cavaletta, La: repr. in Opere, ed. Maier, v.90-151.

Convito di' pastori, Il: first pr. in *Il rimanente delle rime* (1587) and the *Rime di diversi*, ed. Licino (1587); repr. in the *Opere minori*, iii.433-441.

Gerusalemme liberata, La: Il Goffredo, ed. M.A. Malaspina, Venice: D. Cavalcalupo, 1580; *Il goffredo. . .novamento corretto et ristampato*, ed. M.A. Malaspina, Venice: G. Perchacino, 1581; ibid, Venice: G. Perchacino, 1582; *La Gerusalemme liberata*, ed. A. Solerti, 3 vols., Florence, 1895-1896.

Lettere, ed. C. Guasti, 5 vols., Florence, 1852-1855.

Opere, ed. B. Maier, Milan, 1963 ff [5 vols. to 1965].

Opere, ed. G. Rosini, 17 bound vols., Pisa, 1821-1832.

Opere minori in versi, ed. A. Solerti, 3 vols., Bologna, 1891-1895.

Rime. . .parte prima, Venice: Aldo Namuzio, 1581 *(Solerti,* no. 8: the numbers refer to the bibliography in Solerti's edn. of the *Rime,* i.); *Delle rime. . .parte seconda,* Venice: Aldo Manuzio, 1582 *(Solerti,* no. 10); *Scielta delle rime. . .parte prima (e seconda),* Ferrara: V. Baldini, 1582 *(Solerti,* no. 11); *Rime et prose. . .parte terza,* Venice: G. Vasalini, 1583 *(Solerti,* no. 22); *Aggiunta alle rime et prose,* Venice: Aldo Manuzio, 1585 *(Solerti,* no. 23); *Delle rime et prose. . .parte quarta,* Venice: G. Vasalini, 1586 *(Solerti,* no. 27); *Gioie di rime et prose . . . quinta e sesta parte,* ed. G.B. Licino, Venice: G. Vasalini, 1587 *(Solerti,* no. 28); *Delle rime. . . parti quarta et quinta,* ed. G. Guastavini, Genoa: A. Orero, 1586 *(Solerti,* no. 48); *Rime et prose . . . parte quarta,* Milan: Tini, 1586 (not consulted; *Solerti,* no. 49); *Il rimanente delle rime nuove,* Ferrara: V. Baldini, 1587 *(Solerti,* no. 54); *Rime et prose. . .parte prima,* rev. edn., ed. G. Vasalini, Ferrara: V. Baldini, 1589 *(Solerti,* no. 69); *Rime et prose. . .parte terza ristampate . . . con aggiunta,* ed. G. Vasalini, Ferrara: V. Baldini, 1589 *(Solerti,* no. 69); *Rime et prose. . .parte quarta, ristampate,* Venice: G. Vasalini, 1589 *(Solerti,* no. 70); *Delle rime. . .parte prima,* Mantua: F. Osanna, 1591 (not consulted; author's own rev. edn.: *Solerti,* no. 85); *Delle rime. . . parte seconda,* Brescia: P.M. Marchetti, 1593 (not consulted; author's own rev. edn.: *Solerti,* no. 87); *Sonetti* and *Rime fatti a diversi prencipi (Solerti,* no. 116: full title quoted in app. II, note to *I a 5,* 1580, no. 14).

Rime later repr. in *Opere,* ed. Rosini, i-iv; *Cinquanta madrigali inediti . . . alla Granduchessa Bianca Capello,* ed. G. Gargani, Florence, 1871; *Rime,* ed. A. Solerti, 4 vols., Bologna, 1898; in *Opere,* ed. Maier, i and v.

Rinaldo, Venice: F. Sanese, 1562; repr. in *Opere minori,* i.13-337.

Bibl: For life of Tasso, see Solerti, *Tasso;* Princivalli, *Tasso a Roma,* and *Tasso nella vita e nelle opere.* For the works, see Caretti, *Studi sulle rime;* Di Benedetto, *Tasso;* Durante, *Sulle rime,* Fubini, *Rinascimento,* pp. 248-286; Getto, *Interpretazione.* For Tasso and music, see Abert, in *MGG,* cols. 142-144; Ledbetter, *Marenzio* (unpubl. thesis), p. 130; Newcomb, *RIDM,* x (1975), 329-345; Pirrotta, "Note," in *Festschrift Ronga;* Ronga, "Tasso," in *Torquato Tasso: comitato,* pp. 187-207.

Troiano (Troiani), Girolamo (fl. c.1574-1585; listed as an Accademico Filarmonico in Verona on 28 December 1574 [Turrini]; visited Rome, 1585 [T. Tasso, *Lettere,* ed. Guasti, ii.313, no. 325])

Works consulted: *Lettera consolatoria,* bound with the *Rime di diversi. . .nella morte della signora Lucretia Cavalcanti de' Gattoli,* dedicated to the Veronese patron, Lodovico Malaspina.

Bibl: Quadrio, *Storia,* ii.257-258; Turrini, *Accademia Filarmonica,* p.269. See also app. II., notes to *I a 4,5,6* (1588), no. 6; *V a 6* (1591), nos. 5-6.

Veniero (Venieri, Venier), Maffeo (1550-1586)

Works consulted: in the *Rime di Domenico Veniero,* ed. P.A. Serassi, Bergamo: P. Lancellotto, 1750.

Bibl: Dazzi, art. "Venier, Maffeo" in *EISLA,* app. i (1978), 1121. See also above, app. II, note to *RISM* 1593[3].

Zuccarini, Giovambattista (fl. 1585-1586)

Bibl: *NV,* ii, no. 2809 (Vecchi); often confused with G.B. Zuchelli: Eitner, *Bibliographie,* p. 936, equates the 2 names, but Einstein, *VE,* ii. 789 (*VE,* 1607^2), assumes they are 2 different people.

Poetic Anthologies

1546: *Rime diverse di molti eccellentiss. auttori. . .libro primo,* ed. L. Domenichi, rev. repr. of 1545 edn., Venice: G. Giolito, 1546 (= *Domenichi,* i; GB-Lbm, *240.d.4*).

1547: *Rime di diversi nobili huomini. . .libro secondo,* ed. G. Giolito, Venice: G. Giolito, 1547 (= *Domenichi,* ii; cf. rev. edn., 1587; GBLbm, *240.d.5*).

1550: *De le rime di diversi nobilissimi et eccellentissimi autori,* ed. A. Arrivabene, Venice: Segno del pozzo, 1550 (= Domenichi, iii; GB-Lbm, *240.d.6*).

1551: *Libro quarto delle rime di diversi,* ed. E. Bottrigaro, Bologna: A. Giaccarello, 1551 (= *Domenichi,* iv; GB-Lbm, *240.d.7*)

1552: *Rime di diversi illustri Signori Napoletani. . .terzo (sic) libro,* ed. L. Dolce, Venice: G. Giolito, 1552 (= *Domenichi,* v; cf. rev. edn., 1555; GB-Lbm, *240.d.8*).

1553: *Delle rime di diversi eccellenti autori,* ed. A. Arrivabene, Venice: Segno del pozzo, 1553 (= *Domenichi,* vi; GB-Lbm, *240.d.9*).

1553: *Rime di diversi eccellenti autori bresciani,* ed. G. Ruscelli, Venice: Pietrasanta, 1553 (I-Bag, *8.K.K.III.10*).

1555: *Delle rime di diversi illustri Signori napoletani e d'altri nobilissimi intelletti,* rev. edn. of *Domenichi,* v (1552), Venice: G. Giolito, 1555 (GB-Lbm, *240.d.15*).

1555: *Rime di diversi ecc*[ellenti] *autori in vita e in morte dell'Ill*[ustrissima] *S*[ignora] *Livia Col*[onna], ed. F. Cristiani, Rome: A. Barrè, 1555 (GB-Lbm, *11426.b.18*).

1556: *Rime di diversi et eccelenti autori,* Venice: Go Giolito de' Ferrari et fratelli, 1556. Cf. vol. ii, 1565 (GB-Lbm, 11422. a. 11).

1556: *Rime di diversi signori Napolitani,* ed. L. Dolce, Venice: G. Giolito, 1556 (= *Domenichi,* vii; GB-Lbm, *240.d.10*).

1556: *Stanze di diversi illustri poeti,* ed. L. Dolce, Venice: G. Giolito e fratelli, 1556. Cf. vol. ii, 1572 (GB-Lbm, *241.b.23*).

1558: *I fiori delle rime de' poeti illustri,* ed. G. Ruscelli, Venice: G.B. and M. Sessa, fratelli, 1558 (= Domenichi, viii; GB-Lbm, *240.d.11*).

1559: *Rime diverse d'alcune nobilissimi et virtuosissime donne,* ed. L. Domenichi, Lucca: V. Busdragho, 1559 (I-Bag, *8.KK.III.1*).

1560: *Rime di diversi autori eccellentissimi . . . libro nono,* ed. G. Offredi, Cremona: V. Conti, 1560 (= *Domenichi,* ix; GB-Lbm, *240.d.12*).

1565: *De le rime di diversi nobili poeti toscani . . . libro primo,* ed. D. Atanagi, Venice: L. Avanzo, 1565 (GB-Lbm, *1071.e.4*).

1565: *De le rime . . . libro secondo,* ed. D. Atanagi, Venice: L. Avanzo, 1565 (GB-Lbm, *G.10667.68*).

1565: *Il secondo volume delle rime scelte da diversi,* Venice: G. Giolito de' Ferrari et fratelli, 1565. Cf. vol. i, 1556 (I-Bag, *Landoni, 1897*).

1565: *Rime de gli academici affidati di Pavia,* Pavia: G. Bartoli, 1565 (D-Mbs, *Po.it.305*).

1567: *Rime di gli Academici Eterei,* ed. L'Occulto, Prencipe, Padua: n.p., 1567. Cf. 1588 repr. (GB-Lbm, *11431.ee.6*).

1572: *La seconda parte delle stanze di diversi illustri poeti,* ed. A. Terminio, Venice: G. Giolito, 1572. Cf. vol. i, 1556 (GB-Lbm, *241.b.24*).

1582: *Raccolta d'alcune piacevole rime,* ed. E. Viotti, Parma: heredi di G.B. Viotti, 1582 (GB-Lbm, *C.108.a15*).

1585: *Le piacevole rime di Cesare Caporali,* 3rd rev. edn., Milan: P. Tini, 1585 (I-Vnm, *222.c.111*).

1586: *Rime piacevoli di Ces. Caporali, del Mauro, et d'altri Auttori,* 4th edn., Ferrara: V. Baldini, 1586 (I-Vnm, *67606*).

1587: *Rime di diversi celebri poeti dell'età nostra,* ed. G.B. Licino, Bergamo: C. Ventura, 1587 (GB-Lbm, *84.b.4*).

1587: *Il secondo volume d[e]lle rime scelte di diversi autori,* rev. edn. of *Domenichi,* ii (1547), Venice: i Gioliti, 1587 (I-Bag, *8/F.IV.43*).

1588: *Rime degl'illustrissimi Signori Academici Eterei,* repr. of 1567 edn., Ferrara: A. Caraffa, 1588 (I-Rvat, *Ferr.V.2024*)

1590: *Della nova scelta di rime di diversi eccellenti scrittori. . .parte prima,* ed. B. Varoli, Casalmaggiore: A. Guerino e compagno, 1590 (Rome, Biblioteca Universitaria Alessandrina, *N.C.155*).

1591: *Scelta di rime di diversi moderni autori non più stampate. Parte prima,* ed. P. Bartoli, Genoa: heredi di G. Bartoli, 1591 (I-Rvat, *Ferr.VI,260*).

1591: *Scelta di rime di diversi. . .parte seconda,* ed. P. Bartoli, Pavia: heredi di G. Bartoli, 1591 (bound with above vol.).

1593: *Gioie poetiche di madrigali del Sig. Hieronimo Casone e d'altri celebri poeti de' nostri tempi,* ed. G. Borgogni, Pavia: G. Bartoli, 1593 (I-Vnm, *98.c.255*).

1594: *Le muse toscane,* ed. G. Borgogni, Bergamo: C. Ventura, 1594 (I-Rvat, *Ferr.V.5119*).

1598: *Fiori di madrigali di diversi,* ed. E. Caraffa, Venice: G. Vincentini, 1598 (I-Fn, *Palat 12.13.1.28*).

1599: *Rime di diversi illustri poeti de' nostri tempi,* ed. G. Borgogni, Venice: Minima Compagnia, 1599 (I-Bag, *8.KK.II.14*).

1609: *Ghilranda dell'aurora, scelta di madrigali de' più famosi autori di questo secolo,* ed. P. Petracci, Venice: B. Giunti and G.B. Ciotti, 1609 (GB-Lbm, *1079.a.19*).

1611: *Gareggiamento i.e. poetics del Confuso Accademico Ordito* (= C. Fiamma), 9 books bound in 1 vol., Venice: Barezzo Barezzi, 1611 (GB-Lbm, *1471.a.6*).

1611: *Parnaso de' poetici ingegni,* ed. A. Scaiolo, Parma: G.B. Viotti, 1611 (I-Bag, *A.VI.40*).

1621: *I nomi delle donne per bellezza da' peregrini spiriti con poetica lira cantati,* ed. M. Alchino, Verona: B. Merlo, 1621 (I-Bag, *8/11*.III.38*).

Appendix V

Manuscripts

D-Rp, *A.R.774:* A. Raselius, "Dodecachordi vivi." Not consulted: See Debes, *Merulo* (unpubl. thesis), *pp. 94-103.*

F-Pn, *Rés. Vma., 851* ("Bourdeney"). Not consulted: see Mischiati, in *RIDM,* x (1975), 265-328.

GB-Lbm, *R.M., 24.d.2:* "John Baldwin's Commonplace Book." Contains thirteen madrigals by Marenzio, eleven taken from the *1 a 4,5,6.* For further details, see inventory by Bray, *R.M.A. Chronicle,* xii (1974), 137-151.

I-Bc, *C.30:* O. Vecchi, "Mostra delli tuoni" (copied by E. Giacobbi in 1630).

I-Bu, MS *1171:* "Benedetto Pannini. Rime" (Miscellaneous anthology containing poems by Pannini, T. Tasso, Ariosti, Guarini, Pocaterra, and others.)

I-Bu, MS *1210,* Vol. i: "Poesie Varie."

I-Bu, MS *4005: "Rime di diversi autori dei secoli XVI e XVII."*

I-Fl, *Conv. Soppr. 504:* "Rime di diversi autori dell'anno 1500. . ."

I-Fn, *Anteriore di Galilei, 1,* ff.104^r-147^r: "Discorso di Vincenzo Galilei intorno all'uso delle Dissonanze" (second draft); ff. 148^r-196^v (third draft).

I-Fn, *Anteriori di Galilei, 2,* ff.55^r-136: "Discorso di Vincenzo Galilei intorno all'uso delle Dissonanze" (first draft).

I-Fn, *Magl. vii. 327:* "Delle Rime di m Giovab^a di Lorenzo di Filippo Strozzi Fiorentino Libro primo."

I-Fn, *Magl.vii.328:* "Libro secondo de madrigali di m. Giovambattista di Lorenzo di Filippo Strozzi."

I-Fn, *Fondo Nazionale, II.IV.16* (= *Magl.vii.302*): untitled collection of poetry.

I-Fn, *Palat.242:* "Madrigali di M. Giovanbatista Stroz[zi.]"

I-Fn, *Palat.256,* ff.218^r-221^v and 257^r-313^r: "Rime varie."

I-Fr, *Riccardiana 2218:* Severo Bonini, "Prima parti de' Discorsi e regole sopra la musica."

I-Rsm, *Historiae Basilicae Liberianae S. M. Majoris* (4 vols.).

I-Rvat, *Barb.Lat.4288:* untitled collection of anonymous pieces for one or two voices with keyboard, or solo keyboard.

I-Rvat, *Capp. Sist. 53:* Gregorio Allegri, "Missa 'Che fa oggi il mio sole.' "

I-Rvat, *Chigiana Q.IV.4;* untitled collection of anonymous madrigals of the 17th century for four to eight voices.

I-Rvic, San Lorenzo in Damaso, *Matrimonii,* i (1575-1592; also contains deaths for that period).

I-Sc, *I.XI.8-9:* "Rime di M. Giovambattista Strozzi riviste, et corrette dall'Autore."

I-Sc, *I.XI.11:* "Poesie di diversi autori." Poetry by Guarini, Rinuccini, G.B. Strozzi the Elder and the Younger, T. Tasso, M. Veniero (unattrib.) and others.

I-Sc, *L.V.34:* "Primo, e secondo libro di madrigali a 5 voci del Sig^e: Tomasso Pecci. . ."
Wrongly catalogued: the "Primo libro" (ff.1^r-53^v) is in fact a copy of Marenzio's *IX a 5* (1599)

in Pecci's handwriting; on last page is written: "laus deo finis 1630." The "secondo libro" is to be identified with Tommaso Pecci's *I a 5*, 1602 (*NV*, no. 2157).

I-VEaf, MS *220:* "Madrigali a 5 e a 6 voci." See app. II.

Appendix VI

General Printed and Unpublished Secondary Sources

Note: an asterisk (*) placed before an author's name indicates that the book contains transcriptions of madrigals by Marenzio.

Abert, A.A., art. "Guarini" in *MGG*, v. cols. 1002-1005.

————, art. "Tasso" in *MGG*, viii, cols. 142-144.

*Adler, G., *Handbuch der Musikgeschichte*, repr. of 1930 edn., 2 vols., Tutzing, 1961.

Aiguino, Frate Illuminato, *Il tesoro illuminato di tutti i tuoni di canto figurato*, Venice: G. Varisco, 1581.

Anerio, F., *Canzonette a quattro voci, libro primo* (1586), ed. C. Moser, Padua, 1968.

Apel, W., *The notation of polyphonic music, 900-1600*, 5th rev. edn., Cambridge, Mass., 1953.

————, (ed.), see *Harvard Dictionary of Music*.

Ariani, M., "Giovan Battista Strozzi, il Manierismo e il madgriale del "500," in Strozzi, *Madrigali inediti*, pp.vii-cxlviii.

Arnold, D., *Marenzio* (Oxford Studies of Composers, 2), London, 1965.

————, *Monteverdi*, rev. edn., London, 1975.

Arnold, D. and Fortune, N., eds., *The Monteverdi Companion*, London, 1968.

Arnold, D. (ed.), *Vier Madrigale von Mantuaner Komponisten*, (*CW*, 80), Wolfenbüttel, 1960.

Artusi, G.M., *L'arte del contraponto. . .noavemente* (sic) *ristampata*, Venice: G. Vincenti, 1598.

————, *Seconda parte dell'Artusi overo delle imperfettioni della moderna musica*, Venice: G. Vincenti, 1603.

Atti del Congresso internazionale sul tema "Manierismo in arte e musica"— Rome, 1973, in *SM*, iii (1974).

Baldacci, L., *Il petrarchismo italiano nel cinquecento*, Milan-Naples, 1957.

Ban, I., *Zangh-Bloemzel & kort Sangh-Bericht*, facs. repr. of 1642 edn., ed. F. Noske (Early Music Theory in the Low Countries), Amsterdam, 1969.

Banchieri, A., *Il metamorfosi musicale:* see Banchieri, *Opera Omnia*.

Opera Omnia, ed. G. Vecchi (Antiquae Musicae Italicae Monumenta Bononiensia, 12), Bologna, 1963 ff (1 vol. publ. 1963: *Il metamorfosi musicale*).

————, *Vivezze di Flora e Primavera.. . (1622)* ed. E. Piattelli, (Capolavori Polifonici del Secolo XVI, 12), Rome, 1971.

Barbi, M., art. "Dante Alighieri" in *EISLA*, xii.327-347.

Battaglia, S., *Le rime "petrose" e la sestina*, Naples, 1964 (a comparison of Arnaut Daniel, Dante, and Petrarch).

Battaglin, D., "Il linguaggio tragi-comico del Guarini e l'elaborazione del 'Pastor Fido,' " in *Lingua e strutture del teatro italiano del rinascimento*, ed. G. Folena, Padua, 1970, pp. 293-353.

Bennet, John, *Madrigals to four voices (1599)*, ed. E. Fellowes, (*EMS,* 23), London, 1922.

*Bennett, K., *The six-voiced secular madrigals of Luca Marenzio*, D.Phil. Thesis (unpubl.), Oxford, 1978.

Bianchini, G., *Girolamo Parabosco, scrittore e organista del secolo XVI*, (Miscellanea di Storia Veneta, ii/6), Venice, 1899.

Bianconi, L., " 'Ah dolente partita': espressione ed artificio," *SM,* iii (1974), 105-130.

Blunt, A., *Artistic theory in Italy, 1450-1600*, Oxford, 1962.

Bocchi, F., *Luigi Groto,* Adria 1886 (not consulted).

Bonifazi, N., "G.B. Pigna, il Tasso e il 'Ben divino' " *Studi Tassiani,* x (1960), 53-71.

Bonini, S., *Discorsi e regole sopra la musica*, tr. and ed. M. A. Bonino (bilingual edn.), Provo, Utah, 1979. (Not consulted).

_____, *Discorsi e regole sopra la musica*, ed. L. Luisi, Cremona, 1975.

Borghini, V., *Il più nobile umanista del rinascimento*, Turin etc., n.d. [1943].

Bottegari, C., *The Bottegari lutebook,* ed. C. MacClintock, (The Wellesley Edition, 8), Wellesley, Mass., 1965.

Brandes, H., *Studien zur musikalischen Figurenlehre im 16. Jahrhundert*, Berlin, 1935.

Bray, R., "British library, *R.M. 24.d.2.* (John Baldwin's Commonplace Book): an index and commentary," *Royal Musical Association Research chronicle,* xii (1974), 137-151.

Brown, D., *Thomas Weelkes,* London, 1969.

_____, *Wilbye,* (Oxford Studies of Composers, 11), London, 1974.

Brown, H.M., *Instrumental music printed before 1600,* Cambridge, Mass., 1965.

_____, "Psyche's lament: some music for the Medici wedding in 1565," in *Words and music: the scholar's view. . .in honour of A. Tillman Merritt*, ed. L. Berman, Cambridge, Mass., 1972, pp. 2-27.

*Burney, C., *A general history of music* (1776-1789), repr. of 1935 edn., 4 vols. in 2, New York, 1957.

Bussi, F., art. "Parabosco" in *MGG,* x, cols. 740-742.

_____, *Umanità e arte di Gerolamo Parabosco*, Piacenza, 1961.

Butchart, D.S., *The madrigal in Florence, 1560-1630,* D. Phil. thesis (unpubl.), Oxford, 1979.

*_____, *A set of madrigals from the Euing Collection of Glasgow University: 'Il quinto libro de madrigali a sei voci' by Luca Marenzio*, bachelor's diss. (unpubl.), Glasgow, 1974.

Caccini, G., *Le nuove musiche*, ed. H.W. Hitchcock, (Recent Researches in the Music of the Baroque Era, 9).

Campori, G. and Solerti, A., *Luigi, Lucrezia e Leonora d'Este*, Turin, 1888.

Carapetyan, A., "The concept of 'imitazione della natura' in the sixteenth century," *JRBM* (= *Musica Disciplina*) i (1946), 47-67.

Cardamone, D., "Forme musicali e metriche della canzone villanesca e della villanella alla napolitana," *RIDM,* xii (1977), 25-72.

Caretti, L., *Studi sulle rime del Tasso*, rev. edn., Rome, 1973.

Caroso, F., *Nobiltà di Dame,* Venice: il Muschio, 1600.

Carrara, E., art. "Sannazaro" in *EISLA,* xxx.737-740.

_____, *Jacopo Sannazaro* (1456-1530) (Scrittori Italiani con notizie storiche e analisi estetiche), Turin etc., n.d. [1932].

Cavicchi, A. (ed.), *Luzzasco Luzzaschi . . . madrigali per cantare e sonare a uno, due e tre soprani*, Brescia and Cassel, 1965 (introduction, pp.7-23).

Cecchi, E. and Sapegno, N. (eds), *Il Cinquecento* (Storia della Letteratura italiana, 4), Milan, 1966.

Cerone, P., *El Melopeo y Maestro,* Naples: I.B. Gargano and L.N. Nucci, 1613.

Cesari, G. (ed.), *La musica in Cremona nella seconda metà del secolo XVI* (*IMAMI,* 6), Milan, 1931.

————, "Le origini del madrigale cinquecentesco," *RMI,* xix (1912), 1-34 and 380-428.

Ceserani, R., art. "Barignano" in *DBI,* vi. 365-367.

*Chater, J., "Castelletti's 'Stravaganze d'amore' (1585): a comedy with interludes," *SM,* viii (1979), 85-148.

*————, " 'Cruda Amarilli': a cross-section of the Italian madrigal," *MT,* cxvi (1975), 231-234.

————, "Fonti poetiche per i madrigali di Luca Marenzio," *RIDM,* xiii (1978), 60-103.

Chomiński, J. (ed.), *Słownik muzyków polskich,* 2 vols., Cracow, 1964-1967.

Cinelli, G., *Biblioteca volante,* 2nd edn., 3 vols., Venice, 1734-1747.

Cooke, D., *The language of music,* 6th edn., London, 1968.

Corpus of Early Music (in facs.), ed. B. Huys, 30 vols., Brussels, 1970-1972.

Crescimbeni, G.M. *Comentari intorno alla sua Istoria della Volgar poesia:* see *L'istoria della volgar poesia,* 2nd rev. edn., Venice, 1730, ii-v.

————, *L'istoria della volgar poesia,* 2nd edn. (incorporating the *Comentari*), 6 vols., Venice, 1730-1731.

Crocioni, G., *"L'Alidoro," o dei primordi del melodramma,* Bologna, 1938.

Damilano, P., *Giovenale Ancina: musicista filippino (1545-1604),* Florence, 1956.

D'Ancona, A., *Le origini del teatro italiano,* facs. repr. of 1891 edn., 2 vols., Rome, 1966.

*Davison, A.T. and Apel, W. (eds.), *Historical anthology of music,* rev. edn., 2 vols., Cambridge, Mass. and London, 1949-1950.

Dazzi, M.T., art. "Venier, Maffeo," in *EISLA,* app. i (1978), 1121.

De Angelis, P., *Basilicae S. Mariae Maioris de Urbe a Liberio Papa I usque ad Paulem V Pont. Max. descriptio,* Rome: B. Zannetti, 1621.

Debes, L., *Die musikalischen Quellen von Claudio Merulo, (1533-1604): Quellennachweis und thematischer Katalog,* Ph.D. thesis (unpubl.), Würzburg, 1964.

De Castro, A. (ed.)., *Biblioteca de autores españoles,* Madrid, 1950.

DeFord, R., *Ruggiero Giovanelli and the madrigal in Rome, 1572-1599,* Ph.D. thesis (unpubl.), Harvard, 1975. (Not consulted.)

Degrada, F., "Dante e la musica del Cinquecento," *Chigiana,* xxii (1965), 257-275.

Della Valle, P., *Della musica dell'età nostra* (1640), in Solerti, *Origini,* pp. 148-179.

Dent, E.J., "The sixteenth-century madrigal," in *New Oxford History of Music,* iv (ed. G. Abraham, London, 1968), 33-95 (chapter 2).

Der Kleine Pauly, see *Kleine Pauly, Der.*

De Sanctis, F., *Saggio critico sul Petrarca,* ed. E. Bonora, Bari, 1955.

————, *Storia della letteratura italiana,* ed. G. Luti and G. Innamorati, Florence, 1965.

De Benedetto, A., *Tasso, minori e minimi a Ferrara,* Pisa, 1970.

D'India, Sigismondo, *Madrigali a clinque voci, libro I (1607),* ed. F. Mompellio, (I Classici Musicali Italiani, 10), Monza and Verona, 1942.

————, *Il primo libro di musiche da cantar solo* (1609), ed. F. Mompellio (Instituta et Monumenta, Ser. I, vol. iv) Cremona, 1970.

Dionisotti, C., art. "Bembo, Pietro" in *DBI,* viii.133-151.

Dizionario biografico degli Italiani, 21 vols., Rome, 1960 ff.

Dohrn, E., *Marc'Antonio Ingegneri als Madrigalkomponist,* Hanover, 1936.

Dolci, G., art. "Manfredi, Muzio" in *EISLA,* xxii.111-112.

Doni, G.B., *Annotazioni sopra il Compendio de' generi e de' modi della musica,* Rome: A. Fei, 1640.

————, *Compendio del trattato de' generi e de' modi della musica,* Rome: A. Fei, 1635.

————, *Lyra Barberina,* ed. A.F. Gori, 2 vols., Florence, 1763.

Duranti, A., "Sulle rime del Tasso (1561-1579)," *Deputazione Provinciale Ferrarese di Storia Patria. Atti e Memorie,* Ser.III, vol. xvii (Ferrara, 1974).

Dürr, W., "Lingua e musica: considerazioni sul madrigale di Luca Marenzio, 'O dolce anima mia,' " *Ricerche Musicali,* iv (1980), 46-70.

_____, *Studien zu Rhythmus und Metrum im italienischen Madrigal, insbesondere bei Luca Marenzio*, Ph.D. thesis (unpubl.), Tübingen, 1956.

Einstein, A., "Eine Caccia im Cinquecento," in *Festschrift zum 90. Geburtstage . . . Rochus Freiherrn von Liliencron überreicht*, Leipzig, 1910, pp. 72-80.

*_____, "Dante im Madrigal," *AMW*, iii (1921), 405-420.

_____, "Dante on the way to the madrigal," *MQ*, xxv (1939), 142-155.

_____, *Essays on music*, ed. R. Leavis, rev. edn., London, 1958.

*_____ (ed.), *The Golden Age of the madrigal*, New York, 1942.

*_____, *The Italian madrigal*, transl. A. Krappe, R. Sessions and O. Strunk, 3 vols., Princeton, 1949.

_____, "Narrative rhythm in the madrigal," *MQ*, xxix (1943), 475-484.

Eitner, R., *Bibliographie der Musik-Sammelwerke des XVI. und XVII. Jahrhunderts*, Berlin, 1977.

Elwert, W.T., *Versificazione italiana dalle origini ai giorni nostri*, Florence, 1973.

Enciclopedia italiana di scienze, lettere ed arti, 42 vols., Rome, 1929-1978.

Engel, H., art. "Ingegneri" in *MGG*, vi, cols. 1210-1215.

_____, *Luca Marenzio*, Florence, 1956.

_____, art. "Marenzio" in *MGG*, viii, cols. 1634-1642.

_____, art. "Marenzio" in *La Musica: Enciclopedia Storica*, iii.268-285.

_____, "Marenzios Madrigale," *ZMW*, xvii (1935), 257-288.

_____, "Marenzios Madrigale und ihre dichterischen Grundlagen," *Acta Musicologica*, viii (1936), 129-139 and ix (1937), 11-22.

*_____ (ed.), *Das mehrstimmige Lied des 16. Jahrhunderts in Italien, Frankreich und England*, (Das Musikwerk, 3), Cologne, n.d.

_____, "Nochmals die Intermedien von Florenz, 1589," *Festschrift Max Schnieder zum 80. Geburtstage*, ed. W. Vetter, Leipzig, 1955, pp.71-86.

Fano, F. (ed.), *La Camera Fiorentina* (IMAMI, 4), Milan, 1934.

Fatini, G., art. "Gambara" in *EISLA*, xvi.352-353.

Federzoni, G. (ed.), *Alcune odi di Q. Orazio Flacco volgarizzate nel cinquecento*, Bologna and Modena, 1880.

Fenlon, I., *Music and patronage in sixteenth-century Mantua*, 2 vols., Cambridge, 1980.

Ferrari, L., *Onomasticon. Repertorio biobibliografico degli scrittori italiani dal 1501 al 1850*, Milan, 1947.

Fétis, F., *Traité complet de la théorie et de la pratique de l'harmonie*, Paris, 1844

Flanders, P., *The madrigals of Benedetto Pallavicino*, Ph.D. thesis (unpubl.), New York, 1971 (*UM 72-13,353*).

_____, *A thematic index to the works of Benedetto Pallavicino* (Musical Indexes and Bibliographies, 11), Hackensack, New Jersey, 1974.

Flora, F. (ed.), *Gaspara, Stampa e altre poetesse del '500*, Milan, 1962.

Forster, L., *The icy fire: five studies in European Petrarchism*, Cambridge, 1969.

Fortune, N. (ed.): see Arnold, D. (ed.), *The Monteverdi Companion*, London, 1968.

Frati, L. (ed.), *Rime inedite del '500* (Collezione di opere inedite o rare, 53), Bologna, 1918.

_____, "Torquato Tasso in musica," *RMI*, xxx (1923), 389-400.

_____, *Indice dei codici italiani conservati nella R. Biblioteca Universitaria di Bologna*, 7 vols., Forlì & Florence, 1909-1923.

Friedrich, H., *Epochen der Italienischen Lyrik*, Frankfurt, 1964.

Fubini, M., *Metrica e poesia. Lezioni sulle forme metriche italiane dal Duecento al Petrarca*, Milan, 1962.

_____, *Studi sulla letteratura del Rinascimento*, Florence, 1971.

*Fuller Maitland, J., and Barclay Squire, W. (eds.), *The Fitzwilliam Virginal Book*, repr. of 1899 edn., 2 vols., New York, 1963.

Gabrieli, A., *La représentation d'Edipe tiranno au Teatro Olimpico (Vicenza, 1585)*, ed. L. Schrade, Paris, 1960.

———, *Ten madrigals for mixed voices*, ed. D. Arnold, London, 1970.

Garden G., "François Roussel: a northern musician in sixteenth-century Rome," *Musica Disciplina* xxxi (1977), 107-133.

Gaspari, G. and Sesini, U., *Catalogo della Biblioteca del Liceo Musicale di Bologna*, 5 vols., Bologna, 1893-1943.

Gentile, L., and others, *I codici palatini della R. Biblioteca Nazionale di Firenze* (Indici e Cataloghi, 4), 5 vols., Rome, 1889-1967.

Gesualdo, C., *Sämtliche Werke*, ed. W. Weismann and G. Watkins, 10 vols., Leipzig and Hamburg, 1957-1966.

Getto, G., *Interpretazione del Tasso*, Naples, 1967.

Ghilini, G., *Teatro d'huomini letterati*, 2 vols., Venice, 1647

Giazotto, R., *Quattro secoli di storia dell'Accademia Nazionale di Santa Cecilia*, 2 vols., Verona, 1970.

———, "Storia dell'Accademia Nazionale di S. Cecilia," *SM*, i (1972), no. 2, pp. 237-284.

Ginanni, P., *Memorie storico-critiche degli scrittori ravennati*, 2 vols., Faenza, 1769.

Girardi, E., art. "Barbati, Petronio" in *DBI*, vi.127-128.

Giustiniani, V., *Discorsi sopra la musica*, ed. Solerti, *Origine*, pp. 98-128.

———, ibid, tr. C. MacClintock (Musicological Studies and Documents, 9), American Institute of Musicology, 1962.

Glareanus, H.L., *Dodecachordon*, Basle, 1547. (Facs. repr. New York: Broude, 1967).

Groto, L., *Notizie intorno alla vita del celebre Luigi Grotto Cieco d'Adria*, Venice, 1769.

Grove's Dictionary of Music and Musicians, 6th edn., ed. S. Sadie, 20 vols., London, 1981.

Guarini, A., *Prose*, Ferrara: V. Baldini, 1611.

Guarini, E., "Aldobrandini, Cinzio," in *DBI*, ii.102-104.

Guerrieri-Crocetti, C., art. "Tansillo" in *EISLA*, xxxiii.238-239.

Guerrini, P., *Una celebre famiglia Lombarda: i conti di Martinengo*, Brescia, 1930.

———, "Giovanni Contino di Brescia" in *Note d'Archivio*, i (1924), 130-142.

———, *Luca Marenzio, il più dolce cigno d'Italia nel IV centenario della nascita* (Monografie di Storia Bresciana, 41), Brescia, 1953. (Not available for consultation.)

Haar, J., "Classicism and Mannerism in 16th-century music," *International Revue of Music Aesthetics and Sociology*, i (1970), 55-67.

———, "Self-consciousness about style, form and genre in 16th-century music," *SM*, iii (1974), 219-232.

Hannas, R., "Cerone, philosopher and teacher," *MQ*, xxi (1935), 408-422.

Harant, K., *Opera omnia*, ed. J. Berkovec, Prague, 1956.

*Harman, R.A. (ed.), *Popular Italian madrigals of the 16th century*, London, 1976.

Harran, D., " 'Mannerism' in the Cinquecento madrigal?," *MQ*, iv (1969), 521-544.

———, "Verse types in the early Italian madrigal," *JAMS*, xxii (1969), 27-53.

Hartman, A., "Battista Guarini and 'Il pastor fido,' " *MQ*, xxxix (1953), 415-425.

Harvard Dictionary of Music, ed. W. Apel, 2nd rev. edn., London, 1970.

Hassler, H.L., *Sämtliche Werke*, ed. C.R. Crosby jr., Wiesbaden, 1961 ff (11 vols. by 1976; vols. i-vi originally appeared edited by H. Gehrmann, R. Schwartz and J. Auer as *DDT*, ii, vii, xxiv and xxv, Leipzig, 1894-1901 and *DTB*, v/2 and xi/1, Leipzig, 1905 and 1910.)

Hauvette, H., *Luigi Alamanni (1495-1556). Sa vie et son oeuvre*, Paris, 1903.

*Hawkins, Sir J., *A general history of the science and practice of music* (1776), rev. edn., 2 vols., London, 1875.

Heurich, H., *John Wilbye in seinen madrigalen*, Augsburg, 1932.

Historical anthology of music, ed. A.T. Davison and W. Apel, rev. edn., 2 vols., Cambridge, Mass. and London, 1949-1950.

Hol, J., "Cypriano de Rore," in *Festschrift Karl Nef zum 60. Geburtstag,* Basle, 1933, pp. 134-149.

———, *Horatio Vecchi's weltliche Werke* (Sammlung musikwissenschaftlicher Abhandlungen, 13), Strassburg, 1934.

Horace, *The odes,* ed. and tr. J. Michie (Penguin Classics), Harmondsworth, 1967.

———, *Alcuni odi di Q. Orazio Flacco volgarizzate nel cinquecento,* ed. G. Federzoni, 1880.

*Hucke, H., "H.L. Hasslers 'Neue Teutsche Gesang' (1596) und das Problem des Manierismus in der Musik," *SM,* iii (1974), 255-285.

*Huys, B. (ed.), *Corpus of Early Music* (in facsimile), 30 vols., Brussels, 1970-1972.

Ingegneri, M.A., *Sieben madrigale,* ed. B. Hudson, (*CW,* 115), Wolfenbüttel, 1974.

Jackson, R., and Ledbetter, S., art. "Marenzio" in *Grove,* 6th edn.

Jeppesen, K., *The style of Palestrina and the dissonance,* tr. M. Hamerik, New York, Copenhagen and London, 1927.

Kenton, E., "A faded laurel wreath" in *Aspects of Medieval and Renaissance music. A birthday offering to Gustave Reese,* ed. J. La Rue, New York, 1966, pp.500-518.

Kerman, J., *The Elizabethan madrigal,* New York, 1962.

*Kiesewetter, R.G., *Schicksale und Beschaffenheit des weltlichen Gesanges,* Leipzig, 1841.

Kirkendale, W., "Franceschina, Girometta, and their companions in a madrigal 'a diversi linguaggi' by Luca Marenzio and Orazio Vecchi," *Acta Musicologica,* xliv (1972), 181-235.

*———, (ed.), *Madrigali a diversi linguaggi von Luca Marenzio-Orazio Vecchi, Johann Ecard und Michele Varotto (CW,* 125), Wolfenbüttel, 1975.

*Kishimoto, H., *The secular works of Luca Marenzio: chronological survey and complete works,* Ph.D. thesis (unpubl.), Bryn Mawr (forthcoming).

Kleine Pauly, Der, ed. K. Ziegler and W. Sontheimer, 5 vols., Stuttgart, 1964-1975.

Kroyer, T., *Die Anfänge der Chromatik im italienischen Madrigal* (Publikationen der Internationalen Musikgesellschaft, 4), Leipzig, 1902.

———, "Dialog und Echo in der alten Chormusik," *Jahrbuch der Musikbibliothek Peters,* xvi (1909), 13-32.

Lasca, Il (= Grazzini, A.F.), *Descrizione degl'intermedii rappresentati colla Commedia nelle nozze dell'Illustriss. ed Eccellentis. Sig. Principe di Firenze e di Siena,* Florence: figliuoli di L. Torrenti and C. Pettinari, 1566.

Lassus, O., *Sämtliche Werke,* ed. F.X. Haberl and A. Sandberger, 21 vols., Leipzig, 1894-1926.

Lausberg, H., *Handbuch der literarischen Rhetorik,* 2 vols., Munich, 1960.

Lazzari, A., *Le ultime tre duchesse di Ferrara e la corte estense a' tempi di Torquato Tasso,* Florence, 1913.

*Lechner, L., *Werke,* general ed. K. Ameln, 12 vols., Kassel, 1956-1960.

Ledbetter, S., *Luca Marenzio: new biographical findings,* Ph.D. thesis (unpubl.), New York University, 1971 (*UM. 72-24747*)

———, "Marenzio's early career," *JAMS,* xxxii (1979), 304-320. An expanded version of the same author's *Marenzio,* chapter 1.

———, art. "Moscaglia" in *Grove,* xii. 598-599.

———, see Jackson, R., art. "Marenzio" in *Grove,* 6th edn.

Leopold, S., "Madrigali sulle egloghe sdrucciole di Iacopo Sannazaro," *RIDM,* xiv (1979), 75-127.

Li Gotti, E. and Pirrotta, N., *Il Sacchetti e la tecnica musicale del '300,* Florence, 1935.

*Lincoln, H.B. (ed.), *The madrigal collection "L'amorosa Ero,"* Albany, N.Y., 1968.

———, *Annibale Zoilo: the life and works of a 16th-century composer,* D.Phil. thesis (unpubl.), Northwestern University, Evanston, Illinois, 1951.

Litta, P., *Famiglie celebri di Italia,* 10 vols., Milan, 1819-1867.

Lockwood, L., *The Counter-Reformation and the masses of Vincenzo Ruffo,* Venice, 1967.

Lowinsky, E.E., "Echoes of Adrian Willaert's chromatic duo in 16th-century and 17th-century composition," in *Studies in music history: essays for Oliver Strunk,* pp.183-238, ed. H. Powers, Princeton, 1968.

———, "The goddess Fortuna in music," *MQ,* xxix (1943), 45-77.

———, "Mattheus Greiter's 'Fortuna': an experiment in chromaticism and in musical iconography," *MQ,* xlii (1956), 500-519 and xliii (1957), 68-85.

———, "Musical genius—evolution and origins of a concept," *MQ,* 1 (1964), 321-339 and 476-495.

———, *Tonality and atonality in sixteenth century music,* Berkeley and Los Angeles, 1961.

Luoma, R., "Relationships between music and poetry (Cipriano de Rore's 'Quando signor lasciaste,')" *Musica Disciplina,* xxxi (1977), 135-154.

Luzzaschi, L, *Madrigali per cantare e sonare a uno, due e tre soprani (1601),* ed. A. Cavicchi, Kassel, 1965.

MacClintock, C., *Giaches de Wert (1535-1596): life and works* (Musicological Studies and Documents, 17), American Institute of Musicology, 1966.

Mace, D.T., "Pietro Bembo and the literary origins of the Italian madrigal," *MQ,* lv (1969), 65-86.

Mandosi, P., *Bibliotheca romana,* Rome: I. de Lazzari, 1682.

Maniates, M.R., *Mannerism in Italian music and culture,* 1530-1630, Chapel Hill, 1979.

———, "Musical mannerism: effeteness or virility?," *MQ,* lvii (1971), 270-293.

Marrocco, W.T. (ed.), *Polyphonic music of the 14th century,* Munich, 1972.

*Marsolo, P.M., *Madrigali a quattro voci* (1614), ed. L. Bianconi (Musiche Rinascimentali Siciliane, 4), Rome: De Santis, 1973.

*Martini, G.B. *Esemplare o sia saggio fondamentale pratico di contrappunto sopra il canto fermo,* 2 vols., Bologna, 1774.

Maylender, M., *Storia delle accademie d'Italia,* 5 vols., Bologna, 1926-1930.

Mazzatini, G., *Inventari dei manoscritti delle biblioteche d'Italia,* Vols. vii and viii, (Florence, Biblioteca Nazionale), Forlì, 1898-1906.

Mazzuchelli, Conte G., *Gli scrittori d'Italia,* 6 vols, Brescia, 1753-1763.

Mei, G., *Letters on ancient and modern music to Vincenzo Galilei and Giovanni Bardi. A study with annotated texts,* ed. C. Palisca (Musicological Studies and Documents, 3), American Institute of Musicology, 1960.

Meier, B., "Melodiezitate in der Musik des 16. Jahrhunderts" in *Tijdschrift van de Vereniging voor Nederlandse Muziekgeschiedenis,* xx (1964-1965), 1-19.

———, *Die Tonarten der klassischen Vokalpolyphonie nach dem Quellen dargestellt,* Utrecht, 1974.

Meierhans, L., *Die Ballata,* Bern, 1956.

Mensi, L., *Dizionario biografico piacentino,* Piacenza, 1899.

Minor, A. and Mitchell, B., *A Renaissance entertainment for the marriage of Cosimo I in 1539,* Columbia, Mo., 1968.

Mirollo, J., *The poet of the marvelous: Giambattista Marino,* New York and London, 1963.

Mischiati, O., "Un'antologia manoscritta in partitura del secolo xvi.," *RIDM,* x (1975), 265-328.

———, *Adriano Banchieri (1568-1634). Profilo biografico e bibliografica delle opere,* Bologna, 1971.

Mitchie, J. (ed.), *The odes of Horace,* (Penguin Classics), Harmondsworth, 1964. Latin text with English translation.

Mompellio, F., *Pietro Vinci, madrigalista siciliano,* Milan, 1937.

Mönch, W., *Das Sonett. Gestalt und Geschichte,* Heidelberg, 1955.

Monte, P. de: madrigals, transcr. by A. Einstein, Smith College Archives, xxxvi-xliv (consulted on microfilm in GB-Ob).

———, *Opera,* ed. C. van den Borren, J. Nuffel and G. van Doorslaer, 31 vols., Bruges, 1927-1939 (incomplete).

_____, *Il secondo libro di madrigali spirituali a sei e a sette voci (1589)*, ed. P. Nuten, Brussels, 1958.

Monteverdi, C., *Tutte le opere*, ed. G.F. Malipiero, 16 vols., Asolo, 1926-1942; suppl. vol., 1966.

Morley, T., *First book of madrigals to four voices* (1594), ed. E. Fellowes (*EMS*, 2), London, 1921.

_____, *A plaine and easie introduction to practical musicke*, London: P. Short, 1597. Facs. repr. ed. E. Fellowes (The Shakespeare Association Facsimiles, 14), London, 1937; also ed. R.A. Harman, London, 1952. References are to the facs. repr.

Morpurgo, S., *I manoscritti della R. Biblioteca Riccardiana*, Rome, 1900.

Musica, La, eds. G.M. Gatti and A. Basso. Pt. 1: *Enciclopedia storica,* 4 vols., Turin, 1966. Pt. 2: *Dizionario,* 2 vols., Turin 1968 and 1971.

Musik in Geschichte und Gegenwart, Die, ed. F. Blume, 15 vols, Kassel, 1949-1973.

Mutini, C., art. "Caro, Annibale" in *DBI,* xx. 497-508.

Myers, P.A., *An analytical study of the Italian cyclic madrigals published by composers working in Rome ca.1540-1614,* Ph.D. thesis (unpubl.) Illinois, 1971 (*UM 72-12309*).

*_____, *Il Settimo Libro de Madrigalia Cinque Voci by Luca Marenzio. An analysis and transcription.* Master's diss. (unpubl.), Oregon, 1967.

Nardini, C., *I manoscritti della biblioteca Moreniana di Firenze. Manoscritti Moreni,* Florence, 1903.

Nef, K., *Histoire de la musique,* 2nd French edn., tr. Y. Rokseth, Lausanne, 1944.

Negri, G. *Istoria degli scrittori fiorentini,* Ferrara, 1722.

Newcomb, A., "Alfonso Fontanelli and the ancestry of the Seconda Prattica madrigal," in *Studies in Renaissance and Baroque music in honor of Arthur Mendel,* ed. R. Marshall, Kassel, 1974, pp. 47-68.

_____, "Carlo Gesualdo and a musical correspondence of 1594," *MQ,* liv (1968), 409-436.

*_____, *The madrigal at Ferrara, 1579-1597,* 2 vols., Princeton, 1980.

*_____, *The "Musica secreta" of Ferrara in the 1580's,* D.Phil. thesis (unpubl.), Princeton, 1969 (*UM 70-19794*).

_____, "The three anthologies for Laura Peperara (1580-1583)" in *RIDM,* x (1975), 329-345.

Nolan, D., *The "Amori" of Giambattista Pigna come to light. An account of two late Renaissance manuscripts* (Quaderno dell'Istituto Italiano di Cultura, Dublin), Dublin, 1972.

Novelli, M., *Il benedettino Angelo Grillo, liberatore del Tasso,* Naples, 1969.

Nuernberger, L.D., *The five voice madrigals of Cipriano de Rore,* Ph.D. thesis (unpubl.), The University of Michigan, 1963 (*UM 64-6728*).

Nuten, P., art. "Monte" in *MGG,* ix, cols. 489-502.

Obertello, A., *Madrigali italiani in Inghilterra,* Milan, 1949.

Osthoff, W., *Theatergesang und darstellende Musik in der italienischen Renaissance* (Münchner Veröffentlichungen zur Musikgeschichte, 14), 2 vols., Tutzing, 1969.

Paganuzzi, E., Bologna, C., Rognini, L., Cambié, G.M., and Conati, M., *La musica a Verona,* Verona: Banca Mutua Popolare di Verona, 1976.

Palestrina, G.P. da, *Opere Complete,* ed. R. Casimiri and others, 32 vols., Rome, 1939 ff (32 vols. to 1972).

Palisca, C., "The Artusi-Monteverdi controversy" in *The Monteverdi Companion,* ed. D. Arnold and N. Fortune, London, 1968, pp.133-164.

_____, "The 'Camerata Fiorentina': a reappraisal," *SM,* i/2 (1972), 203-236.

_____, "Vincenzo Galilei's counterpoint treatise: a code for the 'seconda pratica'," *JAMS,* ix (1956), 81-96.

_____, "Girolamo Mei: mentor to the Florentine Camerata," *MQ,* xl (1954), 1-20.

_____, "Towards an intrinsically musical definition of Mannerism in the sixteenth century," *SM,* iii (1974), 313-346.

_____, " 'Ut oratoria musica': the rhetorical basis of musical Mannerism" in *The meaning of Mannerism*, ed. F.W. Robinson and S.G. Nichols Jr., Hanover, N.H., 1972, pp.37-65 (not available for consultation).

Parabosco, G., *I diporti*, in *Novellieri minori del cinquecento*, ed. G. Gigli and F. Nicolini (Scrittori d'Italia), Bari, 1912, pp.9-199.

Pastor, L. von, *The history of the popes from the close of the Middle Ages*, ed. from the German by F. Antrobus, 40 vols., London, 1910-1953.

Patrizi, G., art. "Casteletti" in *DBI*, xxi.671-673.

Perella, N.J., *The critical fortune of Battista Guarini's "Il pastor fido,"* Florence, 1973.

Palaez, M., art. "Canzone" in *EISLA*, viii (1949), 812-813.

_____, art. "Molza, F.M." in *EISLA*, xxiii.592.

Pelaez, M., Gabetti, G., and Luciani, S.A., art. "Ballata" in *EISLA*, v (1949), 982-985.

Petrobelli, P., " 'Ah dolente partita': Marenzio, Wert, Monteverdi" in *Congresso internazionale sul tema "Claudio Monteverdi e il suo tempo,"* ed. R. Monterosso, Verona, 1969.

Philips, P., *Select Italian madrigals*, ed. J. Steele (Musica Britannica, 29), London, 1970.

Piccioli, A., *Prose tiberine del Pastor Ergasto Antonio Piccioli al famosissimo Tirsi, Prencipe dei Pastori della Valle Tiberina* [. . .] *Don Virginio Orsino, Duca di Bracciano*, Treviso: Dazuchino, 1597.

Pirrotta, N., "Early opera and aria" in *New looks at Italian opera. Essays in honor of Donald J. Grout*, ed. W. Austin, New York, 1968, pp.39-107.

_____, *Li due Orfei: da Poliziano a Monteverdi*, rev. edn., Turin, 1975.

_____, "Note su Marenzio e il Tasso" in *Scritti in onore di Luigi Ronga*, Milan, 1973, pp.557-571.

_____, "Per l'origine e la storia della 'caccia' e del 'madrigale' trecentesco," *RMI*, xlviii (1946), 305-323, and xlix (1947), 121-142.

_____, "Scelte poetiche di Monteverdi," *NRMI*, ii (1968), 10-42 and 226-254.

_____, "Temperaments and tendencies in the Florentine Camerata," *MQ*, xl (1954), 169-189.

Ponnelle, L., and Bordet, L., *St. Philip Neri and the Roman society of his times, 1515-1595*, tr. R. Kerr, London, 1932.

Pontio, P., *Ragionamento di musica*, Parma: Erasmo Viotto, 1588. Facs. repr. ed. S. Clercx, (Documenta Musicologica, Ser. I, vol. xvi), Kassel, 1959.

*Powley, E.G., *Il Trionfo di Dori. A critical edition*, Ph.D. thesis (unpubl.), Rochester, Eastman School of Music. Not consulted: announced in *JAMS*, xxii (1969), 461.

Praetorius, M., *Gesamtausgabe der musikalischen Werke*, 20 vols., ed. F. Blume, Wolfenbüttel, 1928-1940.

_____, *Syntagma musicum* (1614-1619), facs. repr. ed. W. Gurlitt, (Documenta Musicologica, Ser. I, vols. xiv, xv, xxi), 3 vols., Kassel, 1958-1959.

Praz, M., art. "Petrarchismo" in *EISLA*, xxvii (1950), 23-24.

Princivalli, V., *Torquato Tasso a Roma*, Rome, 1895.

_____, *Torquato Tasso nella vita e nelle opere*, Rome, 1895.

Quadrio, S., *Della storia e della ragione d'ogni poesia*, 7 bound vols., Bologna & Milan, 1739-1752.

Reese, G., *Music in the Renaissance*, 4th rev. edn., New York, 1959.

Reich, W., *Alban Berg: Leben und Werk*, Zurich, 1963.

Répertoire International des Sources Musicales, gen. ed. F. Lesure.
  Ser. A: *Einzeldrucke vor 1800*, Kassel 1971 ff (7 vols. to 1978).
  Ser. B,I,I: *Recueils imprimés, XVIe—XVIIe siècles*, Munich, 1960.

Roche, J., *The madrigal*, London, 1972.
  1960.

Roche, J., *The madrigal*, London, 1972.

*_____, (ed.), *The Penguin Book of Italian madrigals*, Harmondsworth, 1974.

Roncaglia, A., "Per la storia dell'ottava rima," *Cultura Neolatina*, xxv/1 (1965), 5-14.

Ronga, L., "Tasso e la musica" in *Torquato Tasso: comitato per le celebrazioni di Torquato Tasso, Ferrara, 1954*, Milan, 1957, pp.187-207.

Rore, C. de, *Opera Omnia*, ed. B. Meier (*CMM*, 14), 8 vols., American Institute of Musicology, 1959-1977.

Rosselli, F., see Roussel, F.

Rossi, V., *Battista Guarini ed il Pastor Fido*, Turin, 1886.

Roussel, F., *Opera Omnia*, ed. G. Garden (*CMM*, 83), 4 vols., American Institute of Musicology, 1980 ff (4 vols. to 1980).

Rua, G., art. "Beccuti" in *EISLA*, vi.464-465.

Sapegno, N., art. "Ariosto, Ludovico" in *DBI*, ii.172-188.

_____, art. "Sachetti, Franco" in *EISLA*, xxx.390-391.

Sartori, C., *Bibliografia della musica strumentale italiana*, (Biblioteca di Bibliografia Italiana, 23), 2 vols., Florence, 1952-1968.

_____, art. "Brescia" in *MGG*, ii, cols. 279-283.

*Schering, A. (ed.), *Geschichte der Musik in Beispielen*, Leipzig, 1931.

*Schinelli, A. (ed.), *Collana di composizioni polifoniche vocali sacre e profane*, 3 vols., Milan, 1955-1960.

Schmalzriedt, S., *Heinrich Schütz und andere zeitgenössische Musiker in der Lehre Giovanni Gabrielis. Studien zu ihren Madrigalen*, Stuttgart, 1972.

Schuler, R., *The life and liturgical works of G.M. Nanino (1545-1607)*, Ph.D. thesis (unpubl.), University of Minnesota, 1963 (*UM 63-7953*).

Schulz-Buschhaus, U., *Das Madrigal*, Berlin, 1969.

Schütz, Heinrich, *Neue Ausgabe sämtlicher Werke*, ed. F. Schöneich and others, 38 vols., Kassel, 1955-1971.

Schwartz, R., "Hans Leo Hassler unter dem Einfluss der italiänischen Madrigalisten," *VJM*, ix (1893), 1-61.

Schweitzer, A., *J.S. Bach*, tr. E. Newman, rev. enlarged edn., 2 vols., London, 1964.

Shearman, J., *Mannerism* (Style and Civilization), 3rd edn., Harmondsworth, 1973.

Shindle, W.R., *The madrigals of Giovanni de Macque*, Ph.D. thesis (unpubl.), Indiana University, 1970 (*UM 71-6206*).

*Sloan, M., *Il Secondo Libro de Madrigali a Quattro Voci of Giovanni Battista Moscaglia. Transcription and stylistic study*, Master's diss. (unpubl.), Kent State University, 1969.

Solerti, A., *Ferrara e la corte Estense nella seconda metà del secolo decimosesto*, rev. edn., Città di Castello, 1900.

_____, *Le origini del melodramma*, Turin, 1903.

_____, *Vita di Torquato Tasso*, 2 vols., Turin, 1895.

Spiro, A., *The five-part madrigals of Luzzasco Luzzaschi*, Ph.D. thesis (unpubl.), Boston, 1961 (*UM 61-3378*).

*Steele, J., "The later madrigals of Luca Marenzio," *Studies in Music*, iii (1969), 17-24.

Sternfeld, F.W. (ed.), *Music from the Middle Ages to the Renaissance*, (A History of Western Music, 1), London, 1973.

_____, "Repetition and echo in Renaissance poetry and music" in *Essays in Renaissance studies: presented to Dame Helen Gardner*, ed. J. Carey, Oxford, 1980, pp. 33-43.

Strunk, O., *Source readings in music history*, New York, 1950.

Sweelinck, J., *Werken*, ed. M. Seiffert, and others, 10 vols., Amsterdam, 1896-1957; suppl. vol. 1958.

Tanaka, S., "Studien im Gebiete der reinen Stimmung," *VJM*, vi (1890), 1-90.

Tasso, T., *La Cavaletta, overo de la poesia toscana*, in *Opere*, ed. B. Maier, Milan, 1963, v. 90-151.

————, *Lettere*, ed. C. Guasti, 5 vols., Florence, 1852-1855.

Tinto, G.F., *La nobiltà di Verona*, Verona: Girolamo Discepolo, 1592.

Tiraboschi, G., *Biblioteca modenese*, 6 vols., 1781-1786.

————, *Storia della letteratura italiana*, 2nd edn., 8 vols., Modena, 1787-1793.

Tollius, G., *Zesstemmige madrigalen (1597)*, ed. M. Seiffert (Veereeniging voor Noord-Nederlands Muzickgeschiedenis, 24), Leipzig: Breitkopf and Härtel, 1901.

*Torchi, L. (ed.), *L'arte musicale in Italia*, 7 vols., Milan, 1897-1907 (Vol. ii contains madrigals by Marenzio).

Troiano, G., *Lettera consolatoria con alcune rime di diversi . . . nella morte della signora Lucretia Cavalcanti*, Venice: G. Giolito, 1568[-1569].

Trucchi, F. (ed.), *Poesie italiane inedite*, 4 vols., Prato, 1846-7.

Turri, L., *Luigi Groto*, Lanciano, 1885 (not consulted).

Turrini, G., *L'Accademia Filarmonica dalla fondazione (maggio 1543) al 1600*, Verona, 1941.

*Unger, H., *Die Beziehung zwischen Musik und Rhetorik im 16.-18. Jahrhundert* (published thesis), Berlin, 1941.

Valentini, A., *I musicisti bresciani*, Brescia, 1894.

Vedova, G., *Biografia degli scrittori padovani*, 2 vols., Padua, 1832-1836.

Vellutello, A., *Il Petrarcha con l'espositione d'Alessandro Vellutello*, repr. of 1525 edn., Venice: n.p., 1538.

Vincento, N., *L'antica musica ridotta alla moderna prattica*, (1555), facs. repr., ed. E. Lowinsky, Kassel, 1959.

————, *Opera Omnia*, ed. H.W. Kaufmann, (*CMM*, 26), American Institute of Musicology, 1963.

Vogel, E., *Bibliothek der gedruckten weltlichen Vokalmusik Italiens*, rev. A. Einstein, 2 vols, Hildesheim, 1962.

Vogel, E., Einstein, A., Lesure, F. and Sartori, C., *Bibliografia della musica italiana vocale profana pubblicata dal 1500 al 1700*, rev. edn., 3 vols., n.p.: Staderini, 1977.

*Wade, W.W., *The sacred style of Luca Marenzio as represented in his four-part motets (1585)*, Ph.D. thesis (unpubl.), Northwestern Univ., 1958. (Not consulted)

*Walker, D.P., *Les fêtes de Florence (1589): musiques des intermèdes de "La pellegrina,"* Paris, 1963.

Watkins, G., *Gesualdo: the man and his music*, London, 1973.

Weelkes, T., *Madrigals of six parts . . . 1600*, ed. E. Fellowes (*EMS*, 12), London, 1916.

Weinberg, B., *A History of literary criticism in the Italian Renaissance*, 2 vols., Chicago and Toronto, 1961.

Weiss, R., art. "Alamanni" in *DBI*, i.568-571.

Wert, G. de, *Collected Works*, ed. C. MacClintock and M. Bernstein (*CMM*, 24), 17 vols., American Institute of Musicology, 1961-1977.

Whitfield, J.H., *A short history of Italian literature*, London, 1960.

Wilbye, J., *First set of madrigals to 3.4.5. and 6 voices* (1598), ed. E. Fellowes, (*EMS*, 6), London, 1914.

————, *Second set of madrigals to 3.4.5. and 6 voices . . . 1609*, ed. E. Fellowes, 2nd rev. edn., (*EMS*, 7), London, 1920.

Wilkins, E., *The invention of the sonnet and other studies in Italian literature*, Rome, 1959.

————, *Life of Petrarch*, Chicago and London, 1961.

————, *The making of the Canzoniere and other Petrarchan studies*, (Edizioni di Storia e Letteratura, 38), Rome, 1951.

————, *Studies in the life and works of Petrarch*, Cambridge, Mass., 1955.

Willetts, P.J. "A neglected source of monody and madrigals," *ML*, xliii (1962), 329-339.

Williamson, E., *Bernardo Tasso*, Rome, 1951.

Winspeare, F., *Isabella Orsini e la corte medicea del suo tempo* (Biblioteca dell'Archivio Storico Italiano, 12), Florence, 1961.

Winter, C., *Ruggiero Giovanelli, c.1560-1625, Nachfolger Palestrinas zu St. Peter in Rom,* Munich, 1935.

*Winterfeld, C. von., *Johannes Gabrieli und sein Zeitalter,* 3 vols., Berlin, 1834.

Wittkower, R., *Art and architecture in Italy, 1600-1750,* 3rd rev. edn., (Pelican History of Art), London, 1958.

Wolf, R.E., "Renaissance, Mannerism, Baroque: three styles, three periods," *Les Colloques de Wégimont,* iv (1957), 35-59.

Wolff, H.C., "Manierismus und Musikgeschichte," *Musikforschung,* xxiv (1971), 245-250.

Wölfflin, H., *Renaissance and Baroque,* ed. P. Murray, tr. K. Simon, London, 1964.

Zacconi, L., *Prattica di musica,* repr. of 1592 edn., Venice: G. Polo, 1596.

———, *Prattica di musica . . . seconda parte,* Venice: Alessandro Vincenti, 1622.

Zarlino, G., *The art of counterpoint (Le Istitutioni harmoniche,* 1558, iii), tr. G.A. Marco and C.V. Palisca, New Haven and London, 1968.

———, *Le istitutioni harmoniche* (1558), facs. repr., New York, 1965.

*Zimmerman, F.B., *Features of Italian style in Elizabethan part songs and madrigals,* B. Litt. thesis (unpubl.), Oxford, 1955.

Index

Mozart, Wolfgang Amadeus, 74
Mutio, Girolamo, 182

Naccherelli, Piero, 174
Nanino, Giovanni Maria, 6, 8, 13, 15, 38, 52, 57, 65, 115, 219; texts set by, also set by Marenzio, 174
Nannini, Remigio, 131 n.49, 219, 234
Naples, 29, 132 n.16
Nasco, Jan, 172
Nenna, Pomponio, 126
Nenninger, Matthias, 116, 223
Neri, St. Philip, 2
Newcomb, Anthony A., 115
Nicoletti, Filippo, 131 n.42, 222
Noema, 159 n.56
Nores, Jason de, 232
Nuremberg, 106, 115

Occa, Alberto L', 131 n.41
Ode, 14, 26
Ongaro, Antonio, 208, 216, 234
Oratorio, Congregazione dell', 2
Orsi, Aurelio, 186, 234
Orsini, Flaminio, 209
Orsini, Paolo Giordano, Duke of Bracciano, 2
Orsini, Virginio, Duke of Bracciano, 2, 6, 74, 109, 121, 204, 205
Ottava rima, 25, 70, 95, 101; musical treatment of, 103-4, 108
"Ottuso, L'", 125
Ovid, 96
Oxymoron, 118. *See also* Antithesis

Pace, Pompeo, 172, 192, 234
Padua, 34
Palestrina, Giovanni Pierluigi da, 15, 38, 121, 126, 191; texts also set by Marenzio, 182
Pallavicino, Benedetto, 5, 11, 35, 127; texts set by, in common with Marenzio, 172, 173, 176, 177, 181, 196, 197, 200, 206, 211, 212, 216
Pallavicino, Nicolo, 141 n.124, 190
Pannini, Benedetto, 240
Parabosco, Girolamo, 26, 27, 179, 234
Parmigianino (Girolamo Mazzola), 69
Parody, 7, 9, 20
Parola-chiave, 102, 103
Paronomasia, 101
Pasqualino, Lelio, 6, 26, 172, 234
Passeri, Aurelio, 129 n.15
Patrons, 2-6
Paulis, Annibale de', 201
Pavesi, Cesare, 26, 191, 234

Peacham, Henry, 11, 121
Pecci, Tommaso, 165 n.63, 216, 240
Peperara, Laura, 5, 30, 43, 124, 130 n.32, 181
Peretti family. *See* Montalto
Peretti, Felice. *See* Sixtus V (pope)
Peretti, Flavia, 2, 74, 109, 130 n.25, 205, 210
Peri, Jacopo, 131 n.6
Peroratio, 100-102, 126
Perugia, Nicola da, 25, 185
Pesciolini, Biagio, 172, 177, 197
Petrarch (Petrarca, Francesco), 7, 9, 12, 14, 19-21, 26, 27, 35, 39, 58, 63, 73, 74, 99, 100, 105, 118, 137 n.48, 151 n.7, 155 n.94, 171, 173, 177, 179, 181-84 passim, 188, 190, 192, 195-98 passim, 202, 203, 210, 216-17, 218, 222, 234; comparison of, with Guarini, 34; influence of, on Sannazaro, 30; influence of, on Tasso, 31; metrical forms used by, 25; *Trionfi,* 25, 120, 216
Petrarchism, 20-21
Pevernage, Andreas, 224
Phalèse, Pierre, 109, 116, 207, 210
Philips, Peter, 173, 185, 224
Piccioli, Antonio, 130 n.32
Piccioni, Giovanni, 207, 213, 214
Piccolomini, Silvia, 209
Pigna (Nicolucci), Giovambattista, 4, 10, 200, 235
Pirrotta, Nino, 30, 122
Pisanelli, Pompilio, 172
Pisani, Marquis of. *See* Vivonne, Jean de
Pocaterra, Annibale, 3, 201, 235, 240
Poesia per musica, 14
Poland, 2, 109
Poliziano, Angelo, 96, 177
Polybius, 140 n.81
Pontano, Giovanni, 27
Pontio, Pietro, 84
Portinaro, Francesco, 196
Posch, Isaac, 173
Praetorius, Michael, 44, 94, 173, 184, 209
Prattica, prima, 125
Prattica, seconda, 7, 125

Question, musical treatment of, 100, 102, 120
Quirino, Vincenzo, 25, 176, 189, 235

Range, vocal, 45-47
Raselius, Andrea, 40, 172, 176, 240
Raval, Sebastian, 4, 194, 196
Repercussio, 26, 42, 44, 88
Repetition, 27, 75-76, 95-96, 101-8 passim, 126